LEGITIMACY, JUSTICE AND PUBLIC INTERNATIONAL LAW

Do states or individuals stand under duties of international justice to people who live elsewhere and to other states? How are we to assess the legitimacy of international institutions such as the International Monetary Fund and the United Nations Security Council? Should we support reforms of international institutions and how should we go about assessing alternative proposals of such reforms?

The book brings together leading scholars of public international law, jurisprudence and international relations, political philosophers and political theorists to explore the central notions of international legitimacy and global justice. The chapters examine how these notions are related and how understanding the relationships will help us comparatively assess the validity of proposals for the reform of international institutions and public international law.

LUKAS H. MEYER is Professor of Practical Philosophy at the University of Graz Department of Philosophy.

LEGITIMACY, JUSTICE AND PUBLIC INTERNATIONAL LAW

Edited by

LUKAS H. MEYER

CAMBRIDGE
UNIVERSITY PRESS

CAMBRIDGE
UNIVERSITY PRESS

University Printing House, Cambridge CB2 8BS, United Kingdom

One Liberty Plaza, 20th Floor, New York, NY 10006, USA

477 Williamstown Road, Port Melbourne, VIC 3207, Australia

314-321, 3rd Floor, Plot 3, Splendor Forum, Jasola District Centre, New Delhi - 110025, India

79 Anson Road, #06-04/06, Singapore 079906

Cambridge University Press is part of the University of Cambridge.

It furthers the University's mission by disseminating knowledge in the pursuit of education, learning and research at the highest international levels of excellence.

www.cambridge.org
Information on this title: www.cambridge.org/9780521199490

First published 2009

A catalogue record for this publication is available from the British Library

ISBN 978-0-521-19949-0 Hardback

CONTENTS

LIST OF CONTRIBUTORS

ARTHUR ISAK APPLBAUM is Professor of Ethics and Public Policy and Acting Director of the Edmond J. Safra Foundation Center for Ethics, Harvard University.

SAMANTHA BESSON is Professor of Public International Law and European Law, University of Fribourg, Switzerland.

ALLEN BUCHANAN is James B. Duke Professor of Philosophy, Duke University.

DANIEL BUTT is Fellow and Tutor in Politics, Oriel College, University of Oxford.

SIMON CANEY is Professor in Political Theory, University of Oxford, and University Lecturer and Fellow and Tutor in Politics, Magdalen College, University of Oxford.

ROBERT O. KEOHANE is Professor of International Affairs, Woodrow Wilson School of Public and International Affairs, Princeton University.

PETER KOLLER is Professor of Legal Philosophy and Sociology of Law, Institute for Philosophy, Sociology of Law and Legal Informatics, University of Graz, Austria.

MATTHIAS LUTZ-BACHMANN is Professor of Philosophy, Goethe-University, Frankfurt, Germany.

LUKAS H. MEYER is Professor of Practical Philosophy, University of Graz, Austria.

DAVID MILLER is Professor of Political Theory, University of Oxford and Official Fellow in Social and Political Theory, Nuffield College, University of Oxford.

HERLINDE PAUER-STUDER is Associate Professor, Department of Philosophy, University of Vienna, Austria.

STEVEN R. RATNER is Professor of Law, University of Michigan.

PRANAY SANKLECHA is University Assistant (researcher and lecturer) in Practical Philosophy, University of Graz, Austria.

ACKNOWLEDGEMENTS

Most chapters in this volume were first presented at a symposium held at the University of Bern in December 2006. I wish cordially to thank my co-chairs of the symposium: Prof. Gerhard Beestermöller (Institute for Theology and Peace, Hamburg), Prof. Eyal Benvenisti (Tel Aviv University), Prof. Chaim Gans (Tel Aviv University), Prof. Wilfried Hinsch (RWTH Aachen), Prof. Gerhard Kruip (University of Mainz and Hannover Institute of Philosophical Research), PD Dr. Heinz-Gerhard Justenhoven (Institute for Theology and Peace, Hamburg), Prof. Corinna Mieth (University of Bonn) and Prof. Markus Stepanians (RWTH Aachen). Corinna Mieth and I prepared the symposium by holding two workshops at the Hannover Institute of Philosophical Research in January and June 2005 that were sponsored by the Hannover Institute and the Institute for Theology and Peace.

The Bern Symposium was generously sponsored by Swiss National Fonds, Swiss Academy for the Humanities and Social Sciences, Max and Elsa Beer-Brawand-Fonds (University of Bern), The Cegla Center for Interdisciplinary Research in the Law (Tel Aviv University, The Buchmann Faculty of Law), Minerva Center for Human Rights (Hebrew University of Jerusalem, Tel Aviv University), RWTH Aachen's Chair of Practical Philosophy, Hannover Institute of Philosophical Research, and the Institute for Theology and Peace, Hamburg. For their engaging and extremely helpful support in organising the symposium I wish heartily to thank Dominic Roser and Barbara Wallmark.

I would like to thank the following colleagues for their invaluable critical support – for having commented on the papers as submitted for the symposium or for having contributed to the blind peer-review process undertaken for all the chapters of the book: the reviewers for Cambridge University Press as well as Gerhard Beestermöller, Eyal Benvenisti, Monika Betzler, Chaim Gans, Wilfried Hinsch, Christoph Horn, Gerhard Justenhoven, Gerhard Kruip, Rahul Kumar, Peter Mayer,

Corinna Mieth, Georg Mohr, Jörg Paul Müller, Dietmar von der Pfordten, Thomas W. Pogge, Mathias Risse, Markus S. Stepanians, Jane Stromseth and Leif Wenar.

I also wish to warmly thank Finola O'Sullivan, Brenda Burke and Richard Woodham at Cambridge University Press along with Thomas Distel and Pranay Sanklecha at the University of Bern for their very fine work all along the way in the production of the volume.

Introduction: Legitimacy, justice and public international law. Three perspectives on the debate

LUKAS H. MEYER AND PRANAY SANKLECHA

In this introduction, we attempt to elucidate three theoretical perspectives that are helpful in framing the contributions to this volume. In the course of this elucidation we also attempt to indicate some important problems that the debate currently faces. We do this through discussions of international legitimacy, international justice and the relations between ideal and non-ideal theory.

International legitimacy. From normative authority by consent to instrumental legitimacy

Questions of legitimacy have long been central to both political philosophy and political practice. It is not merely vanity that leads dictators of virtually all stripes to first decide to hold elections and then announce that they have won 96 per cent of the vote in them. Saddam Hussein, for instance, held a referendum in 2002 on whether he should continue as ruler of Iraq for the next seven years, and after the election was held it turned out that out of 11,445,638 eligible voters, every single one voted in favour.[1] The natural question to ask is: why bother? Why bother to hold sham elections with sham results when you hold power anyway? There are many possible answers, but two are especially relevant here. The effect of legitimacy is, or can be, twofold. First, it makes it easier to exercise the power one does possess. Second, and as important, it can often increase the scope of the power one possesses. Legitimacy matters

For very helpful comments on earlier versions of this introduction we would like to warmly thank Keith Bustos, Julian Culp, Thomas Distel, Sarah Kenehan and Nora Kreft.

[1] BBC News. Online, available at: http://news.bbc.co.uk/2/hi/middle_east/2331951.stm.

in the real world because it affects power, and power matters because it creates the ability – on some views, is just the ability – to get things done.

In this section, we will consider three important traditions in the debate on legitimacy. These are the consent, instrumentalist and procedural traditions respectively. We will argue that the consent tradition is generally deemed to be unsatisfactory when applied to the international context, at least when consent is thought of as a sufficient condition for legitimacy. The instrumentalist and procedural traditions have found more favour in the international context, and we will attempt to outline some important ways in which these traditions have influenced the debate on international legitimacy. Besides identifying areas of consensus in the debate, we also attempt to describe some important problems that this consensus faces and will need to resolve.

Before beginning a discussion of legitimacy, however, we must first make a distinction between descriptive and normative senses of the concept of legitimacy. On the dominant descriptive view (which comes from Max Weber[2]), 'a norm or an institutional arrangement is legitimate if, *as a matter of fact*, it finds the approval of those who are supposed to live in this group'.[3] Legitimacy in this sense is simply the fact that the subjects of the norm or institutional arrangement believe that norm or arrangement to be legitimate.

The normative sense of legitimacy deals with whether this belief is correct – i.e. whether that norm or institutional arrangement satisfies certain specified conditions for possessing legitimacy. As Arthur Applbaum points out, one could of course hold the view that one of the conditions – or even the only one – for possessing normative legitimacy is that most people subject to the rule of an entity believe it to possess normative legitimacy, but 'this is a claim about the normative criteria for having moral legitimacy – a particular conception – not a claim about the meaning of moral legitimacy'.[4] It is possible, then, for a political authority to be legitimate in the descriptive sense while being illegitimate in the

[2] See M. Weber, *Wirtschaft und Gesellschaft. Grundriss der verstehenden Soziologie* (Tübingen: J. C. B. Mohr, 1922). For an English translation, see M. Weber, *Economy and Society. An Outline of Interpretive Sociology*, G. Roth and C. Wittich (eds.), 3 vols. (New York, NY: Bedminster Press, 1968).

[3] W. Hinsch, 'Justice, Legitimacy and Constitutional Rights', in *Justice, Equality and Democracy*, M. Matravers and L. H. Meyer (eds.) (London and New York, NY: Routledge, in press).

[4] A. I. Applbaum, 'Legitimacy in a Bastard Kingdom', *John F. Kennedy School of Government Center for Public Leadership Working Papers*, Spring 2004, 79. Applbaum also argues, convincingly, that while the view isn't incoherent, it is wrong.

normative sense; this is what we might say, for instance, of the rule of kings in the Middle Ages. The chapters in this volume, and therefore this introduction, concentrate on normative legitimacy.

There are various ways in which one could argue that entities are legitimate in the normative sense, and there are also various ideas of what follows for the political entity and its subjects from the political entity possessing normative legitimacy. We will outline the more influential views briefly because this background is necessary for placing the contributions to this volume within the tradition of the debate on legitimacy and authority. This will also, we hope, have the effect of identifying some small consensus on which tradition appears best suited to dealing with the specific challenges raised by considering legitimacy in an international rather than domestic context.

One very important understanding is found in the consent tradition, and its basic idea can be stated simply: it is the consent of persons within a state to the authority of the state that legitimates the state with respect to those persons. This simple formulation is obviously not a full expression of a fully worked out consent understanding, but every such understanding has this insight at its heart, and it is sufficient for the purposes of this introduction to work with this simple formulation.

Two main interpretations of consent within this tradition can be distinguished. The first is that consent is to be understood as hypothetical consent,[5] the second that it is to be understood as historical consent. David Hume raised powerful criticisms against both interpretations. He objected to the interpretation that historical consent could legitimate by first arguing that there never was historical consent in the first place.[6] Further, even if it was true that the historical parties in given historical circumstances gave their consent, it does not follow from this that presently existing parties are bound by this historical consent. Hume also levelled this kind of objection at the idea of hypothetical consent, the idea being that while the hypothetical parties in the hypothetical position might have hypothetically consented to certain rules, this does not bind actual parties in actual positions.[7] Those rules may be worth following

[5] See for example: J. Rawls, *A Theory of Justice* (Cambridge, MA: Harvard University Press, 1971); B. Barry, *Justice as Impartiality* (Oxford University Press, 1995); T. M. Scanlon, *What We Owe To Each Other* (Cambridge, MA: Harvard University Press, 1998).

[6] D. Hume, 'Of the Original Contract' (1777), in *Essays, Moral, Political and Literary* (Indianapolis, IN: Liberty Classics, 1987).

[7] See also R. Dworkin, 'The Original Position', in N. Daniels (ed.), *Reading Rawls* (New York, NY: Basic Books, 1975).

for several reasons, and so actual parties may agree to follow them, but they agree to follow them because of those reasons and not because hypothetical parties would have agreed to follow them in hypothetical circumstances – hypothetical consent is, or so the argument goes, both non-binding on and irrelevant to actual people in real situations. The second objection to hypothetical consent, meanwhile, is also simple but powerful. Consenting to being tortured, or killed, does not legitimate being tortured or killed, and promising to obey orders to act in ways that are morally prohibited does not justify acting in such ways. At the very least, then, consent cannot be the only condition for the legitimacy of an authority.

These objections are not decisive but are important to outline because they describe problems that will be faced by any account of international legitimacy that is based on hypothetical consent. Having mentioned these problems we will not further pursue the hypothetical consent model, because one view in the context of international legitimacy has been that it is the actual consent of states to international institutions that legitimates those institutions. When consent theory is discussed in this volume, it is this view which is considered.

The first three chapters in this volume are unanimous in rejecting this view (i.e. the one from actual consent) of international legitimacy. They offer a variety of reasons which together amount to a substantial case against the extension of the consent idea. Many states are themselves illegitimate, for instance, and this makes it difficult to see how their consent could legitimate an international institution. If in response to this one claims instead that it is the consent of democratic states that legitimates international institutions, one faces other problems. First, there is the problem of what Allen Buchanan and Robert O. Keohane call 'bureaucratic discretion',[8] which is the idea that even within democratic states 'at some point the impact of the popular will on how political power is used becomes so attenuated as to be normatively anaemic'.[9] This problem would exist for international institutions even if there was a world democracy, but given its absence the problem of bureaucratic discretion becomes even more important at the international level because 'global governance institutions require lengthening the chain of delegation',[10] i.e. the chain between the popular will and the exercise of political power. Second, as Simon Caney remarks, the restriction to democratic states also creates the problem of explaining how and why

[8] A. Buchanan and R. O. Keohane, Chapter 1, this volume. [9] *Ibid.* [10] *Ibid.*

international institutions 'possess legitimacy over the unfortunate members of illiberal states whose lives are structured by these institutions but have no input into the process'.[11]

Additionally – and this problem arises whether we limit the legitimating power of consent to democratic states or not – the imbalance of power between states means that weak states may have no choice but to accept a particular international institution, and this makes it difficult to argue that they have truly consented to it. The imbalance of power creates the further problem that even if we could argue that weaker states did somehow consent to international institutions, the design and operation of these institutions would be dominated by the more powerful states and used to serve their ends, thereby creating injustice and making it difficult to claim that the institutions were legitimate.

Theorists of international legitimacy seem to agree that the consent tradition cannot be used as an exclusive explication of the conditions required for international legitimacy. This looks like being one of the areas of consensus referred to earlier. Note that this is, as one would expect in such a contested field, a very limited claim – we suggest that the consensus is only that the consent tradition cannot be used to provide sufficient conditions for international legitimacy; whether state consent is a necessary condition or not is still up for grabs. Buchanan and Keohane, for instance, argue that ongoing democratic state consent *is* a necessary but insufficient condition for international legitimacy.[12]

Turning away from the consent tradition, we consider now a second major tradition in the debate on legitimacy, namely that of instrumentalist accounts of legitimacy. The most sophisticated account in this tradition comes from Joseph Raz, and consists of what he terms the service conception of authority.

The idea at the root of the service conception is that an authority is legitimate for a person when (a) by obeying its orders that person will do better at acting for the reasons that she ought to act for independently (the normal justification condition), and (b) the authority takes those independent reasons into account when it issues its directives (the dependence condition). It follows from these two conditions, argues Raz, that the directives of a legitimate authority are not an additional

[11] S. Caney, Chapter 3, this volume.
[12] Buchanan and Keohane, Chapter 1, this volume.

independent reason for action, but rather a reason for action that excludes some independent reasons (the pre-emption thesis).[13]

This is an account of authority that specifies both a justification right on the part of the agent exercising power *plus* a content-independent obligation to obey on the part of the subjects under the authority of that agent. Rather than directly attacking this interpretation of authority, one important strategy in the debate on international legitimacy has been to attempt to drive a wedge between what we will call 'authority' and 'legitimacy'.[14] Many seem to adopt this strategy and doing this might well be another area of consensus in the debate. Roughly speaking, the idea has been to first suggest that legitimacy consists only of the justification right on the part of the agent exercising that power without any corresponding obligation to obey, then to attempt to secure legitimacy rather than authority for international institutions.

This is an understandable move, because the normal justification condition and the dependence condition are clearly very difficult to satisfy. Because of its importance in the international legitimacy debate, we would like to briefly point out one important problem that has to be dealt with if the move is to be successful. This is the question of whether the distinction between authority and legitimacy, as it is outlined above, can be sustained at all. Does an agent-justification right make sense without a corresponding duty?[15] Broadly speaking, there are two possible options. One would either have to deny that an agent-justification right implies any duties on the part of others, or one could accept an implication but argue that what was implied was something less than a duty. If one takes the first option, one faces the problem that it then becomes more difficult to understand what the right in question actually means. Normally, when we say, for instance, that one has a right to free speech, we understand this right as entailing some sorts of duties on the part of others; and even if this duty is simply not to interfere with, rather than promote, free speech, when fleshed out this often amounts to substantial

[13] J. Raz, *The Morality of Freedom* (Oxford University Press, 1986), part I. For criticisms of the pre-emptive thesis see L. Green, *The Authority of the State* (Oxford: Clarendon Press, 1988), 113–14; Stephen Perry, 'Second-Order Reasons, Uncertainty and Legal Theory', *Southern California Law Review*, 62 (1989), 913; F. Schauer, *Playing by the Rules* (Oxford: Clarendon Press, 1991), 913–94.

[14] See for example A. Buchanan, *Justice, Legitimacy and Self-Determination: Moral Foundations for International Law* (Oxford University Press, 2004).

[15] For attempts to argue that it does, see Applbaum, 'Legitimacy in a Bastard Kingdom', 85–88; R. Ladenson, 'In Defense of a Hobbesian Conception of Law', in J. Raz (ed.), *Authority* (Oxford: Basil Blackwell, 1990), 32–55, esp. 32–40.

duties. If one were to take the second option instead, a difficulty would lie in explaining exactly what was implied, and how these demands, whatever they were, were to be meaningfully distinguished from duties.

The stringent requirements of the service conception along with how influential it has been have together made a major contribution, then, to the direction the international legitimacy debate has taken. In addition, the tradition the service conception exemplifies (i.e. instrumentalist interpretations of legitimacy) has also been very influential in the debate on international legitimacy.

We can see this influence in Arthur Applbaum's contribution to this volume (Chapter 10). He attempts in it to identify conditions under which the use of force in international relations is morally permissible. He puts the question thus: is forcing a people to be free possible, and if so, is it ever morally permissible? Now, forcing a people to be free, if possible, seems like a classic case of a paternal action, and Applbaum argues that paternal actions are most likely to be just when three conditions are met: the freedom of the agent being paternalised is already impaired, the good at stake is that agent's future freedom, and the agent's retrospective endorsement is likely. The agent's retrospective endorsement is most likely, of course, when the paternal action results in the agent's future freedom being secured. Applbaum claims, that is, that a necessary condition for the legitimacy of forcing a people to be free is that the use of force should *result in certain effects*, namely that the agent's future freedom be secured.

Buchanan and Keohane argue in Chapter 1 for a standard of legitimacy which contains, amongst other things, the following two conditions: in order to be legitimate, international institutions must (1) not violate the least controversial human rights and (2) provide benefits that would otherwise not be obtained, compared to other practically feasible institutions and not compared to the optimal case. The second condition is clearly in the tradition of instrumental justifications of legitimacy, and while the first can be seen as a constraint, it is also plausible to either see it, or recast it, as an instrumental condition that needs to be satisfied for institutions to be legitimate. Similarly, Caney also argues in Chapter 3 for a standard of legitimacy which includes the condition that for an institution to be legitimate it must ensure that 'persons' most fundamental rights are upheld', and he explicitly refers to this as 'an instrumental component'[16] of his standard of legitimacy.

[16] Both quotes are from Caney, Chapter 3, this volume.

This seems to be another of those areas of consensus in the debate on international legitimacy. Again, however, it is necessary to be clear about what we are claiming exactly. It is the limited claim that any account of international legitimacy seems to pay homage to the tradition of instrumentalist justifications of legitimacy by accepting that at least one part of the standard for legitimacy is that the institution in question satisfies certain instrumental considerations. We are not claiming that there is a consensus that instrumental considerations constitute sufficient conditions for the legitimacy of international institutions, but rather that there seems to be agreement that they are necessary ones.

Samantha Besson's chapter in this volume (Chapter 2) brings out very clearly, in fact, that there isn't agreement on instrumental considerations being sufficient to legitimate international institutions. She attempts to provide a feasible model of instantiating global democracy. The idea is that given the weaknesses of the view that state consent can legitimate international institutions, the model of global democracy she proposes could serve as a better way of legitimating those institutions. Her chapter can be seen as flowing from a third important tradition in the debate on legitimacy and authority, namely the idea that the legitimacy of institutions derives from the procedures they follow in issuing their directives.[17] One strand in this tradition, and the one that Besson's chapter can be understood as belonging to, is that these procedures are democratic ones,[18] but this is not settled, for there seem to be ways in which procedures could legitimate without them being democratic.

Buchanan and Keohane, and Caney, include different procedural elements in the conditions for legitimacy that they propose in their respective contributions to this book. One of Caney's conditions, for instance, is that in order to be legitimate international institutions must 'provide a fair political framework in which to determine which principles of justice should be adopted to regulate the global economy'.[19] Buchanan and Keohane, meanwhile, argue that legitimate international institutions must make 'provision for ongoing, inclusive deliberation about what global justice requires'.[20]

[17] For an influential sociological account of the significance of procedural legitimacy, see N. Luhmann, *Legitimation durch Verfahren* (Frankfurt: Suhrkamp, 1983) (first published 1969).

[18] See J. Waldron, *Law and Disagreement* (New York, NY: Oxford University Press, 1999); P. Singer, *Democracy and Disobedience* (Oxford University Press, 1973).

[19] Caney, Chapter 3, this volume.

[20] Buchanan and Keohane, Chapter 1, this volume.

It is not the aim of Steven Ratner's chapter (Chapter 4) to provide procedural conditions for legitimacy, but his contribution can also be fruitfully seen as being part of the debate that centres on this tradition. He takes existing international institutions as a fundamental starting point and subjects these to analysis aimed at answering the question: do they act 'impartially in the broad sense of not playing favourites in the way they treat certain actors and situations with which they deal?'[21] Among the institutions he considers are the Security Council and the IMF, and the decision-making processes of both these organisations can certainly be said to use partial procedures.[22]

Given this partiality, the tradition of procedural legitimacy could be understood as providing a basis for the claim that these international institutions are illegitimate. Ratner argues, however, that in many cases unequal treatment can be justified from a second-order impartial perspective. For example, the nature of the Security Council could be defended on impartial utilitarian-type grounds by arguing that it would be paralysed with a large membership, or that the veto promotes stability and peace. This is an impartial justification because the limited and exclusive composition of the Security Council is justified on the basis of the benefits that such a composition would in theory generate for *all* countries, namely the preservation of international peace and security.

Ratner does not argue that the possible second-order impartial justifications of unequal treatment are conclusive or even uniformly persuasive. Rather, the point is that any appraisal of international organisations needs to move beyond knee-jerk opposition to unequal treatment – it can be legitimate for these organisations to make distinctions in whom they admit, who will decide how they act, and what will be the target of their decisions. Further, these distinctions need to be justified from an impartial perspective, because while partiality may be justifiable – even desirable – in private interaction, justice in the context of international institutions demands the higher standard of impartiality.

Ratner can be understood, then, as arguing that while international institutions ought to be impartial this does not mean that the partial procedures that they actually follow should be rejected out of hand. He

[21] S. R. Ratner, Chapter 4, this volume.

[22] As Ratner explains, in the case of the Security Council this claim is made on the basis of the special powers of the Security Council, the privileged position within the Security Council of the five permanent members, and the veto power they enjoy. In the case of the IMF, the grounds are that votes on decisions are allocated based on each state's financial contribution to the IMF, leading to a situation where the rich states dominate the institution.

provides a possible defence of the (first-order) partial procedures of institutions like the IMF and the Security Council, and this defence makes most sense when it is understood as a challenge to the influential view that legitimacy requires that specific sorts of procedures – in this case (first-order) impartial ones – be followed. This defence, as we have said, consists of suggesting second-order justifications, such as defending the partial nature of the Security Council on the basis of the benefits this provides to all countries. This type of justification could also be read as being in line with the instrumentalist tradition of legitimacy, because such a defence rests on the first-order partial procedures having certain effects.

Ratner's chapter shows that there can be, and is, much debate over what procedural legitimacy requires. The general debate, however, seems to be inching towards a consensus that a procedural element, whatever it might consist of, is one of the necessary conditions for the legitimacy of international institutions, and more slowly towards the idea that this procedural element has to be, if possible, democratic. This makes sense if we take into account the minimal consensus we claimed existed on the necessity of an instrumental element in the conditions for the legitimacy of international institutions. The least controversial, and most plausible, necessary instrumental condition for the legitimacy of these institutions seems to be that they uphold basic human rights, i.e. the rights that there is the least disagreement over, and that are the least susceptible to charges of parochialism. Now, it is notoriously difficult to ground even the most basic of human rights satisfactorily, but their plausibility does seem to depend on some sort of generally shared assumption about the equal worth of human beings as human beings and the treatment this implies towards them.

It is clearly not the case that the use of democratic procedures guarantees that basic human rights will be upheld. Indeed, a well-known difficulty with accounts that claim that democratic procedures are a necessary and sufficient condition for legitimacy is that democratic procedures can result in outcomes that clearly and systematically violate basic human rights, leading to the thought that a state which produces such outcomes, even if through democratic procedures, cannot be legitimate.

It also seems plausible, however, to argue that democratic procedures have a better chance of upholding basic human rights than any other feasible political procedures.[23] Second, one might further (and differently)

[23] See A. Sen and J. Dreze, *Hunger and Public Action* (Oxford University Press, 1989); P. Dasgupta, *An Inquiry into Well-Being and Destitution* (Oxford University Press, 1993).

argue that a belief in the equal worth of human beings implies that they should be able to participate equally in the business of governing themselves and, once again, democratic procedures seem to be the types of procedures which, if other conditions hold, can secure this. Neither of these arguments is uncontroversial, and we do not mean to suggest otherwise. They are, however, prominent, and they can help explain why a commitment to the upholding of human rights as being a necessary part of any standard of legitimacy can lead to a further commitment to democratic procedures as also being a necessary part of a standard of legitimacy.

It is important to note, however, that we are not claiming that there is a consensus that democratic procedures are necessary ideal conditions for legitimacy, only that there are theoretical pressures which tend to push the debate that way.[24] The discussion also brings out the idea that while the instrumental and procedural conceptions of legitimacy are different they impact on each other. Additionally, the discussion had a speculative purpose, namely to air the idea that, given the apparent consensus on the necessity of instrumental conditions as part of any set of necessary and sufficient conditions for legitimacy, and further given the apparent consensus that these instrumental considerations are to do with upholding basic human rights, one important future direction for theorists in this field to take might be to consider how basic human rights are best grounded, and what, if anything, follows from those grounds for the conditions required for procedural legitimacy.[25]

This has been a rather involved discussion, so a summary is in order. We have suggested that there is a small consensus on some aspects of the debate on the legitimacy of international institutions – the consent theory in its unadulterated form has been largely abandoned in this field, and some form of instrumentalist justification seems to be generally considered necessary. This instrumentalist condition is often thought to be insufficient on its own, and there seems to be a general view that a further procedural condition is necessary. The most common instrumental condition (that institutions uphold basic human rights) seems to create theoretical pressures towards further adopting a particular conception of

[24] In his ideal theory of relations between 'peoples' Rawls considers decent societies as legitimate even though they are in his understanding non-democratic. See J. Rawls, *The Law of Peoples* (Cambridge, MA: Harvard University Press, 1999), 62–78.

[25] For an extended discussion of the relation between justice, human rights and international legitimacy, see Buchanan, *Justice, Legitimacy and Self-Determination*.

procedural legitimacy, namely a democratic one. We also suggested two possible (and compatible) directions for the debate – the first has to do with justifying the most common instrumental condition, and what that would imply, and the second has to do with investigating the common strategy of separating legitimacy and authority when it comes to international institutions.

Justice. Rawlsian social liberalism and cosmopolitan liberalism

We have been talking so far of legitimacy but the discussion has already taken us in the direction of justice. This is not surprising, as there is a close connection between the two. Recall, for instance, that one of the objections to consent theory was that consent alone could not legitimate, because certain sorts of injustice – systematic torture, for instance – could not be legitimated by any means. This kind of criticism is similar to a problem that proponents of the democratic conception of procedural legitimacy face. The problem is that democratic procedures do not seem able to legitimate every result they generate; so for instance, a democratically decided policy of apartheid could not be legitimate. Recall, too, that one instrumental condition proposed for the legitimacy of international institutions is that they uphold basic human rights. In other words, one common condition for international legitimacy is a substantive justice condition, and more generally, justice considerations seem relevant to legitimacy no matter what conception of legitimacy one works with.

Apart from this close connection, justice and legitimacy are similar in that the philosophical debates surrounding the two concepts both have long and venerable traditions.[26] Just as with legitimacy, however, for most of this long tradition philosophers have concentrated on asking what justice is *within* societies. Even as late as 1971, for instance, when the book that has dominated work in political philosophy since was first

[26] See, to refer to only two classical texts: Plato, *The Republic*, G. R. F. Ferrari (ed.), T. Griffith (trans.) (Cambridge University Press, 2000); T. Hobbes, *Leviathan*, R. Tuck (ed.) (Cambridge University Press, 1991). For accounts of the history of these debates, see G. Vlastos, *Studies in Greek Philosophy, Volume II: Socrates, Plato, and Their Tradition*, Daniel W. Graham (ed.) (Princeton University Press, 1996); O. Höffe, *Political Justice. Foundations for a Critical Philosophy of Law and the State* (Cambridge: Polity, 1995), part I; J. Rawls, *Lectures on the History of Philosophy* (Cambridge, MA: Harvard University Press, 2007).

published, John Rawls outlined a theory of justice that was explicitly meant to apply to 'the basic structure of society conceived for the time being as a closed system isolated from other societies'.[27]

Rawls does briefly discuss international justice in *A Theory of Justice*, where he suggests that principles of international justice can be found by 'extend[ing] the theory of justice to the law of nations'.[28] To arrive at these principles, he proposes an international original position in which agents would represent nations rather than individuals. It was only much later, however, that Rawls began to develop these suggestions.[29] By this time, the questions constituting this problem had begun to come to the forefront of political philosophy.[30] This is not the place to attempt a history of ideas but one can nonetheless make some remarks as a partial explanation. Increased globalisation has led to both increased interdependence between societies and, as importantly, an increased awareness of this increasing interdependence. Recall that for Rawls the 'primary subject of justice is the basic structure of society'.[31] There can be, and is, disagreement over what constitutes the basic structure and whether there is an international basic structure at all.[32] The very existence of this disagreement, however, owes something to the increased interdependence between societies, and therefore this increased interdependence is one of the reasons for the increasing attention questions of

[27] Rawls, *A Theory of Justice*, 7–8. [28] *Ibid.*, 377.

[29] First in J. Rawls, 'The Law of Peoples', in S. Shute and S. Hurley (eds.), *On Human Rights: The Oxford Amnesty Lectures 1993* (New York, NY: Basic Books, 1993), 41–82; and then in J. Rawls, *The Law of Peoples*.

[30] See, for instance, C. Beitz, *Political Theory and International Relations* (Princeton University Press, 1979 and 1999); T. Pogge, *Realizing Rawls* (Ithaca, NY: Cornell University Press, 1989); H. Shue, *Basic Rights. Subsistence, Affluence and U.S. Foreign Policy*, 2nd edn (Princeton University Press, 1996); T Pogge and D. Moellendorf (eds.), *Global Justice. Seminal Essays* (St. Paul, MN: Paragon House, 2008); T. Pogge and K. Horton (eds.), *Global Ethics. Seminal Essays* (St. Paul, MN: Paragon House, 2008). For an extensive list of related literature see M. Blake, 'International Justice', E. N. Zalta (ed.), *The Stanford Encyclopedia of Philosophy* (Winter 2008 Edition), online, available at: http://plato.stanford.edu/archives/win2008/entries/international-justice.

[31] For Rawls's own view of what the basic structure consists of, see Rawls, *A Theory of Justice*, 7; J. Rawls, *Political Liberalism* (New York, NY: Columbia University Press, 1993), 255–88; Rawls, *The Law of Peoples*, 108.

[32] See Beitz, *Political Theory and International Relations*, 151; B. Barry, 'Humanity and Justice in Global Perspective', in J. Pennock and J. Chapman (eds.), *NOMOS XXIV, Ethics, Economics and the Law* (New York, NY: Harvester Wheatsheaf, 1982), 233; Pogge, *Realizing Rawls*, 23–24; G. A. Cohen, *Rescuing Justice and Equality* (Cambridge, MA: Harvard University Press, 2008), 129–32.

international justice have recently been given in political philosophy. Another development that has contributed to this increased attention has been the establishment and development of non-state actors, and the increased power these actors have.[33] Traditionally, the theoretical focus had been concentrated solely on states, as they were thought to be the only influential actors in the international arena. Changing circumstances have made this exclusive focus seem, at the least, incomplete, leading naturally to the question of how to accommodate the widened range of actors within any systematic explanation of what justice (and legitimacy) involve at the international level.

There has been a methodological similarity in the development of the debates on international legitimacy and international justice, and it is an entirely unsurprising one. We saw in the section on legitimacy that theories of legitimacy that had been developed within the context of closed societies were used as starting points from which a theory of legitimacy in the international context could be developed. Similarly, given the long tradition of theorising about justice within closed societies, the obvious move to make in tackling international justice is, in Rawls's words, to 'extend the theory of justice to the law of nations'.[34] Controversy arises, however, when we attempt to work out how theories of justice are to be so extended. Outlining the different attempts to work this out is one useful way of beginning to place the contributions in this volume within the context of the wider philosophical discourse on international justice.[35]

Those who argue that the principles of justice which have been designed for the domestic context can and ought to be extended completely to the international context can be called cosmopolitans. There are many variants of cosmopolitanism, but the idea at the heart of all these variants is that national boundaries are arbitrary and irrelevant, and therefore indefensible, limitations on the application of principles of justice.[36] A cosmopolitan might agree, for instance, that Rawls is correct

[33] See C. Beitz, 'Social and Cosmopolitan Liberalism', *International Affairs (Royal Institute of International Affairs 1944 -)*, 75 (1999), 515–29, 517.

[34] Rawls, *A Theory of Justice*.

[35] For a good and more extended account of the varying answers possible, see M. Blake, 'International Justice'.

[36] See S. Caney, *Justice Beyond Borders. A Global Political Theory* (New York, NY: Oxford University Press, 2006); Pogge, *Realizing Rawls*; Beitz, *Political Theory and International Relations* (1979 edition); K.-C. Tan, *Justice without Borders* (New York, NY: Cambridge University Press, 2004).

in claiming that the difference principle ought to govern the design of institutions within closed societies, but would further claim that it (i.e. the difference principle) ought to be applied across the entire world, rather than just across say Germany. This position can be placed at one end of the spectrum of possible views regarding the extendibility of domestic principles of distributive justice to the international order.

Peter Koller's contribution to this volume (Chapter 6) provides a systematic and rich discussion of a cosmopolitan interpretation of what justice requires globally. Koller delineates four abstract kinds of justice: transactional, political, distributive and corrective. According to his taxonomy, transactional justice is applicable in exchange relationships, political justice in power relationships, distributive justice in communal relationships and corrective justice in wrongness relationships. He then argues that the types of social interactions that are required for these types of justice to apply are all instantiated at the global level: nations and their members maintain international trade relationships; authorised power is either exercised by international institutions or required for a just global order; the existence of, for example, international economic cooperation and negative effects of societal activities across borders raise distributive problems across nations; nations can be held subject to the demands of corrective justice in the case of wrongs done to each other. He goes on to argue that the international system fails to meet the demands of these four kinds of justice insofar as they apply, but the relevant point here is the prior claim that the international system *can* be held to the demands of these four kinds of justice insofar as they apply. This is a claim that places Koller, and his contribution to this volume, firmly in the cosmopolitan camp.

Rawls, of course, is an exemplar of a different kind of position. He argues that the difference principle cannot be extended to global society, and that at most just societies have a duty of assistance to burdened societies. One argument that is often used for the existence of special duties to members of one's own society rests on the alleged relevance of the existence of social cooperation to determining the scope of principles of justice.[37] Charles Beitz provided an early and succinct description of

[37] See, for example, S. Scheffler, *Boundaries and Allegiances. Problems of Justice and Responsibility in Liberal Thought* (Oxford University Press, 2001), chs. 5 and 6; M. Blake, 'Distributive Justice, State Coercion, and Autonomy', *Philosophy and Public Affairs*, 30 (2001), 257–96; A. Sangiovanni, 'Global Justice, Reciprocity, and the State', *Philosophy and Public Affairs*, 35 (2007), 3–39.

the difference between the two positions (the second of which he calls social liberalism) in the following way: 'social liberalism holds that the problem of international justice is fundamentally one of fairness to societies (or peoples), whereas cosmopolitan liberalism holds that it is fairness to persons'.[38]

One could legitimately – but perhaps not uncontroversially – argue that Rawls's own position is consistent with some sort of cosmopolitanism, since it is possible to interpret the duty of assistance as a cosmopolitan duty, and also because he thinks that certain kinds of human rights are limits on the sovereignty of states even within their own territories. He is anti-cosmopolitan to the extent that he denies principles of distributive justice can be extended from domestic to international contexts, but he nonetheless holds some principles to be valid universally.[39] This brings out an important point, namely that the dispute between cosmopolitans and social liberals often centres on the extendibility of principles of distributive justice, rather than on the universal validity of *all* principles of justice.[40]

David Miller's contribution to this volume (Chapter 8) can be understood as coming from this tradition, broadly speaking. For while he accepts the cosmopolitan responsibility that 'we all share in a general responsibility to protect human rights that crosses national borders',[41] he specifies that these rights are 'to be understood in a fairly narrow sense, as basic rights – rights to life, bodily integrity, basic nutrition and health, and so forth'.[42] As Miller says in his chapter, he has elsewhere argued that a wider set of rights should not 'be seen as human rights proper, (but) as something else – rights of citizenship, for example'.[43] This is not a view that cosmopolitans could accept. It is important to note, however, that while he clearly comes from the tradition of social liberalism, in this

38 Beitz, 'Social and Cosmopolitan Liberalism', 515.

39 However, Rawls leaves open whether his duty of assistance is best understood as a principle of distributive justice. See Rawls, *The Law of Peoples*, 106.

40 There is a third position, at the opposite end of the spectrum to cosmopolitanism, which holds that *no* principles of justice can be extended from the domestic to the international context. We do not discuss it here because it isn't relevant to the chapters in this volume. But see T. Nagel, 'The Problem of Global Justice', *Philosophy and Public Affairs*, 33 (2005), 113–47, A. MacIntyre, 'Is Patriotism a Virtue?' (The Lindley Lecture) (University of Kansas, 1984); and M. Walzer, *Spheres of Justice* (New York, NY: Basic Books, 1983).

41 D. Miller, Chapter 8, this volume. 42 *Ibid.*

43 *Ibid.* Miller's argument for the wider set of rights being citizenship rights can be found in D. Miller, *National Responsibility and Global Justice* (Oxford University Press, 2007).

chapter he explicitly tries to avoid the dispute over whether the wider set of rights should be understood in cosmopolitan or Rawlsian terms.

Herlinde Pauer-Studer's contribution (Chapter 7), too, can be seen as coming from this tradition. She first makes the distinction explained above, retaining the term 'cosmopolitan' and referring to what we have so far called 'social liberalism' as a 'political conception of justice'. She then attempts in her chapter to defend this political conception of justice, i.e. a conception that holds that 'justice applies to the basic structure of a particular society (nation-state), and, moreover, that duties of justice in a strict sense hold merely between the members of a particular society (nation-state)'.[44] Pauer-Studer focuses on one influential cosmopolitan account of international justice, namely that of Thomas Pogge's, which she characterises as being 'monist', i.e. as claiming that the same 'normative principles should apply to institutions and individual choices'.[45] This monist view is criticised, and various grounds for retaining the institution of the nation-state are offered. Thus, as the contributions of Koller, Miller and Pauer-Struder show, understanding the distinction between cosmopolitans and Rawlsians is essential to understanding both the general debate on international justice and the chapters in this volume that contribute to this debate.

Matthias Lutz-Bachmann takes a similar line in a different context (Chapter 9). He suggests that Michael Walzer's just war theory first argues for a moral reading of the validity claims of human rights and then uses this to justify the use of force in international relations. Lutz-Bachmann argues that this theory fails, and one of the grounds for this claim is that the theory does not distinguish between moral obligations and legal obligations for collectives like states. He makes, that is, a distinction between '"moral obligations" and "legal duties", that means between "obligations" which address moral subjects like individual actors and "duties" which bind collective actors like states or international organisations constituted by legal and coercive frameworks'.[46] This distinction suggests a commitment, in Pauer-Studer's terms, to a political conception of justice, because it implies that different normative principles apply to individuals as opposed to institutions.

Daniel Butt, meanwhile, attempts in Chapter 5 to limit the importance of the controversy. He calls social liberalism 'international libertarianism', on the basis that 'those within this school adopt principles of distributive justice between states which are analogous to those principles of distributive

[44] H. Pauer-Studer, Chapter 7, this volume. [45] *Ibid.*
[46] M. Lutz-Bachmann, Chapter 9, this volume.

justice which libertarians such as Robert Nozick maintain should obtain between individuals in domestic society'.[47] He argues that while cosmopolitan liberals can easily accept the claim that the current international order is distributively unjust, international libertarians – i.e. social liberals – might want to claim that it isn't. However, international libertarians have to be sensitive to the provenance of the current distribution, and Butt argues that this distribution has not come about according to principles of just acquisition and just transfer. Consequently, he claims, even international libertarians have to admit that the present international order is distributively unjust.

Butt is not alone, in fact, in attempting to limit the importance of the controversy between cosmopolitans and Rawlsians. Recall that in his contribution, Miller specifies a non-cosmopolitan list of basic human rights. At the same time, he deliberately avoids engaging with the debate on whether a more extended list of rights should be seen as human rights or citizenship rights, and argues that the conclusions in his chapter can be accepted regardless of the view one takes on this issue. Similarly, Pauer-Studer makes concessions to cosmopolitanism and attempts to dissolve some of the differences between it and the political conception of justice by arguing that even if one holds that there are principles of international distributive justice, nation-states would still be necessary in order to achieve more international justice according to those principles.

The point here is not to determine whether these different attempts at limiting the importance of the controversy were successful or not, but rather that all three authors felt it necessary to make the attempt at all. When a controversy is important and alive, one important strategy for making progress is to attempt to come to relatively uncontroversial conclusions; conclusions, that is, that all parties can agree with while retaining their differing views. It is precisely the fact that these chapters attempt to limit the importance of the controversy, therefore, that brings out its significance, and the extent to which it is unresolved.

Ideal and non-ideal theory. How to understand the practical relevance of international justice and legitimacy

The debate on ideal and non-ideal theory is the third and final theoretical perspective we will consider. Non-ideal theorists argue that normative theorists have to take seriously empirical realities that hinder the

[47] D. Butt, Chapter 5, this volume.

applicability of their principles, because if they don't they will provide principles which are not politically feasible and these principles will therefore fail to be action-guiding.[48] Normative principles which require a world state with a universal adult franchise for example, are often criticised on this ground. Ideal theorists, on the other hand, argue that allowing political feasibility this central role in justifying principles of justice will lead to normative theorists endorsing injustice. So, for example, theorists operating with this political feasibility constraint in the mid eighteenth century would, or so the charge goes, have endorsed slavery because of the political infeasibility at the time of abolishing it.[49]

The twin horns of this dilemma, i.e. the charges of 'practical irrelevance' and 'adaptive preference formation' (or 'conservatism') respectively, are highly relevant to the theoretical debate on the justice and legitimacy of international institutions. The problems that international institutions try to address – for example global poverty, climate change, widespread human rights violations – strike many as particularly urgent and compelling. On the one hand, these problems are so important, and any whole-scale reform of the international order so unlikely, that it can seem as though if one is to make any contribution to the problem one has to take the existing order as given and only suggest reforms that are realisable here and now; but on the other adopting this strategy might mean accepting more injustice than one ought to accept, and it might also limit the possibility of substantial reform which might be required to solve these problems.

One solution to the dilemma is, of course, simply to impale oneself on one of its horns. That is to say, one could hold that a theory of justice should either only contain non-ideal principles, or that it should only contain ideal principles. This could be called an exclusive understanding of ideal and non-ideal theorising, but the problem with this understanding is that both horns are sharp and painful. Both the practical irrelevance and the adaptive preference charge are serious criticisms, and any exclusive understanding will be susceptible to at least one of them.

One natural response to this is to try and develop a complex and complementary understanding, one which argues that a theory of justice

48 See for instance C. Farrelly, 'Justice in Ideal Theory: A Refutation', *Political Studies*, 55 (2007), 844–64.

49 Andrew Mason points out this difficulty very clearly in the course of developing his own multi-level understanding in A. Mason, 'Just Constraints', *British Journal of Political Science*, 34 (2004), 251–68.

must contain both ideal and non-ideal principles. This understanding attempts to accommodate the insights of both ideal and non-ideal theorising, and by doing so defuses the strength of both the practical irrelevance and adaptive preference charges. This benefit comes, however, at the cost of problems elsewhere, the most important of which is this: if a theory of justice contains both ideal and non-ideal principles, how are we to understand the relation between them? The 'theory of the second-best' prevents us from saying that under non-ideal conditions the optimal strategy is to realise as many of the elements of the ideal as we can, to the extent that we can.[50] But if this is the case then it seems difficult to explain what exactly the relevance of ideal principles is to non-ideal principles.[51]

This is a considerable problem, and not one to be glossed over. In what follows we use a complementary understanding of ideal and non-ideal theorising as a tool with which to frame and organise some of the papers in this collection but we do not claim to have addressed the problem of the second-best, or even that this problem could be overcome. Rather, we claim that this is a useful and interesting way to understand some of these contributions and we then make the limited claim that such an understanding is helpful in developing the debate on international institutions because it allows for criticisms and contributions on different levels.

In order to explain and defend this limited claim, however, it is first necessary to outline the understanding we will be working with. On this understanding, there are four different types, and two distinct levels, of principles in a theory of justice. The four different types of principles are:

(1) ideal non-institutional principles;
(2) ideal institutional principles;
(3) non-ideal non-institutional principles; and
(4) non-ideal institutional principles.

Principles (1) and (2) constitute the first level, and principles (3) and (4) the second level.

An example of an ideal non-institutional principle is the following: human rights ought to be fully realised. The principles of justice in Rawls's special conception[52] are further examples of ideal non-institutional

[50] On this see for instance R. E. Goodin, 'Political Ideals and Political Practice', *British Journal of Political Science*, 25 (1995), 37–56.

[51] A. Sen, 'What Do We Want From a Theory of Justice?', *The Journal of Philosophy*, 103 (2006), 215–38.

[52] See footnote 55, below, and accompanying text.

principles, for example the equal basic liberties principle. Ideal non-institutional principles specify, in other words, what it is that we ought to aim at under ideal conditions – they tell us that the social ideal consists of *a*, *b* and *c* rather than *x*, *y* and *z*. They are, that is, constitutive of the ideal. Ideal institutional principles, on the other hand, specify how (under ideal conditions) institutions ought to be designed in order to achieve the aims specified by ideal non-institutional principles. Suppose, for instance, that the social ideal of *a*, *b* and *c* would be fully realised by the institution of constitutional democracy. In this case, the ideal institutional principle would direct us to implement such a system. Ideal institutional principles that are correct have two main features: implementing them leads to the full realisation of the ideal non-institutional principles, and they tell us what the institutions required for this full realisation will look like.[53]

Let us suppose for a moment that the ideal institutional principles require the creation of a world democracy with a universal adult franchise, and they specify that this means institutions like a world parliament and so on. It's uncontroversial to claim that under current non-ideal conditions the institutions required by the ideal institutional principles are not realisable. But what kinds of institutions ought we design instead? It is to answer this question that non-ideal institutional principles are introduced. These principles specify what, under non-ideal conditions, our institutions ought to look like so that we can realise the non-institutional principles we want to realise.[54]

There is a deliberate ambiguity in that last sentence, because there is a contentious issue at the heart of it. Let us agree that non-institutional principles specify what institutions ought to look like under non-ideal conditions in order to realise the non-institutional principles we want to

[53] For further discussion of the distinction between ideal non-institutional and ideal institutional principles see A. Swift, 'The Value of Philosophy in Nonideal Circumstances', *Social Theory and Practice*, 34 (2008), 366–68. (Swift distinguishes between 'evaluative' and 'action-guiding' principles.)

[54] Compare Lutz-Bachmann's proposals for a transitional regime in order to promote the establishment of a just international order in Chapter 9, this volume. Lutz-Bachmann's proposed ideal and non-ideal institutional principles reflect the Kantian tradition of political philosophy. He argues that the UN, especially the Security Council and juridical institutions like the ICC, should be reformed such that a global public law which can be effectively specified, applied and executed can be put in place. We should also aim at deeper legal and more inclusive cooperation between democratic states, and we should try to build a global democratic public, which would help to undermine totalitarian regimes and violent cultures, which are the main source of threats to the international order.

realise. But are these non-institutional principles ideal or non-ideal? One view is that there is no such category as non-ideal non-institutional principles. Under non-ideal conditions, it is still the ideal non-institutional principles that specify the social ideal, and it is still those principles and that ideal which guide us in specifying what our institutions, under non-ideal conditions, ought to look like. The opposing view, which is exemplified by Rawls's distinction between his special and general conception of justice,[55] is that what one ought to aim at might itself be different under non-ideal conditions, and that therefore there are such things as non-ideal non-institutional principles.[56] Under ideal conditions the Rawlsian theory of justice gives strict lexical priority to ensuring political liberty. Under extremely non-ideal conditions, however, Rawls gives up this lexical ordering and grants that, for example, in the case of a very poor society it could be required that we promote economic welfare at the expense of some political liberties. The claim is that under non-ideal conditions we may well have different aims from those we have in ideal conditions, which means that we must introduce the category of non-ideal non-institutional principles.[57]

We will use a complementary understanding of ideal and non-ideal theory that contains all four types of principles (ideal non-institutional and institutional, and non-ideal non-institutional and institutional) because, as we mentioned earlier, we think that such an understanding is the most helpful when it comes to the debate on international institutions, but we are very much aware that this understanding is by no means universally accepted and needs to be defended against some substantial charges.

In this volume, Buchanan and Keohane (Chapter 1) propose a standard of legitimacy that international institutions have to satisfy under current conditions.[58] One part of this standard is that given current reasonable and widespread disagreement over what global justice requires, international institutions, in order to be legitimate, have to make provisions for ongoing, inclusive deliberation that allows for a reinterpretation of what the role of that institution is in securing global justice.

[55] Rawls, *A Theory of Justice*, sections 11, 26, 39, 46, 83.

[56] According to Rawls these are to be understood as transitional principles whose validity depends on their contributing (in the long run) to the realisation of the conditions under which the ideal principles are valid. This is best explained using Rawls's own example.

[57] See Rawls, *A Theory of Justice*, 245. (Rawls does not exactly specify at what point the general conception is to be used. Sometimes the special conception is still applicable under non-ideal circumstances.)

[58] Buchanan and Keohane, Chapter 1, this volume.

What follows is not a view that Buchanan and Keohane are committed to, but rather an illustration of how the theoretical framework we are suggesting might be used. On the complementary understanding of ideal and non-ideal theory outlined above, their standard can be seen as a non-ideal institutional principle – it is global justice that international institutions should try to bring about but we cannot agree on what global justice requires either generally or of international institutions specifically. Given this international institutions should, under non-ideal conditions, be designed such that they contribute to developing a consensus both on the requirements of global justice, and the role international institutions have to play in delivering it.

A similar idea to this is found in Caney's chapter, where he argues for his 'Hybrid Model' of legitimacy, which includes the requirement that international institutions should 'provide a fair political framework in which to determine which principles of justice should be adopted to regulate the global economy'. This requirement is defended on grounds similar to those offered by Buchanan and Keohane, namely the idea that there currently exists widespread and reasonable disagreement over both what global justice requires, and about what the role of international institutions ought to be in pursuing global justice.[59]

An important point can be made here, namely that it is difficult to identify which category any given principle falls into. This difficulty can be illustrated at both the non-ideal and ideal levels. For example, take the principle that international institutions ought to follow democratic procedures. This could be thought of as a non-ideal institutional principle if we understand it as specifying a particular type of procedure required to create a fair political framework, but as a non-ideal non-institutional proposal if we interpret it as being the idea that under current non-ideal conditions international institutions ought to aim at legitimacy rather than justice. However, it is also possible to understand both the proposals (i.e. Buchanan and Keohane's, and Caney's) as operating at the ideal level, as either institutional or non-institutional principles. On such an understanding, the fact of reasonable disagreement is not one that can be assumed away even in ideal theory and it is one that has to be dealt with either through procedures – i.e. institutional design – specified in ideal theory; or it has to be dealt with by arguing for a complex ideal in which the fact of reasonable disagreement, and the desirability of it persisting, is taken into account. Despite this difficulty, the distinction is useful. To

[59] Caney, Chapter 3, this volume.

paraphrase Wittgenstein, dispute over national borders does not call into existence entire national territories. The vagueness at the boundaries does mean, however, that where possible theorists should attempt to be explicit about what kind of principle they think themselves to be proposing.

We can now ask the questions: does this all matter? Should we bother with making these distinctions and attempting to organise principles on different levels? We think it does, and we should, because the types of justifications and criticisms that are applicable will vary appreciably according to the type of principle that is being proposed. Suppose, for instance, that Caney's proposals for procedural fairness operate at the level of non-ideal institutional principles. If so, it becomes legitimate to criticise it, for instance, on the grounds of feasibility, and on particularly strict grounds – if someone could plausibly argue that such procedures are not politically feasible in the here and now, then this would be a strong criticism of the principle as it operates on the non-ideal institutional level. Alternatively, suppose the proposals operate at the level of ideal institutional principles because they are allied to the view that reasonable disagreement over conceptions of justice cannot be assumed away even in ideal theory. It may still be possible to criticise this on grounds of feasibility – though some, like G. A. Cohen, would argue not[60] – but the feasibility requirements would certainly be less strict than if the principle were thought to operate at the non-ideal level.

We think this complementary understanding is useful, then, because it allows us to justify and criticise proposals on their own terms. By identifying the level on which principles operate we are able to consider those principles while bracketing, even if only temporarily, many of the complications introduced by the problems of ideal and non-ideal theory. One might not want to do this bracketing, of course, because one might have a strong view on ideal and non-ideal theory that implied a strong view of the kind of thing that justice is, and this strong view on justice further implied views on the role of international institutions. Nevertheless, the distinctions introduced by the complementary multi-level understanding of ideal and non-ideal theory allow one to be clear that rather than criticising the proposals on their own terms, one is criticising the assumptions about ideal and non-ideal theory, and what those mean for justice, that are inherent in those proposals.

[60] Cohen, *Rescuing Justice and Equality*, for example 250–54.

An example of the sort of helpful clarity that this complementary understanding can bring is found in Butt's chapter (Chapter 5). As mentioned earlier, he makes the claim that the current distribution of resources has not come about in a just (here 'just' means 'just according to libertarians') way and that this creates a justified demand for rectification. Given that this rectification has not been carried out, he argues that this allows us to tentatively claim that the international legal system is illegitimate, given the notion that legitimacy requires meeting some minimal threshold of distributive justice. But this claim might be contested, he says, on the grounds that under current non-ideal conditions the priority for the international legal system must be protecting basic human rights and that therefore distributive justice should not be part of the criteria by which the legitimacy of international institutions should be judged. This counter-claim clearly operates at the non-ideal level, and seems to be based upon some kind of background thought like the following: under non-ideal conditions what matters is protecting human rights, and under these conditions anything that prevents institutions from protecting human rights is undesirable. A lack of legitimacy is one of those things, and given that under current non-ideal conditions it is not feasible to rectify past injustice and protect basic human rights, we ought not to claim that the legitimacy of international institutions is weakened if they don't rectify past injustice and protect these basic human rights. Butt responds to this claim by arguing that even under current non-ideal conditions rectifying past injustice and protecting basic human rights are things that are feasible. The point in this context is not to determine whether it's Butt or his imagined critic who is right, but rather that Butt's response is the right *type* of response to the claim of his imagined critic, and this is because both the claim and the response operate on the same level. They are fighting on the same ground; this is no guarantee, of course, of there ever being a winner, but it does mean that the blows they land have a chance of affecting each other.

In Chapter 2, Samantha Besson responds to a common charge made against global democracy, namely that it is unfeasible, by providing a feasible institutional structure that could realise it. One way this attempt can be understood is to see it as a set of non-ideal institutional principles. Once we understand it this way we get a much clearer picture of how it is to be judged, and how it might be criticised. The most obvious criticism is of course simply to argue that the proposals aren't feasible, but there are others. For example, one could call into question the non-institutional principles that Besson's non-ideal institutional principles are meant to realise. First, which level do these non-institutional principles work on? Are the values that would be realised by global democracy values that we want to realise under ideal conditions, or are they values that we settle for in non-ideal conditions? And for both the former and latter, we can ask, are these values actually realised by Besson's proposals? This, of course, is not meant to suggest that Besson's proposal is not valid. Rather, the point is that these questions need to be answered if one is to adequately evaluate Besson's proposal, or to suggest proposals oneself, and the complementary multi-level understanding helps us to identify what it is that Besson, or anyone else, is attempting to do with the proposals they suggest, and this helps us to see what the relevant questions are in each particular case.

To summarise, then, we suggest using a complementary multi-level understanding of ideal and non-ideal theory along the lines we have outlined as a way in which to frame and understand much of the work in this collection, and questions of international justice and legitimacy generally. Such an understanding, we argue, is useful in clearly distinguishing the aims of particular proposals and theorists, and therefore helps in responding to these proposals and theorists in a meaningful way. Further, such an understanding forces one to reflect on the problems of ideal and non-ideal theory as they apply to questions of international justice and legitimacy, and this is desirable because of the relevance and importance of these problems to the concerns of this collection, and of the debate generally.

References

Applbaum, Arthur Isak 2004. 'Legitimacy in a Bastard Kingdom', *John F. Kennedy School of Government Center for Public Leadership Working Papers*, Spring 2004.

Barry, Brian 1982. 'Humanity and Justice in Global Perspective', in Pennock, J. and Chapman, J. (eds.), *NOMOS XXIV, Ethics, Economics and the Law*. New York, NY: Harvester Wheatsheaf.

Barry, Brian 1995. *Justice as Impartiality*. Oxford University Press.

Beitz, Charles 1979 and 1999. *Political Theory and International Relations*. Princeton University Press.

Beitz, Charles 1999. 'Social and Cosmopolitan Liberalism', *International Affairs (Royal Institute of International Affairs 1944 –)* 75: 515–29.

Blake, Michael 2001. 'Distributive Justice, State Coercion, and Autonomy', *Philosophy and Public Affairs* 30: 257–96.

Blake, Michael 2008. 'International Justice', in Zalta, E. N. (ed.), *The Stanford Encyclopedia of Philosophy* (Winter Edition), online, available at http://plato.stanford.edu/archives/win2008/entries/international-justice.

Buchanan, Allen 2004. *Justice, Legitimacy and Self-Determination: Moral Foundations for International Law*. Oxford University Press.

Caney, Simon 2006. *Justice Beyond Borders. A Global Political Theory*. New York, NY: Oxford University Press.

Cohen, Gerald A. 2008. *Rescuing Justice and Equality*. Cambridge, MA: Harvard University Press.

Dasgupta, Partha 1993. *An Inquiry into Well-Being and Destitution*. Oxford University Press.

Dworkin, Ronald 1975. 'The Original Position', in Daniels, Norman (ed.), *Reading Rawls*. New York, NY: Basic Books.

Farrelly, Colin 2007. 'Justice in Ideal Theory: A Refutation', *Political Studies* 55: 844–64.

Goodin, Robert E. 1995. 'Political Ideals and Political Practice', *British Journal of Political Science* 25: 37–56.

Green, Leslie 1988. *The Authority of the State*. Oxford: Clarendon Press.

Hinsch, Wilfried, in press. 'Justice, Legitimacy and Constitutional Rights', in Matravers, Matthew and Meyer, Lukas H. (eds.), *Justice, Equality and Democracy*. London and New York, NY: Routledge.

Hobbes, Thomas 1991. *Leviathan*. Tuck, R. (ed.). Cambridge University Press.

Höffe, Otfried, 1995. *Political Justice. Foundations for a Critical Philosophy of Law and the State*. Cambridge: Polity.

Hume, David 1987 (1777). 'Of the Original Contract', in *Essays, Moral, Political and Literary*. Indianapolis, IN: Liberty Classics.

Ladenson, R. 1990. 'In Defense of a Hobbesian Conception of Law', in Raz, Joseph (ed.), *Authority*. Oxford: Basil Blackwell, 32–55.

Luhmann, Niklas 1983. *Legitimation durch Verfahren*. Frankfurt: Suhrkamp.

MacIntyre, Alasdair 1984. 'Is Patriotism a Virtue?' (The Lindley Lecture), University of Kansas.

Mason, Andrew 2004. 'Just Constraints', *British Journal of Political Science* 34: 251–68.

Miller, David 2007. *National Responsibility and Global Justice*. Oxford University Press.

Nagel, Thomas 2005. 'The Problem of Global Justice', *Philosophy and Public Affairs* 33: 113–47.

Perry, Stephen 1989. 'Second-Order Reasons, Uncertainty and Legal Theory', *Southern California Law Review* 62: 913–94.

Plato 2000. *The Republic*. Ferrari, G. R. F. (ed.), Griffith, Tom (trans.). Cambridge University Press.

Pogge, Thomas 1989. *Realizing Rawls*. Ithaca, NY: Cornell University Press.

Pogge, Thomas and Horton, Keith (eds.) 2008. *Global Ethics. Seminal Essays.* St. Paul, MN: Paragon House.

Pogge, Thomas and Moellendorf, Darrell (eds.) 2008. *Global Justice. Seminal Essays.* St. Paul, MN: Paragon House.

Rawls, John 1971. *A Theory of Justice.* Cambridge, MA: Harvard University Press.

Rawls, John 1993. 'The Law of Peoples', in Shute, Stephen and Hurley, Susan (eds.), *On Human Rights: The Oxford Amnesty Lectures 1993.* New York, NY: Basic Books.

Rawls, John 1993. *Political Liberalism.* New York, NY: Columbia University Press.

Rawls, John 1999. *The Law of Peoples.* Cambridge, MA: Harvard University Press.

Rawls, John 2007. *Lectures on the History of Philosophy.* Cambridge, MA: Harvard University Press.

Raz, Joseph 1986. *The Morality of Freedom.* Oxford University Press.

Sangiovanni, Andrea 2007. 'Global Justice, Reciprocity, and the State', *Philosophy and Public Affairs* 35: 3–39.

Scanlon, T. M. 1998. *What We Owe To Each Other.* Cambridge, MA: Harvard University Press.

Schauer, Fred 1991. *Playing by the Rules.* Oxford: Clarendon Press.

Scheffler, Samuel 2001. *Boundaries and Allegiances. Problems of Justice and Responsibility in Liberal Thought.* Oxford University Press.

Sen, Amartya 2006. 'What Do We Want From a Theory of Justice?', *The Journal of Philosophy* 103: 215–38.

Sen, Amartya and Dreze, Jean 1989. *Hunger and Public Action.* Oxford University Press.

Shue, Henry 1996. *Basic Rights. Subsistence, Affluence and U.S. Foreign Policy.* Princeton University Press.

Singer, Peter 1973. *Democracy and Disobedience.* Oxford University Press.

Swift, Adam 2008. 'The Value of Philosophy in Nonideal Circumstances', *Social Theory and Practice* 34: 366–68.

Tan, Kok-Chor 2004. *Justice without Borders.* New York, NY: Cambridge University Press.

Vlastos, Gregory 1996. *Studies in Greek Philosophy, Volume II: Socrates, Plato, and Their Tradition.* Daniel W. Graham (ed.). Princeton University Press.

Waldron, Jeremy 1999. *Law and Disagreement.* New York, NY: Oxford University Press.

Walzer, Michael 1983. *Spheres of Justice.* New York, NY: Basic Books.

Weber, Max 1968. *Economy and Society. An Outline of Interpretive Sociology.* Roth, Guenther and Wittich, Claus (eds.). New York, NY: Bedminster Press.

1

The legitimacy of global governance institutions

ALLEN BUCHANAN AND ROBERT O. KEOHANE

An institution is legitimate in the *normative* sense if it has *the right to rule* – where ruling includes promulgating rules and attempting to secure compliance with them by attaching costs to non-compliance and/or benefits to compliance. An institution is legitimate in the *sociological* sense when it is widely *believed* to have the right to rule.[1] When people disagree over whether the WTO is legitimate, the disagreement is typically normative. They are not disagreeing about whether they or others *believe* that this institution has the right to rule; they are disagreeing about whether it *has* the right to rule.[2] This chapter focuses on legitimacy in the normative sense.

We articulate a global public standard for the normative legitimacy of global governance institutions – henceforth GGIs, for brevity. This standard can provide the basis for principled criticism of GGIs and guide reform efforts in circumstances in which people disagree deeply about the demands of global justice and the role that GGIs should play in meeting them. We stake out a middle ground between an increasingly discredited conception of legitimacy that conflates legitimacy with international legality understood as state consent, on the one hand, and the unrealistic view that

[1] A thorough review of the sociological literature on organisational legitimacy can be found in M. C. Suchman, 'Managing Legitimacy: Strategic and Institutional Approaches', *Academy of Management Review*, 20 (1995), 571–610.

[2] For an excellent discussion of the inadequacy of existing standards of legitimacy for global governance institutions, see D. Bodansky, 'The Legitimacy of International Governance: A Coming Challenge for International Environmental Law?', *American Journal of International Law*, 93 (1999), 596–624. For an impressive earlier book on the subject, see T. Franck, *The Power of Legitimacy among Nations* (New York: Oxford University Press, 1990). Franck's account focuses on the legitimacy of rules more than institutions and in our judgment does not distinguish clearly enough between the normative and sociological senses of legitimacy.

legitimacy for these institutions requires the same democratic standards that are now applied to states, on the other.

Our approach to the problem of legitimacy integrates conceptual analysis and moral reasoning with an appreciation of the fact that GGIs are novel, still evolving, and characterised by reasonable disagreement about what their proper goals are and what standards of justice they should meet. Because both standards and institutions are subject to change as a result of further reflection and action, we do not claim to *discover* timeless necessary and sufficient conditions for legitimacy. Instead, we offer a principled *proposal* for how the legitimacy of these institutions ought to be assessed – for the time being. Essential to our account is the idea that to be legitimate a GGI must possess certain *epistemic* virtues that facilitate the ongoing critical revision of its goals, through interaction with agents and organisations outside the institution. A principled global public standard of legitimacy can help citizens committed to democratic principles to distinguish legitimate institutions from illegitimate ones and to achieve a reasonable congruence in their legitimacy assessments. Were such a standard widely accepted, it could bolster public support for valuable GGIs that satisfy the standard or at least make credible efforts to do so.

'Global governance institutions' covers a diversity of multilateral entities, including the World Trade Organisation (WTO), the International Monetary Fund (IMF), various environmental institutions, such as the climate change regime built around the Kyoto Protocol, judges' and regulators' networks, the UN Security Council, and the new International Criminal Court (ICC). These institutions are like governments in that they issue rules and publicly attach significant consequences to compliance or failure to comply with them – and claim the authority to do so. Nonetheless, they do not attempt to perform anything approaching a full range of governmental functions. They do not seek, as governments do, to monopolise the legitimate use of violence within a territory, and their creation and continued functioning require the consent of states.

Determining whether GGIs are legitimate – and whether they are widely perceived to be so – is an urgent matter. These institutions can promote international cooperation and also help to construct regulatory frameworks that limit abuses by non-state actors (from corporations to narcotraffickers and terrorists) who exploit transnational mobility. At the same time, however, they constrain the choices facing societies, sometimes limit the exercise of sovereignty by democratic states, and impose burdens as well as confer benefits. For example, states must belong to the WTO in order to participate effectively in the world economy, yet WTO membership requires accepting a large number of quite intrusive rules, authoritatively applied by its dispute settlement system. Furthermore, individuals can be adversely affected by global rules – for example, by the blacklists maintained by the Security Council's Sanctions Committee or by the WTO's policies on intellectual property in 'essential medicines'. If these institutions lack legitimacy, then their claims to authority are unfounded and they are not entitled to our support.

Judgments about institutional legitimacy have distinctive practical implications. Generally speaking, the judgment that an institution is legitimate should shape the character of both our responses to the claims it makes on us and the form that our criticisms of it take. We should support or at least refrain from interfering with legitimate institutions. Further, bona fide institutional agents deserve a kind of impersonal respect, even when we voice serious criticisms of them. Judging an institution to be legitimate focuses critical discourse by signalling that the appropriate objective is to reform it, rather than to reject it outright.

It is important not only that GGIs be legitimate, but also that they are perceived to be legitimate. The perception of legitimacy matters because, in a democratic era, multilateral institutions will only thrive if they are viewed as legitimate by democratic publics. If standards of legitimacy are unclear or unrealistically demanding, public support for global governance institutions may be undermined and their effectiveness in providing valuable goods may be impaired.

Assessing legitimacy

The social function of legitimacy assessments

Global governance institutions are valuable because they create norms and information that enable member states and other actors to coordinate their behaviour in mutually beneficial ways.[3] They can reduce transaction costs, create opportunities for states and other actors to demonstrate credibility, thereby overcoming commitment problems, and provide public goods, including rule-based, peaceful resolutions of

[3] The emphasis here on the coordinating function should not be misunderstood: global governance institutions do not merely coordinate state actions in order to satisfy *pre-existing* state preferences. As our analysis will make clear, they can also help shape state preferences and lead to the development of new norms and institutional goals.

conflicts.[4] An institution's ability to perform these valuable functions, however, may depend on whether those to whom it addresses its rules regard them as binding and whether others within the institution's domain of operation support or at least do not interfere with its functioning. It is not enough that the relevant actors agree that *some* institution is needed; they must agree that *this* institution is worthy of support. So, for institutions to perform their valuable coordinating functions, a higher-order coordination problem must be solved.

GGIs are not pure coordination devices in the way in which the rule of the road is, however. Even though all may agree that some institution or other is needed in a specific domain (the regulation of global trade, for example), and all may agree that any of several particular institutions is better than the non-institutional alternative, different parties, depending upon their differing interests and moral perspectives, will find some feasible institutions more attractive than others. The fact that all acknowledge that it is in their interest to achieve coordinated support for some institution or other may not be sufficient to assure adequate support for any particular institution.

The concept of legitimacy allows various actors to coordinate their support for particular institutions by appealing to their common capacity to be moved by *moral reasons*, as distinct from purely strategic or exclusively self-interested reasons. If legitimacy judgments are to perform this coordinating function, however, actors must not insist that only institutions that are *optimal* from the standpoint of their own moral views are acceptable, since this would preclude coordinated support when moral views diverge. More specifically, actors must not assume that an institution is worthy of support only if it is *fully just*. We thus need a standard of legitimacy that is both accessible from a diversity of moral standpoints and less demanding than a standard of justice. It should appeal to various actors' capacities to be moved by moral reasons, but without presupposing more moral agreement than exists.

Legitimacy and self-interest

As Andrew Hurrell points out, the rule-following that results from a sense of legitimacy is 'distinguishable from purely self-interested or instrumental behaviour on the one hand, and from straightforward

[4] R. O. Keohane, *After Hegemony: Cooperation and Discord in the World Political Economy*, 20th anniversary edition, 2005 (Princeton: Princeton University Press, 1984).

imposed or coercive rule on the other'.[5] Sometimes self-interest may speak in favour of treating an institution's rules as binding; that is, it can be in one's interest to take the fact that an institution issues a rule as a weighty reason for complying with it, independently of a positive assessment of the content of particular rules. This would be the case if one is likely to do better, from the standpoint of one's own interest, by taking the rules as binding than one would by evaluating each particular rule as to how complying with it would affect one's interests. Yet clearly it makes sense to ask whether an institution that promotes one's interests is legitimate. So legitimacy, understood as the right to rule, is a moral notion that cannot be reduced to rational self-interest.

There are advantages in achieving coordinated support for institutions on the basis of moral reasons, rather than exclusively on the basis of purely self-interested ones. First, the appeal to moral reasons is instrumentally valuable in securing the benefits that only institutions can provide because, as a matter of psychological fact, moral reasons matter when we try to determine what practical attitudes should be taken towards particular institutional arrangements. For example, we care not only about whether an environmental regulation regime reduces air pollutants and thereby produces benefits for all, but also whether it fairly distributes the costs of the benefits it provides. Given that there is widespread disagreement as to which institutional arrangement would be optimal, we need to find a shared evaluative perspective that makes it possible for us to achieve the coordinated support required for effective institutions without requiring us to disregard our most basic moral commitments. Second, and perhaps most important, if our support for an institution is based on reasons other than self-interest or the fear of coercion, it may be more stable. What is in our self-interest may change as circumstances change and the threat of coercion may not always be credible, and moral commitments can preserve support for valuable institutions in such circumstances.

For questions of legitimacy to arise there must be considerable moral disagreement about how institutions should be designed. Yet for agreement about legitimacy to be reached, there must be sufficient agreement on the sorts of moral considerations that are relevant for evaluating alternative institutional designs. The practice of making legitimacy judgments is grounded in a complex belief – namely, that while it is

5 A. Hurrell, 'Legitimacy and the Use of Force: Can the Circle Be Squared?', *Review of International Studies*, 31 (2005), 16.

true that institutions ought to meet standards more demanding than mere mutual benefit (relative to some relevant non-institutional alternative), they can be worthy of our support even if they do not maximally serve our interests and even if they do not measure up to our highest moral standards.[6]

Legitimacy requires not only that institutional agents are justified in carrying out their roles, but also that those to whom institutional rules are addressed have content-independent reasons to comply with them, and that those within the domain of the institution's operations must have content-independent reasons to support the institution or at least to not interfere with its functioning.[7] One has a content-independent reason to comply with a rule if and only if one has a reason to comply regardless of any positive assessment of the content of that rule. For example, I have a content-independent reason to comply with the rules of a club to which I belong if I have agreed to follow them and this reason is independent of whether I judge any particular rule to be a good or useful one. If I acknowledge an institution as having authority I thereby acknowledge that there are content-independent reasons to comply with its rules or at least to not interfere with their operation.

[6] Legitimacy can also be seen as providing a 'focal point' that helps strategic actors select one equilibrium solution among others. For the classic discussion of focal points, see T. C. Schelling, *The Strategy of Conflict* (Cambridge: Harvard University Press, 1960), ch. 3. For a critique of theories of cooperation on the basis of focal point theory, and an application to the European Union, see G. Garrett and B. Weingast, 'Ideas, Interests, and Institutions: Constructing the European Community's Internal Market', in J. Goldstein and R. O. Keohane (eds.), *Ideas and Foreign Policy* (Ithaca: Cornell University Press, 1993), esp. 178–85.

[7] Most contemporary analytic philosophical literature on legitimacy tends to focus exclusively on the legitimacy of the *state* and typically assumes a very strong understanding of legitimacy. In particular, it is assumed that legitimacy entails (1) a content-independent moral *obligation* to comply with all institutional rules (not just content-independent moral reasons to comply and/or a content-independent moral obligation to not interfere with others' compliance), (2) being justified in using *coercion* to secure compliance with rules, and (3) being justified in *using coercion to exclude* other actors from operating in the institution's domain. (See, for example, C. H. Wellman and A. J. Simmons, *Is There a Duty to Obey the Law? For and Against* (Cambridge University Press, 2005)). It is far from obvious, however, that this very strong conception is even the only conception of legitimacy appropriate for the state, given what is sometimes referred to as the 'unbundling' of sovereignty into various types of decentralised states and the existence of the European Union. Be that as it may, this state-centred conception is too strong for global governance institutions, which generally do not wield coercive power or claim such strong authority. For a more detailed development of this point, see A. Buchanan, 'The Legitimacy of International Law', in S. Besson and J. Tasioulas (eds.), *The Philosophy of International Law* (Oxford University Press, in press (2009)).

The debate about the legitimacy of GGIs engages both the perspective of states and that of individuals. Indeed, as recent mass protests against the WTO suggest, politically mobilised individuals can adversely affect the functioning of global governance institutions, both directly, by disrupting key meetings, and indirectly, by imposing political costs on their governments for their support of institutional policies. Legitimacy in the case of global governance institutions, then, is the right to rule, understood to mean both that institutional agents are morally justified in making rules and attempting to secure compliance with them and that people have moral, content-independent reasons to follow them and/or to not interfere with others' compliance with them.

If it becomes widely believed that an institution is illegitimate, the result may be a lack of coordination, at least until the institution changes to conform to the standards or a new institution that better conforms to them replaces it. Thus, it would be misleading to say simply that the function of legitimacy judgments is to achieve coordinated support for institutions; rather, their function is to make possible coordinated support based on moral reasons, while at the same time supplying a critical but realistic minimal moral standard by which to determine whether institutions are *worthy* of support.

Justice and legitimacy

The foregoing account of the social function of legitimacy assessments helps clarify the relationship between justice and legitimacy. Collapsing legitimacy into justice undermines the valuable social function of legitimacy assessments. There are two reasons not to insist that only just institutions have the right to rule. First, there is sufficient disagreement on what justice requires that such a standard for legitimacy would thwart the eminently reasonable goal of securing coordinated support for valuable institutions on the basis of moral reasons. Second, even if we all agreed on what justice requires, withholding support from institutions because they fail to meet the demands of justice would be self-defeating from the standpoint of justice itself, because progress towards justice requires effective institutions.

Competing standards of legitimacy

Having explicated our *conception* of legitimacy, we now explore *standards* of legitimacy: the conditions an institution must satisfy to have the right to rule. We articulate three candidates for the appropriate standard of legitimacy – state consent, consent by democratic states, and global democracy – arguing that each is inadequate.

State consent

On this view, GGIs are legitimate if (and only if) they are created through state consent. Legally constituted institutions, created by states according to the recognised procedures of public international law and consistent with it, are *ipso facto* legitimate or at the very least enjoy a strong presumption of legitimacy. Call this the International Legal Pedigree View (the Pedigree View, for short). A more sophisticated version of the Pedigree View requires the periodic reaffirmation of state consent, on the grounds that states have a legitimate interest in determining whether these institutions are performing as they are supposed to.[8]

The Pedigree View fails because it is hard to see how state consent could render GGIs legitimate, given that many states are non-democratic and systematically violate the human rights of their citizens and are for that reason themselves illegitimate. State consent in these cases cannot transfer legitimacy for the simple reason that there is no legitimacy to transfer. To assert that state consent, regardless of the character of the state, is sufficient for the legitimacy of GGIs is to regress to a conception of international order that fails to impose even the most minimal normative requirements on states.

It might be argued, however, that even though the consent of illegitimate states cannot itself make global governance institutions legitimate, there is an important instrumental justification for treating state consent as a necessary condition for their legitimacy: doing so provides a check on the tendency of stronger states to exploit weak ones. In other words, persisting in the fiction that all states – irrespective of whether they respect the basic rights of their own citizens – are moral agents whose consent confers legitimacy serves an important value. This fiction, however, is not one that those who take human rights seriously can consistently accept.

The proponent of state consent might reply as follows: 'My proposal is not that we should return to the pernicious fiction of the Morality

[8] For a more detailed discussion, see A. Buchanan, *Justice, Legitimacy and Self-Determination: Moral Foundations for International Law* (Oxford University Press, 2003), esp. ch. 5.

of States. Instead, it is that we should agree, for good cosmopolitan reasons, to regard a global governance institution as legitimate only if it enjoys the consent of all states.' Withholding legitimacy from GGIs simply because not all states consent to them, however, would purport to protect weaker states at the expense of giving a legitimacy veto to tyrannies. The price is too high. Weak states are in a numerical majority in multilateral institutions. Generally speaking, they are less threatened by the dominance of powerful states within GGIs than they are by the actions of such powerful states acting outside of institutional constraints.

The consent of democratic states

The idea that state consent confers legitimacy is much more plausible when restricted to democratic states. On reflection, however, the mere fact of state consent, even when the state in question is democratic and satisfies whatever other conditions are appropriate for state legitimacy, is not sufficient for the legitimacy of GGIs.

From the standpoint of a particular weak democratic state, participation in GGIs such as the WTO is hardly voluntary, since the state would suffer serious costs by not participating. Yet 'substantial' voluntariness is generally thought to be a necessary condition for consent to play a legitimating role.[9] There may be reasonable disagreements over what counts as substantial voluntariness, but the vulnerability of individual weak states is serious enough to undercut the view that the consent of democratic states is by itself sufficient for legitimacy.

There is another reason why the consent of democratic states is not sufficient for the legitimacy of GGIs: the problem of reconciling democratic values with unavoidable 'bureaucratic discretion' that plagues democratic theory at the domestic level looms even larger in the global case. For a modern state to function, much of what state agents do will not be subject to democratic decisions, and saying that the public has consented in some highly general way to whatever it is that state agents do is clearly inadequate. The difficulty is not in identifying chains of delegation stretching from the individual citizen to state agents, but

[9] For a perceptive discussion of how consent to new international trade rules in the Uruguay Round (1986–94) was merely nominal, since the alternatives for poor countries were so unattractive, see R. H. Steinberg, 'In the Shadow of Law or Power? Consensus-based Bargaining and Outcomes in the GATT/WTO', *International Organization*, 56 (2002), 339–74.

rather that at some point the impact of the popular will on how political power is used becomes so attenuated as to be normatively anaemic. Given how problematic democratic authorisation is within the modern state and given that global governance institutions require lengthening the chain of delegation, democratic state consent is not sufficient for legitimacy.

Still, the consent of democratic states may appear to be necessary, if not sufficient, for the legitimacy of GGIs. Indeed, it seems obvious that for such an institution to attempt to impose its rules on democratic states without their consent would violate the right of self-determination of the people of those states. Matters are not so simple, however. A democratic people's right of self-determination is not absolute. If the majority persecutes a minority, the fact that it does so through democratic processes does not render the state in question immune to sanctions or even to intervention. One might accommodate this fact by stipulating that a necessary condition for the legitimacy of GGIs is that they enjoy the consent of states that are democratic *and* that do a credible job of respecting the rights of all their citizens.

This does not mean that *all* such states must consent. A few such states may wilfully seek to isolate themselves from global governance (for example Switzerland only joined the UN in 2002). Furthermore, democratic states may engage in wars that are unnecessary and unjust, and resist pressures from international institutions to desist. It would hardly delegitimise a GGI established to constrain unjust warfare that it was opposed by a democratic state that was waging an unjust war. A more reasonable position would be that there is a *strong presumption* that global governance institutions are illegitimate unless they enjoy the ongoing consent of democratic states. Let us say, then, that ongoing consent by rights-respecting democratic states constitutes *the democratic channel* of accountability.[10]

However valuable the democratic channel of accountability is, it is not sufficient. First, as already noted, the problem of bureaucratic discretion that attenuates the power of majoritarian processes at the domestic level seems even more serious in the case of global bureaucracies. Second, not all the people who are affected by GGIs are citizens of democratic states, so even if the ongoing consent of democratic states

[10] How the requirement of ongoing consent should be operationalised is a complex question we need not try to answer here; one possibility would be that the treaties creating the institution would have to be periodically reaffirmed.

fosters accountability, it may not foster accountability to *them*. If – as is the case at present – democratic states tend to be richer and hence more powerful than non-democratic ones, then the requirement of ongoing consent by democratic states may actually foster a type of accountability that is detrimental to the interests of the world's worst-off people. From the standpoint of any broadly cosmopolitan moral theory, this is a deep flaw of domestic democracies as ordinarily conceived: government is supposed to be responsive to the interests and preferences of the 'sovereign people' – *the people whose government it is* – not all people or even all people whose legitimate interests will be seriously affected by the government's actions.[11] For these reasons, the consent of democratic states seems insufficient. The idea that the legitimacy of GGIs requires democracy on a grander scale may seem plausible.

Global democracy

Because democracy is now widely thought to be the gold standard for legitimacy in the case of the state, it may seem obvious that GGIs are legitimate if and only if they are democratic. And since these institutions increasingly affect the welfare of people everywhere, surely this must mean that they ought to be democratic in the sense of giving everyone an equal say in how they operate. Call this the Global Democracy View.

The most obvious difficulty with this view is that the social and political conditions for democracy *on the domestic model* – with a central role for majoritarian decision-making in which each individual has an equal vote – are not met at the global level and there is no reason to think that they will be in the foreseeable future. At present there is no global political structure that could provide the basis for that sort of democratic control over global governance institutions, even if one assumes that democracy requires little direct participation by individuals. Any attempt to create such a structure in the form of a global democratic federation that relies on existing states as federal units would lack legitimacy, and hence could not confer legitimacy on global governance institutions, because, as has already been noted, many states are themselves undemocratic or lack other qualities necessary for state legitimacy. Furthermore, there is at present no global public – no worldwide political community constituted by a broad consensus recognising a common domain as the proper subject of global collective decision-making and

[11] Buchanan, 'The Legitimacy of International Law'.

habitually communicating with one another about public issues. Nor is there consensus on a normative framework within which to deliberate together about a global common interest. Indeed, there is not even a global consensus that some form of global government, much less a global democracy, is needed or appropriate. Finally, once it is understood that it is *liberal* democracy, democracy that protects individual and minority rights, that is desirable, the Global Democracy View seems even more unfeasible. Democracy worth aspiring to is more than elections; it includes a complex web of institutions, including a free press and media, an active civil society, and institutions to check abuses of power by administrative agencies and elected officials.

GGIs provide benefits that cannot be provided by states and, as we have argued, securing those benefits may depend upon these institutions being regarded as legitimate. The value of these institutions, therefore, warrants being more critical about the assumption that they must be democratic *on the domestic model* and more willing to explore an alternative conception of their legitimacy. In the next section we take up this task.

A Complex Standard of legitimacy

Desiderata for a standard of legitimacy

Our discussion of the social function of legitimacy assessments and our critique of the three dominant views on the standard of legitimacy for GGIs (state consent, democratic state consent, and global democracy) suggest that a standard of legitimacy for such institutions should have the following characteristics:

(1) It must provide a reasonable public basis for coordinated support for the institutions in question, according to moral reasons that are widely accessible in spite of the persistence of significant moral disagreement – in particular, about the requirements of justice.
(2) It must not confuse legitimacy with justice but nonetheless must not allow that extremely unjust institutions are legitimate.
(3) It must take the ongoing consent of democratic states as a presumptive necessary condition, though not a sufficient condition, for legitimacy.
(4) It should not make authorisation by a global democracy (on the domestic model) a necessary condition of legitimacy, but nonetheless should *promote* the key values that underlie demands for democracy in the state.

(5) It must properly reflect the dynamic character of GGIs: the fact that not only the means they employ, but even their goals, may and ought to change over time.
(6) It must address the two problems we encountered earlier: the problem of bureaucratic discretion and the tendency of democratic states to disregard the legitimate interests of foreigners. The standard of legitimacy must therefore incorporate mechanisms for accountability that are more robust and inclusive than that provided by the consent of democratic states.

Moral disagreement and uncertainty

The first desideratum of a standard of legitimacy is complex and warrants further explication and emphasis. We have noted that a central feature of the circumstances of legitimacy is the persistence of disagreement about, first, what the proper goals of the institution are (given the limitations imposed by state sovereignty properly conceived), second, what global justice requires, and third, what role if any the institution should play in the pursuit of global justice.

There are two circumstances in the case of GGIs that exacerbate the problem of moral disagreement. First, in the case of the state, democratic processes, at least ideally, supply a way of accommodating these disagreements, by providing a public process that assures every citizen that she is being treated as an equal, but no such process is available at the global level. Second, although there is a widespread perception, at least among cosmopolitans broadly speaking, that there is serious global injustice and that the effective pursuit of global justice requires a significant role for global institutions, it is not possible at present to provide a principled specification of the division of institutional labour for pursuing global justice. In part the problem is that there is no unified system of GGIs within which a fair and effective allocation of institutional responsibilities for justice can be devised. How responsibilities for justice ought to be allocated among GGIs and between states and GGIs depends chiefly on the answers to two questions: what are the proper responsibilities of states in the pursuit of global justice, taking into account the proper scope of state sovereignty (because this will determine how extensive the role of global institutions should be), and what are the capabilities of various global institutions for contributing to the pursuit of global justice? Neither of these questions can be answered satisfactorily at present, in part because GGIs are so new and in part because people have only recently begun to think seriously about achieving justice on a global scale. So the difficulty is not just that there is considerable moral disagreement about the proper goals of GGIs and about the role these institutions should play in the pursuit of global justice; there is also moral *uncertainty*.[12] A plausible standard of legitimacy for GGIs must somehow accommodate *the facts of moral disagreement and uncertainty*.

Three substantive criteria

We begin with a set of institutional attributes that have considerable intuitive appeal: minimal moral acceptability, comparative benefit, and institutional integrity.

Minimal moral acceptability

GGIs, like institutions generally, must not persist in committing serious injustices. If they do so, they are not entitled to our support. On our view, the primary instance of a serious injustice is the violation of human rights.

There is disagreement as to exactly what the list of human rights includes and how the content of particular rights is to be filled out. There is agreement, however, that the list includes the rights to physical security, to liberty (understood as at least encompassing freedom from slavery, servitude, and forced occupations), and the right to subsistence. So, we can at least say this much: GGIs (like institutions generally) are legitimate only if they do not persist in violations of the least controversial human rights. This is a rather minimal moral requirement for legitimacy, but in view of the normative disagreement and uncertainty that characterise our attitudes towards these institutions, it would be hard at present to reach agreement on a more extensive set of rights that they are bound to respect. Yet it would certainly be desirable to develop a more meaningful consensus on stronger human rights standards. What this suggests is that we should require GGIs to respect minimal human rights, but also expect them to meet higher standards as we gain greater clarity about the scope of human rights.

[12] For a valuable discussion that employs a different conception of normative uncertainty, see M. Hlavac, 'A Developmental Approach to the Legitimacy of Global Governance Institutions', in D. A. Reidy and W. J. Riker (eds.), *Coercion and the State* (Dordrecht: Springer Netherlands, 2008).

For many global governance institutions, it is proper to expect that they should *respect* human rights, but not that they should play a major role in *promoting* human rights. Nonetheless, a theory of legitimacy cannot ignore the fact that in some cases the dispute over whether a GGI is legitimate is in large part a disagreement over whether it is worthy of support if it does not actively promote human rights. A proposal for a standard of legitimacy must take into account the fact that some of these institutions play a more direct and substantial role in securing human rights than others.

We seem to be in a quandary. Contemporary GGIs have to operate in an environment of moral disagreement and uncertainty, which limits the demands we can reasonably place on them to respect or protect particular human rights. Furthermore, to be sufficiently general, an account of legitimacy must avoid moral requirements that only apply to some GGIs. These considerations suggest the appropriateness of something like the minimal moral acceptability requirement, understood as refraining from violations of the least controversial human rights. On the other hand, the standard of legitimacy should reflect the fact that part of what is at issue in disputes over the legitimacy of some of these institutions is whether they should satisfy more robust demands of justice; it should acknowledge the fact that where the issue of legitimacy is most urgent, there is likely to be deep moral disagreement and uncertainty.

The way out of this impasse is to build the conditions needed for principled, informed deliberation about moral issues *into the standard of legitimacy itself*. That standard should require minimal moral acceptability, but should also accommodate and even encourage the possibility of developing more determinate and demanding requirements of justice for at least some of these institutions, as a principled basis for an institutional division of labour regarding justice emerges.

Comparative benefit

This second substantive condition for legitimacy is relatively straightforward. The justification for having GGIs is primarily if not exclusively instrumental. The basic reason for states or other addressees of institutional rules to take them as binding and for individuals generally to support or at least to not interfere with the operation of these institutions is that they provide benefits that cannot otherwise be obtained. If an institution cannot effectively perform the functions invoked to justify its existence, then this insufficiency undermines its claim to the right to rule.

'Benefit' here is comparative. The legitimacy of an institution is called into question if there is an institutional alternative, providing significantly greater benefits, that is feasible, accessible without excessive transition costs and meets the minimal moral acceptability criterion. The most difficult issues, as discussed below, concern trade-offs between comparative benefit and our other criteria. Legitimacy is not to be confused with *optimal* efficacy and efficiency. The other values that we discuss are also important in their own right; and in any case, institutional stability is a virtue. Nevertheless, if an institution steadfastly remains instrumentally suboptimal when it could take steps to become significantly more efficient or effective, this could impugn its legitimacy in an indirect way: it would indicate that those in charge of the institution were either grossly incompetent or not seriously committed to providing the benefits that were invoked to justify the creation of the institution in the first place. For instance, as of the beginning of 2006 the United Nations faced the issue of reconstituting a Human Rights Commission that had been discredited by the membership of states that notoriously abuse human rights, with Libya serving as chair in 2003.[13]

Institutional integrity

If an institution exhibits a pattern of egregious disparity between its actual performance, on the one hand, and its self-proclaimed procedures or major goals, on the other, its legitimacy is seriously called into question. The United Nations Oil-for-Food scandal is a case in point. The Oil-for-Food Program was devised to enable Iraqi oil to be sold, under strict controls, to pay for food imports under the UN-mandated sanctions of the 1990s. More than half of the companies involved paid illegal surcharges or kickbacks to Saddam Hussein and his cronies, resulting in large profits for corporations and pecuniary benefits for some programme administrators, including at least one high-level UN official.[14] The most damning charge is that neither the Security Council oversight bodies nor the Office of the Secretary-General followed the UN's prescribed procedures for accountability. At least when viewed in the light

[13] In March 2005, Secretary-General Kofi Annan called for the replacement of the Commission on Human Rights (fifty-three members elected from slates put forward by regional groups) with a smaller Human Rights Council elected by a two-thirds vote of members of the General Assembly (see his report 'In Larger Freedom', A/59/2005, para. 183).

[14] For the report of the Independent Inquiry Committee into the United Nations Oil-for-Food Program (the Volcker Committee), dated 27 October 2005, see www.iic-offp.org/story27oct05.htm.

of the historical record of other failures of accountability in the use of resources on the part of the UN, these findings raise questions about the legitimacy of the Security Council and the Secretariat.

An institution should also be presumed to be illegitimate if its practices or procedures predictably undermine the pursuit of the very goals in terms of which it justifies its existence. If the fundamental character of the Security Council's decision-making process renders that institution incapable of successfully pursuing what it now acknowledges as one of its chief goals – stopping large-scale violations of basic human rights – this impugns its legitimacy. To take another example, Randall Stone has shown that the IMF during the 1990s inconsistently applied its own standards with respect to its lending, systematically relaxing enforcement on countries that had rich and powerful patrons.[15] Similarly, if the WTO claims to provide the benefits of trade liberalisation to *all* of its members, but consistently develops policies that exclude its weaker members from the benefits of liberalisation, this undermines its claim to legitimacy. If an institution fails to satisfy the integrity criterion, we have reason to believe that key institutional agents are either untrustworthy or grossly incompetent, that it lacks correctives for these deficiencies, and that it is therefore unlikely to be effective.

Epistemic aspects of legitimacy

Minimal moral acceptability, comparative benefit, and institutional integrity are plausible presumptive substantive requirements for the legitimacy of GGIs. It would be excessive to claim that they are necessary conditions *simpliciter*, because there may be extraordinary circumstances in which an institution would fail to satisfy one or two of them, yet still reasonably be regarded as legitimate. This might be the case if there were no feasible and accessible alternative institutional arrangement, if the non-institutional alternative were sufficiently grim, and if there was reason to believe that the institution had the resources and the political will to correct the deficiency. How much we expect of an institution should depend, inter alia, upon how valuable the benefits it provides are and whether there are acceptable, feasible alternatives to it.

[15] R. W. Stone, 'The Political Economy of IMF Lending in Africa', *American Political Science Review*, 98 (2004), 577–91. See also R. W. Stone, *Lending Credibility: The International Monetary Fund and the Post-Communist Transition* (Princeton University Press, 2002).

For example, we might be warranted in regarding an institution as legitimate even though it lacked integrity, if it were nonetheless providing important protections for basic human rights and the alternatives to relying on it were even less acceptable. In contrast, the fact that an institution is effective in incrementally liberalising trade would not be sufficient to rebut the presumption that it is illegitimate because it abuses human rights.[16]

There are two limitations on the applicability of these three criteria, however. The first is *the problem of factual knowledge*: being able to make reasonable judgments about whether an institution satisfies any of the three substantive conditions requires considerable information about the workings of the institution and their effects in a number of domains and the likely effects of feasible alternatives. Some institutions may not only fail to supply the needed information; they may, whether deliberately or otherwise, make such information either impossible for outsiders to obtain or prohibitively costly.

The second difficulty with taking the three substantive conditions as jointly sufficient for legitimacy is *the problem of moral disagreement and uncertainty* noted earlier. Even if there is sufficient agreement on what counts as the violation of basic human rights, there are ongoing disputes about whether some global governance institutions should meet higher moral standards. As emphasised above, there is not only disagreement but also uncertainty as to the role that some of these institutions should play in the pursuit of global justice.

Further, merely requiring that GGIs not violate basic human rights is unresponsive to the familiar complaint that rich countries unfairly dominate them, and that even if they provide benefits to all, the richer members receive unjustifiably greater benefits. Although all parties may agree that fairness in the internal operations of the institution matters, there are likely to be disagreements about what fairness would consist of, disputes about whether fairness would suffice or whether equality is required, and about what is to be made equal (welfare, opportunities, resources, and so on). There is also likely to be disagreement about *how* unfair an institution must be to lack legitimacy. A proposal for a public global standard of legitimacy must not gloss over these disagreements.

In the following sections we argue that the proper response to both the problem of factual knowledge and the problem of moral disagreement

[16] We are indebted to Andrew Hurrell for this example.

and uncertainty is to focus on what might be called the *epistemic-deliberative* quality of the institution, the extent to which the institution provides reliable information needed for grappling with moral disagreement and uncertainty concerning its proper functions. To lay the groundwork for that argument, we begin by considering two items often assumed to be obvious requirements for the legitimacy of GGIs: accountability and transparency.

Accountability

Critics of GGIs often complain that they lack accountability. Accountability includes three elements: first, standards that those who are held accountable are expected to meet; second, information available to accountability holders, who can then apply the standards in question to the performance of those who are held to account; and third, the capacity to impose sanctions: to attach costs to the failure to meet the standards.

It is misleading to say that GGIs are illegitimate because they lack accountability and to suggest that the key to making them legitimate is to make them accountable. Most GGIs, including those whose legitimacy is most strenuously denied, include mechanisms for accountability.[17] The problem is that the accountability is morally inadequate. For example, the World Bank has traditionally exhibited a high degree of accountability, but it has been accountability to the biggest donor countries, and the Bank therefore has to act in conformity with their interests, at least insofar as they agree. Such accountability does not ensure meaningful participation by those affected by rules or due consideration of their legitimate interests.[18]

So accountability must be of the right sort. At the very least, this means that there must be effective provisions in the structure of the institution to hold institutional agents accountable for acting in ways that ensure satisfaction of the minimal moral acceptability and comparative benefit conditions. But accountability understood in this narrow way is not sufficiently *dynamic* to serve as an assurance of the legitimacy of GGIs, given that in some cases there is serious disagreement about what the goals of the institution should be and, more specifically, about what role if any the institution should play in the pursuit of global justice.

17 R. W. Grant and R. O. Keohane, 'Accountability and Abuses of Power in World Politics', *American Political Science Review*, 99 (2005), 29–44.

18 For a discussion, see N. Woods, 'Holding Intergovernmental Institutions to Account', *Ethics & International Affairs*, 17 (2003), 69–80.

The point is that what the *terms of accountability* ought to be – what standards of accountability ought to be employed, who the accountability holders should be, and whose interests the accountability holders should represent – cannot be definitively ascertained without knowing what role, if any, the institution should play in the pursuit of global justice.

Therefore, what might be called narrow accountability – accountability without provision for contestation of the terms of accountability – is insufficient for legitimacy, given the facts of moral disagreement and uncertainty. Because what constitutes appropriate accountability is itself subject to reasonable dispute, the legitimacy of GGIs depends in part upon whether they operate in such a way as to facilitate principled, factually informed deliberation about the terms of accountability. There must be provisions for critically revising existing terms of accountability.

Transparency

Achieving transparency is often touted as the proper response to worries about the legitimacy of global governance institutions.[19] But transparency by itself is inadequate. First, if transparency means merely the *availability* of accurate information about how the institution works, it is insufficient even for narrow accountability – that is, for ensuring that the institution is accurately evaluated in accordance with the current terms of accountability. Information must be (a) accessible at reasonable cost, (b) properly integrated and interpreted, and (c) directed to the accountability holders. Furthermore (d) the accountability holders must be adequately motivated to use it properly in evaluating the performance of the relevant institutional agents. Second, if, as we have argued, the capacity for critically revising the terms of accountability is necessary for legitimacy, information about how the institution works must be available not only to those who are presently designated as accountability holders, but also to those who may contest the terms of accountability.

Broad transparency is needed for critical revisability of the terms of accountability. Both institutional practices and the moral principles that shape the terms of accountability must be revisable in the light of critical reflection and discussion. Under conditions of broad transparency, information produced initially to enable institutionally designated accountability holders to assess officials' performance can be appropriated

[19] A. Florini, *The Coming Democracy* (Washington, DC: Island Press, 2003).

by agents *external* to the institution, such as non-governmental organisations (NGOs), and used to support more fundamental criticisms, not only of the institution's processes and structures, but even of its most fundamental goals and its role in the pursuit of global justice.

One especially important dimension of broad transparency is *responsibility for public justification.*[20] Institutional actors must offer public justifications of at least the more controversial and consequential institutional policies and must facilitate timely critical responses to them. Potential critics must be in a position to determine whether the public justifications are cogent, whether they are consistent with the current terms of accountability, and whether, if taken seriously, these justifications call for revision of the current terms of responsibility.

Broad transparency can sometimes serve as a proxy for satisfaction of the minimal moral acceptability, comparative benefit, and integrity criteria. For example, it may be easier for outsiders to discover that an institution is not responding to demands for information relevant to determining whether it is violating its own prescribed procedures, than to determine whether in fact it is violating them. Similarly, it may be very difficult to determine whether an institution is comparatively effective in solving certain global problems, but much easier to tell whether it generates – or systematically restricts access to – the information outsiders would need to evaluate its effectiveness. If an institution persistently fails to cooperate in making available to outsiders the information that would be needed to determine whether the three presumptive necessary conditions are satisfied, that by itself creates a presumption that it is illegitimate.

Epistemic virtues

Legitimate GGIs should possess three epistemic virtues. First, because their chief function is to achieve coordination, they must generate and properly direct reliable information about coordination points; otherwise they will not satisfy the condition of comparative benefit. Second, because accountability is required to determine whether they are in fact performing their current coordinating functions efficiently and effectively requires narrow transparency, they must at least be transparent

[20] For an illuminating account of the legitimacy of healthcare institutions that emphasises responsibility for justifications, see N. Daniels and J. Sabin, 'Limits to Health Care: Fair Procedures, Democratic Deliberation, and the Legitimacy Problem for Insurers', *Philosophy & Public Affairs*, 26 (1997), 303–50.

in the narrow sense: they must also have effective provisions for integrating and interpreting the information current accountability holders need and for directing it to them. Third, they must have the capacity for *revising the terms of accountability*, and this requires broad transparency: there must be provision for ongoing, inclusive deliberation about what global justice requires and how the institution in question fits into a division of institutional responsibilities for achieving it.

Overcoming informational asymmetries

A fundamental problem of institutional accountability is that insiders generally have better information about the institution than outsiders. Outsiders can determine whether institutions enjoy the consent of states, and whether states are democratic; but it may be very difficult for them to reach well-informed conclusions about the minimal moral acceptability, comparative benefit, and integrity conditions. Our emphasis on epistemic virtues is well suited to illuminate these problems of asymmetrical information.

First, if institutional agents persist in failing to provide public justifications for their policies and withhold other information critical to the evaluation of institutional performance, we have good reason to believe the institution is not satisfying the substantive criteria for legitimacy.[21] Second, there may be an asymmetry of knowledge in the other direction as well, and this can have beneficial consequences for institutional accountability. Consider issue areas such as human rights and the environment, which are richly populated with independent NGOs that seek to monitor and criticise national governments and GGIs and to suggest policy alternatives. Suppose that in such domains there is a division of labour among external epistemic actors. Some individuals and groups seek information about certain types of issues, while others focus on other aspects, each drawing on distinct but in some cases overlapping groups of experts. Still others specialise in integrating and interpreting information gathered by other external epistemic actors.

[21] The analogy in the economics of information is to the market for used cars. A potential buyer of a used car would be justified in inferring poor quality if the seller were unwilling to let him have the car thoroughly examined by a competent mechanic. See G. A. Akerlof, 'The Market for Lemons: Quality Uncertainty and the Market Mechanism', *Quarterly Journal of Economics*, 84 (1970), 488–500.

The fact that the information held by external epistemic actors is dispersed will make it difficult for institutional agents to know what is known about their behaviour or to predict when potentially damaging information may be integrated and interpreted in ways that make it politically potent. Their awareness of this asymmetry will provide institutional agents incentives for avoiding behaviour for which they may be criticised. A condition of *productive uncertainty* will exist. Although institutional agents will know that external epistemic actors do not possess the full range of knowledge that they do, they will know that there are many individuals and organisations gathering information about the institution. Further, they will know that some of the information that external epistemic actors have access to can serve as a reliable proxy for information they cannot access. Finally, they will also know that potentially damaging information that is currently harmless because it is dispersed among many external epistemic agents may at any time be integrated and interpreted in such a way as to make it politically effective, but they will not be able to predict when this will occur. Under these conditions, institutional agents will have significant incentives to refrain from behaviour that will attract damning criticism, despite the fundamental asymmetry of knowledge between insiders and outsiders.

This is not to say that the effects of transparency will always be benign. Indeed, under some circumstances transparency can have malign effects. As David Stasavage points out, 'open-door bargaining ... encourages representatives to posture by adopting overly aggressive bargaining positions that increase the risks of breakdown in negotiations'.[22] Our claim is not that outcomes are better the more transparent institutions are. Rather, it is that the dispersal of information among a plurality of external epistemic actors provides some counterbalance to informational asymmetries favouring insiders. There should be a very strong but rebuttable presumption of transparency, because the ills of too much transparency can be corrected by deeper, more sophisticated public discussion, whereas there can be no democratic response to secret action by bureaucracies not accountable to the public.

Furthermore, if national legislatures are to retain their relevance – if what we have called the democratic accountability channel is to be effective – they must be able to review the operations of GGIs. To do

[22] D. Stasavage, 'Open-Door or Closed-Door? Transparency in Domestic and International Bargaining', *International Organization*, 58 (2004), 667–704.

this, they need a flow of information from transnational civil society. Monitoring is best done pluralistically by transnational civil society, whereas the sanctions aspects of accountability are more effectively carried out by legislatures. With respect both to the monitoring and sanctioning functions, broad transparency is conducive to the principled revisability of institutions and to their improvement through increasingly inclusive criticism and more deeply probing discussion over time.

Institutional agents generally have incentives to prevent outsiders from getting information that may eventually be interpreted and integrated in damaging ways and to deprive outsiders of information that can serve as a reliable proxy to assess institutional legitimacy. The very reasons that make the epistemic virtues valuable from the standpoint of assessing institutional legitimacy may therefore tempt institutional agents to ensure that their institutions do not exemplify these virtues. But institutional agents are also aware that it is important for their institutions to be widely regarded as legitimate. Outsiders deprived of access to information are likely to react in the same way as the prospective buyer of a used car who is prevented from taking it to an independent mechanic. They will discount the claims of the insiders and may conclude that the institution is illegitimate. So if there is a broad consensus among outsiders that institutions are not legitimate unless they exemplify the epistemic virtues, institutional agents will have reason to ensure that their institutions do so.

Contestation and revisability: links to external actors and institutions

We have argued that the legitimacy of GGIs depends upon whether there is ongoing, informed, principled contestation of their goals and terms of accountability. This process of contestation and revision depends upon activities of actors outside the institution. It is not enough for the institutions to make information available. Other agents, whose interests and commitments do not coincide too closely with those of the institution, must provide a check on the reliability of the information, integrate it, and make it available in understandable, usable form to all who have a legitimate interest in the operations of the institution. Such activities can produce positive feedback, in which appeal to standards of legitimacy by the external epistemic actors not only increases compliance with existing standards but also leads to improvements in the quality of the standards themselves. For these reasons, in the absence of global democracy and given the limitations of the democratic channel described earlier, legitimacy depends crucially upon not only the epistemic virtues of the institution itself but also on the activities of *external epistemic actors*. Effective linkage between the institution and external epistemic actors constitutes what might be called the *transnational civil society channel of accountability*.

The needed external epistemic actors, if they are effective, will themselves be institutionally organised.[23] Institutional legitimacy, then, is not simply a function of the institution's characteristics; it also depends upon the broader institutional environment in which the particular institution exists. To borrow a biological metaphor, ours is an ecological conception of legitimacy.

All three elements of our Complex Standard of legitimacy are now in place. First, global governance institutions should enjoy the ongoing consent of democratic states. That is, the democratic accountability channel must function reasonably well. Second, these institutions should satisfy the substantive criteria of minimal moral acceptability, comparative benefit, and institutional integrity. Third, they should possess the epistemic virtues needed to make credible judgments about whether the three substantive criteria are satisfied and to achieve the ongoing contestation and critical revision of their goals, their terms of accountability, and ultimately their role in a division of labour for the pursuit of global justice, through their interaction with effective external epistemic agents.

A place for democratic values in the absence of global democracy

Earlier we argued that it is a mistake to hold GGIs to the standard of democratic legitimacy that is now widely applied to states. We now want to suggest that when the Complex Standard of legitimacy we propose is satisfied, important democratic values will be served. To do this, we will assume, rather than argue, that among the most important democratic values are the following: equal regard for the fundamental interests of all persons; decision-making about the public order through principled,

[23] We use the term 'external epistemic actor' here broadly, to include individuals and groups outside the institution in question who gain knowledge about the institution, interpret and integrate such knowledge, and exchange it with others, in ways that are intended to influence institutional behaviour, whether directly or indirectly (through the mediation of the activities of other individuals and groups).

collective deliberation; and mutual respect for persons as beings who are guided by reasons.

If the Complex Standard of legitimacy we propose is satisfied, all three of these values will be served. To the extent that connections between the institutions and external epistemic actors provide access to information that is not restricted to certain groups but available globally, it becomes harder for institutions to continue to exclude consideration of the interests of certain groups, and we move closer towards the ideal of equal regard for the fundamental interests of all. Furthermore, by making information available globally, networks of external epistemic actors are in effect addressing all people as individuals for whom moral reasons, not just the threat of coercion, determine whether they regard an institution's rules as authoritative. Finally, if the Complex Standard of legitimacy is satisfied, every feature of the institution becomes a potential object of principled, informed, collective deliberation, and eligibility for participation in deliberation will not be determined by institutional interests.[24]

Consistency with democratic sovereignty

One source of doubts about the legitimacy of GGIs is the worry that they are incompatible with democratic sovereignty. Our analysis shows why and how global governance *should* constrain democratic sovereignty. The standard of legitimacy we propose is designed inter alia to help GGIs correct for the tendency of democratic governments to disregard the interests of those outside their own publics. It does this chiefly in two ways. First, the emphasis on the role of external institutional epistemic actors in achieving broad accountability helps to ensure more inclusive representation of interests over time. Second, the requirement of minimal moral acceptability, understood as non-violation of basic human rights, provides protection for the most vulnerable: if this condition is met, democratic publics cannot ignore the most serious 'negative externalities' of the policies they pursue through GGIs. So GGIs that satisfy our standard of legitimacy should not be viewed

[24] On our view, the legitimacy of global governance institutions, at present at least, does not require participation in the critical evaluation of institutional goals and policies by all who are affected by them; but if the standard of legitimacy we recommend were accepted, opportunities for participation would expand.

as undermining democratic sovereignty, but rather as enabling democracies to function justly.

Having articulated the Complex Standard, and indicated how it reflects several key democratic values, we can now show, briefly, how it satisfies the desiderata for a standard of legitimacy we set out earlier.

(1) The Complex Standard provides a reasonable basis for coordinated support of institutions that meet the standard, support based on moral reasons that are widely accessible in the circumstances under which legitimacy is an issue. To serve the social function of legitimacy assessments, the Complex Standard only requires a consensus on the importance of not violating the most widely recognised human rights, broad agreement that comparative benefit and integrity are also presumptive necessary conditions of legitimacy, and a commitment to inclusive, informed deliberation directed towards resolving or at least reducing the moral disagreement and uncertainty that characterise our practical attitudes towards these institutions. Thus the Complex Standard steers a middle course between requiring more moral agreement than is available in the circumstances of legitimacy and abandoning the attempt to construct a more robust, shared moral perspective from which to evaluate GGIs. In particular, the Complex Standard acknowledges that the role that these institutions ought to play in a more just world order is both deeply contested and probably not knowable at present.

(2) In requiring only minimal moral acceptability at present, the Complex Standard acknowledges that legitimacy does not require justice, but at the same time affirms the intuition that extreme injustice, understood as violation of the most widely recognised human rights, robs an institution of legitimacy.

(3) The Complex Standard takes the ongoing consent of democratic states to be a presumptive necessity, though not a sufficient condition for legitimacy.

(4) The Complex Standard rejects the assumption that GGIs cannot be legitimate unless there is global democracy, but at the same time promotes some of the key democratic values, including informed, public deliberation conducted on the assumption that every individual has standing to participate, and the requirement that key institutional policies must be publicly justified.

(5) The Complex Standard reflects a proper appreciation of the dynamic, experimental character of GGIs and of the fact that not only the

means they employ but even the goals they pursue may and probably should change over time.

(6) The Complex Standard's requirement of a functioning transnational civil society channel of accountability – an array of overlapping networks of external epistemic actors – helps to compensate for the limitations of accountability through democratic state consent.

The central argument of this chapter can now be summarised. The Complex Standard provides a reasonable basis for agreement in legitimacy assessments of global governance institutions, given their distinctive characteristics. When the Comparative Benefit condition is satisfied, the institution provides goods that are not readily obtainable without it; but these goods can be reliably provided only if coordination is achieved, and achieving coordination without excessive costs requires that the relevant agents take the fact that the rule is issued by the institution as a content-independent reason for compliance. Satisfaction of the Minimal Moral Acceptability condition rules out the more serious moral objections that might otherwise undercut the instrumental reasons for supporting the institution. Satisfaction of the other conditions of the Complex Standard, taken together, provides moral reasons to support or at least not interfere with the institution, among the most important of which is that the institution has epistemic virtues that contribute to its on-going improvement and to the broader task of forging agreement on what justice requires and on the institutional division of labour needed to attain it. Thus, when a global governance institution meets the demands of the Complex Standard, there is justification for saying that it has the right to rule, not merely that it is beneficial.

References

Akerlof, George A. 1970. 'The Market for Lemons: Quality Uncertainty and the Market Mechanism', *Quarterly Journal of Economics* 84: 488–500.

Annan, Kofi 2005. 'In Larger Freedom', *UN-report* document A/59/2005.

Bodansky, Daniel 1999. 'The Legitimacy of International Governance: A Coming Challenge for International Environmental Law?', *American Journal of International Law* 93: 596–624.

Buchanan, Allen 2003. *Justice, Legitimacy and Self Determination: Moral Foundations for International Law.* Oxford University Press.

Buchanan, Allen, in press (2009). 'The Legitimacy of International Law', in Besson, Samantha and Tasioulas, John (eds.) *The Philosophy of International Law.* Oxford University Press.

Daniels, Norman and Sabin, James 1997. 'Limits to Health Care: Fair Procedures, Democratic Deliberation, and the Legitimacy Problem for Insurers', *Philosophy & Public Affairs* 26: 303–50.

Florini, Ann 2003. *The Coming Democracy*. Washington, DC: Island Press.

Franck, Thomas 1990. *The Power of Legitimacy Among Nations*. New York: Oxford University Press.

Garrett, Geoffrey and Weingast, Barry 1993. 'Ideas, Interests, and Institutions: Constructing the European Community's Internal Market', in Goldstein, Judith and Keohane, Robert O. (eds.) *Ideas and Foreign Policy*. Ithaca: Cornell University Press.

Grant, Ruth W. and Keohane, Robert O. 2005. 'Accountability and Abuses of Power in World Politics', *American Political Science Review* 99: 29–44.

Hlavac, M. 2008. 'A Developmental Approach to the Legitimacy of Global Governance Institutions', in Reidy, D. A. and Reiker, W. J. (eds.) *Coercion and the State*. Dordrecht: Springer Netherlands.

Hurrell, Andrew 2005. 'Legitimacy and the Use of Force: Can the Circle Be Squared?', *Review of International Studies* 31: 15–32.

Keohane, Robert O. 2005 (20th anniversary edition). *After Hegemony: Cooperation and Discord in the World Political Economy*. Princeton University Press.

Schelling, Thomas C. 1960. *The Strategy of Conflict*. Cambridge: Harvard University Press.

Stasavage, David 2004. 'Open-Door or Closed-Door? Transparency in Domestic and International Bargaining', *International Organization* 58: 667–704.

Steinberg, Richard H. 2002. 'In the Shadow of Law or Power? Consensus-based Bargaining and Outcomes in the GATT/WTO', *International Organization* 56: 339–74.

Stone, Randall W. 2002. *Lending Credibility: The International Monetary Fund and the Post-Communist Transition*. Princeton University Press.

Stone, Randall W. 2004. 'The Political Economy of IMF Lending in Africa', *American Political Science Review* 98: 577–91.

Suchman, Mark C. 1995. 'Managing Legitimacy: Strategic and Institutional Approaches', *Academy of Management Review* 20: 571–610.

Wellman, Christopher Heath and Simmons, A. John 2005. *Is There a Duty to Obey the Law? For and Against*. Cambridge University Press.

Woods, Ngaire 2003. 'Holding Intergovernmental Institutions to Account', *Ethics & International Affairs* 17: 69–80.

2

Institutionalising global *demoi*-cracy

SAMANTHA BESSON

Introduction

Over the last few years, international institutional reform has become a major concern among international lawyers.[1] They are not alone in addressing the issue, however. Global justice theorists have also started focusing on the crucial institutional dimension of global justice. So doing, they have gradually developed normative criteria to guide reform of international institutions. Interestingly, some of them have also emphasised the need to pay heed to existing institutional structures and to factor those into any valuable normative reflection on the design of future global institutions. It is such a dynamic and reflexive approach to institutionalising global[2] institutions which I would like to adopt in this chapter, starting from normative requirements, confronting them to institutional reality and, finally, returning to our normative starting

Professor of Public International Law and European Law, University of Fribourg (Switzerland). The present chapter was written within the framework of the Project for a European Philosophy of European Law (PEOPEL, http://fns.unifr.ch/peopel) and with the support of the Swiss National Science Foundation. Early drafts of the chapter were presented at a workshop in Berlin on 4 August 2006 and at a conference in Berne on 16 and 17 December 2006. Many thanks are due to all participants for their comments, and in particular to Arthur Applbaum, Allen Buchanan, Simon Caney, Wilfried Hinsch, Alexandra Kemmerer, Gerhard Kruip, Lukas Meyer, Daniel Philpott, Steven Ratner, Matthias Risse and Dietmar von der Pfordten. Special thanks are also due to Nils Kapferer, Stéphanie Murenzi and Thierry Leibzig for their help with the formal layout of the chapter. The final version of this chapter was submitted in March 2007, and only slightly revised in November 2008.

1 The term 'institutions' is used here in a broad sense to refer to all official bodies in charge of law-making in a globalised legal order, whether at the international, supranational, transnational or national level.

2 In what follows, the term 'global' has been chosen to include all institutions and processes implicated in the production of the law that applies in national cases, whether supranational, international or transnational, but also national institutions and processes which remain at the core of the former either for implementation or further legislative purposes. See S. Besson, 'Theorizing the Sources of International Law', in S. Besson and J. Tasioulas (eds.), *The Philosophy of International Law* (Oxford University Press, in press (2010)).

point to rethink it through and produce a normative proposal that is both critical and feasible.

That method will be used in the chapter to discuss a specific issue underlying and somehow conditioning all current projects of international institutional reform: *global democracy*. Although the theorising of democracy beyond the state has been at work for quite some time now, first in the context of the European Union and more recently at the international level, most publicised projects fall short of an institutional proposal, i.e. of an account of how to turn their normative proposal into a plausible institutional structure. Moreover, in the few cases where these projects do provide institutional proposals, they often fail to accommodate current international institutional circumstances both in the theoretical model and in their suggestions for further institutionalisation. And this shortcoming is one of the reasons for their failure to convince as they should. This chapter's principled proposal for a model of global democracy should serve as a focal point for provisional support of existing institutions, while at the same time providing guidance for improvement and stimulating institutional reform.[3]

A three-pronged argument will enable us to identify a more institution-sensitive model of global democracy which can match the pluralism that characterises current law-making processes in a globalised world. The first section will explain why the legality of international law can no longer be thought of separately from its legitimacy and how international law should be produced so as to be able to claim legitimacy.[4] More precisely, I will argue that global democracy is one of the most important dimensions of the legitimacy of international institutions and respectively of international law, and hence a necessary requirement of international law-making processes. Given the current state of international institutions, however, the objection pertaining to the lack of feasibility of global democracy needs to be met adequately. The second step will be to argue for a theoretical model of global democracy that does not aim at imitating existing institutional models of national democracy in a world state. Rather, mirroring international institutional and legal evolution, global democracy should be conceived of as pluralistic, deterritorialised and

[3] See A. Buchanan, *Justice, Legitimacy, and Self-Determination: Moral Foundations for International Law* (Oxford University Press, 2004), 324.

[4] 'International law' is used here in a broad sense to refer not only to intergovernmental law, but also to the outcome of any post-national law-making processes, i.e. processes which take place beyond the national state, whether they are supranational, international *stricto sensu* or transnational.

deliberative, i.e. in a nutshell as deliberative *demoi*-cracy. The final step in the argument will be to suggest ways in which this institution-sensitive normative argument can translate into further institutional requirements, both in terms of the adequate fora for global *demoi*-cratic deliberation and in terms of participatory and representative modalities of that deliberation.

International law, legitimacy and democracy

In a nutshell, the legitimacy of law amounts to its ability to provide peremptory or exclusionary reasons for action. The law's (legitimate) authority is distinct from that of its moral content and relies on content-independent reasons. A given legal norm may only be said to be authoritative in this sense, when it matches pre-existing individual reasons in such a way that the person is in a better position to comply with the latter if it complies with the former.[5] As a result, there is no general prima facie obligation to obey the law qua law and legality alone is not enough for legitimacy. Legitimacy is an essential part of legality, however, in the sense that the law should be such that it can claim to be legitimate and hence to bind those to whom it applies. In circumstances of pervasive and persistent disagreement about substantive moral issues, the democratic nature of the law-making process is often regarded as the best justification for that claim.[6]

The question that needs to be addressed in this section is whether the principles underlying national law's legitimacy apply to the (legitimate) authority of international law and in particular to its authority both over states and individuals. A second question pertains to the type of

[5] See J. Raz, *The Authority of Law* (Oxford University Press, 1979); J. Raz, *Ethics in the Public Domain* (Oxford University Press, 1995); S. Besson, *The Morality of Conflict. Reasonable Disagreement and the Law* (Oxford: Hart Publishing, 2005), ch. 13. Note that the Razian conception of authority may be borrowed separately from the remainder of Raz's legal theory. See for a revised democratic conception of Razian authority, J. Waldron, 'Authority for Officials', in L. H. Meyer, S. L. Paulson and T. W. Pogge (eds.), *Rights, Culture, and the Law. Themes from the Legal and Political Philosophy of Joseph Raz* (Oxford University Press, 2003), 45; S. Besson, 'Democracy, Law and Authority' (Review of Lukas Meyer, Stanley Paulson and Thomas Pogge (eds.), *Rights, Culture and the Law: Themes from the Legal and Political Philosophy of Joseph Raz*), *Journal of Moral Philosophy*, 2 (2005), 89.

[6] See Besson, *Morality of Conflict*, chs. 13 and 14; T. Christiano, *The Rule of The Many: Fundamental Issues in Democratic Theory* (Boulder: Westview Press, 1996).

legitimacy claims that may be made adequately by international law and in particular whether they should and can be of a democratic nature.

International law and legitimacy

Until the 1990s, and but for a few exceptions,[7] the legitimacy of international institutions and accordingly of international law was no real concern for international lawyers; legitimacy was a concern confined to the arena of national politics. In international affairs, the only relevant subjects were states and not individuals. As a consequence, in those rare cases where legitimacy was discussed in international law, it was in order to be linked back to state consent, just as the authority of a promise derives from the promisor's consent. This minimalist understanding of international legitimacy mirrored the traditional contractualist or consensualist approach to international law, according to which states are both the authors and the subjects of international norms and hence bind themselves by agreeing to them.[8] Following Buchanan, one may coin this approach the *State Consent* model.[9]

From the 1980s onwards, international law itself started regulating issues of legitimacy, and democratic legitimacy more precisely, albeit at the national level. This had been the case quite early on, for instance, in the areas of the right to self-determination and democracy-conditioned state recognition, of free elections monitoring, and of democratic and more generally human rights conditionality clauses in trade agreements.[10] Paradoxically, however, the gradual emergence and reinforcement of the

[7] See, for example, T. Franck, 'Why a Quest for Legitimacy?', *UC Davis Law Review*, 21 (1987), 535; T. Franck, 'Legitimacy in the International System', *American Journal of International Law*, 82 (1988), 705; T. Franck, 'The Emerging Right to Democratic Governance', *American Journal of International Law*, 86 (1992), 46.

[8] See most recently, J. L. Goldsmith and E. A. Posner, *The Limits of International Law* (New York: Oxford University Press, 2005), ch. 7. Contra: T. Franck, 'The Power of Legitimacy and the Legitimacy of Power: International Law in an Age of Power Disequilibrium', *American Journal of International Law*, 100 (2006), 88; A. Buchanan, 'Democracy and the Commitment to International Law', *University of Georgia Journal of International and Transnational Law*, 34 (2006), 305.

[9] See A. Buchanan and O. Keohane, 'The Legitimacy of Global Governance Institutions', *Ethics and International Affairs*, 20 (2006), 405; A. Buchanan, 'Legitimacy of International Law', in S. Besson and J. Tasioulas (eds.), *The Philosophy of International Law* (Oxford University Press, in press (2010)).

[10] See G. Fox and B. Roth, 'Introduction: The Spread of Liberal Democracy and Its Implications for International Law', in G. Fox and B. Roth (eds.), *Democratic Governance and International Law* (Cambridge University Press, 2000), 1; C. Pippan, 'Right to Democracy

so-called international right to democracy[11] did not immediately lead to challenging international law-making processes themselves. This may seem quite surprising given the latter's prima facie dubious democratic quality; not only did these processes vest very little legitimacy onto the democratic standards developed for national political processes,[12] but the concentration of international competences in the executive and hence the 'deparlamentisation'[13] of international matters at the national level had perverse effects on national democracies themselves.[14] Of course, the legitimacy of international law necessarily increases with the democratisation of national law-making processes and in this sense the latter are a necessary element of international legitimacy. Following Buchanan, one may coin this approach the *Democratic State Consent* model.[15] It remains, however, that the focus on national democracy in those international norms pertaining to the right to democracy confirms the traditionally indirect approach to international legitimacy based on national democracy and hence ultimately on state consent.[16]

It is only since the mid-1990s that attitudes relative to the legitimacy of international law itself started to shift.[17] As a result, the legitimacy of

in International Law', *European Journal of International Law*, 15 (2004), 213; M. Beutz, 'Functional Democracy: Responding to Failures of Accountability', *Harvard Journal of International Law*, 44 (2003), 387; R. Rich, 'Bringing Democracy into International Law', *Journal of Democracy*, 12 (2001), 20; J. Crawford and S. Marks, 'The Global Democracy Deficit: An Essay in International Law and its Limits', in D. Archibugi, D. Held and M. Kohler (eds.), *Re-Imagining Political Community, Studies in Cosmopolitan Democracy* (Cambridge: Polity Press, 1998), 72; H. J. Steiner, 'Political Participation as a Human Right', *Harvard Human Rights Yearbook*, 1 (1988), 77.

11 See Franck, 'Legitimacy in the International System'; T. Franck, *The Power of Legitimacy among Nations* (Oxford: Clarendon Press, 1990); Franck, 'Emerging Right'; J. Crawford, 'Democracy and International Law', *British Yearbook of International Law*, 44 (1993), 113; J. Crawford, 'Democracy and the Body of International Law', in G. Fox and B. Roth (eds.), *Democratic Governance and International Law* (Cambridge University Press, 2000), 91; J. Crawford, 'Democracy in International Law – A Reprise', in G. Fox and B. Roth (eds.), *Democratic Governance and International Law* (Cambridge University Press, 2000), 114.

12 See the critical essays in Fox and Roth, 'Introduction'.

13 E. Stein, 'International Integration and Democracy: No Love at First Sight', *American Journal of International Law*, 95 (2001), 493.

14 See Crawford, 'Body of International Law'; Crawford, 'Democracy, A Reprise'; Franck, 'Legitimacy in the International System'.

15 See Buchanan and Keohane, 'Global Governance Institutions'; Buchanan, 'Legitimacy of International Law'.

16 See Crawford and Marks, 'Global Democracy Deficit', 82–5.

17 See Franck, 'Quest for Legitimacy'; Franck, 'Legitimacy in the International System'; Crawford, 'Democracy and International Law'; J. Weiler and A. Paulus, 'The Structure of Change or Is there a Hierarchy of Norms in International Law?', *European Journal of*

international law can no longer be put at rest by reference to the two models mentioned before. The *State Consent* model cannot account for the legitimacy of all international law norms. The primary reason for this is double: not only are states no longer the only international law-making institutions, but they are no longer the only international legal subjects either. As such, their consent remains at the most a residual source of legal authority in the cases where they are both authors and subjects of international legal norms.[18] Besides, even in those cases, the development of other sources of international law such as customary law makes it increasingly difficult to link normativity back to state consent. Finally, even when this link seems plausible, most legal philosophers actually doubt that consent can be a constitutive source of legal authority of its own.[19] This becomes even more problematic when those protected by the respect for autonomy, and equal autonomy more precisely, are states, whereas those usually protected by consensual approaches to authority in political theory are individuals.[20]

Nor can this renewed concern for international legitimacy be sidelined by reference to the *Democratic State Consent* model. This model amounts to a merely indirect form of global democracy, i.e. one that derives the legitimacy of international law from the electoral legitimacy of state representatives negotiating and consenting to those norms.[21] Of course, democratic state consent is an important factor of global democracy,

International Law, 8 (1997), 545; D. Bodanksy, 'The Legitimacy of International Governance: A Coming Challenge for International Environmental Law?', *American Journal of International Law*, 93 (1999), 596; Stein, 'International Integration'; M. Kumm, 'The Legitimacy of International Law: A Constitutionalist Framework of Analysis', *European Journal of International Law*, 15 (2004), 907; A. von Bogdandy, 'Globalization and Europe: How to Square Democracy, Globalization and International Law', *European Journal of International Law*, 15 (2004), 885; J. Weiler, 'The Geology of International Law – Governance, Democracy and Legitimacy', *Zeitschrift für ausländisches öffentliches Recht und Völkerrecht*, 64 (2004), 547; Buchanan, *Moral Foundations*, chs. 5 and 7; Buchanan, 'Democracy and Commitment'; Buchanan, 'Legitimacy of International Law'; Franck, 'Power of Legitimacy'; Besson, 'Theorizing the Sources'; J. Tasioulas, 'The Legitimacy of International Law', in S. Besson and J. Tasioulas (eds.), *The Philosophy of International Law* (Oxford University Press, in press (2010)); S. Besson, 'The Authority of International Law – Lifting the State Veil', *Sydney Law Review* 31: 3 (2009).

18 See Buchanan, *Moral Foundations*, 317–19.

19 See Buchanan, *Moral Foundations*, ch. 7; J. Tasioulas, 'Review: Justice, Legitimacy and Self-Determination: Moral Foundations for International Law', *International and Comparative Law Quarterly*, 55 (2006), 238. Contra: T. Christiano, 'Democratic Legitimacy and International Institutions', in S. Besson and J. Tasioulas (eds.), *The Philosophy of International Law* (Oxford University Press, in press (2010)).

20 See, for example, Buchanan, *Moral Foundations*, 317–20, 325.

21 See, for example, A. Paulus, 'Comment: The Legitimacy of International Law and the Role of the State', *Michigan Journal of International Law*, 25 (2004), 1057.

provided of course that the states consenting are democratically organised, that state representatives are publicly accountable and that the ways in which decision-making among states is organised are adequately inclusive and egalitarian.[22] It is not, however, sufficient in itself from an individual perspective. International law impacts directly on individual lives and private persons have become international legal subjects, both passively as bearers of international rights and duties and actively as direct claimants before international authorities. It is time, therefore, that they become international law-makers as well.[23] Moreover, international norms now cover areas traditionally left to national law, go well beyond the regulation of interstate relations and pertain to individuals' basic interests, and this without respecting national legitimating channels. Finally, not all individuals affected by international law are citizens of democratic states and hence have a say in national democratic processes pertaining to international issues or are represented by democratically elected representatives in international fora, thus creating an inequality in legitimacy.[24] In those new circumstances, the call for the legitimacy of international law comes closer to the one in national law; international legal norms should be able to be justified directly to those to whom they apply on grounds of global justice and cosmopolitan ethics.[25]

International legitimacy and democracy

If legitimacy and its relationship to legality have now become front stage in international law scholarship, it comes as no surprise that global democracy be considered as one of the most important sources of legitimacy of international law. According to the *Global Democracy* model, international law may only be regarded as legitimate and binding upon its subjects, when all the individuals (directly or indirectly) affected have been included in the decision-making process.

If legality alone is not enough for the legitimacy of international law,[26] international law should be such that it can claim legitimacy. There are

[22] See Christiano, 'Democratic Legitimacy'.

[23] See Besson, 'Theorizing the Sources'; R. McCorquodale, 'The Individual in International Law', in M. D. Evans (ed.), *International Law*, 2nd edition (Oxford University Press, 2006), 307.

[24] See S. Caney, Chapter 3, this volume.

[25] See P. Alston, 'The Myopia of the Handmaidens: International Lawyers and Globalization', *European Journal of International Law*, 8 (1997), 447.

[26] Contra Kumm, 'Legitimacy'; Franck, 'Legitimacy in the International System'; Franck, 'Power of Legitimacy'. See Buchanan, 'Legitimacy of International Law'.

many other dimensions to international law's legitimacy than democracy, such as the *substantive* legitimacy of legal contents or other forms of output legitimacy. However, *procedural* legitimacy, and democracy in particular, are the most consensual sources of legitimacy in pluralist societies where reasonable disagreement about global justice is pervasive and persistent.[27] Democratic law-making procedures respect the minimal political equality of each participant[28] and hence allow for coordination under conditions that vest their outcomes with authority and reasons to abide by them. This coordination-based approach to legal legitimacy is even better suited to international law as the latter applies to very different subjects and in very different places.[29]

True, this does not preclude the co-existence of other secondary sources of legitimacy of international law in certain cases, such as substantive justice, as in the case of *jus cogens* norms, or state consent in certain more limited cases. Nor does it imply that all sources of international law should become democratic to be vested with legitimacy; some simply cannot for reasons pertaining to the nature of their process or to their law-makers.[30] Finally, democracy requires a minimal guarantee of human rights to function properly and these are therefore an intrinsic part of the legitimating process of international law besides democracy;[31] this is the case of the minimal right to political equality and of political rights such as freedom of expression and reunion.[32]

[27] See Besson, *Morality of Conflict*, chs. 6, 13 and 14.

[28] See C. Beitz, 'Procedural Equality in Democratic Theory: A Preliminary Examination', in R. Pennock and J. Chapman (eds.), *Liberal Democracy, Nomos XXV* (New York University Press, 1983), 71.

[29] See Buchanan and Keohane, 'Global Governance Institutions'; Caney, Chapter 3, this volume.

[30] See Besson, 'Theorizing the Sources'.

[31] See Buchanan and Keohane, 'Global Governance Institutions'; Buchanan, 'Legitimacy of International Law'.

[32] Note, however, that pervasive disagreement about human rights is a reason why human rights cannot constitute a sufficient basis for the legitimacy of international law on their own (contra: Buchanan, *Moral Foundations*, chs. 5 and 7; Buchanan, 'Democracy and Commitment'; Buchanan, 'Legitimacy of International Law'; see, however, A. Buchanan, 'Human Rights and the Legitimacy of the International Legal Order', *Legal Theory*, 14 (2008), 39–70). See Besson, *Morality of Conflict*, ch. 9; J. Waldron, *Law and Disagreement* (Oxford University Press, 1999), chs. 11 and 13.

Theorising global *demoi*-cracy

Global democracy qua theoretical challenge

In a nutshell, democracy requires that all those whose basic interests are affected by policy decisions are able to participate directly or indirectly in the process of making them. Global democracy draws the consequences of globalisation for democracy. National states are no longer the only sources of decisions that affect their legal subjects;[33] many decisions are taken outside the reach of national political processes as for instance by international law-making processes, but also by other national political processes which can produce decisions that affect people outside their electoral constituencies. Globalisation thus generates a legitimacy gap that needs to be filled by globalising democracy.[34]

Global democracy groups all democratic processes that occur within and beyond the national state and whose outcomes affect individuals within that state, but in ways that link national democracy to other transnational, international or supranational democratic processes. Thus, it is not simply about improving national processes, nor about legitimising international processes indirectly through those national processes.[35] Indirect international democracy models of this kind have to answer the famous dilemma they create for states between defending their citizens' interests at the expense of other states and their citizens, on the one hand, and following the rules of international democracy at the expense of their own citizens' interests, on the other.[36] Nor should global democracy be confused with the idea of a cosmopolitan state and supranational democracy.[37] The idea of a world state has long been regarded as neither feasible nor desirable given the resilience of the national state and its key role in the global law-making processes.[38]

33 See J. Habermas, 'The Postnational Constellation and the Future of Democracy', in J. Habermas and M. Pensky (eds.), *The Postnational Constellation – Political Essays*, (Cambridge University Press, 2001), 58; D. Held, 'Cosmopolitanism: Globalization Tamed?', *Review of International Studies*, 29 (2003), 465.

34 See D. Archibugi, 'Cosmopolitan Democracy and Its Critics: A Review', *European Journal of International Relations*, 10 (2004), 438.

35 See Archibugi, 'Cosmopolitan Democracy', 442.

36 See D. Archibugi, 'The Reform of the UN and Cosmopolitan Democracy: A Critical Review', *Journal of Peace Research*, 30 (1993), 305.

37 See, for example, D. Held, 'The Transformation of Political Community: Rethinking Democracy in the Context of Globalization', in I. Shapiro and C. Hacker-Cordon (eds.), *Democracy's Edges* (Cambridge University Press 1999), 84; Habermas, 'Postnational Constellation'.

38 See Archibugi, 'Reform of the UN', 306.

Rather, global democracy amounts to a pluralist model that identifies different levels of legitimation and places national democracy at the core of global democratic processes.[39] Even though they have been deeply affected and somehow weakened by globalisation, national law-making processes are much more central to global law-making processes than some claim they are. Thus, they remain crucial to the ratification and implementation of international norms.[40] They have also become major channels of transnational and comparative law-making.[41] In fact, the pluralist relationship between the national and international legal orders implies accommodating national democratic law-making processes within the international ones. Because they affect the same people normatively, the different law-making processes should be connected rather than hermetically separated and they should be coordinated rather than set in priority to each other.[42] In revealing those beneficial connections between national democracy and transnational or post-national democracy and the need to open up national democracies to one another, global democracy proposes the implementation of a multi-layered and multi-centred democratic society not only *among* and *beyond* states, but also *within* states themselves.

Of course, if one understands global democracy as inclusive of a multitude of national and post-national law-making processes, it is important to adapt the concept of democracy to the new post-national constellation and its many layers of governance. Global polities cannot be governed in the same way as national ones. Democratic models need, moreover, to be revised at the national level as well. In a globalised world, indeed, national democracies themselves can be deemed deficient in many ways.[43] In fact, global democracy is a holistic process that

[39] See S. Sassen, 'The Participation of States and Citizens in Global Governance', *Indiana Journal of Global Studies*, 10 (2003), 5.

[40] See Paulus, 'Comment'; Sassen, 'Global Governance', 10 and 15.

[41] See, for example, A. M. Slaughter, 'Government Networks: The Heart of the Liberal Democratic Order', in G. Fox and B. Roth (eds.), *Democratic Governance and International Law* (Cambridge University Press, 2000), 199; A. M Slaughter, 'Disaggregated Sovereignty: Towards the Public Accountability of Global Government Networks', *Government and Opposition*, 39 (2004), 159; J. Delbrück, 'Exercizing Public Authority Beyond the State: Transnational Democracy and/or Alternative Legitimation Strategies?', *Indiana Journal of Global Studies*, 10 (2003), 29.

[42] See Besson, 'Theorizing the Sources'.

[43] See e.g. Archibugi, 'Cosmopolitan Democracy'; V. Schmidt, 'The European Union: Democratic Legitimacy in a Regional State?', *Journal of Common Market Studies*, 42 (2004), 976; J. M. Guéhenno, *La fin de la démocratie* (Paris: Champs Flammarion, 1999).

integrates these different layers in such a way that their democratic quality can no longer be judged in an isolated fashion and depends on their imbrication with other layers.[44] Hence, the model of global democracy proposed needs to take into account the existing institutional reality beyond the state and accordingly reassess democratic normative requirements developed in the national context.

In what follows, I would like to argue that there are three main key dimensions that a model of global democracy should have in order to be able to both accommodate and further challenge global institutional developments: first, the who-question: it should have a multitude of democratic subjects, hence the concept of *demoi*-cracy; second, the where-question: global *demoi*-cracy should be conceived of as deterritorialised, hence the concept of deterritorialised *demoi*-cracy; and, finally, the how-question: global *demoi*-cracy is best understood as based on deliberation, hence the concept of deliberative *demoi*-cracy.

Three dimensions of global democracy

Global *demoi*-cracy

The absence of a global demos is one of the main objections to global democracy. According to this objection, government representatives are still the primary participants in discussions relative to global politics, rather than the whole community of global stakeholders.[45]

The problem is that there is no agreed set of criteria as to how to judge what makes a multitude of people a demos or a political community. Self-rule or self-legislation which lies at the core of democracy also implies self-constitution; the community which binds itself by the laws it generates defines itself at the same time as a democratic subject by drawing its own boundaries.[46] True, these boundaries usually match pre-political and cultural or ethnic boundaries.[47] Comparative politics and history

[44] See J. S. Dryzek, 'Transnational Democracy', *Journal of Political Philosophy*, 7 (1999), 30; Archibugi, 'Cosmopolitan Democracy'; J. Bohman, 'From *Demos* to *Demoi*: Democracy across Borders', *Ratio Juris*, 18 (2005), 293; S. Besson, 'Deliberative *Demoi*-cracy in the European Union. Towards the Deterritorialization of Democracy', in S. Besson and J. L. Martí (eds.), *Deliberative Democracy and its Discontents* (Aldershot: Ashgate, 2006), ch. 9.

[45] See N. Urbinati, 'Can Cosmopolitical Democracy Be Democratic?', in D. Archibugi (ed.), *Debating Cosmopolitics* (London: Verso, 2003), 67.

[46] See S. Benhabib, *The Rights of Others: Aliens, Residents and Citizens* (Cambridge University Press, 2004), ch. 4.

[47] See, for example, M. Canovan, *Nationhood and Political Theory* (Cheltenham: Edward Elgar, 1996); D. Miller, *Citizenship and National Identity* (Cambridge: Polity Press, 2000).

have shown, however, that this is not always the case. All it takes often is some kind of 'we-feeling', a form of solidarity among different 'stakeholders'.[48] In fact, solidarity need not necessarily be pre-political at all; it can be generated by the political exercise itself. This minimal requirement of a solidarity feeling should also apply at the post-national level, therefore. There is no reason why solidarity need respect state boundaries,[49] as recently exemplified in the European Union.[50]

In fact, this global or at least post-national solidarity need not be exclusive of pre-existing democratic solidarities at the national level. In many transnational areas of governance, one finds different *demoi* represented in the same political processes, and even being 'civilised' in this shared political process to borrow an expression used in the European Union.[51] If communities of fate already overlap de facto, it would be regressive to try to identify this pluralistic global community in a static manner as a single and territorially delimited global polity.[52] As a consequence, it is not only the congruence between pre-political and political boundaries of the demos which is put into question at the post-national level, but also the single nature of the post-national demos.

Global democracy is the outcome of the imbrication of many national, transnational, international and supranational democratic processes in which the democratic subjects are many and do not necessarily constitute a single overarching demos. Thus, rather than seek to identify a unitary global demos, be it national or supranational, the alternative to an indirectly democratic global polity qua union of democratic states should be a directly *demoi*-cratic global polity qua union of peoples.[53]

48 See Archibugi, 'Cosmopolitan Democracy'.

49 See C. Calhoun, 'The Class Consciousness of Frequent Travellers: Towards a Critique of Actually Existing Cosmopolitanism', in D. Archibugi (ed.), *Debating Cosmopolitics* (London: Verso, 2003), 86.

50 See Besson, 'Deliberative *Demoi*-cracy'; S. Besson, 'The EU and Human Rights: Towards a New Kind of Post-national Human Rights Institution', *Human Rights Law Review*, 6 (2006), 323.

51 See J. Weiler, 'To Be a European Citizen: Eros and Civilization', in J. Weiler (ed.), *The Constitution of Europe* (Cambridge University Press, 1999), 324; Held, 'Cosmopolitanism: Globalization Tamed?'.

52 See Archibugi, 'Cosmopolitan Democracy'.

53 See in the EU context, Besson, 'Deliberative *Demoi*-cracy'; J. Bohman, 'Constitution Making and Democratic Innovation: The European Union and Transnational Governance', *European Journal of Political Theory*, 3 (2004), 315; Bohman, '*Demos* to *Demoi*'; K. Nicolaïdis, 'The New Constitution as European Demoi-cracy?', *The Federal Trust Constitutional Online Paper*, 38 (2003); K. Nicolaïdis, 'We, The Peoples of

That is after all what some have read in the maybe not so rhetorical 'We, the Peoples' of the Preamble to the UN Charter.

Deterritorialised global *demoi*-cracy

Not only should global democracy be understood as a process connecting a plurality of democratic subjects, but it can only be effectively understood as such if it is conceived of as deterritorialised and as constituted of a global functional demos of *demoi*. Plurality is not only a quantitative characteristic of global democracy, but also a qualitative one qua functioning mode in each of these many subjects of global democracy wherever they are localised. On this model, different national *demoi*, either located separately at national level or together in different fora at the transnational, international or supranational global levels, together constitute a global functional and deterritorialised demos. For instance, national citizens elect and vote in national elections as global citizens, thus turning national polities into more or less global ones depending on the topics addressed. Similarly, in international institutions, national representatives deliberate neither as representatives of their national demos only nor as those of a single global demos, but as representatives of a functional demos *of demoi*.

This is the only way in which our democratic practices can accommodate the rapidly increasing deterritorialisation of law, which belies the basic democratic principle of inclusion of all those affected by democratic decisions. The progressive deterritorialisation of politics[54] and law-making processes leads indeed to the erosion of the congruence between those affected by a given set of laws, i.e. the legal subjects, and the authors of those laws. This growing gap violates the principle of political equality and of democratic inclusion.[55] The deterritorialisation

Europe ...', *Foreign Affairs*, 83 (2004), 97; M. Poiares Maduro, 'Where to Look for Legitimacy?', in E. O. Eriksen, J. E. Fossum and A. Menendez (eds.), *Constitution Making and Democratic Legitimacy*, ARENA Report 5/02 (Oslo: Arena, 2002); Weiler, 'Eros and Civilization'; P. van Parijs, 'Should the European Union Become More Democratic?', in A. Follesdal and P. Koslowski (eds.), *Democracy and the European Union* (Berlin: Springer, 1998), 287.

54 See D. Held, A. McGrew, D. Goldblatt and J. Perraton, *Global Transformations. Politics, Economics, and Culture* (Stanford University Press, 1999), 32; D. Held, *Cosmopolitan Democracy: An Agenda for a New World Order* (Cambridge: Polity Press, 1995), 237.

55 See J. S. Dryzek., 'Legitimacy and Economy in Deliberative Democracy', *Political Theory*, 29 (2001), 651, 662; Archibugi, 'Cosmopolitan Democracy', 439; Held, *Cosmopolitan Democracy*; D. Held. *The Global Covenant: The Social Democratic Alternative to the Washington Consensus* (Cambridge: Polity Press, 2004).

of law should therefore be matched by the progressive deterritorialisation of democratic processes themselves.[56] If legal pluralism implies the possibility for legal norms of different origins to apply to the same person, there should also be a legitimation pluralism; it is important indeed that this person can participate in the different law-making processes at the origin of these norms wherever they are located and this in turn implies including other affected *demoi* in each demos' deliberations, whether these take place at national, international, supranational or transnational level.[57]

True, deterritorialisation raises the well-known paradox of the democratic polity, according to which the modern democratic polity is both constituted and constrained by pre-political territorial boundaries and hence cannot be constituted and function as democratically as it should.[58] In fact, territory was traditionally used as a convenient indicator of affectedness and was therefore a democratic mode of delineation of the polity before law was globalised and started applying across functional rather than territorial lines. Territoriality is no fatality,[59] however, and democratic iterations may gradually help fill the gap between those affected and those participating.[60]

If one extends democratic deliberation across territorial polities functionally to all those significantly affected by a decision, one may therefore count a new kind of political constituents or subjects, i.e. moral-political[61]

[56] See e.g. Besson, 'Deliberative *Demoi*-cracy'; Bohman, '*Demos* to *Demoi*'; Archibugi, 'Cosmopolitan Democracy', 445; Dryzek, 'Transnational Democracy', 44.

[57] This could not be done by mere reference to the principle of subsidiarity, for that principle can only be used within a hierarchical legal order to shift the decision-making top-down or bottom-up, rather than laterally across different legal orders. Moreover, the principle of subsidiarity is a principle of territorial governance par excellence.

[58] See, for example, Benhabib, *Rights of Others*, ch. 4; Poiares Maduro, 'Where to Look'; T. Pogge, 'Creating Supra-National Institutions Democratically: Reflections on the European Union's "Democratic Deficit"', *Journal of Political Philosophy*, 5 (1997), 163; F. G. Whelan, 'Prologue: Democratic Theory and the Boundary Problem', in R. Pennock and J. Chapman (eds.), *Liberal Democracy, Nomos XXV* (New York University Press, 1983), 13; C. Offe, 'Homogeneity and Constitutional Democracy: Coping with Identity Conflicts through Group Rights', *Journal of Political Philosophy*, 6 (1998), 113.

[59] Contra: Pogge, 'Democratic Deficit'; Held, *Cosmopolitan Democracy*, 154 and 236; Habermas, 'Postnational Constellation'.

[60] See Besson, 'Deliberative *Demoi*-cracy'; Benhabib, *Rights of Others*; Delbrück, 'Exercizing Public Authority', 40.

[61] See Besson, 'Deliberative *Demoi*-cracy'; contra F. Cheneval, 'The People in Deliberative Democracy', in S. Besson and J. L. Martí (eds.), *Deliberative Democracy and its Discontents* (Aldershot: Ashgate, 2006), ch. 8.

constituents, besides electoral or formal political constituents in each territorial entity.[62] If the global functional demos of *demoi* may be constituted on grounds of deterritorialised solidarity, one needs to determine what makes it the case that someone is a citizen of a functional demos rather than of another.[63] Most authors mention the fact of being 'affected' by a polity's decision as sufficient.[64] Stakeholders in these overlapping communities of fate are not, however, most of the time strictly speaking *bound* by the democratic decisions taken by other polities. They are at the most strongly affected by them and this is a purely factual criterion which anyone can fill and which does not therefore suffice to trigger normative consequences and democratic rights in particular. In practice, however, the difference is often moot, since very often stakeholders simply have to abide by the new factual or legal situation thus created. As such, their being 'affected' is already, albeit indirectly, normative and not only factual.

Of course, the line must be drawn somewhere.[65] The first criterion must be one of degree of affectation of the interests which must be comparable to a de facto obligation. Thus, for instance, what makes the national *demoi* in Europe part of a functional European demos is the fact that they mutually influence each other's normative orders not only through the primacy of European law *stricto sensu*, but also indirectly through their respective national laws and the latter's future impact on European law.[66] A second criterion besides the quasi-normative character of the affectedness is that the interests affected must be basic or fundamental interests, i.e. interests in the conditions for self-development or self-determination. This is an objective element that is distinct from how

62 See A. Gutmann and D. Thompson, 'What Deliberative Democracy Means', in A. Gutmann and D. Thompson (eds.), *Why Deliberative Democracy?* (Princeton University Press, 2004), ch. 1, 37–8; D. Thompson, 'Democratic Theory and Global Society', *Journal of Political Philosophy*, 7 (1999), 120.

63 As to the identification of those who are normatively affected, it is part of the ordinary process of law-making to assess the impact of each decision or law and this should also encompass an appreciation of its extra-territorial impact.

64 See, for example, C. Gould, *Globalizing Democracy and Human Rights* (Cambridge University Press, 2004); Gutmann and Thompson, 'Deliberative Democracy'.

65 See Thompson, 'Democratic Theory', 120. See for a detailed discussion of this test: S. Besson, '*Ubi Ius, Ibi Civitas*: A Republican Account of the International Community', in S. Besson and J. L. Martí (eds.), *Legal Republicanism: National and International Perspectives* (Oxford University Press, 2009), 204.

66 See S. Besson, 'From European Integration to Integrity – Should European Law Speak with Just One Voice?', *European Law Journal*, 10 (2004), 257; Besson, 'Deliberative *Demoi*-cracy'.

the impact on one's interests is actually felt by each individual. A third element relates to the degree of affectedness of the interests; the normative or quasi-normative impact on the interest must be direct and unmediated.[67]

A common and difficult objection to the deterritorialisation of democracy lies in national sovereignty and more precisely the concept of popular sovereignty.[68] It seems prima facie counter-intuitive indeed to argue that a polity's democratic process should be concerned with the interests of another and vice versa. This objection relies on an outdated conception of sovereignty, however.[69] Contemporary state sovereignty can no longer be equated only with a sovereignty of competence or immunity, but has also become a sovereignty of responsibility towards one's state's population, and towards others' whose interests it might affect. In circumstances of increasing global interdependence, sovereignty can only be exercised in cooperation,[70] whether this takes place at the national, international, supranational or transnational level. As a result, the exercise of sovereignty becomes reflexive and dynamic; it implies a search for the best allocation of power in each case, thus questioning and potentially improving others' exercise of sovereignty as well as one's own.[71]

Since democratic rule is one of the values protected by popular sovereignty, the correct exercise of sovereignty implies, on the one hand, looking for the best level of decision to endow those affected by that decision with the strongest voice and hearing.[72] Often, this will imply giving priority to the level of governance closer to those affected, but not necessarily as EU decision-making has demonstrated.[73] Functional

[67] See Caney, Chapter 3, this volume.

[68] See, for example, Goldsmith and Posner, *The Limits*, ch. 8.

[69] See Buchanan, 'Democracy and Commitment'; Buchanan, 'Legitimacy of International Law'; R. Falk and A. L. Strauss, 'On the Creation of Global Peoples Assembly: Legitimacy and the Power of Popular Sovereignty', *Stanford Journal of International Law*, 36 (2000), 209.

[70] See S. Besson, 'Sovereignty in Conflict', *European Integration Online Papers*, 8 (2004), online, available at: http://eiop.or.at/eiop/texte/2004-015a.htm; S. Besson, 'Sovereignty: From Independence to Responsibility. On Asking the Right Question in Switzerland', in T. Cottier (ed.), *Die staatspolitischen Auswirkungen eines EU-Beitritts der Schweiz* (Zurich: vdf, in press (2009)); P. Magnette, *L'Europe, l'Etat et la Démocratie* (Bruxelles: Complexe, 2000), 161–6.

[71] See Besson, 'Sovereignty in Conflict'; N. Walker, 'Late Sovereignty in the European Union', in N. Walker (ed.), *Sovereignty in Transition* (Oxford: Hart Publishing, 2003), 22–3.

[72] See Poiares Maduro, 'Where to Look'.

[73] Note that the national level may itself be decomposed into different municipal, regional and national *stricto sensu* levels. See V. Schmidt, 'The Effects of European Integration on National Governance: Reconsidering Practices and Reconceptualizing Democracy', in

sovereignty also leads, on the other hand, to a change in the nature of the democratic process itself and in the scope of those included, whether at national, transnational, international or supranational level; this is particularly important at national level where all affected interests cannot always participate or even be represented. This functional inclusion is not only democratically beneficial to non-national interests included, but also to pre-existing national interests. Thus, minorities who were previously underrepresented or social groups whose inclusion was not sufficiently guaranteed in certain EU member states have been empowered by the broader inclusion of all European interests affected in national decision-making processes.[74]

Deliberative global *demoi*-cracy

Extending the idea of a community of multiple stakeholders beyond territorial boundaries has recently been made much easier by reference to deliberative democracy theories. According to these theories, the essence of democracy is not to be found only in voting, but also in deliberation before and after the vote.[75]

Deliberation can cope with fluid boundaries and allows for transnational communication, in each and every location whether national, transnational, international or supranational.[76] What matters for deliberative democracy is indeed the character of political interaction, rather than its locus. As such, deliberative democracy broadens the scope of democratic accountability beyond national borders. This is the true meaning of *demoi*-cracy, i.e. democratic deliberation across different territorial *demoi* with citizens of these different *demoi* deliberating with each other, thus constituting one demos along different functional lines

J. Gröte and B. Gbikpi (eds.), *Participatory Governance* (Opladen: Leske and Budrich, 2002), 141; Schmidt, 'Democratic Legitimacy'.

[74] See Besson, 'Deliberative *Demoi*-cracy'; J. S. Dryzek, 'Deliberative Democracy in Divided Societies. Alternatives to Agonism and Analgesia', *Political Theory*, 33 (2005), 218; Schmidt, 'Effects of European Integration'; Schmidt, 'Democratic Legitimacy', 980–1; F. Duina and P. Oliver, 'National Parliaments in the European Union: Are there Any Benefits to Integration', *European Law Journal*, 11 (2005), 173; Poiares Maduro, 'Where to Look'.

[75] See S. Besson, 'Democracy and Disagreement – From Deliberation to Vote and Back Again. The Move towards Deliberative Voting Ethics', in M. Iglesias and J. Ferrer (eds.), *Globalization, Democracy and Citizenship* (Berlin: Duncker & Humblot, 2003), 101; Besson, 'Deliberative *Demoi*-cracy'; Gutmann and Thompson, 'Deliberative Democracy'; Dryzek, 'Divided Societies'.

[76] See, for example, Thompson, 'Democratic Theory'; Gutmann and Thompson, 'Deliberative Democracy'; Besson, 'Deliberative *Demoi*-cracy'.

in each case. Another benefit of the deliberative model of global democracy lies in its reflexivity. Deliberative democracy allows indeed for widespread disagreement and deliberation over the legitimacy of the polity and its regime, which is important in the global polity. A final and connected reason lies in the dynamic nature of deliberation. It is a long-term process in which discussions may constantly be re-opened.[77]

Nevertheless, one finds strong resistance to the idea of deterritorialised *demoi*-cracy within certain deliberative democracy theories. Among the practical and ethical reasons for limiting deliberative democracy to territorially bound democratic polities are, on the one hand, the complexity of transnational deliberation and, on the other, the absence of the grounds of reciprocity that underlie the duty of justification in public deliberations.[78] The practical limitations of transnational deliberation need not, however, be higher than national ones. In fact, the European experience shows how the interests of national citizens may be beneficially protected and the equality among them may be re-established through the consideration of non-national EU citizens' interests.[79] As to the ethical grounds for limiting deliberative democracy to territorial entities, the objection does not cut any ice. The mutual influence of national decisions on each other in a pluralistic legal order provides the grounds for reciprocity required in deliberation.

Institutionalising global *demoi*-cracy

Global democracy qua institutional challenge

The final and main question in this chapter is how the institutional reality-sensitive normative model of global *demoi*-cracy proposed in the previous section may be translated into institutional requirements. The key element in a global *demoi*-cracy is not so much quantity, but its functional quality; it pertains to the interests included and hence deliberated and decided upon in each forum and according to existing processes. In this respect, the proposed account does not (yet) require transposing state-like democratic institutions on a global level, such as a world legislature or global assemblies.[80]

77 See Gutmann and Thompson, 'Deliberative Democracy', 6.

78 See Gutmann and Thompson, 'Deliberative Democracy', 36.

79 See Schmidt, 'Effects of European Integration'; Schmidt, 'Democratic Legitimacy'; Besson, 'Deliberative *Demoi*-cracy'.

80 See, for example, Archibugi, 'Reform of the UN'; T. Franck, *Fairness in International Law and Institutions* (Oxford: Clarendon Press, 1995); Falk and Strauss, 'Global Peoples Assembly'.

Of course, any account of the institutionalisation of global *demoi*-cracy, however minimal, will be too blunt and general to be able to reflect the constant fine-tuning there should be in reality. A few caveats are in order therefore. First of all, one should emphasise that, as in the national state, every single *type of law making process* should be matched by different democratic procedures.[81] Thus, the transactional, the legislative and the regulatory types of international law-making processes should be institutionalised differently to gain in democratic legitimacy, just as different sources of national law are legitimised in different ways. Second, *official* channels of deliberation and decision need to be complemented by *non-official* ones that account for the civil dimension of the international public sphere. This is the case at national level, but these channels are even more important to put into place at the global level; indeed, accountability mechanisms are spatially and chronologically deferred in a deterritorialised democracy and need to be complemented by strong and interconnected public spheres.[82] Finally, *different law-making agents* should be distinguished in the global law-making process besides individuals, and in particular international organisations, states and non-governmental organisations. The democratisation of law-making processes implicating each of these agents, whether at national, transnational, international or supranational level, calls for the development of different decision-making mechanisms.[83]

In this section, I shall concentrate on the quasi-legislative and multilateral modes of international law-making, as they are constantly increasing in importance and affect other non-conventional legal sources such as custom, and because their legal subjects are also individuals and hence the largest group of international law's subjects. Scope precludes, however, going into all the necessary details.[84] For the time being, the

[81] See Weiler, 'Geology'; Besson, 'Theorizing the Sources'.

[82] See, for example, J. S. Dryzek, *Deliberative Democracy and Beyond* (Oxford University Press, 2000); M. Reisman, 'The Democratization of Contemporary International Law-Making Processes and the Differentiation of Their Application', in R. Wolfrum and V. Röben (eds.), *Developments of International Law in Treaty Making* (Berlin: Springer Verlag, 2005). It is important, however, to distinguish the democratisation of international law-making from its privatisation (contra: Reisman, 'Democratization', 21–2; and presumably G. Teubner and A. Fischer-Lescano, 'Regime-Collisions: The Vain Search for Legal Unity in the Fragmentation of Global Law', *Michigan Journal of International Law*, 25 (2004), 999). See Besson, 'Theorizing the Sources'.

[83] See Stein, 'International Integration'; Buchanan, 'Democracy and Commitment'.

[84] See, however, A. McGrew, 'Democracy Beyond Borders?', in A. McGrew and D. Held (eds.), *The Global Transformations Reader: An Introduction to the Globalization Debate* (Cambridge: Polity Press, 2000), 405; Stein, 'International Integration'; Delbrück, 'Exercizing Public Authority'.

proposals of international institutional design I will make here focus on two main connected issues: first, the fora of deliberative *demoi*-cracy and, second, the latter's different modalities.

The fora of deliberative demoi*-cracy*

Literally, a democratic forum is the institutionalised place in which the agent of deliberation, i.e. the people or demos, deliberates.[85] In principle, fora of deliberation correspond to the territorial boundaries of the polity and do not transcend them. When democracy is deterritorialised and its agents are not only a demos but many *demoi*, the forum of deliberation remains largely that of the relevant existing territorial polities, be it the supranational entity, its member states or other international or transnational frameworks. In this sense, global *demoi*-cracy does not subvert national and other post-national sovereignties, but on the contrary opens them to each other in each and every single locale.[86]

What is specific about global democracy is that it takes place *at the same time* at many different levels of territorial governance: national, international, supranational and transnational.[87] These different layers constitute a *network* of national, transnational and international agencies and bodies that match, cut across or group spatially delimited locales.[88] Moreover, deterritorialised *demoi*-cracy is not only about being multi-layered, but also multi-centred and imbricated at all levels; it is not only about taking decisions at different places and multiplying deliberative fora, but also and mostly about taking them together in a deterritorialised fashion in those same places.[89] This will come more naturally when all are present or at least represented in larger fora such as supranational, international or transnational fora, but it is also important to ensure sufficient inclusion in national fora despite the lack of physical presence of all those affected.

The national forum of deliberative *demoi*-cracy

The first forum of deterritorialised deliberation one may think of is that of national deliberations. Non-citizens of a national demos are included

[85] See Bohman, '*Demos* to *Demoi*'; Gutmann and Thompson, 'Deliberative Democracy', 62.
[86] See, for example, McGrew, 'Democracy Beyond Borders?'.
[87] See Sassen, 'Global Governance'; Held, 'Transformation of Political Community'.
[88] See Held, *Cosmopolitan Democracy*, 237; Dryzek, 'Transnational Democracy'; Held, 'Cosmopolitanism: Globalization Tamed?', 475–8.
[89] See Schmidt, 'Democratic Legitimacy'; Nicolaïdis, 'European Demoi-cracy', 6.

in the deliberations of that demos in those domains in which they constitute, with other non-national citizens, a further functional global demos because they are affected by the latter's decisions.

Multiplying transnational, supranational or international decision-making authorities to further transnational deliberation may be necessary, but it also tends to undermine democratic accountability within national democratic processes themselves.[90] As a result, and by reaction to a fear of disempowerment, national democracies often become paradoxically the primary hindrance to the democratisation of international law, both within national fora and beyond them.[91] This is deeply counterproductive given the pivotal role national processes still play in the ratification, reception and implementation of post-national legal norms and hence should have in their legitimation process; the national forum is the place where the plurality of legal norms applicable to an individual in a globalised world converge and hence the place where they can be made normatively coherent.[92] Moreover, the proximity of national institutions to individuals makes them a primary forum of direct legitimation in the global law-making process. It is thus central to start by enhancing the representation of foreign interests in national deliberations and thus by turning national democracy into a central forum of global democracy, before working on the inclusive quality of further law-making fora beyond the state.

The inclusion of non-national interests in national fora may take place, in a first step, through special tribunes in which all affected foreign interests are discussed.[93] In the long run, however, the aim should be to include these interests in ordinary democratic deliberations, even in the absence of those whose interests are included. By reference to the EU, one may distinguish two correlative elements of the progressive deterritorialisation of national democratic processes.

First of all, and most importantly, non-national Europeans have now become part of the European demos that is a functional layer of all national *demoi*. As such, they are true functional citizens of each territorially-bound national demos. For instance, every single European

[90] See Gutmann and Thompson, 'Deliberative Democracy', 62.

[91] See Archibugi, 'Reform of the UN', 313–14.

[92] On legal pluralism and normative coherence, see Besson, 'European Integration'; S. Besson, 'The Concept of Constitutionalism in Europe: Interpretation *in lieu of* Translation', *No Foundations* 1 (2007), online, available at: www.helsinki.fi/nofo/; Besson, 'Theorizing the Sources'.

[93] See Thompson, 'Democratic Theory', 121–2.

citizen may vote and be eligible in municipal and European elections in any other European country. There is, in other words, a right to choose one's polity in the EU and this leads to what I have called elsewhere 'democratic forum-shopping' in Europe.[94] The effective denationalisation of EU citizenship will most probably trigger its further deterritorialisation in a second stage.[95] The ability to choose one's polity, and the advantages this generates for the chosen polities (economic but also political), might indeed lead, secondly, to the preventive *internalisation* of the interests of members of other European *demoi* potentially affected by national decisions in the national political processes at stake, even when the latter are not residents in that member state.[96] This might be the case in particular in the increasing number of areas where national decisions affect European ones and thus eventually all other national decisions.[97] Eventually, one may hope that the inclusion of non-national citizens' interests in national deliberations fora will result in the mutual internalisation of those interests, thus leading to a certain emulation among national democratic processes.

The supranational and international fora of deliberative *demoi*-cracy

There is another group of fora in whose deliberations non-national citizens may be included: supranational and international deliberations in which different national *demoi* are represented and in which most affected interests will thus be represented by representatives of their respective national demos.

International fora of deliberation group global or at least regional *demoi* that are as territorially delineated as national *demoi* and allow therefore for an overall representation of affected interests. This is a straightforward way in which foreigners, whose interests cannot actually be included in national deliberations, may still exercise some influence over national decisions; public officials are indeed often to some degree

94 See Besson, 'Deliberative *Demoi*-cracy'; Poiares Maduro, 'Where to Look'; M. Poiares Maduro, 'Europe and the Constitution: What if this is as Good as it Gets?', in J. Weiler and M. Wind (eds.), *European Constitutionalism Beyond the State* (Cambridge University Press, 2003), 74.

95 See, for example, S. Besson and A. Utzinger, 'European Citizenship across Borders', in A. Epiney, T. Haag and A. Heinemann (eds.), *Challenging Boundaries, Festschrift Roland Bieber* (Zurich: Schulthess, 2007), 257; Sassen, 'Global Governance', 20.

96 See Poiares Maduro, 'Where to Look'; Poiares Maduro, 'Europe and the Constitution'.

97 See Besson, 'European Integration'; Poiares Maduro, 'Where to Look'; Poiares Maduro, 'Europe and the Constitution'.

more accountable to representatives of those foreigners' interests in international fora than they would be in national debates.[98] The difficulty here lies in the modalities of such functional deliberations, although they are technically easier to overcome than in national deliberations. Most of the time, indeed, intergovernmental organisations are dominated by government officials rather than by elected representatives.

Supranational fora may correct these shortcomings of international deliberation in representing non-territorial interests in more directly democratic ways. This may be demonstrated by deliberations in the European Parliament, for instance. The latter functions indeed like a national parliament, with universally elected representatives representing the interests of all European citizens whatever their nationality. As such, supranational fora favour the development of a functional global public sphere. This is evidenced by the modalities of defence of European interests which are no longer only grouped and represented along territorial lines and national polities, but increasingly across transnational groupings of interests. Interestingly, the development of cooperation between the European Parliament and national parliaments and, more generally, the latter's inclusion in a number of important decision-making procedures in the EU in the Lisbon Treaty, are evidence of a third form of democratic representation that may be experimented at the supranational level: the representation of peoples besides that of states and of citizens.

The transnational forum of deliberative *demoi*-cracy

Finally, the deterritorialisation of democracy also takes place at the transnational level, whether it is through the interconnection of national or infranational levels of governance. The difficulty with transnational deliberation is that the locus of deliberation does not match any of the territorial boundaries of existing polities, and it takes more effort to implement therefore.[99]

In fact, more and more transnational networks of cooperation have been developed both at the European and global level in the past few years; some link official authorities, such as legislative, executive or judicial networks. For instance, one should mention the democratic deliberations that take place through transnational interparliamentary cooperation in the European Union. These exchanges contribute to the

[98] See Gutmann and Thompson, 'Deliberative Democracy', 39.
[99] See Held, 'Cosmopolitanism: Globalization Tamed?'.

development of a global public sphere qua transnational network of national public spheres that goes deeper than the surface of parliamentary deliberations at global level.[100] Other transnational networks are purely private or, as in most cases of global administrative governance, mixtures of both.[101] The difficulty lies therein that these networks are not usually democratic in their functioning and are rather technocratic,[102] and need therefore to be perfected in this respect; various measures have already been taken to conceive of and improve the accountability and transparency of those transnational fora of deliberation and decision-making.[103]

The modalities of deliberative demoi-*cracy*

There are two constitutive modalities of democracy one should be concerned about when institutionalising global *demoi*-cracy: participation, on the one hand, and representation, on the other. Scope precludes discussing them by reference to the different fora presented before, but they should clearly be implemented differently in each case. Our concern here will mostly be the national forum of deliberative *demoi*-cracy, as it is the pivotal locus of deterritorialised democratic legitimation of law in a globalised world.

Deliberative *demoi*-cratic participation

In principle, democracy implies that all those affected by a decision be able to participate in the decision-making process. It should be clear from the outset, however, that not all global stakeholders can participate equally in all the democratic processes in which the decisions that affect them will be taken, whether supranational, international, transnational or, even worse, national. Direct participation need not, however, be required at all levels in a global democracy. It suffices that those whose

100 See L. Blichner, 'The Anonymous Hand of Public Reason: Interparliamentary Discourse and the Quest for Legitimacy', in E. O. Eriksen and J. E. Fossum (eds.), *Democracy in the European Union. Integration through Deliberation?* (London: Routledge, 2000), 141; Besson, 'Deliberative *Demoi*-cracy'.

101 See, for example, Slaughter, 'Government Networks'; Slaughter, 'Disaggregated Sovereignty'; N. Krisch, 'The Pluralism of Global Administrative Law', *European Journal of International Law*, 17 (2006), 247; Teubner and Fischer-Lescano 'Regime-Collisions'.

102 See Buchanan, *Moral Foundations*, chs. 5 and 7; Besson, 'Theorizing the Sources'.

103 See, for example in the EU, D. Curtin, 'Framing Public Deliberation and Democratic Legitimacy in the European Union', in S. Besson and J. L. Martí (eds.), *Deliberative Democracy and its Discontents* (Aldershot: Ashgate, 2006), ch. 7.

basic interests are normatively affected by global decisions be able to have an influence on them. In fact, democratic deliberation may take place through different channels despite physical absence and these provide promising alleys for global *demoi*-cracy. As Dryzek argues, it may even be beneficial in divided polities to establish a distance between deliberation and decision-making and this both through a deferral of the decision in time and a delocalisation in space.[104]

In any case, direct participation has already become secondary to representation in most national democracies. Democratic representation may even be seen as an enhancer of democratic *participation* and deliberation thanks to the distance it creates between deliberation and decision-making and to the relationship of election and accountability it launches between representatives and their constituencies.[105] Not only can representation enhance democratic participation, but it can also increase the protection of *political equality* within a polity. Simple majorities cannot exclude minorities as easily in a representative democracy as in a purely direct democracy; it takes a majority to elect and authorise representatives, another for these to act and still another to make them accountable. The deferred nature of the decision and the increased scope of deliberation also leave more time and space to diverging opinions and perspectives to make themselves heard and maybe to convince and change majorities until the decision-making stage.[106] In short, although the representation of non-national citizens' interests cannot be as inclusive as the direct participation of all of them, this incomplete inclusion is compensated by the participation-enhancing effect of representation and the correctives representation provides to the excesses of majoritarianism.

Deliberative *demoi*-cratic representation

If global *demoi*-cracy is best understood as both indirectly participative, when possible, and representative, it remains to see how *demoi*-cratic representation can work effectively in a globalised democracy. In principle, a decision-making process is properly inclusive if the interests, opinions and social perspectives of all those affected by the decisions are represented in the decision-making process.

104 See Dryzek, 'Divided Societies', 223; Besson, *Morality of Conflict*, ch. 10.

105 See S. Besson, 'The Paradox of Democratic Representation', in L. Wintgens (ed.), *The Theory and Practice of Legislation: Essays in Legisprudence* (Aldershot: Ashgate, 2005), 125.

106 See Besson, 'Democratic Representation'; N. Urbinati, 'Representation as Advocacy', *Political Theory*, 2 (2000), 758.

In current systems of international, supranational and transnational level decision-making, however, individuals are indirectly represented primarily by their national states and in most cases by members of the executive, who are not always elected and only very indirectly accountable to the general public. True, there are exceptions as in the case of the European Parliament. All these mechanisms remain largely separate from national political channels, however, at the price in particular of transparency and accountability overall, on the one hand, and of coherence of the decisions taken at the different levels, on the other. Once more, it is clear therefore that before multiplying representative fora at the transnational, international and supranational levels, the focus of institutional measures should be on enhancing the democratic quality of representation at *the national level first.*

The challenge, however is that this implies representing the interests of all those affected by national decisions in national deliberation and decision-making, even when they are not part of the electoral constituency. There is a form of representation, however, that has been developed in diverse and divided societies where not all citizens can be represented descriptively and which might contribute to the representation of non-national citizens' interests: *reflective representation.*[107] In a nutshell, reflective representation requires from each representative that she project herself into the place of others in her own internal deliberation, rather than leave the confrontation with diversity to external and interactive deliberation.

The problem with this approach, however, is that, without minimal representation or means of asserting a voice in the making of the decision, it is too easy to assume that a decision will benefit non-national citizens simply because national representatives use reflective means of deliberation. There are two ways of ensuring a more effective representation of non-national citizens' interests through reflective representation.

First of all, *diverse representation.* Without some kind of minimal descriptive representation, reflective representation cannot be as diversified as required by the representation of non-national citizens.[108] Although minimal descriptive deliberation is required, it is very unlikely that moral-political constituents will be represented as fairly as electoral

[107] See R. E. Goodin, *Reflective Democracy* (Oxford University Press, 2003).

[108] See R. Eckersley, 'Deliberative Democracy, Ecological Risk and "Communities of Fate"', in M. Saward (ed.), *Democratic Innovation: Deliberation, Association and Representation* (London: Routledge, 2000), 117; Goodin, *Reflective Democracy*, 171.

constituents in national deliberations. A solution might lie in foreigners' tribunes or, as in certain post-national polities like the EU, in granting to non-national citizens political rights at national level. In fact, it might actually be better for the quality of deliberations not to have a full descriptive representation of all non-national citizens as people tend to cut deals in such circumstances.[109]

A second, and more efficient way of ensuring the effective reflective representation of non-national citizens' interests lies paradoxically in the *electoral system* itself, and more precisely the electoral sanction of those representatives who do not include all affected interests in their deliberation and decision-making. The success of democratic accountability greatly depends on the moral capacities of citizens and public officials. As such, the support of elected representatives by their electoral constituents will in principle follow their championing the cause of moral-political constituents.[110] Moreover, national citizens might also want to make sure, through (re-)electing representatives who represent the interests of all those affected, that their own direct interests are well protected abroad. Increasingly, this might only be the case when non-national interests are mutually taken into account in the decision-making process. Representatives' failure to do so might trigger electoral sanctions, as this omission might result in negative effects on the inclusion of national interests elsewhere.

Conclusion

The legitimacy of international law has attracted increasing attention in recent years. So has one of the most important dimensions of legitimacy: global democracy. Although different theoretical models of global democracy have been developed, very few proposals have been made as to how to implement them in practice. Nor have those proposals, as a matter of fact, factored an institutional dimension in the theoretical model propounded. This has resulted in a certain lassitude among theorists vis-à-vis the desirability and feasibility of global democracy, but has also brought the threat of a backlash in national democratic practice and has led to the rejection of important global legitimacy-enhancing institutions precisely on grounds of democracy. This has been exemplified

[109] See Goodin, *Reflective Democracy*; C. Sunstein, 'The Law of Group Polarization', *Journal of Political Philosophy*, 10 (2002), 175.

[110] See Gutmann and Thompson, 'Deliberative Democracy', 39.

recently in the European Union following the popular rejection in some member states of the Constitutional Treaty in 2005 and of the Reform Treaty in 2007.[111]

In view of this theoretical and practical situation, the purpose of this chapter was to look more closely into the institutionalisation of global democracy. The chapter proposed a theoretical albeit institution-sensitive model of deliberative *demoi*-cracy that matches the deterritorialisation of law-making in practice thanks to its three constitutive elements: its pluralist subject, its deterritorialised process and, finally, its deliberative nature. It also discussed ways of further institutionalising deliberative *demoi*-cracy and focused more particularly on the fora of global *demoi*-cracy, and in particular on national fora, and its specific modalities in terms of participation and representation.

Prima facie, the qualitative change required in this chapter amounts to very little by contrast to what would be required by the implementation of the kind of supranational and cosmopolitan democracy propounded in other accounts of global democracy. At the same time, however, and this is quite paradoxical, this proposal is often perceived as radical in terms of change in national democratic habits and practices. While the international community might not yet know it is a community, national societies have obviously not yet taken the full measure of their internationality. Understanding why this is the case might provide one of the keys to address the international legitimacy crisis.

References

Alston, P. 1997. 'The Myopia of the Handmaidens: International Lawyers and Globalization', *European Journal of International Law* 8: 435–48.

Archibugi, D. 1993. 'The Reform of the UN and Cosmopolitan Democracy: A Critical Review', *Journal of Peace Research* 30: 301–15.

Archibugi, D. 2004. 'Cosmopolitan Democracy and Its Critics: A Review', *European Journal of International Relations* 10: 437–73.

Beitz, C. 1983. 'Procedural Equality in Democratic Theory: A Preliminary Examination', in Pennock, R. and Chapman, J. (eds.), *Liberal Democracy, Nomos XXV*. New York University Press, ch. 2, pp. 71–90.

Benhabib, S. 2004. *The Rights of Others: Aliens, Residents and Citizens*. Cambridge University Press.

[111] See S. Besson, 'Europe as a Demoi-cratic Polity', *Retfaerd – Juridisk Tidskrift*, 1/116 (2007), 3–21.

Besson, S. 2003. 'Democracy and Disagreement – From Deliberation to Vote and Back Again. The Move towards Deliberative Voting Ethics', in Iglesias, M. and Ferrer, J. (eds.), *Globalization, Democracy and Citizenship*. Berlin: Duncker & Humblot, 101–35.

Besson, S. 2004. 'From European Integration to Integrity – Should European Law Speak with Just One Voice?', *European Law Journal* 10: 257–81.

Besson, S. 2004. 'Sovereignty in Conflict', *European Integration Online Papers* 8, online, available at: http://eiop.or.at/eiop/texte/2004-015a.htm.

Besson, S. 2005. *The Morality of Conflict. Reasonable Disagreement and the Law*. Oxford: Hart Publishing.

Besson, S. 2005. 'Democracy, Law and Authority' (Review of Lukas Meyer, Stanley Paulson and Thomas Pogge (eds.), *Rights, Culture and the Law: Themes from the Legal and Political Philosophy of Joseph Raz*), *Journal of Moral Philosophy* 2: 89–99.

Besson, S. 2005. 'The Paradox of Democratic Representation', in Wintgens, L. (ed.), *The Theory and Practice of Legislation: Essays in Legisprudence*. Aldershot: Ashgate, 125–61.

Besson, S. 2006. 'Deliberative *Demoi*-cracy in the European Union. Towards the Deterritorialization of Democracy', in Besson, S. and Martí, J. L. (eds.), *Deliberative Democracy and its Discontents*. Aldershot: Ashgate, 188–231.

Besson, S. 2006. 'The EU and Human Rights: Towards a New Kind of Post-national Human Rights Institution', *Human Rights Law Review* 6: 323.

Besson, S. 2007. 'The Concept of Constitutionalism in Europe: Interpretation *in lieu of* Translation', *No Foundations* 1, online, available at: www.helsinki.fi/nofo/.

Besson, S. 2007. 'Europe as a *Demoi*-cratic Polity', *Retfaerd – Juridisk Tidskrift*, 1/116: 3–21.

Besson, S. 2009. '*Ubi Ius, Ibi Civitas*: A Republican Account of the International Community', in Besson, S. and Martí, J. L. (eds.), *Legal Republicanism: National and International Perspectives*. Oxford University Press, 204.

Besson, S. in press (2009). 'The Authority of International Law – Lifting the State Veil', *Sydney Law Review* 31.

Besson, S. in press (2009). 'Sovereignty: From Independence to Responsibility. On Asking the Right Question in Switzerland', in Cottier, T. (ed.), *Die staatspolitischen Auswirkungen eines EU-Beitritts der Schweiz*. Zurich: vdf.

Besson, S. in press (2010). 'Theorizing the Sources of International Law', in Besson, S. and Tasioulas, J. (eds.), *The Philosophy of International Law*. Oxford University Press.

Besson, S. and Utzinger, A. 2007. 'European Citizenship across Borders', in Epiney, A. Haag T. and Heinemann, A. (eds.), *Challenging Boundaries, Festschrift Roland Bieber*. Baden-Baden: Nomos, 629–44.

Beutz, M. 2003. 'Functional Democracy: Responding to Failures of Accountability', *Harvard Journal of International Law* 44: 387–432.

Blichner, L. 2000. 'The Anonymous Hand of Public Reason: Interparliamentary Discourse and the Quest for Legitimacy', in Eriksen, E. O. and Fossum, J. E. (eds.), *Democracy in the European Union. Integration through Deliberation?* London: Routledge, 141–63.

Bodanksy, D. 1999. 'The Legitimacy of International Governance: A Coming Challenge for International Environmental Law?', *American Journal of International Law* 93: 596–624.

Bogdandy, A. von. 2004. 'Globalization and Europe: How to Square Democracy, Globalization and International Law', *European Journal of International Law* 15: 885–906.

Bohman, J. 2004. 'Constitution Making and Democratic Innovation: The European Union and Transnational Governance', *European Journal of Political Theory* 3: 315–37.

Bohman, J. 2005.'From *Demos* to *Demoi*: Democracy across Borders', *Ratio Juris* 18: 293–314.

Buchanan, A. 2004. *Justice, Legitimacy, and Self-Determination: Moral Foundations for International Law.* Oxford University Press.

Buchanan, A. 2006. 'Democracy and the Commitment to International Law', *University of Georgia Journal of International and Transnational Law* 34: 305–32.

Buchanan, A. 2008. 'Human Rights and the Legitimacy of the International Legal Order', *Legal Theory* 14: 39–70.

Buchanan, A. in press (2010). 'Legitimacy of International Law', in Besson, S. and Tasioulas, J. (eds.), *The Philosophy of International Law.* Oxford University Press.

Buchanan, A. and Keohane, O. 2006. 'The Legitimacy of Global Governance Institutions', *Ethics and International Affairs* 20: 405–37.

Calhoun, C. 2003. 'The Class Consciousness of Frequent Travellers: Towards a Critique of Actually Existing Cosmopolitanism', in Archibugi, D. (ed.), *Debating Cosmopolitics.* London: Verso, 86–116.

Canovan, M. 1996. *Nationhood and Political Theory.* Cheltenham: Edward Elgar.

Cheneval, F. 2006. 'The People in Deliberative Democracy', in Besson, S. and Martí, J. L. (eds.), *Deliberative Democracy and its Discontents.* Aldershot: Ashgate, ch. 8, 159–80.

Christiano, T. 1996. *The Rule of The Many: Fundamental Issues in Democratic Theory.* Boulder: Westview Press.

Christiano, T. in press (2010). 'Democratic Legitimacy and International Institutions', in Besson, S. and Tasioulas, J. (eds.), *The Philosophy of International Law.* Oxford University Press.

Crawford, J. 1993. 'Democracy and International Law', *British Yearbook of International Law* 44: 113–33.

Crawford, J. 2000. 'Democracy and the Body of International Law', in Fox, G. and Roth, B. (eds.), *Democratic Governance and International Law.* Cambridge University Press, 91–122.

Crawford, J. 2000. 'Democracy in International Law – A Reprise', in Fox, G. and Roth, B. (eds.), *Democratic Governance and International Law*. Cambridge University Press, 114–20.

Crawford, J. and Marks, S. 1998. 'The Global Democracy Deficit: An Essay in International Law and its Limits', in Archibugi, D., Held, D. and Kohler, M. (eds.), *Re-Imagining Political Community, Studies in Cosmopolitan Democracy*. Cambridge: Polity Press, 72–90.

Curtin, D. 2006. 'Framing Public Deliberation and Democratic Legitimacy in the European Union', in Besson, S. and Martí, J. L. (eds.), *Deliberative Democracy and its Discontents*. Aldershot: Ashgate, 133–58.

Delbrück, J. 2003. 'Exercizing Public Authority Beyond the State: Transnational Democracy and/or Alternative Legitimation Strategies?', *Indiana Journal of Global Studies* 10: 29–43.

Dryzek, J. S. 1999. 'Transnational Democracy', *Journal of Political Philosophy* 7: 30.

Dryzek, J. S. 2000. *Deliberative Democracy and Beyond*. Oxford University Press.

Dryzek, J. S. 2001. 'Legitimacy and Economy in Deliberative Democracy', *Political Theory* 29: 651–69.

Dryzek, J. S. 2005. 'Deliberative Democracy in Divided Societies. Alternatives to Agonism and Analgesia', *Political Theory* 33: 218–42.

Duina, F. and Oliver, P. 2005. 'National Parliaments in the European Union: Are there Any Benefits to Integration', *European Law Journal* 11: 173–95.

Eckersley, R. 2000. 'Deliberative Democracy, Ecological Risk and "Communities of Fate"', in Saward, M. (ed.), *Democratic Innovation: Deliberation, Association and Representation*. London: Routledge, 117–32.

Falk, R. and Strauss, A. L. 2000. 'On the Creation of Global Peoples Assembly: Legitimacy and the Power of Popular Sovereignty', *Stanford Journal of International Law* 36: 191–220.

Fox, G. and Roth, B. 2000. 'Introduction: The Spread of Liberal Democracy and Its Implications for International Law', in Fox, G. and Roth, B. (eds.), *Democratic Governance and International Law*. Cambridge University Press, 1–24.

Franck, T. 1987. 'Why a Quest for Legitimacy?', *UC Davis Law Review* 21: 535–48.

Franck, T. 1988. 'Legitimacy in the International System', *American Journal of International Law* 82: 705–59.

Franck, T. 1990. *The Power of Legitimacy among Nations*. Oxford: Clarendon Press.

Franck, T. 1992. 'The Emerging Right to Democratic Governance', *American Journal of International Law* 86: 46–91.

Franck, T. 1995. *Fairness in International Law and Institutions*. Oxford: Clarendon Press.

Franck, T. 2006. 'The Power of Legitimacy and the Legitimacy of Power: International Law in an Age of Power Disequilibrium', *American Journal of International Law* 100: 88–106.

Goldsmith, J. L. and Posner, E. A. 2005. *The Limits of International Law*. New York: Oxford University Press.

Goodin, R. E. 2003. *Reflective Democracy*. Oxford University Press.

Gould, C. 2004. *Globalizing Democracy and Human Rights*. Cambridge University Press.

Guéhenno, J. M. 1999. *La fin de la démocratie*. Paris: Champs Flammarion.

Gutmann, A. and Thompson, D. 2004. *Why Deliberative Democracy?* Princeton University Press.

Habermas, J. 2001. 'The Postnational Constellation and the Future of Democracy', in Habermas, J. and Pensky, M. (eds.), *The Postnational Constellation – Political Essays*. Cambridge University Press, 58–112.

Held, D. 1999. 'The Transformation of Political Community: Rethinking Democracy in the Context of Globalization', in Shapiro, I. and Hacker-Cordon, C. (eds.), *Democracy's Edges*. Cambridge: Cambridge University Press, 84–111.

Held, D. 2003.'Cosmopolitanism: Globalization Tamed?', *Review of International Studies* 29: 465–80.

Held, D. 2004. *The Global Covenant: The Social Democratic Alternative to the Washington Consensus*. Cambridge: Polity Press.

Held, D., McGrew, A., Goldblatt, D. and Perraton, J. 1999. *Global Transformations. Politics, Economics, and Culture*. Stanford University Press.

Krisch, N. 2006. 'The Pluralism of Global Administrative Law', *European Journal of International Law* 17: 247–78.

Kumm, M. 2004. 'The Legitimacy of International Law: A Constitutionalist Framework of Analysis', *European Journal of International Law* 15: 907–31.

Magnette, P. 2000. *L'Europe, l'Etat et la Démocratie*. Bruxelles: Complexe.

McCorquodale, R. 2006. 'The Individual in International Law', in Evans, M. D. (ed.), *International Law*, 2nd edition, Oxford University Press, 307–32.

McGrew, A. 2000. 'Democracy Beyond Borders?', in McGrew, A. and Held, D. (eds.), *The Global Transformations Reader: An Introduction to the Globalization Debate*. Cambridge: Polity Press, 405–19.

Miller, D. 2000. *Citizenship and National Identity*. Cambridge: Polity Press.

Nicolaïdis, K. 2004. 'The New Constitution as European Demoi-cracy?', *Critical Review of International Social and Political Philosophy* 7: 76–93.

Nicolaïdis, K. 2004. 'We, The Peoples of Europe ...', *Foreign Affairs* 83: 97–110.

Offe, C. 1998. 'Homogeneity and Constitutional Democracy: Coping with Identity Conflicts through Group Rights', *Journal of Political Philosophy* 6: 113–41.

Parijs, P. van. 1998. 'Should the European Union Become More Democratic?', in Follesdal, A. and Koslowski, P. (eds.), *Democracy and the European Union*. Berlin: Springer, 287–301.

Paulus, A. 2004. 'Comment: The Legitimacy of International Law and the Role of the State', *Michigan Journal of International Law* 25: 1047–58.

Pippan, C. 2004. 'Right to Democracy in International Law', *European Journal of International Law* 15: 213–18.

Pogge, T. 1997. 'Creating Supra-National Institutions Democratically: Reflections on the European Union's "Democratic Deficit"', *Journal of Political Philosophy* 5: 163–82.

Poiares Maduro, M. 2002.'Where to Look for Legitimacy?', in Eriksen, E. O., Fossum J. E. and Menendez, A. (eds.), *Constitution Making and Democratic Legitimacy*. (ARENA Report 5/02) Oslo: Arena, 81–110.

Poiares Maduro, M. 2003. 'Europe and the Constitution: What if this is as Good as it Gets?', in Weiler, J. and Wind, M. (eds.), *European Constitutionalism Beyond the State*. Cambridge University Press, 74–102.

Raz, J. 1979. *The Authority of Law*. Oxford University Press.

Raz, J. 1995. *Ethics in the Public Domain*. Oxford University Press.

Reisman, M. 2005. 'The Democratization of Contemporary International Law-Making Processes and the Differentiation of Their Application', in Wolfrum, R. and Röben, V. (eds.), *Developments of International Law in Treaty Making*. Berlin: Springer Verlag, 15–30.

Rich, R. 2001. 'Bringing Democracy into International Law', *Journal of Democracy* 12: 20–34.

Sassen, S. 2003. 'The Participation of States and Citizens in Global Governance', *Indiana Journal of Global Studies* 10: 5–28.

Schmidt, V. 2002. 'The Effects of European Integration on National Governance: Reconsidering Practices and Reconceptualizing Democracy', in Gröte, J. and Gbikpi, B. (eds.), *Participatory Governance*. Opladen: Leske and Budrich, 141–76.

Schmidt, V. 2004. 'The European Union: Democratic Legitimacy in a Regional State?', *Journal of Common Market Studies* 42: 975–97.

Slaughter, A. M. 2000. 'Government Networks: The Heart of the Liberal Democratic Order', in Fox, G. and Roth, B. (eds.), *Democratic Governance and International Law*. Cambridge University Press, 199–238.

Slaughter, A. M. 2004. 'Disaggregated Sovereignty: Towards the Public Accountability of Global Government Networks', *Government and Opposition* 39: 159–90.

Stein, E. 2001. 'International Integration and Democracy: No Love at First Sight', *American Journal of International Law* 95: 489–534.

Steiner, H. J. 1988. 'Political Participation as a Human Right', *Harvard Human Rights Yearbook* 1: 77–134.

Sunstein, C. 2002.'The Law of Group Polarization', *Journal of Political Philosophy* 10: 175.

Tasioulas, J. 2006. 'Review: Justice, Legitimacy and Self-Determination: Moral Foundations for International Law', *International and Comparative Law Quarterly* 55: 237–40.

Tasioulas, J. in press (2010). 'The Legitimacy of International Law', in Besson, S. and Tasioulas, J. (eds.), *The Philosophy of International Law*. Oxford University Press.

Teubner, G. and Fischer-Lescano, A. 2004. 'Regime-Collisions: The Vain Search for Legal Unity in the Fragmentation of Global Law', *Michigan Journal of International Law* 25: 999–1046.

Thompson, D. 1999. 'Democratic Theory and Global Society', *Journal of Political Philosophy* 7: 111–25.

Urbinati, N. 2000. 'Representation as Advocacy', *Political Theory* 2: 758–86.

Urbinati, N. 2003. 'Can Cosmopolitical Democracy Be Democratic?', in Archibugi, D. (ed.), *Debating Cosmopolitics*. London: Verso, 67–85.

Waldron, J. 1999. *Law and Disagreement*. Oxford University Press.

Waldron, J. 2003. 'Authority for Officials', in Meyer, L. H., Paulson S. L. and Pogge, T. W. (eds.), *Rights, Culture, and the Law. Themes from the Legal and Political Philosophy of Joseph Raz*. Oxford University Press, 45–70.

Walker, N. 2003. *Sovereignty in Transition*. Oxford: Hart Publishing.

Weiler, J. 1999. 'To Be a European Citizen: Eros and Civilization', in Weiler, J., *The Constitution of Europe*. Cambridge University Press, 324–55.

Weiler, J. 2004. 'The Geology of International Law – Governance, Democracy and Legitimacy', *Zeitschrift für ausländisches öffentliches Recht und Völkerrecht* 64: 547–62.

Weiler, J. and Paulus, A. 1997. 'The Structure of Change or Is there a Hierarchy of Norms in International Law?', *European Journal of International Law* 8: 545–65.

Whelan, F. G. 1983. 'Prologue: Democratic Theory and the Boundary Problem', in Pennock, R. and Chapman, J. (eds.), *Liberal Democracy, Nomos XXV*. New York University Press, 13–47.

3

The responsibilities and legitimacy of economic international institutions

SIMON CANEY

Recently much has been written about the ethical issues surrounding global politics. There has, for example, been a considerable literature on global ideals of distributive justice. However, amongst all this, very little has been written by political theorists on some of the most significant international institutions, such as the International Monetary Fund (IMF), the World Bank and the World Trade Organisation (WTO).[1] Many discussions of global distributive justice tend to regard states as the central duty-bearers and assume that the pursuit of global justice requires, for example, an increase in states' overseas development budgets. There has, of course, been a considerable literature on some international institutions. Writers such as Daniele Archibugi and David Held have defended what they term a 'cosmopolitan democracy' where this calls for the democratisation of global political institutions.[2]

Earlier versions of this paper were presented at the Department of Philosophy, St Andrews (February 2004); the Department of Politics, University of Southampton (April 2004); the Centre for International Studies, University of Cambridge (October 2004); the School of Politics, International Relations and the Environment, University of Keele (June 2005); and the Symposium on 'Justice, Legitimacy, and Public International Law', University of Bern (December 2006). For their illuminating comments I am grateful in particular to Duncan Bell, Allen Buchanan, Andy Mason, Tony McGrew, David Miller, David Owens, Mark Philp, Nick Rengger, Steve Ratner, John Skorupski and Graham Smith. I am especially grateful to Corinna Mieth, my commentator at Bern, and to Mathias Risse for their extremely helpful written comments. The final draft of this paper was completed during my tenure of a Leverhulme Research Fellowship and I am extremely grateful to the Leverhulme Trust for its invaluable support.

1 For one notable exception see Peter Singer's analysis of the World Trade Organisation in *One World: The Ethics of Globalization* (New Haven and London: Yale University Press, 2002), 51–105.

2 See D. Archibugi and D. Held (eds.), *Cosmopolitan Democracy: An Agenda for a New World Order* (Cambridge: Polity, 1995) and D. Held, *Democracy and the Global Order: From the Modern State to Cosmopolitan Governance* (Cambridge: Polity, 1995).

However, the focus of this perspective tends to be on reforming the United Nations.[3]

My aim in this chapter is to provide a provisional and tentative analysis of the normative nature of international economic institutions, such as the IMF, World Bank and the WTO. I shall make particular reference to these three institutions, in part, because they play an important role and, in part, to simplify the analysis. However, it is not assumed that these are the only international economic institutions of import nor is it assumed that the analyses that follow cannot be applied to other institutions.[4] To this we should also add that the chapter is exploratory in nature. It certainly cannot claim to provide and defend a normative theory of international institutions. I hope, however, to outline the key tasks of such a theory, analyse several different approaches, identifying their strengths and weaknesses, and introduce and defend what I take to be the most promising account.

Four tasks

Let us begin by outlining the tasks ahead. A normative analysis of international institutions must, I believe, perform at least four tasks. First, it should be able to provide a plausible account of the *responsibilities* or *functions* of the institutions. What duties do international institutions have? And, how does one identify these duties? To illustrate the relevance of this point we might consider current debates surrounding the role of the IMF. Some, such as Nobel Laureate Joseph Stiglitz, maintain that it should restrict itself to the purposes outlined in the original Articles of Agreement that were signed by the member states.[5] Others, such as the late Milton Friedman, argue that the IMF should have no role to play and should be disbanded.[6] This too is a position that should be covered under the heading of 'functions'. Some, by contrast with these preceding views, would argue that institutions such as the IMF, World Bank and

[3] Some, though, have made some suggestions concerning the accountability of international economic institutions: see T. McGrew, 'The World Trade Organization: Technocracy or Banana Republic?', in A. Taylor and C. Thomas (eds.), *Global Trade and Global Social Issues* (London and New York: Routledge, 1999), 197–216.

[4] Also, it should be noted that international institutions vary tremendously. For example, some include virtually all states whereas others have more limited membership. Furthermore, they clearly differ in their roles and in their powers.

[5] J. Stiglitz, *Globalization and its Discontents* (London: Allen Lane, 2002), 232–3.

[6] Cited in R. Gilpin, *The Challenge of Global Capitalism: the World Economy in the 21st Century* (Princeton and Oxford: Princeton University Press, 2000), 329–30.

WTO should help to eradicate poverty. They might hold, for example, that WTO agreements should be framed with a view to realising the aims of the Millennium Development Goals or, perhaps, more ambitiously, to maximise the condition of the world's least well-off.[7] Some of these might also hold that it is the job of the WTO to design a framework of international trade that discourages excessive carbon dioxide emissions. Their view would be that the WTO has environmental responsibilities and should seek to minimise global climate change. In this vein, Stiglitz has argued that members of the WTO should use it to impose sanctions on high-emitting countries like the USA.[8] Some, however, would strongly oppose these ambitious views. To give one prominent example, on 1 February 2001 Arthur Dunkel, Peter Sutherland and Renato Ruggiero wrote, in their 'Joint Statement on the Multilateral Trading System', that '[t]he WTO cannot be used as a Christmas tree on which to hang any and every good cause that might be secured by exercising trade power'.[9] They thus reject the claim that the WTO should seek to address global poverty or should combat exploitative labour laws.

A second morally relevant question that needs to be answered is: 'What gives an international institution the *legitimacy* to perform the tasks it is performing?' Do they, for example, derive their legitimacy from the fact that they are the creation of states? Or does their legitimacy inhere in the fact that they perform important functions? Or do they in fact lack legitimacy?

A third key question is: 'What *powers* may international institutions have?' This can be broken down into two questions. The first considers the extent of their power. Should such powers be overridable by others? Or should they be the final arbiter on any issues? The first question, then, concerns the status of their decisions. A second question is the more specific one of which particular instruments should such institutions be entitled to use. Should international economic institutions have the power to issue binding regulations that govern all persons and enterprises? Can they make conditional offers? May they impose sanctions on regimes that do not comply with their rules? May they even levy taxes?

[7] C. Beitz, *Political Theory and International Relations* (Princeton: Princeton University Press, 1999), 150–3.

[8] J. Stiglitz, *Making Globalization Work: the Next Steps to Global Justice* (London: Allen Lane, 2006), 176–8.

[9] See www.wto.org/English/news_e/news01_e/jointstatdavos_jan01_e.htm.

A fourth, and final, question that an adequate account of the normative character of international institutions needs to address is: 'What are the *binding norms* that should govern international institutions?' To grasp the question being raised here it may be useful to give an example. For instance, it is commonly suggested that international economic institutions should adopt a norm of publicity and that their decision-making should be 'transparent' and 'open'.[10] In the terminology I am employing, those who subscribe to this approach are claiming that international institutions should adopt a binding norm of transparency. Some might suggest some more demanding binding norms. To give one example, consider the claim advanced by many (but not all) liberal theorists that the state should be neutral between conceptions of the good.[11] Given this, one might ask, analogously, whether international institutions are similarly bound by these or similar strictures. May the World Bank, for example, act on controversial beliefs about the good life? One might consider population issues in this light. Population growth may, of course, have a pronounced impact on the extent of a country's economic development and it may also be tied to a religious worldview, such as Catholicism. The question, then, is whether the World Bank (or IMF) can act on the judgement that a state should curb population growth by encouraging contraception, and thereby act on the assumption that Catholic doctrine on contraception should be disregarded.

A further relevant question is whether international institutions should be neutral between conflicting accounts of justice when these are in conflict. So should they be neutral between egalitarian, libertarian and social democratic visions of global justice? We might also wonder whether international institutions should be neutral between different kinds of political system. Here we should record that the World Bank affirms that it should be neutral between different political systems. Article 4, section 10 of the Articles of Agreement of the International Bank for Reconstruction and Development (IBRD) states that:

10 See S. Caney, 'Cosmopolitanism, Democracy and Distributive Justice', *The Canadian Journal of Philosophy*, supplementary volume 31 (2006), 55; S. Caney, 'Cosmopolitan Justice and Institutional Design: An Egalitarian Liberal Conception of Global Governance', *Social Theory and Practice*, 32 (2006), 748–50; Stiglitz, *Globalization and its Discontents*, 227–9; United Nations Development Programme, *Human Development Report 2002: Deepening Democracy in a Fragmented World* (New York: Oxford University Press, 2002), 115; and N. Woods, 'Making the IMF and the World Bank More Accountable', *International Affairs*, 77 (2001), 90–1.

11 R. Dworkin, *A Matter of Principle* (Oxford: Clarendon Press, 1985), 191; J. Rawls, *Political Liberalism* (New York: Columbia University Press, 1993), 191–4.

> The Bank and its officers shall not interfere in the political affairs of any member; nor shall they be influenced in their decisions by the political character of the member or members concerned. Only economic considerations shall be relevant to their decisions, and these considerations shall be weighed impartially in order to achieve the purposes stated in Article I.[12]

Finally, we need to consider whether international institutions must be non-partisan between two parties who are at war.

The above four questions are questions that any adequate normative account of international institutions must address. (They do not, no doubt, exhaust the set of relevant questions.) Prior to examining several specific potential theories we would do well to bear three methodological points in mind. First, as I have said, very few political theorists have written on these topics.[13] Hence what follows will focus on existing normative theories and then see what light they shed, if any, on the question of the functions, legitimacy, powers and binding norms of international institutions.

Second, we may observe that the above four questions are interrelated. For example, the source of *legitimacy* (Q2) may also provide the answer to the *function* question (Q1). Thus someone may argue that the IMF has *legitimacy* because it resulted from an agreement between legitimate agents, namely states. But this answer to the *legitimacy* question may then provide an answer to the *function* question, namely institutions should serve the roles that have been agreed to by the member states. It may also provide answers to (Q3) (the powers such institutions possess will only be those that states have ceded to them and nothing more) and

[12] See the IBRD's Articles of Agreement at: http://web.worldbank.org/WBSITE/EXTERNAL/EXTABOUTUS/0,,contentMDK:20049603~pagePK:43912~piPK:36602,00.html#I11.

[13] An exception is the recent important paper by A. Buchanan and R. O. Keohane, 'The Legitimacy of Global Governance Institutions', *Ethics and International Affairs*, 20 (2006), 405–37. There have also been extensive enquiries by others into the role of these institutions. For one example see the report on 'The Future of the WTO' chaired by Peter Sutherland and commissioned by the then Director General of the WTO, Supachai Panitchpakdi (www.wto.org/english/thewto_e/10anniv_e/future_wto_e.pdf). See also R. Howse, 'The Legitimacy of the World Trade Organization', in J.-M. Coicaud and V. Heiskanen (eds.), *The Legitimacy of International Organizations* (Tokyo: United Nations University Press, 2001), 355–407; R. Howse and K. Nicolaïdis, 'Legitimacy and Global Governance: Why Constitutionalizing the WTO is a Step too Far', in R. B. Porter, P. Sauvé, A. Subramanian and A. Beviglia Zampetti (eds.), *Efficiency, Equity and Legitimacy: The Multilateral Trading System at the Millennium* (Washington, DC: Brookings Institution Press, 2001), 227–52; and R. Howse and K. Nicolaïdis, 'Enhancing WTO Legitimacy: Constitutionalization or Global Subsidiarity?', *Governance*, 16 (2003), 73–94.

to (Q4) (the binding norms on such institutions can only be what states rightfully require of them). So an answer to one question may entail an answer to one or more of the other questions. This can be seen by considering another theory. Someone might argue that the appropriate answer to the *function* question can, on occasion, supply the answer to the *legitimacy* question. Suppose that someone argues that there should be an international legitimate authority in order to arbitrate when there are disputes between different states and/or economic corporations. On this view an international institution is required to perform a certain function. Now if this is the rationale for the introduction of an international legitimacy it might lead one to accept a particular answer to the *legitimacy* question (namely this institution acquires legitimacy in so far as it performs its role). The key point, then, is that the four issues are so closely related that an answer to one of them has implications for one's position towards the others. Moreover, what the two examples have borne out is that some theories prioritise one of the questions and then, drawing on the answer to that question, are led to specific answers to the other questions. For instance, some are preoccupied with the issue of legitimacy and from this work out the rest of their theory. Others, by contrast, are primarily concerned with certain functions and then from this work out the rest of their theory. What one needs is a theory whose answers to the four questions form a coherent whole.

Third, one might wonder why it is appropriate to focus on international institutions. The answer to this is that international institutions are *sui generis*. By contrast with private individuals they have considerable power and often define the background within which individuals and corporations act. By contrast with states, on the other hand, international institutions tend to have a restricted remit. The WTO, for example, regulates some aspects of international trade but its jurisdiction does not extend beyond that and it does not even cover all areas of trade. In addition to their restricted remit, international institutions differ from states in that, almost by definition, they are likely to have a more culturally heterogeneous population than any state.

In connection with this last point, I wish to introduce, though not argue for, a hypothesis that I shall be working with. I shall term this hypothesis the Pluralist Hypothesis. This contends that: different agents (with different properties) may have different *responsibilities* (depending in part on their capacity, the kinds of instruments at their disposal and the nature of the institution) and are subject to different *binding norms* (depending, in part, on what instruments they employ). The thought is that the responsibilities and binding norms (and possibly the sources of legitimacy) are different for different kinds of agents – be they individuals or states or NGOs or economic corporations or international institutions – and that one cannot simply treat them in a monistic way, ascribing the same roles, legitimacy, powers and binding norms to all. International institutions are different from states and individuals and firms in morally relevant ways and these morally relevant differences should inform our account of their duties, legitimacy, powers and binding norms. The analysis that follows should therefore be seen in this light and the conclusions reached apply only to international institutions and not to other actors.

Having made these preliminary methodological remarks we may proceed to the normative analysis.

State-centric contractarianism – version one

Let us begin with what might be termed *state-centric contractarianism*. On this view, states are regarded as moral agents. As such they have various duties, requiring, amongst other things, that they do not interfere with other states and that treat other states as free and equal. A corollary of the moral powers that states have is that they have the right to create institutions. From this theory we can deduce answers to the questions posed above. On the question of the functions of international institutions (Q1): the state-centric approach maintains that the functions that (state-created) international institutions should perform are those that states have mandated them to perform. For their legitimacy (Q2), the claim would be that these institutions have legitimacy because and to the extent that they have been authorised by states. On the question of power (Q3): international institutions can exercise only those powers allocated to them by states. Turning now to the fourth set of issues (Q4): international institutions can invoke whatever norms and principles that they are authorised to do. Thus the state-centric perspective can easily generate a coherent set of answers to the above questions. Let us call this first brand of *state-centric contractarianism* (SCI). Put succinctly SCI claims:

> **SCI**: International institutions possess *legitimacy* to the extent that they are authorised by their member states; and the *responsibilities*, *powers* and *binding norms* of international institutions are those that their member states ascribe to them.

With this broad theoretical model in mind we can turn now to our contemporary world and apply it to the three international institutions considered in this chapter. The legitimacy of these institutions is straightforward. Each is a creation of states. The IMF and World Bank were created at the Bretton Woods Conference and their legitimacy derives from the legitimacy of the contracting parties. To ascertain their responsibilities we should then turn to their Articles of Agreement. In particular we should turn to Article I of the IMF's Articles of Agreement which outlines the IMF's 'purposes' and Article I of the IBRD's Articles of Agreement which specifies its 'purposes'.[14] For the WTO we should turn to Article III of the Marrakesh Agreement establishing the WTO and to the decisions reached at the Ministerial conferences.[15]

Is this an adequate account? One objection to this state-centric model is that it is a version of what Brian Barry terms 'justice as mutual advantage' and suffers from its faults.[16] To explain: the contracting parties (in this case, states) have unequal bargaining power and this state-centric model allows the nature and functions of international institutions to mirror these inequalities. It allows the powerful and wealthy to determine the roles of these institutions to their advantage and to the disadvantage of the poor and disadvantaged. It simply operates according to the principle 'to each according to his threat advantage'.[17] It would yield the highly counter-intuitive outcome that international institutions would be acting legitimately even if they are actively causing global poverty, exploitation, malnutrition and disease.

An obvious response to this line of argument is that we can easily modify state-centric contractarianism to avoid this objection. One might, for example, modify SCI and claim that:

> **SCII**: International institutions possess *legitimacy* to the extent that they are authorised by their member states; and the *responsibilities*, *powers* and *binding norms* of international institutions are those that their member states ascribe to them; however, international institutions (like their member states) must not violate certain negative duties of justice (revision 1).

14 For Article I of the IMF's Articles of Agreement see www.imf.org/external/pubs/ft/aa/aa01.htm. For Article 1 of the IBRD's Articles of Agreement see http://web.worldbank.org/WBSITE/EXTERNAL/EXTABOUTUS/0,,contentMDK:20049563~pagePK:43912~menuPK:58863~piPK:36602,00.html#I1.

15 For Article III see www.wto.org/English/docs_e/legal_e/04-wto_e.htm.

16 B. Barry, *Justice as Impartiality: A Treatise on Social Justice Volume II* (Oxford: Clarendon, 1995), 31–3.

17 J. Rawls, *A Theory of Justice*, revised edition (Oxford University Press, 1999), 122: cf. Barry, *Justice as Impartiality*, 41–6 and 48.

They are not entitled, for example, to steal or kill or harm people in other ways. This qualified version of state-centric contractarianism would, it might be argued, avoid the unattractive outcomes attributed to a pure form of state-centric contractarianism. The thought underlying the revised version is simply that states are entitled to further their own interests (and those of their members) so long as they do not harm other people, and hence they may create international institutions – like the IMF or the World Bank or the WTO or the European Union – so long as these too do not harm other people.

This response may allay some of the worries raised by the first objection but before proceeding further it is worth recording that it may have quite radical implications and could require a major transformation in the way that international economic institutions act at present. One powerful argument for why this might be the case is provided by Thomas Pogge in his important work *World Poverty and Human Rights.*[18] In the latter Pogge advances the moral claim that agents (institutions and individuals) have a negative duty not to uphold unjust rules and practices. He further argues that much of the existing global poverty arises precisely because international actors violate this negative duty. *If* both of these claims are right, then, SCII would have considerable moral implications for the two claims entail that if international institutions abided by Pogge's injunctions then there would be no (or very little) global poverty. Whether honouring Pogge's negative duty does have such momentous implications depends on (at least) two issues. First, it is important to establish the content of the negative duty which binds institutions. Is it, as Pogge holds, a duty not to act in ways that result in others being in severe poverty, in which case ascribing this negative duty to international institutions would be of tremendous significance? Or is it something more modest and restricted such as the duty not to use extortion, manipulation or force? A second factor to bear in mind when considering the importance of Pogge's duty is the empirical matter of how much global poverty arises from the failure of international institutions to honour Pogge's negative duty and how much arises from other factors (such as corrupt or incompetent governments or natural phenomena).[19] The point here, however, is not to settle

[18] T. Pogge, *World Poverty and Human Rights: Cosmopolitan Responsibilities and Reforms* (Cambridge: Polity, 2002).

[19] Pogge's claims are controversial. For a discussion and evaluation see Simon Caney, 'Global Poverty and Human Rights: the Case for Positive Duties', in T. Pogge (ed.),

these empirical questions (as if that could be done in such a cursory way) but simply to note in passing that to insist that international economic institutions honour a negative duty not to impose unjust rules on others might (if Pogge is correct) have quite dramatic implications for existing global poverty and inequalities.

State-centric contractarianism – version two

SCII is, undoubtedly, an improvement on SCI but it remains to be seen why international institutions are bound only by negative duties not to violate the rights of others. Why, it might be asked, do they not have positive duties too to eradicate poverty and destitution? After all, they undoubtedly may greatly shape the opportunities available to people. The WTO, for example, by determining the rules governing global trade is a major determinant of the success or failure of different firms and in doing so exercises power over people's ability to support themselves. Likewise, the IMF, by imposing conditionalities, determines the courses of action open to members of recipient states and through them it exercises power over people's lives and their ability to further their fundamental interests. Given this, one might ask what reason we have for accepting the assumption, made by SCII, to the effect that international economic institutions have only negative duties not to violate the rights of individuals and do not have positive duties to protect the rights of individuals. Put another way: SCII assumes that international institutions should promote the interests of their members so long as they treat persons fairly and that all that treating persons fairly requires is not violating their rights. And this last element requires some defence.

One argument might simply contend that there are no positive duties to uphold rights (such as, for example, the right not to suffer poverty). But this will be hard to sustain because the most natural defence of negative duties also requires a commitment to positive duties. When pressed as to why persons have a negative duty not to harm or kill another person it is very hard to avoid claiming that one reason that these are wrong is because they damage some absolutely fundamental interests. But if we make this claim it then becomes very difficult to see why persons do not also have some positive duties to help secure these

Freedom from Poverty as a Human Right: Who Owes What to the Very Poor? (Oxford University Press, 2007), 275–302.

interests.[20] So to claim that international institutions are bound only by negative duties of justice because there are no positive duties of justice is implausible.

A second more complex reply to the question of why international economic institutions have only negative duties not to violate the rights of others would argue that as *private* actors they are free to act as they wish just so long as they do not infringe people's rights. It justifies SCII by referring to examples which involve non-political actors who are hired by individuals. Consider, for example, cases where individuals hire a lawyer (or accountant or financial advisor) to represent their interests. Such instances have two important features. Here we think, first, that the lawyer has a positive duty to further the interests of their clients. But we also think, second, that they may not do so by violating the rights of other individuals. Lawyers cannot promote the interests of their clients by intimidating or assaulting people who are not their clients. And this mirrors what SCII claims of international institutions. So one might defend SCII by arguing that it fits with our intuitions about other examples where a body is hired by certain parties in order to perform certain roles.

I believe that this kind of reasoning is a key assumption underlying state-contractarianism. Its guiding thought is that international institutions are in a contractual relationship with states in just the same way that lawyers or accountants are hired by individuals and are thus in a contract with them. To assess SCII we need, then, to examine more closely the assumption that international economic institutions are (like lawyers etc.) non-political institutions contracted by agents to represent their interests. In what follows I want to argue that state-centric contractarianism commits a category mistake for the responsibilities it affirms can only make sense if we conceive of international institutions as 'private' ones but not if we recognise that they are 'political' ones. Now in order to explain and develop this argument we need to: (a) provide a plausible account of what constitutes a 'political' institution; (b), elaborate further on the moral relevance of whether an institution is, or is not, a political institution; and (c), determine whether the three institutions in question are 'political' institutions if we employ this definition of the 'political'.

[20] See A. Buchanan, *Justice, Legitimacy, and Self-Determination: Moral Foundations for International Law* (Oxford University Press, 2004), 89–92: see also 197.

To begin with (a): there are, of course, numerous ways of defining the 'political'. In what follows I wish to work with as uncontentious a conception as possible for I wish to show that even using such an uncontroversial conception we can show that state-centric contractarianism is untenable. For the purposes of this chapter I shall assume that X is a political body when X has a *major* impact on persons' *fundamental interests* through the use of *power*. Three aspects of this definition merit comment. First, it, of course, raises the question of how we define 'power'. Here I shall follow Robert Dahl's well-known suggestion that 'A has power over B to the extent that he can get B to do something that B would not otherwise do'.[21] In a power-relationship, A (the power holder) is able to make B perform actions (or omissions) or impose sanctions or costs on them. B (the 'victim' of the power-relationship) has his choice constrained and his options are involuntarily limited. He may be compelled to pursue a particular course of action or to suffer an involuntary penalty. Second, observe that political institutions, on this account, exercise power over people's most *fundamental interests*, structuring what kind of life they are able to lead and determining the opportunities they face. Finally, observe that political institutions have a *major* (as opposed to a trivial) impact on these fundamental interests. Our focus, then, is on actors that through the use of *power* exert a *major* impact over the *fundamental* choices open to others.

Let us turn now to (b). It is critical to note that the issue here is not a terminological or semantic one about the meaning of the word 'politics'. Rather it is important to clarify that the institutions in question are political ones in the sense that they need to satisfy the constraints imposed by political morality on such institutions. There are three

[21] R. A. Dahl, 'The Concept of Power', *Behavioral Science*, 2 (1957), 202–3. Dahl's definition has, of course, been much discussed. Note, however, two points. First, those who criticise his treatment of power employ a basic concept that is similar (though not identical) in structure. To take one prominent example: Steven Lukes holds that 'A exercises power over B when A affects B in a manner contrary to B's interests', S. Lukes, *Power: A Radical View*, second edition (Basingstoke: Palgrave Macmillan, 2005), 30. Dahl's account is preferable to Lukes's because it articulates the core idea as being that of *making people do things they would not otherwise do*, whilst avoiding reference to the claim that power necessarily harms another's interests. One may exercise power over another by compelling him to do something which is in his interests. Second, note that those who criticise Dahl's view (such as Lukes) object that it is under-inclusive. They do not deny that power can fit his definition: it is just that they add that it does not capture all the relevant kinds of power-relations (such as what Lukes call the second and third dimensional views of power – e.g. Lukes, *Power*).

aspects to this point. First, whether an institution is political or not is relevant to the nature and applicability of *binding norms*. We do not, for example, insist that secondary associations should abjure controversial doctrines whereas we might make this claim of political actors (Q4). No one claims that the Catholic Church should eschew controversial conceptions of the good but one might (following liberals, such as Rawls) claim that since states exercise political power they are subject to the standards of public justifiability.[22] Second, the question of whether an institution is political or not is critical to the question of whether it enjoys *legitimacy* (Q2) for if it is a political body we need to be able to provide an account of the source of its political legitimacy. Again this is not a task we need to perform for non-political bodies like clubs or churches. Third, the issue of whether an institution is a 'political' one or not, is also relevant to the question of its *responsibilities* (Q1), for I take it to be a feature of a political institution that it has duties to uphold a fair distribution of resources and opportunities in its jurisdiction. This is intentionally worded in a rather vague way to allow that there are many different accounts of justice (from libertarian to Rawlsian to egalitarian to desert-based and so on). All of the latter agree that the state is under an obligation to ensure people receive their just entitlements, however much they might disagree on what those entitlements are.

Having characterised the 'political' and noted why it might matter, let us turn now to (c). To make good the second objection we must note the ways in which the IMF, World Bank and WTO are political actors in the sense defined above. This is not hard to establish. To take the example of the WTO, this structures the terms of trade that govern international commerce. It exercises power because it lays down the rules under which people can and cannot trade – applying, in particular, its principle of non-discrimination (and its concomitant Most-Favoured-Nation (MFN) rule and National Treatment rule) and its principle of reciprocity.[23] The WTO has, moreover, frequently struck down laws which, it maintains, violate free trade. Furthermore through the dispute settlement system it allows states that have been wronged by another state's violation of the rules of the WTO to punish it through retaliatory measures. In virtue of this procedure the WTO regulates people's lives through the exercise of

[22] Rawls, *Political Liberalism*.

[23] On these see A. Narlikar's helpful discussion, in A. Narlikar, *The World Trade Organization: A Very Short Introduction* (Oxford University Press, 2005), 28–9.

power.[24] If we consider now the IMF: this too defines the conditions under which some people live and as such exercises considerable political power over them. For example, by making conditional loans which specify that recipient governments must adopt certain kinds of economic policies it exerts control over people's lives. Much the same point applies to the World Bank which, in virtue of its technical expertise and its use of conditionality, can also compel states to implement certain reforms and thereby it determines the choices open to people in client states. In the most comprehensive analysis of the IMF and World Bank to date, Ngaire Woods writes that:

> The powers of the IMF and World Bank to require governments to reform are significant. They do not lend large proportions of global development financing but the timing of their loans gives them considerable leverage because they lend at times when governments have few alternative sources of finance.[25]

She continues,

> The IMF and World Bank deploy a mixture of technical advice and coercive power in bargaining with borrowing governments. Each institution can variously lend or withhold resources, disburse or suspend payments, and impose various forms of conditions.[26]

24 For instructive general accounts see B. M. Hoekman and P. C. Mavroidis, *The World Trade Organization: Law, Economics, and Politics* (London and New York: Routledge, 2007) and Narlikar, *The World Trade Organization*. It is true that the WTO does not possess the kinds of powers possessed by states (which is why I have suggested the Pluralist Hypothesis), but by making laws which constrain the actions of members and by allowing the imposition of sanctions it limits the options of members who might then have no choice but to accede to its rules. As such it exercises power over them. An interesting account of one kind of power possessed by the WTO can be found in D. G. Singh, *Network Power: The Social Dynamics of Globalization* (New Haven and London: Yale University Press, 2008), ch. 8. See also M. Risse's helpful discussion of the coercive character of international institutions such as the WTO in M. Risse, 'What to Say About the State', *Social Theory and Practice*, 32 (2006), 671–98. Risse recognises that the WTO and other international institutions are coercive ('What to Say About the State?', especially 679–83 and 690–2) but goes on to argue that the state exercises a kind of coercion which is different in a morally relevant way (in particular, state coercion possesses '[l]egal and political immediacy' ('What to Say About the State?', 688)). I argue against the moral relevance of this difference in 'Global Distributive Justice and the State', *Political Studies*, 57 (2008), 502.

25 N. Woods, *The Globalizers: The IMF, the World Bank, and their Borrowers* (Ithaca and London: Cornell University Press, 2006), 71. Woods does, though, caution against exaggerating the power of the Bretton Woods institutions, writing that 'it is easy to overstate their power and influence' (*The Globalizers*, 71). See, more generally, Woods's instructive analysis of the IMF and World Bank in *The Globalizers*.

26 Woods, *The Globalizers*, 82.

Two further points should be recorded. First, as Woods's analysis makes clear, it is important to note that international institutions (in her case the IMF and World Bank) enjoy power over member states, and derivatively their members, in part because of the vulnerability of some member states and would-be member states. It is in part because countries like Angola or Mozambique are very poor that the Bank and the IMF are able to exercise power over them. Second, it is misleading to regard these three institutions in isolation for it is more accurate to say that they act in concert with each other (and with other institutions) and thereby they jointly form part of an international system that exercises power over people's lives. This last point is of fundamental importance for it might be the case that several institutions considered on their own do not make a group of persons do something that they would not otherwise do but that when they act in concert they do. In such a situation people in developing countries might be said to be powerless although there is no single political actor controlling them.

Having established that the IMF, World Bank and World Trade Organisation are political institutions, we can now return to the argument under consideration. SCII maintains that international institutions are akin to non-political bodies (e.g. lawyers) that are hired by individual parties (e.g. the lawyers' clients) to further their interests in a fair legal system. The point of the preceding analysis is to show that this analogy is incorrect. International institutions are not private actors. Unlike the latter they can and do exercise considerable power over large groups of people who have not consented to them. They are public bodies. Or, put another way, it is wrong to say that they should serve the interests of some within a fair framework (which is how we might think of lawyers) because they are part of the political framework. They define it. They are political actors and, as such, have the responsibilities noted above. With their power comes responsibility.

One can come at this issue from another angle. Rather than start with international institutions and ask what responsibilities they have we might begin with an account of moral responsibility and work out from that what duties fall to international institutions. One leading principle (and one which I have sought to defend elsewhere) holds that those who are able to uphold people's rights have, in virtue of that capacity, a prima facie duty to exercise their power in ways which uphold people's rights.[27] With their ability to make a difference comes a

[27] See S. Caney, 'Cosmopolitan Justice, Responsibility, and Global Climate Change', *Leiden Journal of International Law*, 18 (2005), 747–75; 'Global Poverty and Human Rights: the

responsibility to protect rights.[28] This principle thus entails that international institutions have a duty to exercise their ways which enable persons to enjoy their fundamental rights.

State-centric contractarianism – version three

I have argued above that the fact that certain institutions are political ones entails that they are under certain responsibilities. The political character of these institutions also has a second implication, namely that if an institution is a political one we then require an account of what (if anything) grants it the legitimacy to exercise power over people. It is worth dwelling on this point because one considerable problem in the state-centric perspective is that state-centric contractarianism is unable to provide an adequate account of political legitimacy. It assumes that international institutions possess legitimacy to the extent that they have been authorised to perform certain actions (and are complying with the terms of the contract and not violating persons' rights) by parties that themselves possess legitimacy to do these actions. Legitimacy is thus, as it were, passed down the line. This runs into two obvious problems. The first concern is simply that many states lack legitimacy because of their repugnant treatment of their own citizens (and foreigners) and because of their undemocratic character. Let us call this the 'problem of illegitimate states'. In the second place, even when governments enjoy a democratic mandate this is not because of their views on the policies of the WTO, IMF and World Bank. This can hardly be said to be uppermost in people's minds when they vote for a British MP, American Congressman or woman, member of the German Bundestag and so on. The electoral connection is thus not strong enough to have a legitimising effect. We

Case for Positive Duties'; 'Climate Change and the Duties of the Advantaged', *Critical Review of International Social and Political Philosophy*, 12 (2009).

28 In making this argument I am not denying that private actors are subject to duties of distributive justice. Indeed, such a position seems plausible to me. (For a seminal contemporary discussion see G. A. Cohen, *If you're an Egalitarian, How Come You're so Rich?* (Cambridge MA: Harvard University Press, 2000).) My argument above is, however, directed towards someone who denies that international institutions have positive duties of justice on the grounds that they, as private institutions, are bound only by negative duties (whereas they would be bound by positive duties of justice too if they were public institutions). There are two kinds of response to this position. One is that private actors also bear positive duties of justice. I have much sympathy with this line of reasoning. The second response is to accept this argument's assumptions about the public/private distinction and to show that, even if we grant that, SCII still fails because international institutions are unequivocally public institutions in the relevant sense.

might think of legitimacy in terms of a water pail passed down a line of workmen. It is fullest at the start; when it is handed down the line to one person it inevitably leaks some water; and it does this again when this first recipient passes in on to his neighbour and so on. In the same way, there is a leakage of legitimacy the more that one body passes it on to another. Let us call this second point the 'problem of diluted authorisation'.[29]

One might think that state-centric contractarianism can partly meet these objections by making further modifications to it. To meet the problem of illegitimate states, for example, one might argue that international institutions have the legitimacy to perform certain tasks only where they have been authorised to do so by legitimate states and legitimate states are defined, for example, as liberal democracies (revision 2). To meet the problem of diluted authorisation, one might try to improve the democratic scrutiny of international institutions. This might be done in a variety of ways. For example, states may demand greater transparency in the workings of international institutions to better enable them to hold them to account; and they might empower themselves to compel IMF or WTO or World Bank officials to defend their policies before the committees in their respective legislatures.[30] By adopting such measures they can strengthen their ability to hold international institutions to account (revision 3). Adding in these two revisions, then, we arrive at the following revised conception of state-centric contractarianism:

> SCIII: International institutions possess legitimacy to the extent that they are authorised by their member states; the responsibilities, powers and binding norms of international institutions are those that their member states ascribe to them; however, international institutions (like their member states) have a duty to all not to violate certain negative duties of justice (revision 1);
>
> the created international institutions may include only liberal democratic states as members if they are to enjoy legitimacy (revision 2); and

[29] Both of these points are made by Buchanan and Keohane, 'The Legitimacy of Global Governance Institutions', 413–15.

[30] See, in this context, the Fourth Report of the Treasury Committee – *The International Monetary Fund: A Blueprint for Parliamentary Accountability* (13 March 2001). HC 162. Online, available at: www.publications.parliament.uk/pa/cm200001/cmselect/cmtreasy/162/16202.htm. In the latter the Treasury Committee recommends that Parliamentary Committees should be empowered to question senior IMF officials, the Treasury Committee should write and disseminate its assessments of the IMF's performance, the minutes of the IMF's Executive Board be published, and that the voting record of the UK's IMF representative also be published. See www.publications.parliament.uk/pa/cm200001/cmselect/cmtreasy/162/16205.htm#a1.

initiatives must be taken to boost the accountability of existing international institutions to member states if they are to enjoy legitimacy (revision 3).

This reply is partially successful. There are no doubt ways of improving the accountability of international institutions to member states and so the concerns informing the problem of diluted authorisation might perhaps be allayed. However, the response to the problem of illegitimate states, whilst it is an improvement on the previous formulation, is inadequate. It can, perhaps, explain why international institutions would have legitimacy over the citizens of liberal democratic member states of these international institutions. However, international institutions will inevitably exercise power over individuals who belong to states that would be excluded from the contract because they are illiberal and/or undemocratic. The actions of international institutions cannot be restricted so that they only exercise power over their members for they will almost always produce actions which constrain persons not party to the contract, thereby restricting some people's fundamental opportunities. The latters' interests are, however, unrepresented in this revised version of state-centric contractarianism. An international institution's legitimacy over such people (persons in non-liberal democratic regimes) needs to be justified and it cannot be grounded by reference to the agreement of liberal democratic states.[31]

To bring out the ways in which international institutions will inescapably have a coercive impact on people living in illiberal states that are not party to the contract consider the following examples:

Tariffs: Suppose that an international institution passes laws imposing tariffs on goods imported from non-member countries. This could be authorised by the liberal-democratic member states and yet it exercises considerable power over the lives of people who are not represented in the institution (constraining what they may do and the opportunities open to them).

Subsidies: International institutions may also subsidise certain industries (as is the case of the European Community's Common Agricultural Policy (CAP)). In doing so they, in effect, force firms in other countries out of business because they leave these other firms with no genuine chance of competing. In

[31] This point is also brought out by Buchanan and Keohane, 'The Legitimacy of Global Governance Institutions', 415–16.

such cases international institutions (authorised by liberal democratic member states) may be said to be coercively limiting the opportunities of others and thereby exercising power over them.

Given these two kind of phenomena it follows that under SCIII international institutions would exercise power over members of states who are not represented in the international institutions. As such a state-centric contractarianism is unable to provide an adequate account of how the power of international institutions over such people could be legitimate.

This concludes the analysis of state-centric contractarianism and it may be useful to sum up the two kinds of charge being pressed against it. The first kind centres on state-centric contractarianism's account of the *duties* of international institutions. Here we have seen that

* first: SCI's account results in morally unacceptable results.
* second: SCII's position is more tenable. However, we have no reason to accept its contention that international institutions have only negative duties not to harm others on the grounds either that (a), there are no positive duties of justice or (b), that international institutions *qua* non-political actors are bound solely by negative duties of justice. Neither (a) nor (b) was plausible. SCII's insistence that international institutions should simply refrain from violating others' rights thus remains undefended.
* third: qua political bodies, international institutions, have positive duties to ensure that the global economic, political rules within which individuals and corporations act are fair.

The second set of problems surrounds state-centric contractarianism's analysis of *legitimacy* (Q2). For here we have seen that

* even when modified (à la SCIII) state-centric contractarianism is unable to provide a compelling account of why international institutions (even ones comprising only liberal democratic states) possess legitimacy over the citizens of those states and, more importantly, why they possess legitimacy over the unfortunate members of illiberal states whose lives are structured by these institutions but who have no input into the process.

Cosmopolitan justice and cosmopolitan democracy

Having considered and rejected one account of the normative character of international institutions, let us now consider two others. We may start by drawing on the claim advanced earlier that international institutions are, in a morally relevant sense, political institutions. For with this in mind, we should ask what roles and powers are appropriate for political institutions. Prior to examining the second and third accounts we should note that to call international institutions political actors is, of course, not to equate them with states. There are a number of obvious and important differences. Unlike states, international institutions, (a), do not, at present, possess a monopoly of coercive powers. Furthermore, (b), they have a restricted remit, being concerned only with quite specific areas of policy. In addition to this, (c), they, more than states, have jurisdiction over a culturally diverse population. While it is, of course, true that many states are profoundly divided along ethnic and cultural lines, the diversity at the global level is (as a matter of logic) at least as great and (as a matter of fact) much greater than in any state. The existence of pluralism at the global level is thus more dramatic and profound than that found in any state. Finally, (d), we should record that, unlike very many states, international institutions do not comprise a citizenry united by a civic culture. It is not just that the world includes cultural, religious, ethnic and national diversity. It is also the case that there is no identification with global institutions in the way in which individuals (even individuals in pluralistic societies) often identify with their state's political institutions.

The contrasts with individuals are equally obvious. International institutions can, (a), generally exercise more influence than individuals and, (b), they may use political power. A third difference is the fact that, (c), international institutions are also not subject to the kinds of obligations that individuals are (such as special obligations to friends and family and, some would argue, special obligations to fellow nationals). International institutions, of course, lack these kinds of responsibilities. Any adequate normative account of international economic institutions must, then, be sensitive to the ways in which they differ from both individuals and states. It must reflect their *sui generis* nature.

With these points in mind, let us now present two different normative models of international institutions – what we might term the 'cosmopolitan justice' approach and the 'cosmopolitan democracy' approach. Consider the cosmopolitan justice approach first. This starts with a commitment to realising a cosmopolitan programme of distributive justice and then seeks to work back from this to deduce the responsibilities, legitimacy, powers and binding norms of international institutions. To give a skeletal account of this model, its provisional answers to the four questions run as follows: in terms of the functions of international institutions (Q1), the claim is that they should act in such a way as to bring about a distributively fairer world (as judged by cosmopolitan criteria). So if, for example, one thinks that there should be a global difference principle then, on the cosmopolitan justice approach, the role of international institutions is to further this ideal of cosmopolitan distributive justice.[32] If we turn to the legitimacy question (Q2), this approach would argue that international institutions have legitimacy insofar as they successfully further principles of distributive justice. They affirm then something like Joseph Raz's 'normal justification thesis' and his 'service' conception of legitimacy.[33] In terms of the means to be used (Q3), the answer to this question draws on the functions to be performed for the claim must be that international institutions may use those tools necessary to achieve their desired goals. So it should employ conditionalities only if, and to the extent that, these further the goals of distributive fairness. If we turn now from (Q3) to (Q4), a cosmopolitan justice approach will endorse a binding norm of transparency. It might also defend a norm of neutrality towards conceptions of the good on the grounds that to adopt a partisan position on a deeply controversial issue will make it more difficult for the institution to garner widespread support and without this it is, in general, less likely to be able to secure its objectives. The cosmopolitan justice approach is however unable to adopt a complete neutrality on either ideals of justice or on which political systems are preferable.

What I have termed the 'cosmopolitan justice' perspective is adopted by thinkers from a number of different political perspectives. For example, some of an egalitarian stripe might hold that it is the role of international institutions to further a global difference principle or a global principle of equality. Others, by contrast, would see the role of the international economic institutions as upholding laissez-faire principles of justice.[34]

The 'cosmopolitan justice' approach can be contrasted with a second normative account of international institutions – what I earlier termed

[32] Beitz, *Political Theory and International Relations*, 150–3.

[33] J. Raz, *The Morality of Freedom* (Oxford: Clarendon, 1986), part one.

[34] See F. A. Hayek, *The Road to Serfdom* (London and Henley: Routledge and Kegan Paul, 1976 [1944]), ch. XV and E. U. Petersmann, 'Human Rights and the Law of the World Trade Organization', *Journal of World Trade*, 37 (2003), 241–81. For a useful discussion of the issues surrounding the appropriateness of 'constitutional' approaches to the WTO see D. Cass, *The Constitutionalization of the World Trade Organization: Legitimacy, Democracy, and Community in the International Trading System* (Oxford: Oxford University Press, 2005).

the 'cosmopolitan democracy' approach. The guiding principle at the heart of this model is that institutions that impact greatly on persons' interests must be accountable to those persons via democratic procedures. It maintains that those whose lives are deeply affected by international institutions have a democratic right to hold those institutions to account.[35] Now drawing on this normative principle, one can construct an account of the roles, legitimacy, powers and binding norms of international institutions. On the cosmopolitan democratic view, international institutions have legitimacy, (Q2), only to the extent that they are democratically accountable. Without this they suffer from a 'democratic deficit' and therefore a 'legitimacy deficit'. As to their roles (Q1): their roles are derived in a procedural fashion and are defined as furthering those policies which democratically accountable global institutions in fact choose. On (Q3): a cosmopolitan democratic position would conclude that global institutions should have those powers that the people decide to allocate to them. So representatives of international institutions would have those powers that they have been authorised to possess (so long as they do not use those powers to undermine democratic government.) Finally, cosmopolitan democrats will hold that democratic global institutions should be governed by the kinds of norms that they think should characterise democratic politics – for example, transparency, respect for the views of others and so on.

What both accounts have in common is that they start from a recognition that institutions like the WTO, IMF and World Bank are public institutions: they are not private bodies at liberty to seek their own interests. Where they differ is in their interpretation of the duties of public bodies. It is possible that the two positions will converge in practice. However, even if they do converge they are, of course, theoretically distinct and possess different strengths and weaknesses.

The limitations of both cosmopolitan models

Are either of these two normative models compelling? Let us start with a purist version of the cosmopolitan democracy approach. This is vulnerable to three objections.

First, to assess the relevance of the cosmopolitan democratic approach to global institutional design it is useful to reflect on the following.

[35] See Archibugi and Held, *Cosmopolitan Democracy*; Held, *Democracy and the Global Order*; and McGrew, 'The World Trade Organization'.

Consider the current state of affairs in the world. According to a recent UNDP Human Development Report, 'one in five people in the world – more than 1 billion people – still survive on less than $1 a day, a level of poverty so abject that it threatens survival. Another 1.5 billion people live on $1–$2 a day. More than 40 per cent of the world's population constitute, in effect, a global underclass, faced daily with the reality or the threat of extreme poverty'.[36] The report continues, 'more than 850 million people, including one in three preschool children, are still trapped in a vicious cycle of malnutrition and its effects'.[37] And it adds that 'more than 1 billion people lack access to safe water and 2.6 billion lack access to improved sanitation. Diseases transmitted through water or human waste are the second leading cause of death among children worldwide, after respiratory tract infection. The overall death toll: an estimated 3,900 children every day'.[38] Now in light of this, we might ask 'when determining global institutional design, which is more problematic – the existence of these levels of global poverty and sickness, on the one hand, or the fact that the WTO, IMF and World Bank are not democratically accountable, on the other?'. In light of the current ills of the world it would seem extraordinary to claim that our primary objective when engaged in global institutional design should be to democratise global institutions. This shows that we attribute greater moral weight to eradicating certain material injustices. When constructing a global order these are more morally urgent than securing the electoral accountability of the Executive Boards of the Bretton Woods institutions. Elsewhere I have termed this the 'wrong priorities objection'.[39]

Second, we should note that a commitment to democracy does not entail that all decisions are taken democratically. In many countries, for example, there is a common law tradition and hence the source of law is not a legislature's statutes but the reflections of judges on cases. Furthermore, in some political systems the central bank is not directly accountable but this is not felt to be a problem. To be committed to democracy as a form of government does not, of necessity, require that one apply democratic procedures to each and every

[36] United Nations Development Programme, *Human Development Report 2005 International Cooperation at a Crossroads: Aid, Trade and Security in an Unequal World* (New York: Oxford University Press, 2005), 24.

[37] UNDP, *Human Development Report 2005*, 24.

[38] UNDP, *Human Development Report 2005*, 24.

[39] Caney, 'Cosmopolitan Justice and Institutional Design', 731–3.

political decision: they can govern the system as a whole rather than every single institution.[40]

Third, we should note that democracy is not necessary for accountability. As a growing literature in international relations scholarship has shown, there are very many different kinds of accountability, including non-electoral types of accountability. A useful taxonomy is provided by Ruth Grant and Robert Keohane. They distinguish between the following types of accountability: 'hierarchical' accountability (accountability to one's superiors), 'supervisory' accountability (accountability to monitors), 'fiscal' accountability (accountability to budget-holders), 'legal' accountability (accountability to the judiciary), 'market' accountability (accountability to market forces), 'peer' accountability (accountability to one's peer institutions), and 'public reputational' accountability (accountability to the public).[41] We should not therefore assume that international institutions can enjoy accountability only if they are democratically accountable. One might, for example, seek to make them accountable to other international institutions with related concerns ('peer' accountability). One could argue, for example, that the WTO should be accountable to the ILO and to an environmental body nominated by the United Nations Environmental Programme.

Do these three considerations entail that we should eschew cosmopolitan democracy altogether and commit ourselves to the wholly instrumental approach adopted by the cosmopolitan justice approach? No. For the cosmopolitan justice approach is less able to cope with the

[40] R. O. Keohane and J. S. Nye Jr., 'Redefining Accountability for Global Governance', in M. Kahler and D. A. Lake (eds.), *Governance in a Global Economy: Political Authority in Transition* (Princeton and Oxford: Princeton University Press, 2003), 388 and 392.

[41] R. W. Grant and R. O. Keohane, 'Accountability and Abuses of Power in World Politics', *American Political Science Review*, 99 (2005), 36–7. For other typologies see R. O. Keohane, 'Global Governance and Democratic Accountability', in D. Held and M. Koenig-Archibugi (eds.), *Taming Globalization: Frontiers of Governance* (Cambridge: Polity, 2003), 137, and Keohane and Nye, 'Redefining Accountability for Global Governance', 389–91. See, more generally, Keohane, 'Global Governance and Democratic Accountability', 130–59; Grant and Keohane, 'Accountability and Abuses of Power in World Politics', 29–43; R. O. Keohane and J. S. Nye Jr., 'The Club Model of Multilateral Cooperation and Problems of Democratic Legitimacy', in R. B. Porter, P. Sauvé, A. Subramanian and A. Beviglia Zampetti (eds.), *Efficiency, Equity, and Legitimacy: The Multilateral Trading System at the Millennium* (Washington, DC: Brookings Institution Press, 2001), 264–94; Keohane and Nye Jr., 'Redefining Accountability for Global Governance', 386–411; and F. Scharpf, *Governing in Europe: Effective and Democratic?* (Oxford University Press, 1999), 7–21. See also J. Nye *The Paradox of American Power: Why the World's Only Superpower can't go it Alone* (Oxford University Press, 2002), 104–10 and 163–8.

existence of reasonable disagreement about the nature of global justice. Let me explain. It is hard to deny that many reasonable and reflective people disagree about which principles of distributive justice, if any, should apply at the global level. Given this it seems unreasonable simply to state that political institutions should be designed to best realise the correct principles of distributive justice. According to this line of reasoning, to say that global political institutions should be designed to realise the best principle of distributive justice is wrongheaded.[42] There is no consensus whatsoever on what would constitute a just world, and simply to impose any one conception, over and above others, would be illegitimate. Wholly instrumental conceptions of the roles of international institutions, thus, are undesirable because they require the imposition of a contentious moral doctrine.

How then should we respond to reasonable disagreement about justice? Following many, I would make two suggestions. First, a fair way of responding to disagreement is to design institutions which are procedurally fair and which provide a just arena in which the different viewpoints can be expressed and adjudicated. In light of this one can similarly argue that international institutions should be designed so that they provide a fair forum in which competing views about global rules (on say, agricultural tariffs or textile subsidies or environmental protections or labour standards) can be discussed and adjudicated.[43] This kind of institutional design respects persons by giving them a political framework in which they can present their principles and the reasoning underpinning them.[44] Second, a just response to reasonable disagreement requires not simply institutional design. It also requires a certain kind of political culture – one in which persons treat others with respect, acknowledging the reasonableness of (some of) those who disagree with them, and expressing their own viewpoints with appropriate modesty.[45] Put otherwise: a fair treatment of reasonable disagreement requires that all those involved

[42] See, in this context, two illuminating defences of non-instrumental approaches: T. Christiano, *The Rule of the Many: Fundamental Issues in Democratic Theory* (Boulder: Westview Press, 1996), especially ch. 2; J. Waldron, *Law and Disagreement* (Oxford: Clarendon Press, 1999). Both Christiano and Waldron defend democracy on non-instrumental grounds, holding it to be a fair decision-making procedure.

[43] See on this T. Franck, *Fairness in International Law and Institutions* (Oxford: Clarendon Press, 1995), ch. 15, especially 482–4.

[44] See S. Caney, 'Anti-Perfectionism and Rawlsian Liberalism', *Political Studies*, 43 (1995), 255–6.

[45] See on this A. Gutmann and D. Thompson, 'Moral Conflict and Political Consensus', *Ethics*, 101 (1990), 64–88.

adhere to certain *binding norms* – such as norms of respect, a desire to reach agreement, a commitment to understanding the viewpoint of those with whom one disagrees, and so on.[46]

The Hybrid Model

These four considerations, I believe, support the following:

> The Hybrid Model: This holds that international institutions should be designed so that:
>
> **(a)** persons' most fundamental rights are upheld [an instrumental component] and, then,
> **(b)** over and above that they provide a fair political framework in which to determine which principles of justice should be adopted to regulate the global economy [a procedural component].

The Hybrid Model recognises that the protection of some fundamental interests takes priority over other goals, such as democratising global institutions. By prioritising these rights, and by affirming (a), it captures the point made in the 'wrong priorities' objection.[47] At the same time it also recognises that there is reasonable disagreement about some aspects of global justice and, by affirming (b), it thereby recognises the need for a fair decision-making procedure. As such it combines the best of the two competing cosmopolitan models (protecting fundamental interests and respecting reasonable disagreement).

Let us now turn to the four tasks identified in the first section of the chapter. The Hybrid Model generates answers to all four questions. First, it maintains that international institutions have a duty to uphold certain fundamental interests and then, above that, to be an arena in which different principles can be fairly adjudicated and evaluated (Q1). It also

[46] This response can be contrasted with that advocated by Rawls in *The Law of Peoples*. Rawls argues that the appropriate response to the fact that some decent peoples reject liberal values is that liberal states and international institutions may not promote egalitarian liberal principles of justice (J. Rawls, *The Law of Peoples with 'The Idea of Public Reason Revisited'* (Cambridge, MA: Harvard University Press, 1999), 42–3). However, to disallow the WTO from acting on egalitarian liberal principles of justice because they are controversial seems to me unwarranted and on my model the WTO could act on these kinds of principles *if they were authorised by the participants in a reformed WTO*.

[47] One key question is, of course, what count as 'fundamental rights'. I cannot hope to answer that here but have sought to answer this in Simon Caney, 'Egalitarian Liberalism and Universalism', in T. Laden and D. Owen (eds.), *Cultural Diversity and Political Theory* (Cambridge University Press, 2007), 151–72.

provides an account of the legitimacy of international institutions, maintaining that international institutions possess legitimacy to the extent that they uphold fundamental rights and provide a context for the fair adjudication of competing visions of how to govern the world economy (Q2). Since it prioritises a commitment to upholding certain fundamental rights, the Hybrid Model also ascribes to international institutions the powers necessary to perform this task, though what this means in practice can only be ascertained with the help of a great deal of empirical analysis (Q3). If we consider now what kinds of binding norms should govern their conduct (Q4), the Hybrid Model calls, as we have seen above, for certain kind of political norms – those of respect and civility which are necessary for the fair resolution of competing viewpoints.

What, though, does the Hybrid Model mean in practice? I have argued elsewhere that this kind of model would require the following reforms to existing international institutions:[48]

(1) equalising representation and influence in international institutions;
(2) enabling the participation of the vulnerable;
(3) ensuring that there are effective enforcement mechanisms that are available to all;
(4) making greater use of international ombudsmen;
(5) increasing transparency;
(6) rendering international institutions accountable to other relevant institutions;
(7) requiring international institutions to provide a justification of their policies; and
(8) exploring ways of making international institutions democratically accountable.[49]

[48] I have provided a much fuller defence of each of these eight proposals elsewhere. These proposals draw on an extensive literature on institutional reform. See, in particular, Grant and Keohane, 'Accountability and Abuses of Power in World Politics'; Keohane, 'Global Governance and Democratic Accountability'; Keohane and Nye, 'The Club Model of Multilateral Cooperation and Problems of Democratic Legitimacy'; Keohane and Nye, 'Redefining Accountability for Global Governance' and Woods, 'Making the IMF and the World Bank More Accountable'. For my defence of these proposals and for references to the literature surrounding them see Caney, 'Cosmopolitanism, Democracy and Distributive Justice', 'Cosmopolitan Justice and Institutional Design', 745–51.

[49] It might be claimed that a state-centric contractarianism could also endorse such proposals. Two points should be made in reply. First, it *might* do so but only under special circumstances. It seems, for example, much less likely that it would do so when there are either very great inequalities in political power between states or when the member states not are

Concluding remarks

International institutions play, and should play, a significant role in the global economy. Yet there has been little normative analysis of the responsibilities, legitimacy, powers and binding norms of international institutions. The tendency has been either to focus solely on states or individuals. Working with the Pluralist Hypothesis, this chapter has sought to identify the responsibilities and sources of legitimacy of international institutions. I have argued that the state-centred contractarian approach to international institutions, in all its forms, represents an unpromising approach. I have further argued that purist versions of what I have termed the 'cosmopolitan justice' approach and the 'cosmopolitan democracy' approach to global institutional design are also unpersuasive. Having rejected these three approaches, I have suggested a Hybrid Model that combines the valuable insights contained in both of the cosmopolitan approaches.

References

Archibugi, Daniele and Held, David (eds.) 1995. *Cosmopolitan Democracy: An Agenda for a New World Order*. Cambridge: Polity.

Barry, Brian 1995. *Justice as Impartiality: A Treatise on Social Justice Volume II*. Oxford: Clarendon.

Beitz, Charles 1999. *Political Theory and International Relations*. Princeton University Press (with a new afterword by the author).

Buchanan, Allen 2004. *Justice, Legitimacy, and Self-Determination: Moral Foundations for International Law*. Oxford University Press.

Buchanan, Allen and Keohane, Robert O. 2006. 'The Legitimacy of Global Governance Institutions', *Ethics and International Affairs* 20: 405–37.

Caney, Simon 1995. 'Anti-Perfectionism and Rawlsian Liberalism', *Political Studies* 43: 248–64.

Caney, Simon 2005. 'Cosmopolitan Justice, Responsibility, and Global Climate Change', *Leiden Journal of International Law* 18: 747–75.

Caney, Simon 2006. 'Cosmopolitan Justice and Institutional Design: An Egalitarian Liberal Conception of Global Governance', *Social Theory and Practice* 32: 725–56.

committed to both a fair treatment of their own citizens or ensuring that the members of other states are properly protected. Second, even if it were true that a state-centric contractarianism might endorse the institutional reforms mentioned in the text this does not, of course, rescue that theory. To do that, one would need to show that the objections to SSC presented earlier are unpersuasive. My concern is whether SSC is a plausible justificatory theory and the objections developed earlier dispute this.

Caney, Simon 2006. 'Cosmopolitanism, Democracy and Distributive Justice', *The Canadian Journal of Philosophy* (supplementary volume) 31: 29–63.

Caney, Simon 2007. 'Egalitarian Liberalism and Universalism', in Laden, T. and Owen, D. (eds.) *Cultural Diversity and Political Theory*. Cambridge University Press, 151–72.

Caney, Simon 2007. 'Global Poverty and Human Rights: the Case for Positive Duties', in Pogge, T. (ed.) *Freedom from Poverty as a Human Right: Who Owes What to the Very Poor*? Oxford University Press, 275–302.

Caney, Simon 2008. 'Global Distributive Justice and the State', *Political Studies* 57: 487–518.12

Caney, Simon 2009. 'Climate Change and the Duties of the Advantaged', *Critical Review of International Social and Political Philosophy* 12.

Cass, Deborah 2005. *The Constitutionalization of the World Trade Organization: Legitimacy, Democracy, and Community in the International Trading System*. Oxford University Press.

Christiano, Thomas 1996. *The Rule of the Many: Fundamental Issues in Democratic Theory*. Boulder: Westview Press.

Cohen, G. A. 2000. *If you're an Egalitarian, How Come You're so Rich?* Cambridge, MA: Harvard University Press.

Dahl, Robert A. 1957. 'The Concept of Power', *Behavioral Science* 2: 201–15.

Dworkin, Ronald 1985. *A Matter of Principle*. Oxford: Clarendon Press.

Franck, Thomas M. 1995. *Fairness in International Law and Institutions*. Oxford: Clarendon Press.

Gilpin, Robert 2000. *The Challenge of Global Capitalism: the World Economy in the 21st Century*. Princeton and Oxford: Princeton University Press.

Grant, Ruth W. and Keohane, Robert O. 2005. 'Accountability and Abuses of Power in World Politics', *American Political Science Review* 99: 29–43.

Gutmann, Amy and Thompson, Dennis 1990. 'Moral Conflict and Political Consensus', *Ethics* 101: 64–88.

Hayek, F. A. 1976 [1944]. *The Road to Serfdom*. London and Henley: Routledge and Kegan Paul.

Held, David 1995. *Democracy and the Global Order: From the Modern State to Cosmopolitan Governance*. Cambridge: Polity.

Hoekman, Bernard M. and Mavroidis, Petros C. 2007. *The World Trade Organization: Law, Economics, and Politics*. London and New York: Routledge.

Howse, Robert 2001. 'The Legitimacy of the World Trade Organization', in Coicaud, J.-M. and Heiskanen, V. (eds.) *The Legitimacy of International Organizations*. Tokyo: United Nations University Press, 355–407.

Howse, Robert and Nicolaïdis, Kalypso 2001. 'Legitimacy and Global Governance: Why Constitutionalizing the WTO is a Step too Far', in Porter, R. B., Sauvé, P., Subramanian, A. and Beviglia Zampetti, A. (eds.) *Efficiency,*

Equity and Legitimacy: The Multilateral Trading System at the Millennium. Washington, DC: Brookings Institution Press, 227–52.

Howse, Robert and Nicolaïdis, Kalypso 2003. 'Enhancing WTO Legitimacy: Constitutionalization or Global Subsidiarity?', *Governance* 16: 73–94.

Keohane, Robert O. 2003. 'Global Governance and Democratic Accountability', in Held, D. and Koenig-Archibugi, M. (eds.) *Taming Globalization: Frontiers of Governance.* Cambridge: Polity, 130–59.

Keohane, Robert O. and Nye Jr., Joseph S. 2001. 'The Club Model of Multilateral Cooperation and Problems of Democratic Legitimacy', in Porter, R. B., Sauvé, P., Subramanian, A. and Beviglia Zampetti, A. (eds.) *Efficiency, Equity, and Legitimacy: The Multilateral Trading System at the Millennium.* Washington, DC: Brookings Institution Press, 264–94.

Keohane, Robert O. and Nye Jr., Joseph S. 2003. 'Redefining Accountability for Global Governance', in Kahler, M. and Lake, D. A. (eds.) *Governance in a Global Economy: Political Authority in Transition.* Princeton and Oxford: Princeton University Press, 386–411.

Lukes, Steven 2005. *Power: A Radical View*, second edition. Basingstoke: Palgrave Macmillan.

McGrew, Tony 1999. 'The World Trade Organization: Technocracy or Banana Republic?', in Taylor, A. and Thomas, C. (eds.) *Global Trade and Global Social Issues.* London and New York: Routledge, 197–216.

Narlikar, Amrita 2005. *The World Trade Organization: A Very Short Introduction.* Oxford University Press.

Nye, Joseph 2002. *The Paradox of American Power: Why the World's Only Superpower can't go it Alone.* Oxford University Press.

Petersmann, Ernst-Ulrich 2003. 'Human Rights and the Law of the World Trade Organization', *Journal of World Trade* 37: 241–81.

Pogge, Thomas 2002. *World Poverty and Human Rights: Cosmopolitan Responsibilities and Reforms.* Cambridge: Polity.

Rawls, John 1993. *Political Liberalism.* New York: Columbia University Press.

Rawls, John 1999. *A Theory of Justice*, Revised Edition. Oxford University Press.

Rawls, John 1999. *The Law of Peoples with 'The Idea of Public Reason Revisited'.* Cambridge, MA: Harvard University Press.

Raz, Joseph 1986. *The Morality of Freedom.* Oxford: Clarendon.

Risse, Mathias 2006. 'What to Say About the State', *Social Theory and Practice* 32: 671–98.

Scharpf, Fritz 1999. *Governing in Europe: Effective and Democratic?* Oxford University Press.

Singer, Peter 2002. *One World: The Ethics of Globalization.* New Haven and London: Yale University Press.

Singh, David Grewal 2008. *Network Power: The Social Dynamics of Globalization.* New Haven and London: Yale University Press.

Stiglitz, Joseph 2002. *Globalization and its Discontent*. London: Allen Lane.

Stiglitz, Joseph 2006. *Making Globalization Work: the Next Steps to Global Justice*. London: Allen Lane.

United Nations Development Programme 2002. *Human Development Report 2002: Deepening Democracy in a Fragmented World*. New York: Oxford University Press.

United Nations Development Programme 2005. *Human Development Report 2005 International Cooperation at a Crossroads: Aid, Trade and Security in an Unequal World*. New York: Oxford University Press.

Waldron, Jeremy 1999. *Law and Disagreement*. Oxford: Clarendon Press.

Woods, Ngaire 2001. 'Making the IMF and the World Bank More Accountable', *International Affairs* 77: 83–100.

Woods, Ngaire 2006. *The Globalizers: The IMF, the World Bank, and their Borrowers*. Ithaca and London: Cornell University Press.

4

Do international organisations play favourites? An impartialist account

STEVEN R. RATNER

The recent turn of politics and philosophy to serious appraisals of international law is welcome news for politics, ethics and law. Politics can offer us rich description of the international landscape – the actors and their policies, conflicts and approaches to overcoming them; and political and moral philosophy can produce reasoned prescription for devising a just world order. But international law is a critical bridge between them, for law, with its grounding in the institutional arrangements devised by global actors, provides a path to implementing theories of the right or of the good. Just as scholars of politics have realised that their descriptions must include the norms and decision-making processes of international law, so scholars of international justice are taking account of the norms already institutionalised within the international order. Ethical discourse must understand these institutions, for they both place constraints upon and offer opportunities for carrying out the solutions to ethical problems that philosophers derive. Such an understanding is key not only to making international ethics stronger within philosophy, but to making it convincing to those concerned with operationalising ethical theory – political scientists, legal academics, governmental and non-governmental elites and the educated public.

Beyond institutions, the connection between international law and ethics is also tied to international law's own claim to morality. As Andrew Hurrell has put it, 'the ethical claims of international law rest on the contention that it is the *only* set of globally institutionalised processes by which norms can be negotiated on the basis of dialogue and consent, rather than being simply imposed by the most powerful'.[1]

[1] A. Hurrell, 'International Law and the Making and Unmaking of Boundaries' in A. Buchanan and M. Moore (eds.), *States, Nations, and Borders: The Ethics of Making Boundaries* (Cambridge University Press, 2003), 275, 277.

International lawyers thus analyse and seek the construction of an international order with a normative component. I do not claim that the legality of certain institutional arrangements is a sufficient condition for their morality, but it is certainly possible that their legality is a necessary condition for their morality.

The three fields nonetheless differ when they refer to institutions. Philosophers see them broadly as human constructs that organise and transform principles of interpersonal ethics into principles of justice for society. Buchanan has described an institution as 'a kind of organisation, usually persisting over some considerable period of time, that contains roles, function, procedures and processes, as well as structures of authority'.[2] Under this view, international law is both itself an institution and comprised of institutions. Lawyers and political scientists are much more focused on political structures. International law is not an institution, but the WTO is. The terms international institution and international organisation are often deployed interchangeably – something I will do here.

International lawyers have been arguing over the design and function of global institutions for a century at the very least, a not unsurprising turn of events since lawyers are central to the design and functioning of such organisations. When called upon by policy makers, they have attempted to create or reform organisations to match their clients' visions regarding the two most central features of those organisations – (1) their legitimacy vis-à-vis the particular community they serve and (2) their effectiveness at advancing the goals set out for them. The drafting of the constitutive instruments of international organisations or of treaties with implementation mechanisms (like compliance committees of the states parties) is part of the bread and butter of the public international lawyer. Many of the developments on which philosophers write, for example changing notions of sovereignty, the proliferation and increased power of international organisations, or the large role of non-governmental actors in international society, are old news to international law. The appraisal of those organisations for the extent to which they are legitimate and effective is at the core of legal scholarship. Legitimacy, in particular, has been the stuff of countless books and articles, for it seems to offer some standards for assessing the worth of existing organisations.[3]

[2] A. Buchanan, *Justice, Legitimacy, and Self-Determination* (Oxford University Press, 2004), 2.

[3] See, for example, T. Franck, *The Power of Legitimacy Among Nations* (Oxford University Press, 1990); D. Bodansky, 'The Legitimacy of International Governance: A Coming

In this chapter I take a different tack from that of other legal scholars and seek to appraise international organisations based on debates within ethics rather than law. I propose to consider whether international organisations act impartially in the broad sense of not playing favourites in the way they treat certain actors and situations with which they deal. I address this issue because much current criticism of key international organisations is based on the observation that they do not treat all actors or situations the same way and so therefore are morally suspect. Critics repeatedly urge international organisations to be more democratic, whether in terms of greater equality in the privileges of membership, greater even-handedness in treatment of the concerns of rich vs. poor states, or direct involvement of individuals in decision-making.[4] These claims of inequity, partiality or unfairness are central to contemporary philosophical treatments of international law as not meeting a certain vision of a just world order and need to be addressed very carefully. This chapter attempts to engage this important debate through an approach introduced in an earlier article,[5] by viewing international organisations and the states in them as having various rights and duties towards other actors in the international arena; I will then ask whether rights possessed by or duties owed to only some actors – special rights and duties, which translate into various forms of unequal treatment of actors – can be justified.

In particular, I will examine three aspects of international organisations: membership, decision-making processes and choices of targets for action. My goal is to appraise these features of the organisation to see what they indicate about the organisation's impartiality. Although impartiality with respect to these three aspects does not equate with a just international organisation, an appraisal of institutions' impartiality is a critical prerequisite to understanding the institutions that we currently have and proposing ideas to reconstruct them.

I thus will consider organisations from a moral perspective, but, as a legal scholar, I take existing institutions as a fundamental starting point and ask whether they fit some vision of justice. This approach to the status quo differs in two ways from that of most philosophers working in this area. First, unlike cosmopolitans like David Held and Simon Caney, I see no need to justify strong international institutions in the first place,

Challenge for International Environmental Law?', *American Journal of International Law*, 93 (1999), 596.

4 See, for example, the essays in C. Barry and T. W. Pogge (eds.), *Global Institutions and Responsibilities* (Malden, MA: Blackwell, 2005).

5 S. R. Ratner, 'Is International Law Impartial?', *Legal Theory*, 11 (2005), 39.

because these bodies are already part of the international legal landscape, with more to come in the future to address new challenges (though we do not yet have institutions as strong as Held and Caney would like).[6] Second, I prefer to focus on existing institutions because changes in the status quo must respond to problems with it rather than write on a tabula rasa based on ideal theory. This approach should not be confused with an apology for the status quo, but rather as a pragmatic acceptance that global justice must be pursued, in the first instance, through the institutions that we already have.

I begin with an overview of the concepts of general and special duties in international law, impartiality and their application to international organisations. I then turn to the three traits noted above and end with some conclusions about the limitations and promise of my inquiry.

General and special duties in international law and institutions

International law is a set of norms and processes to resolve the numerous claims that global actors – states, individuals, peoples, corporations and others – make upon each other. These rules and processes allocate to these entities various rights, duties and powers, including the power to make the rules. The most important of these, in my view, are the duties by each actor towards other actors, though those duties are sometimes grounded by rights held by other actors. International law has traditionally recognised duties on *states* and towards other *states*, and indeed the bulk of duties today are still inter-state. But in the last century it has come to include important duties on states towards *individuals* through international human rights law and international humanitarian law; on states towards *peoples* through the norm of self-determination; on *individuals* towards states or other individuals through international criminal law; and in other combinations as well.

Those duties can be grouped into general duties – those directed to *all* other states (or individuals or peoples) – and special duties – those directed towards only *some* states. This notion derives from Robert Goodin's work on H. L. A. Hart.[7] Although Hart and Goodin developed these concepts in relation to ethical duties of the individual – what Thomas Pogge calls

[6] See, for example, S. Caney, *Justice Beyond Borders: A Global Political Theory* (Oxford University Press, 2005), 156–82.

[7] R. Goodin, 'What Is So Special About Our Fellow Countrymen?', *Ethics*, 98 (1988), 663, 665. As Goodin points out, a special duty can refer to both a duty on A that B does not have, and a duty on A towards B but not towards C, D and all others. I am referring to the

interactional conceptions of morality and justice – they have much analytic force when applied to inter-state arrangements – in Pogge's terms, institutional conceptions of morality and justice.[8]

Thus, the duty of states under Article 2(4) of the UN Charter to refrain from the threat or use of military force and the duty under the Vienna Convention on Diplomatic Relations to respect the status of diplomats are quintessential general duties, owed to all other states. Indeed, even a state's duties regarding transborder harms, like pollution, are really duties owed to all states, though those duties are often only discharged towards close neighbours (depending on the range of the noxious activity). Other duties are special, such as those a state assumes towards a limited number of other states via bilateral, regional or other non-global treaty. A very important set of special duties is limited territorially, namely a state's duties under human rights law generally to guarantee the human rights only of residents of its territory. The result of this vision of international law is that each actor is surrounded by spheres of duties, with some orbits filled by all other actors and some filled by only some actors. The breadth of the sphere is a function of the strength of the norm – its overall importance to the international legal order – as well as its hardness – the extent to which it creates a true legal obligation on the state.

The pay-off of this construct for examining the ethics of international law is that it allows for inquiry into whether international actors owe *and should owe* different duties to other actors. It permits us to break down core rules or concepts of international law and ask whether they are justifiable from an ethical perspective based on the general and special duties inherent in them. Special duties require particular scrutiny because they involve, at some level, unequal treatment for states (or individuals), with only some actors benefiting from them.

These same sorts of questions can be posed of international organisations. Thus, states within the organisation have particular rights and

latter for most of this chapter but address the former in the context of the UN Security Council below.

8 T. W. Pogge, 'Cosmopolitanism and Sovereignty', *Ethics*, 103 (1992) 48, 50–2. My use of the terms general vs. special thus differs from Hare's terminology, in which general contrasts with specific and refers to the precision or detail of a moral proposition, whereas universal contrasts with singular and refers to the persons or entities who are the object of the moral claim. R. M. Hare, *Freedom and Reason* (Oxford: Clarendon Press, 1963), 38–40. Nonetheless, I believe Hare's concept of universalisability – i.e. for a prescription about one subject to be a moral one, it must apply to all other subjects with the same non-moral features – resembles the idea of second-order impartiality discussed below.

duties as part of their membership, typically spelled out in a constitutive instrument, such as voting in various bodies (a right) or paying dues (a duty).[9] Moreover, the organisation can have other rights and duties. The UN has the right to bring claims against states for injuries against it, a manifestation of its so-called international legal personality; it has the right to impose binding sanctions against any state if the Security Council so decides; and some have argued that it has a duty to stop massive violations of human rights. The institutions and the states within them possess both general and special duties and the members may have special rights as well,[10] under the organic instruments of the organisation.

Impartiality as a construct for evaluating the conduct of international institutions

Conceptualising the international legal order and institutions in terms of general and special duties allows us to mobilise a set of very useful inquiries posed by philosophers under the rubric of debates over the meaning and scope of impartiality. At its most fundamental level, impartiality describes a way that individuals and institutions decide and act, one based on disinterestedness, consistency and fairness and not merely personal motives.[11] Lawrence Becker has categorised these debates as concerning (1) whether personal interests can play a role in determining moral duties; (2) whether it is possible to adopt a standpoint for moral deliberation that is independent of ourselves; and (3) whether we can take into account personal relationships in assessing moral duties.[12] Most of the impartiality debate and certainly its analysis of special duties, concerns the last issue. These are fundamentally debates over the morality of special duties compared to general ones.

In particular, the partiality/impartiality asks whether special duties are morally justified based on personal relationship per se – what Rawls calls 'relations of affinity'[13] – or some other grounds. As David Miller writes,

[9] It is not always clear to whom these duties are directed – other states or the organisation as a whole.

[10] At times it is more useful analytically to examine the special rights enjoyed by particular member states, which may not map neatly onto a corresponding special duty at all, for example, the special rights of the members of the Security Council discussed below.

[11] It is in this sense that Barry and Terry Nardin define justice as impartiality. See B. Barry, *Justice as Impartiality* (Oxford: Clarendon Press, 1995), 20–7; T. Nardin, *Law, Morality, and the Relations of States* (Princeton University Press, 1983), 258–9, 265.

[12] L. C. Becker, 'Impartiality and Ethical Theory', *Ethics*, 101 (1991), 698.

[13] J. Rawls, *The Law of Peoples* (Cambridge, MA: Harvard University Press, 1999), 112.

one position, which may be loosely described as impartialist, says that 'only general facts about other individuals can serve to determine my duties towards them', while the other, loosely described as partialist, sees relations between individuals as so central to ethics that 'fundamental principles may be attached directly to these relations'.[14] Christopher Wellman has characterised the different stances towards special duties as 'reductionist' and 'associativist' (or 'nonreductionist').[15]

Some of the differences between partialists and impartialists have been narrowed through the notion of orders (or levels) of impartiality.[16] Under this view, one can remain impartial while accepting the morality of special duties as long as one can justify those duties from an independent moral perspective such that all individuals owe those special duties to all persons in that relationship to them. An impartialist could thus defend an individual's patriotic ties – a first-order partialist stance – if he was convinced that it was second-order impartial, i.e. that there was a justification that does not give fundamental moral significance to the relationship between compatriots *alone* but instead justifies the duty on 'more fundamental facts which are themselves morally significant'.[17] But without such an explanation, an impartialist could not justify special duties, and their scholarship seeks to find an argument that transcends the particular ties to other generalisable traits of the relationship.

An inquiry into the morality of international institutions should incorporate – and can eventually contribute to – these debates. For if institutions, or the states in them, have special duties or rights vis-à-vis other international actors, we need to ask if they are justified based on morally significant 'relations of affinity' or on characteristics other than the relationship per se. While partiality may have a place in interpersonal ethics, in devising a just world order in which law and institutions play a central role, we must find an impartial justification for special rights and duties of the institutions and of their members. Institutions are not families, but political entities enmeshed in law, and law is a construct in which impersonal duties prevail over personal ones. Only such a

14 D. Miller, *On Nationality* (Oxford University Press, 1995), 50.

15 See C. H. Wellman, 'Relational Facts in Liberal Political Theory: Is There Magic in the Pronoun "My"?', *Ethics*, 110 (2000), 537.

16 See, for example, Barry, *Justice*, 191–5; M. Baron, 'Impartiality and Friendship', *Ethics*, 101 (1991), 836; see also S. Mendus, *Impartiality in Moral and Political Philosophy* (Oxford University Press, 2002).

17 Wellman, 'Relational Facts', 540.

justification can withstand charges of favouritism. If an institution's acts cannot be justified based on such an impartial justification, then those actions are highly suspect morally and those aspects require, at a minimum, institutional reform.

Three points require clarification. First, I do not claim that impartiality in the acts of an institution is a sufficient condition for an institution to act justly; and indeed there may even be situations in which an organisation may act justly without acting impartially. But the sort of questions we ask in determining the impartiality of human or governmental conduct can get us far in responding to the concerns voiced about today's international institutions. Second, it is not possible or particularly useful to characterise the totality of an institution as partial or impartial (let alone just or unjust). Institutions are multifaced creations of states, and broadbrush accusations of favouritism need to be avoided. Rather, it is necessary to break down the institution into its key functions and examine them. In the case of this chapter, I examine three core functions of institutions and ask whether the actions of the organisation can be convincingly justified from an impartialist perspective. It may well turn out that institutions act impartially in some ways but not others. But even this scrutiny is, I believe, a step forward, as it allows us to determine which aspects require institutional reform or even replacement.

Third, and most important, asking about the impartiality of international organisations does not prejudge what sort of (second-order) impartialist argument can best justify a special right or duty held by it or its members. One must find a convincing impartialist argument – contractarian, Kantian, utilitarian or otherwise. For example, with respect to individual duties, Goodin offers a consequentialist account of special duties towards co-nationals whereby states represent the most efficient means of allocating general duties among all individuals.[18] Alan Gewirth offers a Kantian perspective emphasising individual autonomy as the ethical lodestar of special relationships.[19] Oldenquist and Samuel Scheffler defend the patriot whose allegiance is based on loyalties or special ties alone.[20]

[18] R. Goodin, *Protecting the Vulnerable: A Reanalysis of Our Social Responsibilities* (University of Chicago Press, 1985); Goodin, 'What is So Special'.

[19] A. Gewirth, 'Ethical Universalism and Particularism', *Journal of Philosophy*, 85 (1988), 283, 294–6.

[20] A. Oldenquist, 'Loyalties', *Journal of Philosophy*, 79 (1982), 173; S. Scheffler, 'Relationships and Responsibilities', *Philosophy and Public Affairs*, 26 (1997), 189; for other defences of the moral significance of community, see M. Walzer, *Spheres of Justice*

Indeed, this last clarification may lead one to ask how we determine a convincing impartialist justification and whether we need an overall theory of the justice of international institutions to do so. Otherwise, we may simply be shifting underlying moral arguments into a new box called impartiality without answering any important questions. In response, we can, as an initial matter, easily identify some bad impartialist justifications, e.g. in the case of utilitarian arguments, where it can be shown empirically, or at least safely assumed, that action A (e.g. a particular membership policy or voting scheme) does not in fact increase utility. Other utilitarian justifications may seem defensible but risk decaying into the premise of something like: 'If this function of the organisation is ordered in a way that is most feasible politically – or if it permits the organisation to carry out its functions with the least resistance – then the organisation's conduct is impartial morally.'

But if we have to measure a plausible utilitarian argument that suggests an international organisation acts impartially against a deontological argument that it does not, we may well need more. At this point, I will not offer a comprehensive theory for evaluating impartialist justifications. My goal here is more preliminary insofar as it seeks to respond to critics of international organisations who may not even recognise the possibility that some unequal treatment of states by international organisations can be reconciled with a number of anti-favouritist or impartial justifications. At times alternative impartialist grounds are laid out.

Nonetheless, insofar as I offer some guidance for evaluating those arguments, my starting point is that of a 'weak cosmopolitan', i.e. one who sees the individual, wherever situated, as the ultimate unit of moral concern but who also sees benefits to global order and stability that may ultimately not be theoretically linked to individual dignity or welfare. As a general matter, I would posit that most of the well-known multilateral organisations are agents of inter-state cooperation dedicated at least in principle to goals that promote both individual welfare and global stability – although some may promote more invidious goals either in principle or in practice. Organisations whose goals are laudable should be encouraged to carry out those goals – an overtly utilitarian argument – although this must be balanced with the need not to undercut certain essential values in the international community that are best seen as deontological in nature. These include the most basic norms of

(New York: Basic Books, 1983), 33; Y. Tamir, *Liberal Nationalism* (Princeton University Press, 1993), 95–116.

human dignity, such as non-discrimination based on race, ethnicity or gender; bans on summary execution, slavery and cruel and inhumane treatment; and self-determination of peoples. Thus, for those institutions with laudable purposes, impartialist utilitarian arguments, even if convincing on their own terms, will need to be viewed alongside non-utilitarian arguments that may suggest that indeed the institution is not acting impartially.

Whether or not one agrees with my insistence on the need for an impartial justification, my approach still allows us see the world differently by asking two core questions: (a) how far an international institution's (or other actor's) duties extend; and (b) how we might justify duties by organisations to some but not all other international actors. In the end, we will have determined whether, in a word, organisations (and the states in them) can play favourites – whether they can limit their duties in a moral way. In so doing, we are effectively exploring whether there is indeed one international community or multiple communities.[21] This permits a more nuanced appraisal, for example, of cosmopolitan theories that tend to see states and groupings of them as having equal duties to all individuals around the globe; or Rawls's theories that divide the world into various categories of states, with different duties assigned to them.

Membership

International organisations can be grouped along two axes – the breadth of their *participation*, from fairly regional (or sub-regional), to global; and the *issues* over which they have a mandate, from specialised (or highly technical), to those with a mandate to consider all issues. Examples of the combinations are:

Global and general: United Nations.

Global and specialised: World Trade Organisation, International Monetary Fund, World Bank, International Labour Organisation, World Health Organisation, International Telecommunication Union.[22]

[21] Cf. D. Held, 'Democratic Accountability and Political Effectiveness from a Cosmopolitan Perspective' in D. Held and M. Archibugi (eds.), *Global Governance and Public Accountability* (Oxford: Blackwell, 2005), 240, 248–9 (on the connection between subsidiarity in decision-making and spatial boundaries of a community).

[22] Some global organisations are only open to states with a particular common interest, such as the International Coffee Organisation or the Commonwealth.

Regional and general: Organisation of American States, African Union, Gulf Cooperation Council.

Regional and specialised: European Union (though its mandate is very large), Association of South East Asian Nations, Arctic Council, Inter-American Development Bank.

The membership rules of each organisation are typically set forth in their constituent instrument (e.g. Article 4 of the UN Charter) as well as policy documents or developed by the organisation over time (e.g. the *acquis communautaire* of the EU). As states set up and operate international organisations, they make choices about whose inclusion will benefit the organisation and who will benefit from inclusion in it. In admitting members, the institution agrees to give them special rights vis-à-vis non-members and to create special duties towards them. The organisation may, for instance, be bound to give financial assistance to members but not non-members. As a result, non-member states will often seek to become members, as is clear from the history of the European Union and the WTO.

Global organisations: the United Nations

At one extreme in inclusivity is the United Nations. Article 4 of the UN Charter states:

1. Membership in the United Nations is open to all other peace-loving states which accept the obligations contained in the present Charter and, in the judgment of the Organisation, are able and willing to carry out these obligations.
2. The admission of any such state to membership in the United Nations will be effected by a decision of the General Assembly upon the recommendation of the Security Council.

As of today, the UN has 192 members. For most of its history, it routinely admitted new states resulting from decolonisation, although Cold War politics at times kept other states out (e.g. a group of Western and Eastern states jointly admitted in 1955 and East and West Germany jointly admitted in 1973). Even when Yugoslavia and the USSR dissolved, the UN was generally quick to admit the resulting entities. Clearly, the UN's members have interpreted the term 'peace-loving' loosely and made scarcely any serious inquiries into whether a candidate is 'able and willing' to carry out the obligations of membership, which include, at a minimum, settling disputes peacefully, carrying out decisions of the Security Council and paying dues.

Does the UN have a duty to admit all states that meet the criteria of Article 4(1)? This precise issue faced the International Court of Justice in its first advisory opinion in 1946, when the General Assembly asked it whether a state voting on membership in the General Assembly or Security Council is 'juridically entitled to make its consent to the admission dependent on conditions not expressly provided by [Article 4(1)]'.[23] The Court said no, implying that the UN and its members have a duty to all states to admit them to membership if they meet those criteria. It is a general – though clearly contingent – duty. As a general duty, whose beneficiaries are all states, it is first-order impartial. I need not choose an underlying basis for this impartiality, though from a utilitarian standpoint there is much to be said for maximising overall welfare if an organisation dedicated to prevention and termination of armed conflict includes all states in the world.

Yet certain ethical viewpoints may object to this approach to membership. One could argue that the UN ought to be more selective in its membership, as is seen in calls – from both the American right and some mainstream academics – for an organisation of democracies as a counterweight or alternative to the UN.[24] But are these critics, who want less than universal membership, opposed to an impartial set of duties on the United Nations regarding admission? On the one hand, they might favour a duty by the UN to all states to admit them, but one simply contingent on the state's democratic political structure. On the other hand, they might be said to favour a UN with membership-related duties only to democratic states – special duties that are first-order partial. If this is argued, however, then even the current membership rules under Article 4(1) are also first-order partial; they simply are partial towards peace-loving states instead of democratic states.

These alternative criteria, while different from the first-order impartial criteria of the UN now, are still morally defensible from a second-order impartial perspective. Their advocates argue (wrongly, I believe) on utilitarian grounds, that such a grouping will contribute to international peace more than the somewhat dysfunctional UN. A better impartialist

[23] Conditions of Admission of a State to Membership in the United Nations (Article 4 of the Charter), 1947–8 ICJ Rep. 57 (Adv. Op. of 28 May 1948).

[24] For a recent academic endorsement, see J. Ikenberry and A. M. Slaughter (eds.), *Forging A World of Liberty Under Law* (Princeton, NJ: Princeton University, 2006), 25–6.

justification, one more appealing to cosmopolitans, would be that because democratic states have governments that derive their power from the consent of the governed and thus their legitimacy from the decisions of individuals, an organisation confined to them has an impartial membership criterion. If, however, someone advocated an international organisation open only to states that had a majority of white inhabitants, a second-order impartial justification would be elusive at best. Even a utilitarian would be embarrassed to argue the effectiveness of such an organisation in the face of the overlapping consensus in international law and morality on the invidiousness of racial discrimination.

The way the UN treats candidate states suggests to me tentatively that the following criteria together represent a sufficient condition for an ethically defensible membership policy: (a) publicly stated (even if somewhat open-textured) criteria for membership; (b) eligibility to any state to apply; and (c) selection criteria that can be justified from a second-order impartial perspective. An organisation may fall short in any of these criteria. This last criterion is, of course, the nub of the membership problem. In my example above, plausible utilitarian and deontological arguments can justify both the status quo in the UN as well as a league of democracies idea, while they cannot, at least prima facie, justify a league of white states.

But organisations may even fall short on the first criterion. Under the 1994 Agreement establishing the WTO, 'Any State ... may accede to this Agreement, on terms to be agreed between it and the WTO'. The Agreement thus allows any state to apply for membership, but creates no duties on the organisation to admit anyone. Instead, each application is treated on a case-by-case basis and results in typically prolonged negotiations among the candidate, the WTO Secretariat and member states. As stated on the WTO's webpage:

> The new member's commitments are to apply equally to all WTO members under normal non-discrimination rules, even though they are negotiated bilaterally [between the WTO and the candidate state]. In other words, the talks determine the benefits (in the form of export opportunities and guarantees) other WTO members can expect when the new member joins. (The talks can be highly complicated. It has been said that in some cases the negotiations are almost as large as an entire round of multilateral trade negotiations.)[25]

[25] www.wto.org/english/thewto_e/whatis_e/tif_e/org3_e.htm.

Thus, even as the successful candidate will assume general duties to all other members (e.g. to apply the same tariffs to imports of the same products from all of them), the WTO does not specify exactly what obligation it has to any candidate regarding admission. It assumes no formal duty at all, general or special. It is possible that, as a de facto matter, the WTO admits members based on clear and uniformly applied criteria, but the constitutive instrument does not state them and is thus not ethically defensible without our knowing more. Perhaps the individual admission decisions can be justified from an act-utilitarian perspective – each admission decision is taken in a way to maximise utility according to some standard. But without knowing this for sure, the observer could easily conclude that the WTO resembles a club whose members make ad hoc decisions on whom they wish to admit. The absence in an organisation that purports to be global (*World* Trade Organisation) of any duty to admit new members according to clear criteria creates the potential for that organisation to play favourites in its admissions decisions. It may well contribute to the suspicion with which some in the developing world regard the WTO.

Regional organisations: the Council of Europe

But is admission open to all states a necessary factor for an ethical membership policy? To answer this, I turn to a clearly geographically limited organisation – the Council of Europe (COE), the forty-six-member organisation of European democracies whose most famous treaty is the European Convention on Human Rights and whose best known organ is the European Court of Human Rights. The 1949 treaty creating the COE states:

Article 3 Every member of the Council of Europe must accept the principles of the rule of law and of the enjoyment by all persons within its jurisdiction of human rights and fundamental freedoms, and collaborate sincerely and effectively in the realisation of the aim of the Council …

Article 4 Any European State which is deemed to be able and willing to fulfil the provisions of Article 3 may be invited to become a member of the Council of Europe by the Committee of Ministers.

The COE is thus open only to 'European State[s]'. Article 49 of the Treaty on European Union uses the same phrase with regard to the EU, though it then requires the negotiation of a separate agreement between the EU's members and the candidate on the terms of membership. The Council's membership policy is partial in a first-order sense – it extends only to European countries.[26] The Council, like the EU, has debated the meaning of the term 'European' and has chosen to admit marginally European states – in a geographic sense – like Azerbaijan, Georgia and Armenia, but it has not taken the step of admitting the former Soviet republics of Kazakhstan, Kyrgystan, Uzbekistan or Tadjikistan. This policy contrasts with that of the fifty-six-member Organisation for Security and Cooperation in Europe, whose original purpose was as a forum for East–West dialogue during the Cold War; it included the USSR (as well as Canada and the United States) and now includes all the ex-Soviet republics. But it has no organic instrument specifying membership criteria.

What are we to make morally of an organisation that limits its membership geographically? Probably not much as an initial matter. This sort of first-order partiality seems defensible from a number of second-order impartial stances. At a somewhat crude utilitarian level, many of the cooperation and coordination problems that international organisations are created to solve can be addressed most efficiently from a regional perspective. Trade, transportation and migration of workers are examples – although many such problems do not turn on proximity, and proximity can often be a subterfuge for more controversial traits like culture. This does not mean that it is easy to determine the point at which a state is not in the region, especially in the case of geographically adjacent states – why does the Association of Southeast Asian Nations omit Australia or Bangladesh? – but it provides a decent justification for the idea of regionally limited organisations. From a social contract perspective, it is also quite plausible that shared histories, languages or economic philosophies may promote agreement more readily than heterogeneity. In the case of the Council of Europe, a limitation of its membership to European democracies might be justified based on a utilitarian argument based on the institutional constraints inherent in the enforcement of the European Convention of Human Rights by the European Court; a Council of Europe with too many members would overwhelm the Court with petitions alleging violations. Yet such an impartial utilitarian justification may not offer a defence to the current composition of the Council. After all, it has admitted Russia, a state most

[26] This limitation could be viewed as either one concerning eligibility to apply or criteria for membership.

of which is not in geographically defined Europe and whose human rights problems have already led to hundreds of petitions to the Court.

Defenders of geographically limited membership policies, however, do not limit themselves to second-order impartial arguments. Indeed, many supporters of limited membership for both the Council of Europe and the European Union have a partialist justification – that a state's status as European creates special links that *alone* permit, or even require, those organisations to limit membership to those states. These links are akin to Rawls's 'relations of affinity'.[27] Thus, while those advocating impartialist justifications and those offering partialist justifications might agree on the scope of expansion of the EU, the critical threshold question for the former is whether a state is *in Europe*, while for the latter is whether it is *European*. The debates in Europe about the territorial scope of the EU resemble the debates in ethics about special duties to 'fellow countrymen'. When politicians argue over whether Turkey is sufficiently 'European' to be in the EU, they are asking, in partialist terms, whether it is a member of the European family, a group whose members are presumably entitled to be the beneficiaries of special duties. Their notion of the family may hinge on acceptance of the Christian religion, an easy basis on which to exclude Turkey, or perhaps on shared values related to individual dignity and the proper role of the state in society – although this can cross the line to an impartialist justification.[28] For some, it might even mean race.

Those defending limited membership on partialist grounds – associativist in Wellman's phrasing[29] – have, I suspect, captured the terms of the public debate over expansion. This tendency to argue based on European-ness rather than European location may emanate from the very powers of the Union itself. Because the EU has such strong powers vis-à-vis its members and so many benefits to offer them, public support for its enlargement may well depend on offering up a more accessible justification for inclusion, one that does not seek to reduce European-ness to some impartial geographical concept. As we know from the 'one thought too many' exhortation of Bernard Williams, partial arguments have a distinct advantage over second-order impartial arguments in their common sense connection to human

[27] Rawls, *The Law of Peoples*, 112.

[28] When I pointed out to a colleague, a prominent German international lawyer, that the editor-in-chief of the *European Journal of International Law* at the time was an Australian academic who teaches at NYU Law School, he responded that being a European is 'a state of mind'.

[29] Wellman, 'Relational Facts'.

experience of family and community[30] – and the EU is still called the 'Community'.

Yet even if partial justifications have an appeal in debates over admission into the Council of Europe or the EU, it is too simple to say that they are the only justifications advanced. For after governments and citizens in Europe have decided whether a state is European, they must eventually move on to the second question, namely whether its current economic and political system meets the criteria for membership. These criteria are publicly presented in the organic instrument of the institutions or in other policy documents (in the case of the EU, so-called Copenhagen Criteria – a stable democracy, with respect for human rights and the rule of law and protection minorities; a working market economy; and adoption of the *acquis communautaire*).[31] The Council and EU are thus not obliged to admit any European country simply because it is European, but obliged to admit only those meeting the additional criteria. The European-ness of a state might generate a special duty on the institution to consider the state's admission – as well as a right of the institution to preclude admission of non-European states – but it cannot, under the positive law of the organisation, generate a duty to admit it.

Nonetheless, it is plausible that the two stages cannot be so nicely parsed in the real world. One may discover that once COE or EU decision makers identify a state as sufficiently European, they are willing to interpret creatively the objective membership criteria in a way to allow for admission. This account can explain the willingness of the Council to admit states with fragile democratic institutions and guarantees of the rule of law. I could probably endorse such an outcome if the utilitarian argument that bringing them into an organisation will strengthen the states' domestic institutions was in fact provable; but I could not endorse that partialist view that they should be admitted merely because they are somehow European or 'like us'. Examination of ongoing debates over membership in terms of partiality thus helps to clarify the sorts of arguments that states are making about exclusivity or inclusivity of international organisations as well as their reasons for them.

The debates over admission criteria in the EU, as well as the desirability of a league of democracies, lead us to ask which tests of a political or ideological nature for membership in a international organisation are

30 B. Williams, 'Persons, Character and Morality', in *Moral Luck* (Cambridge: Cambridge University Press, 1981), 1.

31 http://ec.europa.eu/enlargement/the-policy/process-of-enlargement/mandate-and-framework/_en.htm.

based on impartial criteria. The above discussion aims more at identifying the sort of arguments that will not work than the full scope of the ones that will. Certainly, utilitarian arguments – though only ones with some empirical backing – have a role to play here, for international organisations first and foremost need to carry out their functions, and membership criteria that in the end further those functions seem prima facie impartial. Nonetheless, I am not willing to put all the balls in the utilitarian basket, for if other impartialist justifications find such a policy indefensible, the organisation will be playing favourites in an immoral way. International institutions do carry out functions, but also are themselves embodiments of the international order, and certain values are now so much part of that order that no organisation should be able to ignore them completely in choosing its members.

Finally, it may be asked why international organisations should need to justify their membership policies at all – what is so immoral, after all, about a group of states simply picking others with whom to work on a particular issue and keeping others out, just like individuals in a private bridge or golf club or sorority do? The answer to this difficult question may lie in the difference between individual morality and institutional morality discussed earlier. We do not say that a sorority's membership policy is just; instead, we would say simply (or at least the sorority's defenders would) that it is not morally unacceptable for its members to pick the young women they want as new members. But for conversations about the justice of institutions, domestic or international, I believe we need to adopt a higher standard, one where personalities and partiality are not decisive factors. Moreover, as noted earlier, these institutions are often formed through organic instruments and thus founded on law, for which impartiality and impersonalised decision-making is central. Finally, the power of international institutions over member states, both in terms of advantages they bring and disadvantages they can impose, also argues for an admission policy based on criteria defensible in partialist terms.[32]

[32] I appreciate comments from Máximo Langer and Daniel Halberstam on this issue. As Carlos Vásquez has pointed out, this view is in tension with my claim in 'Is International Law Impartial', 55–7, that special duties based on voluntarism, e.g. in bilateral treaties, are easily justifiable. Without fully resolving this issue, I believe the power of international institutions suggests that voluntarism will not suffice for an ethically defensible membership policy.

Decision-making processes and powers

The influence and power of an international organisation turns upon the legal and political effect of its decisions upon member states and others. These effects in turn both depend upon and help determine the mechanisms it uses for making decisions. The decision-making processes used by a number of international institutions have come under great criticism internationally for perceived favouritism to certain interests. To appraise this charge, I examine whether certain members enjoy special rights or duties and how we might justify such treatment.

The United Nations

I begin with the two key organs of the United Nations, the General Assembly and the Security Council. The General Assembly includes all member states, each of which has the right to one vote. The Assembly passes many resolutions each year, but under the UN Charter the Assembly can legally bind members over only a handful of issues, all of them internal to the operation of the UN, notably the budget and the dues, the admission of new members, the composition of UN bodies and the election of various UN officials. Resolutions on external issues – an ongoing war, a human rights atrocity, economic injustice – are mere recommendations.[33] Contrast this with the Security Council, comprised of fifteen states, five of them permanent members and ten elected for two-year terms from the broader UN membership. Council resolutions require a majority of nine votes, with the additional condition that none of the permanent members oppose the resolution. The decisions of the Council enjoy a special status – automatic binding international law – under Article 25 of the Charter: 'The Members of the United Nations agree to accept and carry out the decisions of the Security Council in accordance with the present Charter.'[34] The Council has repeatedly made such decisions since the end of the Cold War, for example to order members to impose economic sanctions or to give states permission to use force that would otherwise be precluded under Article 2(4).

[33] UN Charter articles 10, 11, 13, 14, 17, 18.

[34] Not all the Council's resolutions are decisions; many are meant to be recommendations. But the decisions are binding under Article 25 and, moreover, under Article 103, prevail over any other duties a state may have under other treaties.

Stated simply, the General Assembly is characterised by equal rights for all states but no power over those states beyond internal UN matters; the Security Council is characterised by special rights – for its members vis-à-vis the membership as a whole and for the permanent five on top of that – and vast power over member states.[35] This formula has elicited substantial criticism over the years from the majority of member states, as well as many international lawyers and philosophers, who claim that the Assembly is too weak, the Council too strong and the permanent five too privileged.

The Charter formula is easily traceable historically. The governments preparing the Charter during the Second World War limited the Assembly's powers precisely because of its universal membership and one-state-one-vote rule, for the strong powers did not want the UN to order them to do anything opposed to their interests. Moreover, they granted the Council vast powers only because of its small membership and the veto, the former essential for rapid decision-making and the latter, again, to prevent any decisions against great power interests. And the five states designated in the Charter as permanent members were the principal Second World War victors (with China's membership passing to the PRC upon its replacement of the Taiwan government in 1971). The status quo is thus no accident.[36] But can it withstand the charge of favouritism? I believe much of it can.

With regard to the Assembly, critics, particularly from the developing world, argue that the Assembly's members ought to enjoy *greater* general rights, e.g. the right to make decisions binding on member states. The argument is essentially that sovereign equality, one of the founding principles of the UN according to Article 1 of the Charter, demands greater powers than the Assembly currently enjoys – that just as there is a general right of all states to vote on the budget, there ought to be one to vote on other matters that will bind member states. Such a general right is superficially justifiable if we compare the General Assembly to a domestic polity, where legislators create binding law by majority vote and citizens may do so as well through referenda.

But to say that states enjoy general (or equal) rights to do some things implies nothing at all as to whether they should enjoy general rights to

[35] As noted in footnote 10, discussion of special rights rather than special duties is a better way of understanding disparate treatment in some cases.

[36] See, for example, G. Simpson, *Great Powers and Outlaw States* (Cambridge University Press, 2004); S. Schlesinger, *Act of Creation: The Founding of the United Nations* (Boulder, CO: Westview Press, 2003).

do other things. I have an equal right to vote, but I do not have an equal right to be on a professional baseball team; indeed I would not have an equal right to be on such a team even if I had the best baseball skills in the world. Sovereign equality does not mean equality for all purposes nor should it. Sovereign equality has a very limited scope. It simply means that states are juridical equals, that none of the attributes of a state – size, power, population etc. – *automatically* endow it with greater or lesser legal rights than another state.[37] It is a baseline for the future allocation of rights and duties and does not mean they must be treated as equals for all purposes. The General Assembly's makeup flows from sovereign equality, but not directly so – rather, it originates in a decision by the equally sovereign states ratifying the Charter to create a body where each state gets one vote.

Indeed, to extend the general rights of Assembly members would prove highly unjustifiable from many impartial perspectives. Most obviously from a cosmopolitan viewpoint, as recognised by many philosophers, each member state is not a person, but rather a political entity composed of numerous people, and equal rights in the Assembly to large and small states means unequal rights to the people living there. Indeed, a cosmopolitan might say that the equal voting in the Assembly is already morally flawed because it does not grant equal rights to the citizens of the member states, but is partial to the interests of small states. Thus cosmopolitans would call for something akin to the European Parliament at the international level.[38] (I think, however, equal voting rights could be justified from a second-order impartial perspective if we see some value for resolution of international disputes in providing certain arenas in which states have equal votes.)

If we move beyond the claim that the Assembly ought to enjoy greater powers by virtue of its universal composition and one-state-one-vote decision-making process, we face a harder set of objections when it comes to the Security Council – for the Council is characterised by special rights for (a) its fifteen members and (b) the permanent five in

[37] See, for example, Declaration on Principles of International Law concerning Friendly Relations and Cooperation Among States, UNGA Res. 2625 (1970), 1; *Oppenheim's International Law* 340–2 (R. Jennings and A. Watts, 9th edn, 1992). I thus disagree with Gerry Simpson, who writes that 'the effect of the collective security provisions [in the Charter] is to entrench a form of sovereign *in*equality', Simpon, *Great Powers*, 187 (original emphasis).

[38] D. Archibugi, 'The Reform of the UN and Cosmopolitan Democracy: A Critical Review', *Journal of Peace Research*, 30 (1993), 301; see also T. Franck, *Fairness in International Law and Institutions* (Oxford University Press, 1997), 482–4.

particular, special rights that require independent justification beyond the historical account.[39]

(a) The special rights for the fifteen states are justifiable from a second-order impartialist perspective based on a utilitarian calculation. As the organ entrusted with the 'primary responsibility' for maintaining international peace and security, the Council simply cannot function with a large membership. A large membership is a nearly sufficient condition for paralysis, an unacceptable option for the Council. It is hard to see how any sort of deontological argument should require the Council to enlarge to the point of such paralysis. Can a utilitarian calculus target the best number at fifteen out of 192 states? No, and I do not wish to preclude the wisdom of an improved composition, an idea that nearly every state in the UN endorses. But the notion that the Charter picks favourites by virtue of the small size of the Council alone does not pass muster.

(b) The special rights of the P5 are two-fold: permanent membership and veto. The former ensures in principle that those states will always participate in the deliberations of the Council, and in practice is the basis for their control of much of the Council's agenda (though it does not guarantee that they will convince enough of the other ten members necessary to pass resolutions supporting their positions, as the United States discovered in the spring of 2003 regarding Iraq). The veto, as noted earlier, also ensures that the Council will not pass a resolution that any of the permanent five oppose. To the critics, this form of partiality smacks of the worst type of favouritism, something that cannot be justified from either a first or second-order perspective.[40]

Yet this criticism, while in many ways compelling, overlooks one significant utilitarian defence of permanent membership and the veto – namely that peace, stability and collective security are promoted when the states with power stand behind a resolution of the Security Council and weakened without that endorsement. A stable world order is a state of affairs that Kant and many others since have recognised as a moral good (though Kant rejected deriving duties as a means to further that

[39] For an excellent evaluation of the problem from the perspective of international law, see D. Caron, 'The Legitimacy of the Collective Authority of the Security Council', *American Journal of International Law*, 87 (1993), 552.

[40] See, for example, Simpson, *Great Powers*.

goal and instead insisted that practical reason and satisfaction of the Categorical Imperative would lead to the perpetual peace).[41] This may also be viewed from a social contract perspective, namely that stability and peace are promoted in granting certain states a special responsibility for the maintenance of peace, and with that responsibility comes the special right to block measures that they believe will not advance it.[42] The special rights of the P5 thus emanate from their special duties – special not in the sense that they are owed only *to* some states, but special in that they are owed only *by* some states.[43] Indeed, the Charter specifies that the non-permanent members of the Council should be chosen based on 'due regard … to the contribution of [UN members] to the maintenance of international peace and security and to the other purposes of the Organisation'.[44] The Charter thus implies that the non-permanent members have a special duty to other states to further international peace, and the Council and Assembly have stressed that the permanent members bear such a special responsibility as well.[45]

These impartial justifications are vulnerable to a number of counter-arguments, each from a different moral perspective. First, within utilitarianism, one can make the descriptive claim that the assent of powerful states is not a necessary condition for global order. Perhaps international peace and security might be advanced even against the interests of some of the most powerful states if the majority of the population of the planet backs a particular measure. Second, within the social contract model, one could argue that whatever the theoretical justification of hinging the permanent five's special rights on their special duties, they have clearly abused their special rights and neglected their special duties. Third, bringing in deontological arguments, one can asset that global order, even if advanced by permanent membership for some states, should not supersede other values (like protection of human rights and thus greater participation by states that protect them).

Indeed, the first two of these counter-arguments – those attacking the Council from within utilitarianism or within social contract theory – are especially good arguments against the status quo. For the importance of

41 I. Kant, 'Perpetual Peace: A Philosophical Sketch' in H. Reiss (ed.) and H. B. Nisbet (trans.), *Kant: Political Writings*, 2nd edn (Cambridge: Cambridge University Press, 1991), 93, 108–13, 121–4. On the acceptance by small states of the special powers of the Council, see Schlesinger, *Act of Creation*, 171–3.

42 I appreciate clarification from Carlos Rosenkrantz on this point.

43 See the distinction in Goodin, 'What Is So Special'.

44 UN Charter, Article 23.

45 B. Simma (ed.), *The Charter of the United Nations: A Commentary*, vol. 1, 2nd edn (Oxford University Press, 2002), 439.

power in promoting compliance with resolutions does not translate into a permanent seat for the United States, Russia, the United Kingdom, France and China. Mere recognition that these states were the leading allies (and even at that, only three really were) in a war fought sixty years ago seems like a sentimental partialist argument. For a few decades these arrangements might have made sense as these states had nuclear weapons, colonies or satellites (and thus a global reach), or both. But today other states have nuclear weapons, colonies are gone and two or even three of the permanent five can hardly be said to be global political powers. As for the social contract idea, the members of the Council, and the permanent five in particular, have been quite inconsistent (or worse) in carrying out their special duty of maintaining international peace. The permanent five have shown themselves pursuing their own interests just as much as other states when they block resolutions in the Council; indeed for many years UN peacekeeping operations excluded troops from the permanent five because of their presumed partiality. As a result, either serious reconstruction of the Council is needed (perhaps to give permanent membership to states that do take their global duties seriously, like Sweden or the Netherlands), or any permanent membership is simply impossible to justify given the tendency of states to advance their own interests no matter what.

The last fifteen years have witnessed hundreds of proposals, from governments and NGOs, usually couched in impartial terms, for alternative arrangements in the Council that correct these deficiencies. Consider the views of the Secretary-General's High Level Panel on Threats, Challenges and Change:

> The challenge for any reform is to increase both the effectiveness and the credibility of the Security Council and, most importantly, to enhance its capacity and willingness to act in the face of threats. This requires greater involvement in Security Council decision-making by those who contribute most; greater contributions from those with special decision-making authority; and greater consultation with those who must implement its decisions.
>
> Reforms of the Security Council should meet the following principles:
>
> (a) They should … increase the involvement in decision-making of those who contribute most to the United Nations financially, militarily and diplomatically – specifically in terms of contributions to … assessed budgets, participation in mandated peace operations, contributions

to voluntary activities of the United Nations in the areas of security and development, and diplomatic activities in support of United Nations objectives and mandates;

(b) They should bring into the decision-making process countries more representative of the broader membership, especially of the developing world;

(c) They should not impair the effectiveness of the Security Council;

(d) They should increase the democratic and accountable nature of the body.[46]

Beyond these recommendations, in 2005 all the UN's heads of states and governments endorsed the concept of the Responsibility to Protect, which places a special responsibility on the members of the Council to use that body as an instrument to respond to massive violations of human rights.[47]

The panel thus offers a set of impartial justifications for the special rights that Council members should enjoy. The seemingly impenetrable barrier to Council reform has been that, when states make specific proposals for expansion, most of the participants and their reasons for preferring one set of special rights over another are quite partial. Partial towards whom? – towards themselves and their friends. It is no coincidence that Indonesia, India, Nigeria and Brazil have been sympathetic to the (impartial sounding) idea of permanent members from each region of the globe. Every player in the debate is suspected by every other player of having self-interested reasons for its proposals, so appeal to an impartial justification for special rights rings hollow.

I have no solution to this problem of Security Council reform other than to observe that states who make self-serving proposals for reform are kidding themselves if they think that nobody is noticing. Impartial justifications will probably not convince the most important actors in the end, who will vote for the reform proposals that advance their interests, but to the extent that the debate can be channelled in favour of impartial justifications, such as those offered by the High Level Panel, the better.

[46] *A More Secure World: Our Shared Responsibility: Report of the High-Level Panel on Threats, Challenges and Change* (2004), para. 249. In addition to changes in the composition of the Council, the Panel and others have made proposals for a greater role of the General Assembly in the Council's work, greater transparency in the Council's deliberations and increased roles for NGOs.

[47] UN General Assembly Resolution 60/1 (2005), para. 139.

The only hope for reform lies in the possibility that the many states that do not have a direct stake in the outcome will convince those who do to compromise. And as noted, critics will continue to argue, whether for utilitarian, social contract, or deontological grounds, that no form of permanent membership will permit the Council to avoid characterisation as an institution based on favouritism.

Finally, one last justification for permanent membership for powerful states should be mentioned – one that steps outside the realm of theories of justice, morality or impartiality – a more or less pragmatic argument grounded in the positive criteria of a legal system.[48] As Hart wrote, one of the bare minimum criteria for such a system is that 'those rules of behaviour which are valid according to the system's ultimate criteria of validity must be generally obeyed'.[49] Under the Charter, the decisions of the Council are meant to be part of the international *legal* system, in particular the part governing international peace and security (though Hart himself said that the lack of obedience meant that there was no international legal system). The guaranteed participation of a core group of states with political power in, and the non-objection of those states to anything considered legally binding furthers the end of general obedience. Without the compliance of the powerful, the prospects for obedience by their many allies are diminished. Moreover, those states also are more likely not merely to refrain from complying, but to block the compliance by obstruction. In a world in which the implementation and enforcement of the Council's decisions necessarily falls to member states, the neutrality or opposition of powerful states decreases significantly the prospects for compliance. The special status of the permanent five enhances prospects for their obedience because they cannot complain that they were not involved in or opposed the decision. This decision-making structure is not a sufficient condition for compliance (any more than it is for world order), but it may well be necessary; for without it those states would have to be persuaded to obey something they had opposed. In this sense the status of permanent membership and the veto are not *just* a case of historical power politics. Rather, they preserve the international law of the collective security system from irrelevance.

The likely response to this justification for the veto is that it is circular – that it justifies, and not merely assumes, non-obedience to resolutions

48 I appreciate this distinction from Chaim Gans and Douglas Husak.

49 H. L. A. Hart, *The Concept of Law* (Oxford: Clarendon Press, 1961), 113.

that the permanent members oppose. For if the UN Charter gave the Council binding decision-making power without special rights for the permanent members, those members would still have an obligation to obey it and should not be able to opt out simply because they were not involved or opposed the resolution. But this is a charge that can be levelled at Hart's views as well. Hart's inclusion of the criteria of general obedience can be seen as a justification for non-obedience. But neither his reasons for saying that a legal system can exist only if there is general obedience nor my defence of permanent membership based on that proposition do that – they simply flow from a realisation that however much we might have legal rules validated by rules of recognition, the existence of a legal system turns upon certain realities about society's attitude towards the rules of recognition.[50]

The International Monetary Fund

In contrast to the UN Charter, the Articles of Agreement of the International Monetary Fund provide for decision-making by the member states, but allocate votes based on each state's financial contribution to the IMF or quota. Quotas are determined based on a variety of economic factors about the state, including GDP and foreign exchange reserves. Key decisions – in particular the extension of loans to member states facing shortfalls in foreign exchange reserves due to economic distress – are made by an Executive Board, comprised of twenty-four people entitled to cast the votes of all of the states. The Board has one member from each of the top five quota holders, who casts the vote of that state alone (together they control almost 39 per cent of the votes); and nineteen other members, each representing other groups of countries, with each Executive Director's votes depending on which countries he represents. A majority of votes, required for most Board decisions, can be obtained with the votes of as few as eight Executive Directors, representing thirty-five states. The developing world, however, retains more leverage over votes requiring a super-majority (such as adjustments to quotas, which require 85 per cent of votes), where, if they act together, they can block a decision. The total number of votes as of 2009 was 2,217,033. Consider this sample votes per member state:

[50] See Hart, *Concept*, 100–1.

State	Number of votes	Percentage of total
Argentina	21,421	0.97
Botswana	880	0.04
China	81,151	3.66
Germany	130,332	5.88
Indonesia	21,043	0.95
Japan	133,378	6.02
Russia	59,704	2.69
United States	371,743	16.77[51]

Sovereign equality notwithstanding, the IMF gives special rights to states in proportion to their contribution to the working capital of the Fund. Poor states have little power to influence decision-making and rich states control the voting. As a result, they have succeeded in promulgating IMF policy that conditions the IMF's lending to its members on domestic adjustments based on the rich states' views of the role of the state in the economy, including concepts of good governance, human rights and environmental protection.[52] Many of the developing world complaints about IMF conditionality are actually complaints about how the IMF itself makes decisions. As Marc Williams has said: 'Those in greatest need of the IMF's resources are therefore permanently in a state of subordination.'[53]

The second-order impartialist rationale for this arrangement is that it does not constitute favouritism to give rich states greater votes in a financial institution because their votes are, in fact, in direct proportion to their share in the working capital of the institution. Banks are, after all, in the business of lending out money, and those decisions ought to be made by those who have contributed the money. This argument has a deontological ring to it based on the notion that those with contributions deserve to have influence. And in the case of the IMF, those contributions themselves are determined based on the application of objective economic criteria. From a utilitarian perspective, in order to increase the

[51] www.imf.org.

[52] A. Newburg, 'The Changing Roles of the Bretton Woods Institutions: Evolving Concepts of Conditionality' in M. Giovanoli (ed.), *International Monetary Law: Issues for the New Millennium* (Oxford University Press, 2000), 81.

[53] M. Williams, *International Economic Organisations and the Third World* (London: Harvester Wheatsheaf, 1994), 67.

overall lending from the bank, help countries experiencing currency shortfalls and thereby presumably increase overall economic welfare, the bank needs to attract capital; and it makes sense to couple voting rights to capital contributions to encourage the rich to join and contribute to the IMF. I recognise that this defence treads close to the line of saying that any voting structure that accepts as a given the political desire of rich states to have influence over poor states is an impartial one, and that it neglects the duty of those states to assist poor states by presumably lending money without controlling the recipients' use of it.

A contractarian approach might, however, reject the basic starting point of distributing votes based on wealth. If states did not know whether they would be rich or poor, their risk aversion might cause them to endorse a voting system that did not so directly penalise the poor. It is even conceivable that they would endorse an IMF with equal voting power for states. This Rawlsian argument does not, at this point, convince me that the IMF's criteria are partial or immoral insofar as the utilitarian argument seems particularly strong and the deontological arguments at least passable and not in contradiction with fundamental norms of human dignity.

At the same time, as with the Security Council, one particular distribution of votes need not accomplish that goal best or even particularly well. Indeed, the IMF is aware of this concern and in 2008 adjusted upward the quotas of what it calls the 'the most under-represented' members – China, Korea, Mexico and Turkey – and adopted new criteria for quotas 'to make quotas more responsive to economic realities while enhancing the participation and voice of low-income countries in the IMF's decision making'.[54] Prospects for tinkering with voting are all grounded in different forms of impartialist justification. As the IMF considers these proposals, it will be important to see which such arguments have the greatest political traction with member states.

Decision-making outcomes

Finally, we can ask whether institutions are playing favourites when they decide to exercise their authority over one set of problems but not another. How should an organisation's duties translate into particular decisions? Does, for instance, the United Nations have a duty to respond to mass atrocities in Darfur, Rwanda and Bosnia in

[54] IMF Quotas Factsheet, February 2009, www.imf.org/external/np/exc/facts/quotas.htm.

the same manner? Refraining from playing favourites does not require equal treatment for all states and individuals – just that they be treated as equals.[55]

Some duties of international organisations seem general on their face. The United Nations, through the Security Council, 'shall determine' whether there is a threat to the peace and breach of the peace and 'shall make recommendations or decide' what sort of action to take in response to them.[56] The Charter goes on to say that the Council 'may' take non-military measures or military measures, without any requirement that it do so in each case. These provisions give the Council flexibility to respond to situations as it chooses. Yet such flexibility does not by itself conflict with a general duty to act in *some* manner in the event of a threat to the peace. The UN also 'shall promote' high standards of living, solutions to economic problems and human rights.[57] These are obligations to all member states.

At the same time, the Charter regime does not consist only of a set of general duties. Chapter XII of the Charter, on the International Trusteeship System, obligates the organisation to 'promote the political, economic, social and educational advancement' and the 'progressive development towards self-government or independence' of peoples in the trust territories, an obligation it does not have towards other peoples – and most significantly, did not assume towards peoples living in bona fide colonies.[58] Yet ever since it became clear in the late 1940s that decolonisation was inevitable, the UN has assumed special obligations towards colonial peoples to promote their transition to independence, whether through election monitoring, technical assistance, or even transitional administration; and it has continued to assert special obligations to the states in the developing world. The UN's long-term focus on the peoples of Namibia, South Africa, or the Occupied Palestinian Territories stems from a sense among many member states that the Organisation has a special duty towards certain disempowered groups (though for other states it is merely a political axe to grind).

[55] R. Dworkin, *Taking Rights Seriously* (Cambridge, MA: Harvard University Press, 1977), 227.

[56] UN Charter, Article 39. [57] *Ibid.*, Article 55.

[58] Chapter XII is now a dead letter as all former trust territories have become independent states.

These special duties, however, can be grounded in an impartial rationale, indeed one that is widely shared by the member states. In the case of peoples under colonial occupation, states shared a sense of the illegitimacy of alien rule – in deontological terms, a flagrant violation of the Categorical Imperative. Indeed, we might even recast this duty as a general one that all states owe to all peoples, namely the duty to promote their self-determination.[59] States exercise this general duty in one way with respect to peoples in other existing states – by agreeing to leave them alone in the choice of their government or political structure (up to the point at which the latter start committing human rights violations) – and in another way with respect to peoples in colonial territories – through convincing imperial states to shed their colonies and assist colonial peoples in establishing new states.[60] At the same time, not all states saw their duties to help colonial peoples impartially. Some states, especially other former colonies, likely saw a tie with colonial peoples that itself created a special duty to them – e.g. certain African states' support for decolonisation (or elimination of apartheid in South Africa) came from a sense of community based on geographic proximity, race and shared history. From this perspective, these ties were morally significant enough to create duties to help certain oppressed people.

Textually grounded duties are, for international lawyers, at the core of how international organisations are supposed to act impartially. They do so when they act *according to law*, whether the law of their constitutive instrument or other international law. Acting according to law is not the responsibility of only judicial bodies, but of all international (and indeed domestic) institutions founded on law. Yet, as the example of the Security Council shows, international law, like other law, may be permissive or mandatory regarding the powers of international organisations. Impartiality takes on different contours with respect to these two possibilities.

(a) When international law *requires* an international organisation to act a certain way – regardless of whether that duty is general or special – we might be able to judge whether the organisation is acting impartially

[59] See Ratner, 'Is International Law Impartial?', 49–50, 52–3.

[60] This mirrors the international lawyer's understanding of the right of self-determination of peoples insofar as the right has different contours depending on the type of people (e.g. people of a state as a whole, people of a colony, minority group or indigenous people). See A. Cassese, *Self-Determination of Peoples: A Legal Reappraisal* (Cambridge University Press, 1995).

by simply seeing whether it fulfils that duty uniformly, treating all beneficiaries of the general duty the same and all beneficiaries of the special duty the same (though different from non-beneficiaries of the special duty). Yet the charters of organisations and other principles of international law are often so open-textured that they leave a huge room for discretion to the organisation. The Charter's requirement that the UN promote the 'political, economic, social and educational advancement' of peoples in Trust Territories – a special duty – provides a very amorphous standard on which to judge the impartiality of the UN's actions in different cases. Similarly, the Constitution of the International Labour Organisation obligates the ILO to 'further among the nations of the world programmes which will achieve … full employment and the raising of standards of living', a general duty, though one not specific enough to help much in any inquiry into the impartiality of the ILO's actions.

(b) When international law *authorises* an organisation to act in a certain way, the law itself does not provide any standard for judging impartiality. The Genocide Convention provides that 'Any Contracting Party may call upon the competent organs of the United Nations to take such action under the Charter of the United Nations as they consider appropriate for the prevention and suppression of acts of genocide', which some NGOs and states mistakenly interpret as an obligation on the UN to prevent and punish genocide but is clearly at best only authority for the UN to do so.[61] One cannot look to the Genocide Convention to determine if the UN is acting impartially to prevent genocide. That does not make permissive provisions of international law irrelevant to international organisations. The law can influence the UN's options by inviting various actions or channelling it in certain directions. Most of the Charter's provisions regarding the Security Council are authorisations rather than duties, but, as Rosalyn Higgins long ago observed, the Council's debates and resolutions show 'political operation *within* the law, rather than decision according *to* the law'.[62] But it does mean that the text will not be that helpful in judging the even-handedness of the

[61] Indeed, such authority is legally unnecessary or perhaps even legally invalid, as the Charter alone is the source of authority for the UN's organs.

[62] R. Higgins, 'The Place of International Law in the Settlement of Disputes by the Security Council', *American Journal of International Law*, 64 (1970), 1, 16; see also R. Keohane, *After Hegemony: Cooperation and Discord in the World Political Economy* (Princeton, NJ: Princeton University Press, 1984), 57–9.

organisation's decisions. In the end, whether international legal texts require or merely permit the organisation to act, they have limits as standards to determine whether international organisations are acting impartially.

The next best option, in my view, is to look past international norms to the general principle of law that like cases should be treated alike – again a principle not confined to judicial bodies – akin to the philosopher's notion of universalisability.[63] International affairs does not, as we know, afford any examples of identical or even very like cases, but this general principle nonetheless forces members and observers of international organisations to inquire continuously whether the disparate treatment the institutions afford different wars, economic crises, health emergencies, human rights atrocities, environmental problems and other situations are justified by the relevant differences between the cases and not other considerations. Thus, an impartial set of responses might turn on an objective evaluation of the scope of the crisis, whether in terms of human suffering or economic losses. I admit this proposition begs almost as many questions as it answers, including what counts as a relevant difference; my point is simply that it is probably the best question we can ask to judge if the organisation is picking favourites. We might not have a simple recipe for impartiality, but we will have some indicators of clear partiality or favouritism.

Thus, for example, among international law scholars, Christine Chinkin was highly critical of the Kosovo intervention, noting that 'the commitment to human rights that humanitarian intervention supposedly entails does not mean equality of rights worldwide. The human rights of some people are more worth protecting that those of others.'[64] She lamented the inadequate response of the Council to graver human rights catastrophes in Africa. Detlev Vagts, Jose Alvarez and Gerry Simpson have separately noted the link between the decision-making procedures of the Council discussed earlier and its failure to treat like cases alike. In the most obvious sense, the veto ensures that the permanent five 'enjoy complete de facto immunity from the enforcement jurisdiction of the Security Council'.[65] The permanent five's power not only ensures that

[63] See generally P. Cane, *Responsibility in Law and Morality* (Oxford: Hart Publishing, 2002), 15–28; Hare, *Freedom and Reason*.

[64] C. Chinkin, 'Kosovo: A "Good" or "Bad" War?', *American Journal of International Law*, 93 (1999), 841, 847.

[65] Simpson, *Great Powers*, 188.

certain matters will be off the Council's agenda or at least not the subject of a resolution; it also means that certain issues will dominate it. Thus Alvarez notes the practice of the Security Council in passing resolutions that respond principally to the concerns of the United States, which he calls an example of (in Vagts's words) 'hegemonic international law'.[66] From philosophy, David Held has offered a list of reforms of the UN – compulsory World Court jurisdiction over all inter-state and individual-state disputes, creation of law by a near consensus of the General Assembly (all of which he admits are unrealistic) – based on the idea that it would end the practice of double standards, thereby 'establishing and maintaining the "rule of law" and its impartial administration in international affairs'.[67]

International organisations are hardly unaware of these concerns. In 1991, as the UN began more intrusive peacekeeping operations to protect human rights – long before ideas of more robust measures such as in Somalia, Haiti or Kosovo – Secretary-General Javier Perez de Cuellar wrote:

> It seems to be beyond question that violations of human rights imperil peace, while disregard of the sovereignty of States would spell chaos. The maximum caution needs to be exercised lest the defence of human rights becomes a platform for encroaching on the essential domestic jurisdiction of States and eroding their sovereignty ... Some caveats are, therefore, most necessary ... The principle of protection of human rights cannot be invoked in a particular situation and disregarded in a similar one. To apply it selectively is to debase it. Governments can, and do, expose themselves to charges of deliberate bias; the United Nations cannot.[68]

Or, as the High-Level Panel stated in 2004:

> The credibility of any system of collective security also depends on how well it promotes security for all its members, without regard to the nature

[66] J. Alvarez, 'Hegemonic International Law Revisited', *American Journal of International Law*, 93 (2004), 873.

[67] D. Held, 'Democracy and the New International Order' in D. Archibugi and D. Held (eds.), *Cosmopolitan Democracy: An Agenda for a New World Order* (Cambridge, MA: Polity Press, 1995), 96–107; see also D. Held, 'Cosmopolitanism: Globalization Tamed?', *Review of International Studies*, 29 (2003), 465, 475 ('The susceptibility of the UN to the agendas of the most powerful states ... [is] indicative of the disjuncture between cosmopolitan aspirations and their partial and one-sided application'). I remain highly sceptical of proposals from Held, Caney and others that enhanced power to the International Court of Justice will promote cosmopolitanism in light of the institutional conservatism of that body as reflected in many of its rulings.

[68] *Report of the Secretary-General on the Work of the Organization*, 13 Sept. 1991, 5, UN Doc. A/46/1 (1991).

> of would-be beneficiaries, their location, resources or relationship to great Powers.
>
> Too often, the United Nations and its Member States have discriminated in responding to threats to international security. Contrast the swiftness with which the United Nations responded to the attacks on 11 September 2001 with its actions when confronted with a far more deadly event: from April to mid-July 1994, Rwanda experienced the equivalent of three 11 September 2001 attacks every day for 100 days, all in a country whose population was one thirty-sixth that of the United States.[69]

Nonetheless, claims about selectivity or bias need to be parsed with care, for they can often be a guilty party's first defence against justifiable measures (the reason courts routinely reject them in criminal cases). The Sudanese government's claims that the UN is unfairly singling it out for Darfur through condemnations, the deployment of UN missions or the International Criminal Court's indictment of its president need not be accepted at face value. Sudan might be comparing its treatment with that of less grave situations, in which case the government is asking that unlike cases be treated alike (i.e. through non-action).

Moreover, even if Sudan is comparing its situation to equally grave or worse violations where the UN has not acted (as Chinkin does), we cannot simply say that the most just outcome is inaction in all cases. In other words, some selectivity or partiality, even if merely the result of a confluence of political interests, may advance the purposes of an international organisation (which I have assumed are morally defensible) better than the application of pure even-handedness if the latter means perpetual inaction in the face of situations that the organisation is supposed to address. International organisations, whether composed of states, or, in more far-sighted proposals, of individuals or other non-state actors, are still likely to pick targets with politics in mind as much as law. International lawyers can no more tell them to be consistent than can diplomats.

An act-utilitarian rationale for such politically motivated action would be easy, assuming welfare is overall improved as a result of a particular UN involvement, regardless of what happens in other cases. It is also possible that the Council's resolutions, passed in the context of situation X due to a confluence of political factors, will be invoked by others – not the Council – in the context of situation Y. This pattern of shifting arenas

[69] *A More Secure World*, paras. 40–1.

for invocation of norms is common in international law. But, at the same time, if these are the only possible rationales, we seem to have moved away from the nature of international organisations as creatures of law, for which some consistency in decision-making is needed. This difficult problem, beyond the scope of this chapter, raises the possibility that the individual decision of an international organisation may be morally justifiable, while the overall pattern of conduct is impossible to justify impartially and thus morally suspect (somewhat like the problem of giving charity only to the poor members of one race). As a practical matter, inconsistency is not necessarily crippling to an international institution. The UN Security Council continues to enjoy significant legitimacy among most states despite its membership problems and the inconsistent and unprincipled way in which it often acts.

Does, then, the UN have special duties to certain victims of catastrophes over others? On the one hand, the Charter and other international laws do not specify such duties. Indeed, as can be seen above, the main complaint about the UN from within and without is that it has not acted consistently pursuant to its general duties in the human rights area – duties that, alas, are scarcely mentioned in the Charter but have been accepted over time, most recently in the UN's Millennium+5 Summit Declaration's on the Responsibility to Protect.[70]

On the other hand, global decision makers do seem to increasingly accept that certain sorts of situations ought to trigger some UN action – that it has special duties towards certain particularly aggrieved individuals. Various committees of world leaders, including the Secretary-General's High Level Panel and the International Commission on Intervention and State Sovereignty, have focused on the most controversial response to such suffering, involving humanitarian-oriented military action. They have justified special duties from a second-order impartial perspective by offering a series of criteria for lawful intervention, much of it borrowing from just war theory and incorporating deontological and utilitarian

[70] Though even this commitment is watered down (para. 139): 'The international community, through the United Nations, also has the responsibility to use appropriate diplomatic, humanitarian and other peaceful means … to help to protect populations from genocide, war crimes, ethnic cleansing and crimes against humanity. In this context, we are prepared to take collective action, in a timely and decisive manner, through the Security Council, in accordance with the Charter, including Chapter VII, on a case-by-case basis and in cooperation with relevant regional organizations as appropriate, should peaceful means be inadequate and national authorities are manifestly failing to protect their populations from genocide, war crimes, ethnic cleansing and crimes against humanity.'

justifications and limitations.[71] David Miller has offered a useful framework, combining both partialist and impartialist accounts, for considering how to allocate responsibilities of moral agents to remedy bad situations, and Allen Buchanan has offered a defence of humanitarian intervention from a cosmopolitan perspective with keen regard for the institutional constraints.[72] While I believe that any duties must be general or second-order impartial, I have not yet decided whether the difference between those two options will do any practical work in helping us devise the best norms to overcome the current problem of playing favourites.

Conclusion

The foregoing inquiry into the impartiality of international organisations in admission, decision-making procedures and outcomes for action suggests that appraisal of international organisations needs to move beyond knee-jerk opposition to unequal treatment. Instead, it suggests that international organisations may have legitimate reasons to make distinctions in whom they admit, who will decide how they act and what will be the target of their decisions. The challenge for those who seek to reform institutions is first to carefully consider what exactly is wrong with them and to be forthright in the assumptions they make in their criticisms. Reconstruction must be tailored to the individual problem at issue.

At the same time, my project is essentially a comparative and relative exercise – it asks how institutions treat one set of actors or situations compared to another. As such, it leaves unanswered many questions about the justice of the norms enforced by the organisations (e.g. the international trading rules) or the specific substantive decisions undertaken. It does not ask whether the norms or decisions conform to some notion of distributive justice or even whether they actually advance fundamental community goals like preservation of the planet from environmental catastrophe or nuclear disaster. The conceptualisation of international institutions in terms of general and special rights and duties and the nature of the impartiality inquiry may lead some to conclude that my approach is rather thin and unhelpful on the core

71 *A More Secure World*, para. 207; *The Responsibility to Protect: Report of the International Commission on Intervention and State Sovereignty* (2001), at www.iciss.ca/report-en.asp.

72 D. Miller, 'Distributing Responsibilities', *Journal of Political Phiosophy*, 9 (2001), 453; Buchanan, *Justice*.

questions. In the end, this chapter does not even conclude definitively whether all the various second-order impartialist accounts are convincing arguments – a necessary part of any determination about the impartiality and justice of institutions. Indeed, there is always some second-order impartial argument (probably of a utilitarian nature) to defend the status quo – although utilitarian claims rebutted by empirical data are easily dismissed. I have not yet worked out a theory to distinguish between all the convincing impartialist arguments and all the unconvincing ones.[73]

Yet I believe my work is complementary to that of theorists such as Held, Caney or Buchanan, who have begun to address these issues (in their case, all from a cosmopolitan perspective) and proposed strategies of institutional reform. Even if it is a thin theory of international morality and even if it does not yet answer which organisations are just, it still acts as a check on some of the claims that international organisations are unjust and channels proposals for reform in a direction that takes cognisance of the achievements in institutionalisation realised to date. It also offers a lodestar for considerations for reform, for even if impartial action is not a sufficient criterion for a just international institution, it is a necessary one.

References

Alvarez, J. 2004. 'Hegemonic International Law Revisited', *American Journal of International Law* 93: 873–77.

Archibugi, D. 1993. 'The Reform of the UN and Cosmopolitan Democracy: A Critical Review', *Journal of Peace Research* 30: 301–15.

Baron, M. 1991. 'Impartiality and Friendship', *Ethics* 101: 836–57.

Barry, B. 1995. *Justice as Impartiality*. Oxford: Clarendon Press.

Barry, C. and Pogge, T. W. (eds.) 2005. *Global Institutions and Responsibilities*. Malden, MA: Blackwell.

Becker, L. C. 1991. 'Impartiality and Ethical Theory', *Ethics* 101: 698–700.

Bodansky, D. 1999. 'The Legitimacy of International Governance: A Coming Challenge for International Environmental Law?', *American Journal of International Law* 93: 596–624.

Buchanan, A. 2004. *Justice, Legitimacy, and Self-Determination*. Oxford University Press.

Cane, P. 2002. *Responsibility in Law and Morality*. Oxford: Hart Publishing.

Caney, S. 2005. *Justice Beyond Borders: A Global Political Theory*. Oxford University Press.

[73] I appreciate this insight from Neil Netanel and Gerald Lopez.

Caron, D. 1993. 'The Legitimacy of the Collective Authority of the Security Council', *American Journal of International Law* 87: 552–88.

Cassese, A. 1995. *Self-Determination of Peoples: A Legal Reappraisal.* Cambridge University Press.

Chinkin, C. 1999. 'Kosovo: A "Good" or "Bad" War?', *American Journal of International Law* 93: 841–7.

Dworkin, R. 1977. *Taking Rights Seriously.* Cambridge, MA: Harvard University Press.

Franck, T. 1990. *The Power of Legitimacy Among Nations.* Oxford University Press.

Franck, T. 1997. *Fairness in International Law and Institutions.* Oxford University Press.

Gewirth, A. 1988. 'Ethical Universalism and Particularism', *Journal of Philosophy* 85: 283–302.

Goodin, R. 1985. *Protecting the Vulnerable: A Reanalysis of Our Social Responsibilities.* University of Chicago Press.

Goodin, R. 1988. 'What Is So Special About Our Fellow Countrymen?', *Ethics* 98: 663–86.

Hare, R. M. 1963. *Freedom and Reason.* Oxford: Clarendon Press.

Hart, H. L. A. 1961. *The Concept of Law.* Oxford: Clarendon Press.

Held, D. 1995. 'Democracy and the New International Order', in Archibugi, D. and Held, D. (eds.), *Cosmopolitan Democracy: An Agenda for a New World Order.* Cambridge, MA: Polity Press, 96–120.

Held, D. 2003. 'Cosmopolitanism: Globalization Tamed?', *Review of International Studies* 29: 465–80.

Held, D. 2005. 'Democratic Accountability and Political Effectiveness from a Cosmopolitan Perspective', in Held, D. and Archibugi, M. (eds.), *Global Governance and Public Accountability.* Oxford: Blackwell, 240–67.

Higgins, R. 1970. 'The Place of International Law in the Settlement of Disputes by the Security Council', *American Journal of International Law* 64: 1–18.

High Level Panel on Threats, Challenges and Change. 2004. *A More Secure World: Our Shared Responsibility: Report of the High-Level Panel on Threats, Challenges and Change.*

Hurrell, A. 2003. 'International Law and the Making and Unmaking of Boundaries', in Buchanan, A. and Moore, M. (eds.), *States, Nations, and Borders: The Ethics of Making Boundaries.* Cambridge University Press, 275–97.

Ikenberry, J. and Slaughter, A. M. (eds.) 2006. *Forging A World of Liberty Under Law.* Princeton University.

Kant, I. 1991. 'Perpetual Peace: A Philosophical Sketch', in Reiss H. (ed.) and Nisbet, H. B. (trans.), *Kant: Political Writings, 2nd edn.* Cambridge University Press, 93–130.

Keohane, R. 1984. *After Hegemony: Cooperation and Discord in the World Political Economy*. Princeton University Press.

Mendus, S. 2002. *Impartiality in Moral and Political Philosophy*. Oxford University Press.

Miller, D. 1995. *On Nationality*. Oxford University Press.

Miller, D. 2001. 'Distributing Responsibilities', *Journal of Political Philosophy* 9: 453–71.

Nardin, T. 1983. *Law, Morality, and the Relations of States*. Princeton University Press.

Newburg, A. 2000. 'The Changing Roles of the Bretton Woods Institutions: Evolving Concepts of Conditionality', in Giovanoli, M. (ed.), *International Monetary Law: Issues for the New Millennium*. Oxford University Press, 81–96.

Oldenquist, A. 1982. 'Loyalties', *Journal of Philosophy* 79: 173–93.

Pogge, T. W. 1992. 'Cosmopolitanism and Sovereignty', *Ethics* 103: 48–75

Ratner, S. R. 2005. 'Is International Law Impartial?', *Legal Theory* 11: 39–74.

Rawls, J. 1999. *The Law of Peoples*. Cambridge, MA: Harvard University Press.

Scheffler, S. 1997. 'Relationships and Responsibilities', *Philosophy and Public Affairs* 26: 189–209.

Schlesinger, S. 2003. *Act of Creation: The Founding of the United Nations*. Boulder, CO: Westview Press.

Simma, B. (ed.) 2002. *The Charter of the United Nations: A Commentary*. Oxford University Press.

Simpson, G. 2004. *Great Powers and Outlaw States*. Cambridge University Press.

Tamir, Y. 1993. *Liberal Nationalism*. Princeton University Press.

Walzer, M. 1983. *Spheres of Justice*. New York: Basic Books.

Wellman, C. H. 2000. 'Relational Facts in Liberal Political Theory: Is There Magic in the Pronoun "My"?', *Ethics* 110: 537–62.

Williams, B. 1981. 'Persons, Character and Morality', in *Moral Luck*. Cambridge University Press, 1–19.

Williams, M. 1994. *International Economic Organisations and the Third World*. London: Harvester Wheatsheaf.

5

'Victors' justice'? Historic injustice and the legitimacy of international law

DANIEL BUTT

Thomas Nagel has recently written, 'We do not live in a just world. This may be the least controversial claim one could make in political theory.'[1] Nowhere does this seem more clear than in the field of international justice. In recent years, political theorists have put forward a range of accounts of how international society should, ideally, be ordered. Whilst there is disagreement as to what a just world would look like, defences of the justice of the status quo are few and far between. Even those writers who deny that redistributive duties of justice extend across state borders and who believe that it is appropriate that peoples take responsibility for the results of their own decision-making typically accept the existence of transnational duties to ensure minimal levels of wellbeing for the world's poor – duties which, tragically, are clearly not being fulfilled in the present day. Such judgments as to the injustice of the real world international situation, however, do not necessarily extend to present-day principles of international law, which contain at least formal provisions for the fulfilment of minimal socio-economic rights, whilst privileging ideas of national responsibility and self-determination. In this chapter, I consider the relation between the injustice of contemporary international society and the legitimacy of international law. The chapter is motivated by the thought that the existing international legal system is unfair. The history of its development is, in some ways, one whereby Western powers, who were historically responsible for extensive wrongdoing, shaped international law so as to secure and

For comments on this paper, I am grateful to Rahul Kumar, Chris Brooke and an anonymous reviewer, and to audiences at the Nuffield College Political Theory Workshop in Oxford and the International Symposium on Justice, Legitimacy and Public International Law in Bern.

[1] T. Nagel, 'The Problem of Global Justice', *Philosophy and Public Affairs*, 33 (2005), 113–47 at 113.

legitimate their own advantages – advantages which were often improperly obtained. The chapter is divided into two parts. The first part argues that the current international legal system is unjust, in terms of how existing international law endorses and perpetuates an unjust distribution of resources between states. I argue that this claim should be accepted from two prominent, and rather different, perspectives on international ethics. The second part holds that this injustice calls the legitimacy of international law into question.

Justice and international law

Many feel that contemporary international law is a good thing. Insofar as it contains provisions which, for example, seek to advance peaceful conflict resolution, or to delineate and promote certain basic human rights, the development of international law is commonly portrayed as positive, and conducive to the progress of civilisation.[2] Certainly, the nature and scope (both actual and desirable) of international law is controversial. Theorists disagree over the extent to which the consent of each and every state of the world is necessary for a given norm or proposal to be understood as a principle of international law, with universal applicability. An obvious potential conflict emerges with the collective self-determination of particular peoples, and some maintain that international law can represent the imposition of a particularly Western, liberal worldview upon communities with different traditions and values. But it does seem that a consensus has emerged around certain key principles of international law, most notably those which respect national sovereignty, other than in cases of human rights abuses, and prohibit certain violent forms of international interaction, such as attacking another country in order to expand one's own territory or gain access to resources.[3] One way of viewing the development of international law, then, is as a positive development which seeks to prevent

[2] See, for example, the American Society of International Law's publication, *International Law: 100 Ways It Shapes Our Lives* (available at www.asil.org/files/asil_100_ways_05.pdf). This takes its inspiration 'from the proposition that international law not only exists, but also penetrates much more deeply and broadly into everyday life than the people it affects may generally appreciate', and so lists 100 ways in which international law has an appreciable impact on modern day individuals' everyday lives. It is striking that every example listed portrays the development of international law in a positive light.

[3] See Michael Walzer's account of the 'legalistic paradigm' in *Just and Unjust Wars* (New York: Basic Books, 1977).

such serious harm to basic interests. But this need not be taken as endorsing the substantive justice of the international legal system. The claim that international law has helped to make the world a better place in terms of justice is not incompatible with the claims, first, that the world is still deeply unjust, and second, that this injustice is endorsed and perpetuated by our current system of international law. Even if certain forms of immoral, human rights infringing interaction between states are now prohibited by international law, we are, on some accounts, a long way from realising distributive justice between states. Although the extent to which modern-day states are independent sovereign entities has certainly changed in recent years, with significant limitations being placed on states' ability to run their own affairs in a number of policy areas,[4] the defining characteristic of international law in terms of distributive justice is still the sovereignty which states have over their own borders in two critical respects: in relation to control of their resource holdings, and to immigration policy. As will be seen, this is problematic from two rather different approaches to international distributive justice. From both perspectives, it will be argued, international resource holdings are unjust. Individuals and groups in one state have entitlements to resources currently controlled, according to the tenets of international law, by others. These entitlements are enforceable claims on others, based in distributive justice. International law, however, positively upholds an alternative distributive scheme, and backs this scheme by the use of coercive force. This means that international law is unjust – and calls its legitimacy into question.

For those who hold forward-looking, redistributive accounts of international distributive justice, the claim that the distributive scheme sanctioned by international law is unjust is straightforward. The key factor is the paucity of redistributive mechanisms between states. What international law certainly does not do is to require a redistribution of resources across national boundaries so as to bring about a particular distributive pattern, such as equality, or priority for the worst off. One perspective from which this is obviously problematic is that of egalitarian cosmopolitanism. Advocates of cosmopolitanism maintain that national boundaries are not of ethical significance in terms of distributive justice. Cosmopolitan writers who advocate extensive redistribution of resources at

[4] See D. Held, 'The Changing Structure of International Law: Sovereignty Transformed?' in D. Held and A. G. McGrew (eds.), *The Global Transformations Reader* (Cambridge: Polity, 2003), 162–76.

a domestic level will typically argue for the same kind of redistribution across communities. Such a redistributive position may be founded on a view of the extensive nature of international interdependence in a globalised era, maintaining that the world should be seen as a single scheme of social cooperation. Or one can simply maintain that persons have equal moral worth, and as such are entitled to equal concern and respect regardless of their national background. On either account, redistributive cosmopolitans must seemingly condemn the distributive implications of contemporary international law. As Buchanan notes, 'some would argue that the control over resources that international law accords to states as an element of sovereignty is the single greatest impediment to eradicating the most grievous distributive injustice in our world – the vast disparity of wealth between the "developed" and the "underdeveloped" countries'.[5]

Condemning the distributive implications of international law in terms of ideal theory on this basis is a relatively straightforward business. But there is another school of thought within the literature on international distributive justice which appears to be more sympathetic to the vision of global justice reflected in international law. This position has been described in a number of ways, the most well-known perhaps being that of Charles Beitz, who labels advocates as 'social liberals', in contrast to 'cosmopolitan liberals'.[6] I have elsewhere described this position as 'international libertarianism', as I suggest that those within this school adopt principles of distributive justice between states which are analogous to those principles of justice which libertarians such as Robert Nozick maintain should obtain between individuals in domestic society.[7] Such accounts typically stress the importance of national sovereignty, understood as the (perhaps limited) right collectively to govern oneself free from external interference, of self-ownership, understood in terms of entitlement to one's own territory and resources, and of a minimal or highly limited state at an international level. International libertarians adopt an intermediate position on international ethics between redistributive cosmopolitanism and prescriptive realism, whereby one accepts that states have duties towards one another without accepting that these are analogous to domestic relations of justice within a particular

[5] A. Buchanan, *Justice, Legitimacy, and Self-Determination: Moral Foundations for International Law* (Oxford University Press, 2004), 53.

[6] C. Beitz, 'Social and Cosmopolitan Liberalism', *International Affairs*, 75 (1999), 515–29.

[7] See D. Butt, *Rectifying International Injustice: Principles of Compensation and Between Nations* (Oxford University Press, 2009).

polity.[8] The detail of these principles differs, but it is possible to identify a core shared by the different accounts. The key to the core principles is a respect for national sovereignty and self-determination and a commitment to the basic principles of existing international law. In particular, one might identify two principles common to these accounts:

(1) States should refrain from forceful intervention in the affairs of other states, other than i) when acting in response to aggression, or ii) to prevent human rights violations.
(2) States should comply with voluntarily made treaties and agreements.

These core principles are often supplemented by further, complementary principles which have the effect of making the account more demanding. For example: one might maintain that states have a duty not to harm other states (in a broader sense than in (1) above); that they have a duty not to exploit other states; and that they have duties of assistance to those who lack some basic minimum level of subsistence. The key theme that such accounts possess in terms of distributive justice is that the redistribution they require is, at best, limited. So, for example, while Rawls argues that, 'Peoples have a duty to assist other peoples living under unfavorable conditions that prevent their having a just or decent political and social regime',[9] he explicitly contrasts his position with that of the redistributive cosmopolitans on this point. Duties of assistance only apply insofar as other societies are unable to realise just institutions: 'Once that end is reached, the Law of Peoples prescribes no further target such as, for example, to raise the standard of living beyond what is necessary to sustain those institutions.'[10] In opposing patterned redistribution across national boundaries in the name of national self-determination, or by denying that distributive justice applies in an international context due to the absence of a particular kind of relation between members and non-members of the state, international libertarians endorse backward-looking principles of distributive justice whereby there is no requirement of justice to redistribute resources across state borders with each new generation.

[8] Examples include J. Rawls, *The Law of Peoples* (Cambridge, MA and London: Harvard University Press, 1999), 37; Walzer, *Just and Unjust Wars*, 61–3 and 108; D. Miller, *On Nationality* (Oxford: Clarendon, 1995), 104–5; Nagel, 'The Problem of Global Justice', 130–2; M. Frost, *Ethics in International Relations* (Cambridge University Press, 1996), 106–10; T. Nardin, *Law, Morality and the Relations of States* (Princeton University Press, 1983), 269–70.

[9] Rawls, *The Law of Peoples*, 37. For discussion, see 105–20.

[10] Rawls, *The Law of Peoples*, 119.

The principles of justice advocated by international libertarians seem very close to those enshrined in existing international law. It might, then, be supposed that an advocate of such an approach would reject the claim that international law is unjust in terms of distributive justice. However, this would be a mistake. The problem with existing international law for international libertarians is that it does not take sufficient account of unrectified historic injustice. Some discussion of the more familiar account of Nozickian libertarianism, based upon historical entitlement, may be helpful here. Nozick famously outlines three principles of distributive justice: the principle of just acquisition, by which individuals can come to possess property rights over objects; the principle of justice in transfer, by which entitlement to properly acquired property can be transferred from one individual to another; and the principle of rectification, by which illegitimate transfers of property are to be corrected.[11] The consequence of Nozick's political theory is that it is *possible* for a society characterised by extreme distributive inequality to come about in keeping with the principles of justice. It follows that subsequent attempts by the state to redistribute property from one party to another will be illegitimate insofar as doing so ignores the justly acquired entitlements of property owners. Such a policy disregards the history by which the distribution came about, treating resources as if they were 'manna from heaven'. But it does not follow from this that we need see Nozick as endorsing the actual distributions which we find in modern-day societies. There is no reason to think that such distributions came about in keeping with the principles of justice in acquisition and transfer, since we recognise the pervasive injustice which has characterised how present-day real world holdings have come about. So real world holdings look open to challenge under the principle of rectification. Nozick saw this clearly. He accepts that it might be best to see some patterned principles of distributive justice as 'rough rules of thumb meant to approximate the general results of applying the principle of rectification of injustice'. On the basis of particular empirical assumptions, one might even end up endorsing a one-off version of the difference principle. An important question for each society will be: 'given *its* particular history, what operable rule of thumb best approximates the results of a detailed application in that society of the principle of rectification?'.[12] He concludes that, 'although to introduce socialism as the punishment for our

[11] R. Nozick, *Anarchy, State, and Utopia* (New York: Basic Books, 1974), 150–3.

[12] Nozick, *Anarchy, State, and Utopia*, 231 (Nozick's emphasis).

sins would be to go too far', it is possible that the extent of past injustices is so great as to justify a more extensive, redistributive state in the short run. In other words, his theory does not legitimate real world contemporary property holdings and shield them from a redistributive state.

The parallel with the international situation should now be clear. From an international libertarian perspective, insofar as international law has not accepted the existence of obligations to rectify historic injustice, it endorses and legitimates arbitrariness and injustice in distribution. It is a defining feature of international law, as it has developed through agreed treaties between nations and by international customary practice, that it does not have retroactive effect.[13] This is made clear by, for example, Article 28 of the 1969 Vienna Convention of the Law of Treaties, which holds, 'Unless a different intention appears from the treaty or is otherwise established, its provisions do not bind a party in relation to any act or fact which took place or any situation which ceased to exist before the date of the entry into force of the treaty with respect to that party'.[14] International law serves to constrain and direct future actions and provide redress when acts of international injustice are committed *once these are illegal.* But there is no redress provided for the victims of injustice perpetrated prior to the passage of the legislation in question.[15] In a domestic case, and, in particular, in a society already governed by the rule of law, there are good reasons for the principle of

[13] This chapter employs a predominantly positivist conception of international law, which holds that the content of law is determined by its positive provisions, as enshrined in its formulation in written international law and in authoritative international legal norms and conventions. One could argue from a natural law perspective that international law is actually significantly different in content from its current positive formulation, and thus even suggest that international law properly understood allows for the rectification of historic injustice. Such a view does not affect the substance of my argument, which then becomes the claim that international law as *currently interpreted* is unjust, and may be illegitimate.

[14] Article 28: Non-Retroactivity of Treaties, *Vienna Convention on the Law of Treaties* (1969), available at http://untreaty.un.org/ilc/texts/instruments/english/conventions/1_1_1969.pdf (accessed 21 November 2008).

[15] It is sometimes suggested that the development of the legal category of 'crimes against humanity' at the Nuremberg Trial following the Second World War, under Article 6 of the *Charter of the International Military Tribunal*, represented the development of ex post facto law with retroactive effect. This is far from clear, however, and is probably better seen as a conceptualisation of a particular kind of illegal action: the Judgment of the Tribunal makes specific reference to the principle of *nullum crinem sine lege*, and invokes existing international conventions and particular international treaties, such as the Geneva Conventions. Thus Iu. A. Reshetov writes: 'The well-known principle of justice barring the retroactive effect of the law thus possesses its own substantive peculiarities in international law. These

nullum crimen sine lege, which holds that laws do not have retroactive effect, since there is an obvious danger that individuals will be punished for good faith actions, performed at a time when there was little or no suggestion that the actions in question would subsequently be criminalised. Such a situation would clearly create a highly damaging atmosphere of doubt and insecurity. But when one considers the retroactive illegalisation of seriously unjust, harmful actions, where the relevant sanctions are not so much punitive as restitutive or compensatory and apply to sizeable collectives rather than to individuals, the situation is rather different. The injustice of the historic international action in question does not lie in its unlawfulness, but rather in its unacceptable harmful effects on individuals' interests. Rectificatory duties for such actions would be owed in the absence of any international law whatsoever. In such a context, drawing a line under unrectified injustices and merely requiring that future interaction be just does not necessarily serve the ends of justice.

It is easy to think of situations where the introduction of a rule forbidding certain kinds of harmful interaction without attempts being made to reverse the effects of previous harmful interaction has absurd and unjust consequences. Imagine a case where two communities, each with an equal share of resources, live unknown to each other on two sides of a river. As such, they have no rules of any kind, formal or customary, regulating their interaction. One day, a log jams across the river, forming a bridge. The residents of community A cross the log to explore, and carry off a large part of the property of community B. B protests, and so A proposes a new rule, whereby no resources shall be taken from within the territory of either community without the consent of the elders. Such an outcome will evidently be unjust if it is not accompanied by the return of the misappropriated property. This is so even if (i) the introduction of the rule improves the situation overall, including from B's perspective, and (ii) B consents to the rule in question. This latter point is important,

particularities do not boil down to the establishment of a specific sanction already after the commission of corresponding acts. If the criminal nature of that sort of act is already established by international law, then the pinpointing of the objective side of the crime, that is, the criminal effects proper, can be effected later as well. This occurred at Nuremberg … where the Charter of the International Military Tribunal was elaborated … after the factual commission of acts which, however, long before that were recognised as criminal.' Iu. A. Reshetov, 'The Temporal Operation of Norms on Criminal Responsibility' in G. Ginsburg and V. N. Kudriavtsev (eds.), *The Nuremberg Trial and International Law* (Dordecht: Martinus Nijhoff, 1990), 111–17 at 114. For further discussion of the principle of *nullum crinem sine lege* in international law, see M. Boot, *Nullum Crimen Sine Lege and the Subject Matter Jurisdiction of the International Criminal Court* (Antwerpen: Intersentia, 2002), 18–21.

since it means that one cannot point to the fact of agreement between parties that a line be drawn under the past to resist the claim that justice requires rectification of the injustice perpetrated prior to the agreement in question. It might well be that, without the introduction of the rule, the two communities would engage in a self-perpetuating series of raids on each other's property, leaving both worse off than if the rule is introduced. Or it might be that B is weaker, or just less willing to enter into violent conflict, than A, and so faces the threat of further incursions into its territory if it does not consent to the rule. Such possibilities explain why B may well agree to the introduction of the rule, but also serve to make the obvious point that consent is not sufficient to render an outcome, or a system of rules, just. This is important given the prominence which arguments concerning consent, evidenced by treaty agreements, have traditionally been afforded in the literature on the legitimacy of international law. But as Mattias Kumm notes, 'it is doubtful that much legitimating value can be placed on a state's consent to a treaty, when the state is confronted with a take it or leave it option and the costs of not participating are prohibitively high'.[16] It is commonly asserted that when consent takes place in a context of coercion or threat, the justifiability of the ensuing outcomes cannot be taken for granted. The historic evidence of widespread international injustice, and the relative prominence and bargaining power of precisely those countries most responsible for the commission of said injustice in the development of international law, is sufficient to call into question the justificatory force of consent in international law. International law was developed on the terms of the affluent states, and shaped in their interests. The claim that the principles of international law which lack retroactive effect were consented to by those who were victims of historic injustice does not confer justifiability upon the outcome. The fact that international law endorses and perpetuates distributive injustice does not mean that it has not been a good thing, compared to a counterfactual where no such rules were developed. But it has not been as good as it could or should have been. Insofar as one believes that uncorrected distributive injustices obtain between states, the lack of provision in international law for the righting of these wrongs renders the international legal system unjust. Thus, from the perspectives of both cosmopolitan liberalism and social liberalism, the current international legal order is unjust. For cosmopolitan liberals, it is

[16] M. Kumm, 'The Legitimacy of International Law: a Constitutionalist Framework of Analysis', *The European Journal of International Law*, 15 (2004), 907–31 at 914.

insufficiently forward-looking. For social liberals, it is not backward-looking enough.

Legitimacy and international law

I have argued that existing international law endorses and perpetuates distributive injustice, that its claims to rest upon consent are problematic, and that the world would be more just if some of its provisions were radically reshaped so as to allow for the righting of the lasting effects of historic wrongs. Does this mean that international law is illegitimate? Not necessarily. International law is not solely a set of rules determining the distribution of resources. It also governs the international arena more generally, seeking to regulate how states treat their own citizens, and those of other countries. We might hope that international law reduces or minimises the incidence of violence and war, and prevents a range of actions which could lead to greater distributive injustice than if it did not exist. So there are reasons both of justice in a broad sense, and of distributive justice specifically, to think that, at the very least, the existence of international law is an improvement on what went before. In domestic state of nature arguments, it is often the rich who are portrayed as benefiting particularly from the introduction of law, since without the law they could be set upon by the poor.[17] The principle of equal vulnerability played a key role in Hobbes's account in *Leviathan*. Such suggestions are less plausible in an international context, where rich states are able to defend themselves by means of military technology with a rather greater assurance than was available to the rich in Hobbes's state of nature. The claim that existing international law, though endorsing distributive injustice, furthers justice in a broad sense is a plausible one. This second section therefore scrutinises the claim that the existence of unrectified historic injustice calls into question the legitimacy of international law by looking at the role of justice in contemporary accounts of legitimacy. In addressing this issue, we must confront the variety of meaning which different theorists have attached to the idea of 'legitimacy'. For example, A. John Simmons has written at length on the

[17] See, for example Jean-Jacques Rousseau's discussion of the development of positive law in 'Discourse on the Origin of Inequality', in G. D. H. Cole (trans.), *The Social Contract and the Discourses* (London: Everyman, 1993), 96–9, and A. Smith, *An Inquiry into the Nature and Causes of the Wealth of Nations*, A. S. Skinner and R. H. Campbell (eds.) (Oxford University Press, 1981), 715.

desirability of keeping the terms 'justification' and 'legitimacy' separate. He notes that many contemporary political theorists run the two ideas together, citing (amongst others) Nagel's claim that, 'the task of discovering the conditions of *legitimacy* is traditionally conceived as that of finding a way to *justify* a political system to everyone who is required to live under it', as well as Rawls's statement that 'the basic structure and its public policies are to be *justifiable* to all citizens, as the principle of political *legitimacy* requires', and Leslie Green's stark statement that 'a state is *legitimate* only if, all things considered, its rule is morally *justified*'.[18] Instead, Simmons argues for a strong Lockean notion of legitimacy, understood as the right of the state to direct, be obeyed by, and coerce subjects:

> Legitimacy ... is the exclusive moral right of an institution to impose on some group of persons binding duties, to be obeyed by those persons, and to enforce those duties coercively. Legitimacy is thus the logical correlate of the (defeasible) individual obligation to comply with the lawfully imposed duties that flow from the legitimate institution's processes.[19]

The question, for Simmons, of whether the state is justified in acting in a particular way is quite distinct from the issue of whether it has a specific kind of relationship with those subject to it which gives citizens reason to obey the state's commands just because they are the commands of the state. There are two distinct normative issues in play here. When we ask whether a given system of law is legitimate, we may be asking one of two questions:

(1) Is it justifiable for state actors to impose this system of law on persons?
(2) Do those subject to the law possess a correlative duty to obey the law in question?

These questions are distinct, since it is possible to maintain that a system of law is justified in the sense that it is morally permissible (or, perhaps, even morally obligatory) for institutional actors to impose it upon those subject to it, whilst also maintaining that those subject to the law in question may justifiably refuse to obey its commands (when they can do so without violating any other independent moral duties, for example). There is no incoherence in thinking that a given state acts justifiably in imposing a particular traffic law on all those in its territory, and

[18] A. J. Simmons, *Justification and Legitimacy: Essays on Rights and Obligations* (Cambridge University Press, 2001), 141 (Simmons's emphasis).
[19] Simmons, *Justification and Legitimacy*, 154.

punishing all those it catches breaking the law so that the law is not undermined, whilst maintaining that those subject to the law can justifiably break the law when they can do so without risking harm to others. Rather than stipulatively maintaining that legitimacy need or not need refer to (2) as well as to (1), I shall refer to positive answers to (1) as relating to 'thin legitimacy', and positive answers to (2) as referring to 'thick legitimacy'. Thus, a system of law possesses thin legitimacy insofar as it is morally justifiable for institutional actors coercively to impose its requirements, and thick legitimacy insofar as those subject to the law possess a political obligation to obey the law. Both of these are pressing questions in relation to international law. Consider, for example, immigration restrictions, whereby states use coercive force to prevent non-nationals from entering the state's territory without the state's permission. Are these actions morally justifiable? Do those who wish to enter the state in question but who are refused permission face an obligation to comply with the state's lawful decision? We need an account of the nature of the legitimacy of international law, which tells us a) whether it exists, and b) if so, whether it is thick or thin legitimacy, in order to answer these questions.

How, then, might a system of law come to possess legitimacy? Traditional accounts of thick legitimacy typically make reference to the consent of the governed. John Simmons, for example, maintains that 'the proper grounds for claims of legitimacy concern the transactional components of the specific relationship between individual and institution'. The way to judge the legitimacy of a legal system, on this account, is to look primarily not at its content, but at the particular way that it has come into being, and thus at the nature of the transactional relationship between government and the governed. The question of the justice of outcomes seems to be of secondary importance. Since Simmons is a particular kind of voluntarist, it follows for him that only actual consent constitutes the correct form of relationship. As no existing state achieves this level of consent, it follows that no existing state is legitimate, and, we might surmise, if no existing state meets his criteria of legitimacy, the international legal system cannot do so. Although the idea of consent does have a prominent role in international law in relation to treaties between states, this is clearly insufficient to meet Simmons's criteria for legitimacy given that the states making the treaties lack legitimacy in relation to their own citizens, and so are not empowered to transact on their behalf. Thus even if we leave to one side the question of how meaningful consent is in a context of extreme inequalities of power and a historical background of gross wrongdoing, the actual consent approach cannot ground the legitimacy of international law. If we adopt such an understanding, it seems as if we cannot really talk meaningfully about the legitimacy of the international legal system at all. Seeking to avoid the conclusion that international law is therefore illegitimate, some writers on international law have sought to provide different foundations for its legitimacy. Simmons's account has the same basic structure as a conventional promissory obligation. The reason why one has a defeasible obligation to do X (obey the law) is because one has promised to do so (consented to the authority of the state), rather than because X is in itself good. The alternative is to incorporate some idea of the justice of the order which the system of rules sets up, without equating legitimacy with justice *simpliciter*. This sees legitimacy as a threshold concept – the system need not be perfectly just in order to be legitimate, but it must meet some minimal level of justice. It is this move which removes the requirement for actual consent, or a relevantly similar transactional history between governors and governed, and so opens the door to the possible legitimacy of international law, but it also means that considerations of distributive justice can now undermine legitimacy. For example, in laying out his constitutionalist model for analysing the legitimacy of international law, Mattias Kumm maintains that it is a mistake to look to features of domestic legitimacy, such as informed consent, and expect them to be replicated at an international level. The purpose of international law is 'to establish a fair framework of cooperation between actors of international law in an environment where there is deep disagreement about how this should best be achieved'; if the law is to achieve this purpose, then 'those who are addressed by its norms are generally required to comply, even when they disagree with the content of a specific international rule'.[20] However, all this creates is a presumption in favour of international law, and it follows that this presumption can be overridden if international law gives rise to significant injustice. Thus Kumm writes:

> The fact that there is a rule of international law governing a specific matter means that citizens have a reason of some weight to do as that rule prescribes. But this presumption is rebutted with regards to norms of international law that constitute sufficiently serious violations of countervailing normative principles relating to jurisdiction, procedure

[20] Kumm, 'The Legitimacy of International Law', 918.

> or outcomes ... each of the relevant principles can either support or undermine the legitimacy of international law.[21]

It is unrealistic to expect a system of law to coincide perfectly with the requirements of justice – the question is whether the system is sufficiently just both to allow its coercive imposition by institutional actors and to give rise to a correlative obligation to obey its commands. As the preceding discussion suggests, both redistributive cosmopolitans and international libertarians have good reason to question whether existing real world distributions meet such a threshold. To consider international law legitimate, on both Kumm's and Simmons's thick accounts, is to maintain that those subject to it have a prima facie moral obligation to obey its rules. They should not, for example, seek to redistribute resources in an illegal manner, even if their actions have the effect of bringing about a more just distribution. It is key here that the fact that such actions would be illegal is taken as constituting a reason for persons to forbear from performing them. There may be other reasons – prudential reasons of self-interest, other-regarding reasons based on upholding expectations and life plans – not to act in such a way, but these will not stem from the authority of the law itself. A test case for a redistributive cosmopolitan involves an illegal transfer from those who are, in the real world, better off in material terms than they would be in a just society to those who are worse off than they should be. For an egalitarian cosmopolitan, this would mean a transfer from those who have a greater share of resources than average to those with an inferior share. Does the existence of international law mean that a modern-day Robin Hood with the possibility of acting in such a way faces a moral obligation not to do so? Do those who themselves have less than they should face a political obligation to desist from taking the matter into their own hands, even if they could bring about a more just distribution by action which was illegal and redistributive, but otherwise harmless? A corresponding test case for the international libertarian involves a situation where those suffering from the automatic effects of historical injustice seek, illegally, to reverse these effects. Imagine that before international law developed binding force, Nation B's army stole a cultural artefact (created and paid for by members of Nation G) from G's National Museum. This artefact now resides in the National Museum of B. A member of G surreptitiously removes the artefact and donates it

[21] Kumm, 'The Legitimacy of International Law', 917.

to G's National Museum. If we believe that international law possesses thick legitimacy, it seems to follow that G faces a moral obligation to return the item to B. The question is again that of the extent of the injustice which the law allows. Whilst it seems clear that there are good reasons for laws which prevent individuals from taking matters into their own hands and independently seeking to correct distributions they deem to be unjust, it also does seem that, in cases of gross injustice, to require people to forbear from so acting asks too much of them. Jules Coleman makes the point in relation to corrective justice and property rights:

> In order for a scheme of rights to warrant protection under corrective justice ... [the rights] must be sufficiently defensible in justice to warrant being sustained against individual infringements. Entitlements that fail to have this minimal property are not real rights in the sense that their infringements cannot give rise to a moral reason for acting ... each of us can imagine political institutions that so unjustly distribute resources that no one could have a reason in justice for sustaining them by making repair.[22]

So the crucial question is whether existing resource distributions are sufficiently just so as to be legitimate, and so place obligations on agents to forbear from seeking to promote distributive justice through independent direct action (as opposed to, for example, lobbying democratic institutions to fulfil their justice-based duties). It is very hard for either redistributive cosmopolitans or international libertarians to maintain that agents face such obligations, and so this would appear to suggest that significant elements of international law lack legitimacy in the thick sense. It is relatively straightforward to maintain that this is true for redistributive cosmopolitans, such as global egalitarians, who believe the real world to be deeply, profoundly unjust, and who advocate massive international redistribution. For international libertarians, the question of whether the existing international legal system, lacking retroactive effect, meets the relevant threshold of distributive justice depends upon the extent to which we believe that rectificatory justice requires an extensive redistribution of resources in the present day. My view is that if one adopts an international libertarian account of global distributive justice, one must accept that it seems probable that modern-day states owe extensive rectificatory duties to others on account of past wrongdoing.[23] I have identified elsewhere three grounds on which rectificatory duties can be said to be owed. These are:

[22] J. Coleman, *Risks and Wrongs* (Cambridge University Press, 1992), 352–3.

[23] This is the primary claim of Butt, *Rectifying International Injustice.*

(1) Entitlement: when one state has possession of property to which another state is morally entitled.
(2) Benefit: when one state is benefiting, and another is disadvantaged, as a result of the automatic effects of an act of historic injustice.
(3) Responsibility: when one state is responsible for an ongoing injustice in relation to another, understood in terms of an ongoing failure to fulfil rectificatory duties over time.

Each of these arguments for the existence of potentially extensive present-day rectificatory duties is undoubtedly controversial, but each is conceptually distinct, so that one might reject one or two of these grounds while still accepting the significance of what remains. I have referred primarily in this chapter to the first category, that of entitlement, and so we might consider the fact that international law does not require the restitution of objects, such as items of cultural property, which were misappropriated prior to the development of the relevant legal provision.[24] It is possible to understand 'property' broadly here to refer not only to physical artefacts, but also to other categories of entitlement, including money, the value of improvements made to land, wages which should have been paid to slaves but were not, and so on. Such an account is dependent upon an argument as to how and why entitlements to property can persist even when the property in question rests for long periods of time in the hands of others, and upon an acceptance of the justifiability of inheritance. The latter, in particular, has proved controversial with many theorists, who wish to deny that resources can justifiably be transferred from one generation to the next. But while such arguments are available to the redistributive cosmopolitan, it is much less clear that international libertarians, who, as we have seen, deny that justice requires redistribution across national boundaries even when we are considering generations subsequent to those which generated the resources in the first place, can oppose the idea of a national inheritance of resources. Accordingly, my view is that it is possible to argue for rectificatory duties in connection with a wide range of different kinds of entitlement. I would also maintain that categories (2) and (3) are relevant to judging the justice of the international legal system – both specify what justice-based obligations modern-day states should perform

[24] For discussion of this, in terms of the 1969 Vienna Convention on the Law of Treaties and the 1970 UNESCO Convention on the Means of Prohibiting and Preventing the Illicit Import, Export and Transfer of Ownership of Cultural Property, see J. H. Merryman and A. E. Elsen, *Law, Ethics and the Visual Arts* (London: Kluwer Law International, 2002).

as a result of their rectificatory duties stemming from the past, but in neither case does international law mandate such action. By drawing an arbitrary line under centuries of international wrongdoing and disregarding the ways in which historic actions have affected the distribution of benefits and burdens in the present, international law requires many individuals and groups to live with a dramatically lesser share of the world's resources than they would possess in a just world. There are two senses in which this is problematic for the legitimacy of international law from the perspective of international libertarianism in particular. Some individuals possess a significantly reduced share of resources than they would possess if states fulfilled their rectificatory obligations. One problem, then, is the *distance* between the unjust world and its rectified counterpart which may mean that the world is not sufficiently just to meet the threshold for legitimacy. But there is a further element to unrectified injustice, which concerns the *character* of unrectified distributions.

There is something particularly unacceptable, from a moral perspective, about requiring those who are directly affected by unjust action which violates negative rights to refrain from acting in a way which would lessen their unjust disadvantage. It is one thing to note that a just world would conform to a given distributive pattern, such as equality, and to maintain that individuals are disadvantaged insofar as they lack resources they would have if redistribution were to take place. It is another to say that individuals are disadvantaged by a failure to rectify the effects of rights-violating wrongdoing. It is particularly onerous for individuals to have to live with the fact that others are failing to rectify negative rights infringements. Thomas Pogge has argued that ordinary moral reasoning is committed to a hierarchy of moral reasons, which holds that negative duties not to wrong (unduly harm) others are sharper and weightier than positive duties to protect others from wrongdoing.[25] An analogous point can be made concerning the experience of those who suffer as a result of violations of negative duties – everything else being equal, it is more demanding to expect them to respect an unjust distribution than it would be were the distribution unjust only in relation to a normatively desirable distributive pattern. Let us return to the case of the misappropriated cultural artefact, belonging to G but currently held by B. Imagine that the sum total of G's holdings is 100 units, and that of B is 120 units, and that the artefact has a value of ten units. Both egalitarian cosmopolitans and international libertarians would hold that similar

[25] T. Pogge, *World Poverty and Human Rights* (Cambridge: Polity, 2002), 132.

courses of action should take place – B should transfer the equivalent of ten units to G.[26] But it seems coherent to argue that the distribution is intolerably unjust in terms of the legitimacy threshold from the international libertarian, but not the egalitarian cosmopolitan, perspective. It is thus potentially the character of the unjust distribution, and not simply its distance from the distributive ideal, which renders the law which upholds the distribution illegitimate. As such, international libertarians have particularly strong reasons to doubt the thick legitimacy of international law.

Is, then, international law illegitimate? The alternative to this conclusion is to change, once more, the way we view the idea of legitimacy in an international context, and move from the thick to the thin conception. We saw that Kumm shares with Simmons a belief that, for a system to be legitimate, it must be the case that, generally speaking, its members are obliged to obey its commands. That is to say that they see legitimate systems of law as being those which possess political authority. By contrast, Allen Buchanan argues that law can be legitimate without individuals subject to it being obliged to obey it. Acknowledging the force of Simmons's work, Buchanan argues that the question of political legitimacy should be seen as distinct from that of political authority, since, 'the single most compelling conclusion to be drawn from the recent normative literature on political authority is that virtually no government possesses it'.[27] However, Buchanan dismisses the suggestion that the international legal system should be judged legitimate on the basis of consent, and instead links the legitimacy of international law to its capacity to promote justice. To be legitimate, in this sense, is simply to be morally justified in wielding political power, where to wield political power is to (make a credible) attempt to exercise supremacy, within a jurisdiction, in the making, application, and enforcement of laws.[28] Buchanan's account of moral justification here refers explicitly to the achievement of justice: "The chief moral purpose of endowing an entity with political power is to achieve justice … A wielder of political power that does a credible job of achieving justice is morally justified in wielding that power, if it provides a reasonable approximation of justice

[26] Whether B transfers the artefact itself or property of equivalent value does not matter from the egalitarian viewpoint. From an international libertarian perspective, G may, if it chooses, insist on the return of the artefact specifically. I am obviously working with a simplified version of egalitarian cosmopolitanism in this example.

[27] Buchanan, *Justice, Legitimacy, and Self-Determination*, 240. [28] *Ibid.*, 235.

through processes that are themselves reasonably just."[29] This is a much less demanding conception of legitimacy, but a straightforward link between justice and legitimacy may nonetheless seem to undermine international law's legitimacy straightaway, given the preceding argument relating to the injustice of the current international legal system. This is, however, too quick. Although Buchanan does assess international legitimacy in terms of justice, he defines justice, for this purpose, primarily in terms of basic human rights. Thus, 'A wielder of political power ... is legitimate ... if and only if it (1) does a credible job of protecting at least the most basic human rights of all those over whom it wields power and (2) provides this protection through processes, policies and actions that themselves respect the most basic human rights'.[30] Key here is that his definition of such rights in an international context has little place for questions of distributive justice, being comprised of the following: the right to life (in terms of not being unjustly killed); to security of the person; to resources for subsistence; of due process and equality before the law; to freedom from persecution and against some forms of discrimination; to freedom of expression and to association.[31] This does not deny that distributive justice is a constitutive element of justice in a wider sense, but only denies that it should be included as part of the criteria by which we judge the legitimacy of international law. Clearly, there is more to justice than ensuring everyone has basic human rights. If I enter a society of the affluent and take away all luxury goods for my own personal enjoyment, I act unjustly, even though (on the above account) I need not have infringed anyone's basic human rights. But the point of Buchanan defining justice, in the context of international law, in terms of these basic human rights is that, in current non-ideal circumstances, upholding these rights is the most important job international law has to do. So the crucial question is whether he is right to exclude considerations of distributive justice from his account. In what follows, I suggest that redistributive cosmopolitans and international libertarians should see this matter rather differently.

It is clear that Buchanan accepts that distributive justice would play a key role in the international legal system of an ideal world. He argues for the following three propositions:

(1) an ideal moral theory of international law must include a prominent place for distributive justice;

[29] *Ibid.*, 247. [30] *Ibid.*, 247. [31] *Ibid.*, 129.

(2) due to current international institutional incapacity, there are serious limitations on the role that international law can currently play in contributing to distributive justice;
(3) international law can and should play a beneficial, largely indirect role in securing distributive justice. Examples include the capacity for international law to promote more equitable trade relations, labour standards, environmental regulation and aid for development; to create a global intellectual property rights regime; to support efforts to liberalise immigration policies; and to encourage the development of the institutional capacities needed to secure, eventually, international distributive justice.[32]

The limited role of distributive justice is largely a function of the nature of the non-ideal world. Buchanan points to both institutional incapacity and a lack of political will. He claims that, 'at present institutional resources are insufficient to assign the role of primary arbiter and enforcer of distributive justice to any international agency or collection of international agencies'.[33] In this sense, he suggests, distributive justice is currently relevantly different from the conception of justice focusing on basic human rights. There are neither authoritative international institutions capable of bringing about just distributions, nor the requisite degree of background support for such institutions which is necessary to allow them to function effectively.[34] It seems clear that Buchanan's own favoured account of international justice is a version of redistributive cosmopolitanism. He rejects 'anti-redistributive views', which, he suggests, 'deny any significant scope for redistributive principles except for the purpose of rectifying past unjust takings of goods', and instead endorses an account according to which 'individuals have entitlements to goods and opportunities that are independent of the claims of rectification and that require the state to undertake redistributive policies such as subsidising education, health care services, and income support'.[35] Such a position, when extended globally, puts Buchanan firmly into the redistributive cosmopolitan camp in terms of ideal theory. The gap between the ideal and real worlds on such an account is indeed great. But it is not clear that this is true for those in the international libertarian camp. There is no reason why they should accept that the lack of popular support and the institutional incapacities which Buchanan identifies in connection with his preferred, cosmopolitan account of justice should be

[32] *Ibid.*, 193–4. [33] *Ibid.*, 219. [34] *Ibid.*, 216–30. [35] *Ibid.*, 223.

seen to apply to rectificatory justice. If one believes that distributive justice requires not (for example) redistributing the world's resources equally to each individual, or an implementation of the difference principle, but rather the rectification of the lasting effects of historic injustice, then the change in international law and society envisaged is potentially rather less drastic. Cosmopolitan principles seem, at present, far more popular in the academy than the real world, where the claim that partiality for fellow nationals is legitimate is still predominant. My view is that it is easier to persuade people in the real world that they owe duties to others in different countries as a result of rectificatory justice than as a consequence of redistributive cosmopolitan principles. Buchanan himself accepts that 'there does appear to be less consensus about what distributive justice requires than about the wrongness of violating the most basic civil and political rights'.[36] Rectificatory justice often responds to non-controversially wrongful and unjust actions. Indeed, he explicitly argues that one of the ways that international law can serve the ends of distributive justice in the real world is 'by helping to ensure that states discharge their obligations to rectify injustices committed against indigenous peoples within their borders'.[37] If this is the case for domestic historic injustice, why not also for international historic injustice? It would not be unfeasibly difficult to allocate responsibility for judging disputes and even ensuring compliance to existing international institutions, which already rule on contemporary international injustice. There is a ready-made allocation of rights and duties in such cases: particular individuals and groups are already linked together by the character of their historic interaction.

My contention, then, is that support for potentially redistributive principles of rectificatory justice is easier to secure than the alternative of seeking to persuade the general public of the world to adopt cosmopolitanism. Once principles of rectificatory justice are properly understood, and integrated with those principles of distributive justice which are already held, extensive redistribution can be seen as a requirement of justice by international libertarians within the terms of a narrow reflective equilibrium, simply as a consequence of properly understanding their own position. We do not need to persuade people to abandon their foundational beliefs about justice; we face the less demanding task of arguing that they have not fully thought through the implications of their existing beliefs. This opens the way for a full incorporation of

[36] *Ibid.*, 222. [37] *Ibid.*, 193.

distributive justice in one's assessment of the thin legitimacy of international law. International libertarians cannot straightforwardly reject the incorporation of principles of rectificatory justice into their account of justice which legitimates international law on the grounds of institutional incapacity or the lack of popular consensus in favour of such policies. The (perhaps surprising) conclusion is that, on Buchanan's thin account of legitimacy, contemporary international law is actually more legitimate from the perspective of redistributive cosmopolitanism than that of international libertarianism. This has important implications for states who seek to impose the provisions of international law against those to whom they possess significant rectificatory duties: for example, when developed states use coercive force to prevent the economic migration of individuals from their former colonies. We may accept that states that act in such a way are acting legally, without accepting that their actions are legitimate – in either the thick or thin sense of the term.

References

Beitz, C. 1999. 'Social and Cosmopolitan Liberalism', *International Affairs* 75: 515–29.

Boot, M. 2002. *Nullum Crimen Sine Lege and the Subject Matter Jurisdiction of the International Criminal Court*. Antwerp: Intersentia.

Buchanan, A. 2004. *Justice, Legitimacy, and Self-Determination: Moral Foundations for International Law*. Oxford University Press.

Butt, D. 2009. *Rectifying International Injustice: Principles of Compensation and Between Nations*. Oxford University Press.

Coleman, J. 1992. *Risks and Wrongs*. Cambridge University Press.

Frost, M. 1996. *Ethics in International Relations*. Cambridge University Press.

Held, D. 2003. 'The Changing Structure of International Law: Sovereignty Transformed?', in Held, D. and McGrew, A. G. (eds.), *The Global Transformations Reader*. Cambridge: Polity, 162–76.

Kumm, M. 2004. 'The Legitimacy of International Law: a Constitutionalist Framework of Analysis', *The European Journal of International Law* 15: 907–31.

Merryman, J. H. and Elsen, A. E. 2002. *Law, Ethics and the Visual Arts*. London: Kluwer Law International.

Miller, D. 1995. *On Nationality*. Oxford: Clarendon.

Nagel, T. 2005. 'The Problem of Global Justice', *Philosophy and Public Affairs* 33: 113–47.

Nardin, T. 1983. *Law, Morality and the Relations of States*. Princeton University Press.

Nozick, R. 1974. *Anarchy, State, and Utopia*. New York: Basic Books.
Pogge, T. 2002. *World Poverty and Human Rights*. Cambridge: Polity.
Rawls, J. 1999. *The Law of Peoples*. Cambridge, MA and London: Harvard University Press.
Reshetov, Iu. A. 1990. 'The Temporal Operation of Norms on Criminal Responsibility', in Ginsburg, G. and Kudriavtsev, V. N. (eds.), *The Nuremberg Trial and International Law*. Dordecht: Martinus Nijhoff.
Rousseau, J.-J. 1993. 'Discourse on the Origin of Inequality', in Cole, G. D. H. (trans.), *The Social Contract and the Discourses*. London: Everyman.
Simmons, A. J. 2001. *Justification and Legitimacy: Essays on Rights and Obligations*. Cambridge University Press.
Smith, A. 1981. *An Inquiry into the Nature and Causes of the Wealth of Nations*. Skinner, A. S. and Campbell, R. H. (eds.). Oxford University Press.
Walzer, M. 1977. *Just and Unjust Wars*. New York: Basic Books.

6

International law and global justice

PETER KOLLER

Introduction

It is generally known that people in numerous regions of the world, which usually are called 'Third World' or 'developing countries', particularly Africa, South America, Asia and South East Europe, suffer from extreme poverty. Although a group of developing countries have achieved enormous growth by which they could overcome their backwardness, social and economic inequalities in the world have increased significantly in the course of the last century. It seems obvious that the causes for the misery of poor countries lie in their legal and political structures themselves, at least to a considerable extent. In almost all of them, wealth is distributed extremely unequally, public education is miserable, economic productivity is very low, women are kept under suppression, and birth rates are high. In many countries, large parts of the population suffer from exploitation, because they are denied equal protection of their rights by a corrupt state bureaucracy and judiciary. And many of those countries are under the control of oppressive regimes that rule with brute force, persecute any opposition and misuse their power to their own benefit. When a number of these factors come together, they easily lead to a 'vicious circle of poverty', a self-enforcing process of social impoverishment that a nation hardly can overcome by itself.[1]

It appears plausible to assume that the prevailing features of global poverty and misery are closely connected with the existing legal structures in general and the legal positions of the disadvantaged people in particular. And various empirical studies confirm that. As to whether and to what extent a country's population may suffer from poverty or even starvation highly depends on the civil, political and economic rights

[1] Cf. P. Dasgupta, *An Inquiry into Well-Being and Destitution* (Oxford: Clarendon Press, 1993).

of its citizens rather than its overall social product. So it has been shown that the governmental system of a country has a significant impact on the extent and distribution of social deprivation: in democratic countries, poverty does not so often result in catastrophic famines than in countries with despotic regimes, because democratic governments have strong incentives to take measures in order to prevent them. On the other hand, famines can even occur in wealthy countries when they are ruled by predatory regimes that control the land's natural resources.[2]

These observations, however, by no means imply that the social problems in poor countries are essentially home-made, so that they are beyond the responsibility of the rest of the world. When we study the causes of the present situation of the world more carefully, it becomes pretty clear that the misery in many regions has a lot to do with the prevailing international system, comprising international law as its normative order and international politics as its actual practice. And if one does not subscribe to the implausible view that morality and justice do not apply to international affairs, one can hardly resist the impression that this system is greatly unjust. Even though this general assessment has become widespread, there is little agreement in detail. The current debate on international ethics in general and global justice in particular reveals far-reaching controversies on almost all matters that are relevant for a well-founded evaluation of the present international system. The controversies also concern the normative standards of justice that apply to international relations and the global order.[3]

In this chapter, I want to make an attempt to find a way out of this unsatisfactory situation by pursuing the following strategy: first of all, I want to show that there is a set of reasonable and widely accepted, though highly abstract, demands of justice to which social orders are subject in general. Then, I am going to argue that, if these demands are

[2] See A. Sen, *Poverty and Famines. An Essay on Entitlement and Deprivation* (Oxford: Clarendon Press, 1981); A. Przeworski, M. E. Alvarez, J. A. Cheibub and F. Limongi, *Democracy and Development. Political Institutions and Well-Being in the World 1950–1990* (Cambridge University Press, 2000).

[3] See, for example, S. Luper-Foy (ed.), *Problems of International Justice* (Boulder and London: Westview Press, 1988); C. Chwaszcza and W. Kersting (eds.), *Politische Philosophie der internationalen Beziehungen* (Frankfurt a.M.: Suhrkamp, 1998); T. Pogge (ed.), *Global Justice* (Oxford: Blackwell, 2001); D. Moellendorf, *Cosmopolitan Justice* (Boulder and Oxford: Westview, 2002); G. Kohler and U. Marti (eds.), *Konturen der neuen Welt(un)ordnung. Beiträge zu einer Theorie der normativen Prinzipien internationaler Politik* (Berlin and New York: Walter de Gruyter, 2003); P. Koller (ed.), *Die globale Frage. Empirische Befunde und ethische Herausforderungen* (Vienna: Passagen, 2006).

applied to international relations and the global order, they result in a number of plausible requirements of international and global justice. Eventually, I'll utilise these requirements in order to illuminate the major injustices of the present global system, and conclude with a few hints concerning its requisite reform.

The demands of justice

In contrast to strictly universal demands of morality which are binding for every person in relation to all other human individuals, such as the rule not to harm others without justification, the demands of *justice* are context-dependent in the sense that they are always related to certain forms of social interaction between the people involved.[4] There is, however, a great variety of social relationships that differ so much that it seems pointless to look for a single basic principle of justice which would cover all of them. So if any valid principles of justice can be found at all, it seems plausible to assume a plurality of such principles that apply to different social contexts. I think that it is possible to specify some fundamental and substantial, though very vague, principles of justice by distinguishing between four kinds of justice each of which refers to a certain elementary type of social relationships.[5] These kinds of justice and their respective objects are:

(1) transactional justice applying to exchange relationships;
(2) political justice concerning power relationships;
(3) distributive justice dealing with communal relationships; and
(4) corrective justice focusing on wrongness relationships.

Transactional justice – exchange relationships

Exchange relationships are transactions between independent parties who agree on a mutual transfer of certain goods or services of which the respective parties are entitled to dispose. Contractual transactions are the paradigm case. Justice demands that such transactions occur in a way which makes sure that, in general, they are to the benefit of all parties involved, so that none of them has a legitimate reason to complain about

4 Cf. P. Koller, 'Zur Semantik der Gerechtigkeit', in Koller (ed.), *Gerechtigkeit im politischen Diskurs der Gegenwart* (Vienna: Passagen, 2001), 19–46.

5 P. Koller, 'Soziale Gerechtigkeit – Begriff und Begründung', *ErwägenWissenEthik*, 14 (2003), 237–50, 307–21.

the outcome. In modern societies with their highly differentiated division of labour, exchange relationships are regarded as just, if the parties involved voluntarily agree on them under appropriate conditions which enable them to pursue their best interest. In particular, these conditions require that all parties have equal rights in regard to contractual transactions, that they have sufficient knowledge of the relevant facts, that they possess sufficient capacities of rationality in order to make choices that are guided by their well-considered interests, and that the contractual agreements are performed in absence of power so that no party is able to dictate the terms of trade. These conditions, which together define a *fair market*, make sure that transactions which accord to them are in the best interest of all parties involved.[6]

Political justice – power relationships

A power relationship occurs when an (individual or collective) agent effectively claims the authorised power to determine the ways or circumstances of conduct of other people through binding decisions backed by threat of force. Even though there are good reasons to assume that, at least in large social unions, some form of authorised power is necessary in order to secure a just and efficient social order, it is pretty obvious that any such power involves significant dangers. So power relationships must be kept within acceptable limits in order to qualify as just. Political justice concerns both the scope and the form of power. As to its scope, power must serve *legitimate aims*, which include two sorts: enforcing justifiable or well-established duties and claims of individuals, particularly human rights, and, furthermore, facilitating projects of social cooperation to the benefit of all people concerned, such as the provision of public goods. Regarding its form, power is to be exercised *impartially* on the basis of general and impersonal rules. Accordingly, power is just only if it is used in an impartial way in order to enforce individual duties and rights or promote generally advantageous cooperation.[7]

[6] See L. Walras, *Etudes d'économie sociale: théorie de la répartition de la richesse sociale* (Paris: Economica, 1990 [1896]); F. A. Hayek, *Law, Legislation and Liberty, vol. 2: The Mirage of Social Justice* (London: Routledge, 1976), 73ff., 178f.; P. de Gijsel, 'Individuum und Gerechtigkeit in ökonomischen Verteilungstheorien', in *Ökonomie und Gesellschaft. Jahrbuch 2: Wohlfahrt und Gerechtigkeit* (Frankfurt: Campus, 1984), 14–66, 17ff.

[7] Cf. O. Höffe, *Politische Gerechtigkeit. Grundlegung einer kritischen Philosophie von Recht und Staat* (Frankfurt a.M.: Suhrkamp, 1987), 62ff.

Distributive justice – communal relationships

Communal relationships are constellations among people who have a common claim to certain goods (e.g. because they have inherited them or produced them through their cooperative work) or a common responsibility to bear some burdens (e.g. because they jointly have agreed to take care of something). In other words: individuals are involved in a communal relationship, or a community, when they share common goods or common burdens or both. Justice demands that the goods and burdens of a community are to be distributed in a way that is acceptable to all members. Although there are many different forms of community that are subject to varying context-dependent criteria of distributive justice, there is one general and fundamental principle that works for the distribution of the goods and burdens in all communities, provided that their members respect each other as equals. This is the *principle of equal treatment* according to which the goods and burdens of a community are to be distributed equally among its members unless an unequal distribution is justified by reasons that are acceptable to all parties concerned from an impartial point of view. This principle, which is the basic demand of distributive justice within modern moral and political thinking, relying on the idea that every human person is to be respected equally, is admittedly very vague, since it leaves open what reasons may be appropriate for justifying unequal shares. These reasons vary with the social function and structure of particular communities, but, in general, one can say that they refer to three features of their members: their respective contributions and achievements, their vested rights and liberties, and their basic needs.[8]

Corrective justice – wrongness relationships

What I call a wrongness relationship is a social situation that comes into being when people commit wrongdoings, e.g. by flouting binding norms of social order, violating the rights of other persons, or breaching their duties towards others. Such relationships require a correction of the respective wrongs in order to restore the social order, compensate the victims, or punish serious crimes. Corrective justice consists of two parts: on the one hand, *restitutive* justice which deals with the compensation of

[8] See J. Rawls, *A Theory of Justice* (Cambridge, MA: Harvard University Press, 1971), 62; J. Feinberg, *Social Philosophy* (Englewood Cliffs, NJ: Prentice-Hall, 1973), 99ff.; D. Miller, *Social Justice* (Oxford University Press, 1976), 24ff.

damages, and, on the other hand, *retributive* justice that focuses on the question as to when and to what extent wrongdoings call for punishment. Both parts include a variety of problems which, however, cannot be discussed in the present context.[9]

I conclude my brief survey on the various basic kinds of justice by emphasising once again that their objects are *elementary types of social interaction* rather than complex social relationships. Since, in social reality, people form more or less complex networks of social relationships in which all these types of interaction are interlinked in manifold ways, the kinds of justice and their respective demands are highly interdependent. A family, for instance, represents a network of enduring relationships among its members which certainly includes a number of communal matters subject to distributive justice, but usually also raises problems of transactional, political and corrective justice, when its members conclude contracts among each other, make authoritative decisions binding for others or commit wrongs to others. Furthermore, I should mention that the kinds of justice and their respective demands are also conceptually interrelated. Most significant in this context is the fact that distributive justice, insofar as it does apply to a social arrangement, has priority to the other kinds, because transactional, political and corrective justice presuppose an acceptable initial or previous distribution of the relevant rights and assets of the individuals involved, a fact which itself eventually relies on standards of distributive justice. When the various basic demands of justice, taken together, are applied to complex social orders, they facilitate the construction of more complex ideas of justice in regard to the orders under consideration. If applied to the order of modern societies, they amount to the idea of *social justice*, and they suggest the idea of *international* or *global justice*, if applied to international relations or the entire global order. On the basis of these considerations on justice in general, I now turn to the idea of global justice.

The idea of global justice

For a first approximation, I suggest to interpret the notion of global justice as a comprehensive concept that includes a plurality of demands

[9] See, for example, J. P. Sterba, *The Demands of Justice* (Notre Dame and London: University of Notre Dame Press, 1980), 63ff.; J. Coleman, *Risks and Wrongs* (Oxford University Press, 1992), 197ff.

of justice in regard to international and global affairs. So I would like to define global justice as the *totality of demands of justice that apply to international relations and the global order.* And I want to argue that all kinds of justice and their respective demands come into play: international affairs and the global order are subject to transactional justice to the extent in which different nations as a whole or their members maintain trade and exchange relationships; to political justice insofar as authorised power is either actually exercised by international or supranational agents or requisite for a peaceful and just global order; to distributive justice in regard to those affairs that are in some sense communal to a plurality or the totality of nations; and eventually, it is subject to corrective justice in the case of severe wrongs among nations that require compensation or retribution. The different demands of justice are interconnected in various ways, in which distributive justice again has priority to the extent in which it determines the nations' legitimate claims to common resources in the context of international transactions, power relations, and wrongs. Now, I want to take a closer look at the various demands of justice in order to check to what extent they apply to international law and the global order.

Transactional justice – international trade

The global order is subject to transactional justice when different nations as a whole or their members maintain trade and exchange relationships. Accordingly, international trade relations and global market processes are required to take place under *fair rules and framing conditions* which make sure that all participating peoples and nations can derive benefit from them. To this end, these rules and framing conditions must make sure that no nation is able to dictate unilaterally the terms of trade to its own advantage, and that international exchange transactions are not distorted by asymmetrical market restrictions. International trade differs from domestic trade in the respect that the government of each country defines the conditions under which its citizens may enter into international trade relationships. And a prudent government will tend to rule these relationships in a way that they are to the best benefit of its own country, even if this may harm other countries. One possible means to this end, which, however, can be used only by mighty countries towards weaker ones, consists in exercising political pressure on other countries, or their governments respectively, in order to impose on them biased trade conditions. This is *imperialism*, which, of course, is highly unfair.

Another means, which also works among equally strong nations, is *protectionism*, i.e. measures that obstruct the import of foreign goods and/or foster the export of domestic products. In order to avoid a destructive escalation of such measures, countries are in the habit of concluding international trade agreements which determine the conditions of their mutual transactions. In recent decades, a great many countries have entered into a series of agreements, the GATT, which has led to a successive liberalisation of global trade.[10]

A system of free trade, however, is not necessarily a fair system. Yet, a well-known theory of international trade, the theory of comparative advantage, maintains that free international trade relationships are to the benefit of all countries involved, even if these countries may start from very different initial stages of economic development, provided that their markets are equally open.[11] Although this theory seems to be correct in general, it does not take into consideration some significant features of contemporary international trade: the role of transnational companies and the effects of the international credit system. Consequently, one may say that transactional justice implies the following requirements on a system of international trade: first of all, equal openness of markets, unless exceptions are justified by other requirements of justice; second, sufficient control of transnational companies, in order to prevent them from causing market distortions by their activities; and third, an unbiased international credit system which operates to the benefit of all countries.[12]

Political justice – international power constellations

Political justice applies to international and global affairs insofar as they include or require authorised power. Insofar as such power is required

[10] See J. H. Jackson, *The World Trading System. Law and Policy of International Economic Relations* (Cambridge, MA and London: MIT Press, 1997), 31ff.; H. Sautter, *Weltwirtschaftsordnung. Die Institutionen der globalen Ökonomie* (Munich: Franz Vahlen, 2004), 85ff.; M. J. Trebilcock and R. Howse, *The Regulation of International Trade*, 3rd edn (London and New York: Routledge, 2005), 1–48.

[11] Cf. P. Krugman, *Pop Internationalism* (Cambridge, MA and London: MIT Press, 1996); J. Bhagwati, *Free Trade Today* (Princeton and Oxford: Princeton University Press, 2002).

[12] See Oxfam International, *Rigged Rules and Double Standards. Trade, Globalisation, and the Fight against Poverty* (Oxford: Oxfam, 2002); A. B. Zampetti, *Fairness in the World Economy* (Cheltenham, UK and Northampton, MA: Edward Elgar, 2006), 98ff.; J. E. Stiglitz and A. Charlton, *Fair Trade for All. How Trade Can Promote Development* (Oxford University Press, 2005); E. B. Kapstein, *Economic Justice in an Unfair World. Toward a Level Playing Field* (Princeton and Oxford: Princeton University Press, 2006), 45ff.

for a peaceful and orderly co-existence of nations, it must aim at an *impartial enforcement of international law* and the *provision of public goods* in the interest of all nations concerned.[13] In order to circumvent the difficult question as to whether a just global order needs a comprehensive supranational power system in the form of a world state or nothing more than a more or less decentralised system of global governance managed by a network of international organisations,[14] I just want to underline some obvious demands of political justice with respect to the international order.

First of all, global political justice certainly requires a form of transnational politics that effectively copes with the most severe problems of the present world: first, *gross and massive violations of fundamental human rights*, such as genocide, ethnic cleansing and avoidable famine; second, the *irreversible destruction of global natural resources*, such as the oceans, earthly climate conditions and rainforests; and, third, the *dangers of the ongoing proliferation of means of mass extermination*, such as nuclear and chemical weapons. Furthermore, any form of authorised power at the international level ought to be in control of inter- or supranational institutions that apply the rules of international law in an impartial way in the common interest of all peoples rather than for the sake of mighty nations only.[15]

Distributive justice – international communal issues

The most contested topic of global and international justice is the question as to whether and to what extent distributive justice applies to

[13] Cf. T. M. Franck, *Fairness in International Law and Institutions* (Oxford University Press, 1995), 173ff.; I. Kaul, I. Grunberg and M. A. Stern (eds.), *Global Public Goods. International Cooperation in the 21st Century* (New York and Oxford: Oxford University Press, 1999); W. D. Nordhaus, 'Global Public Goods', in W. Krull (ed.), *Debates on Issues of Our Common Future* (Weilerswist: Velbrück, 2000), 143–54.

[14] As far as this issue is concerned, see M. Zürn, *Regieren jenseits des Nationalstaats. Globalisierung und Denationalisierung als Chance* (Frankfurt a.M.: Suhrkamp, 1998); O. Höffe, *Demokratie im Zeitalter der Globalisierung* (Munich: C. H. Beck, 1999), 229ff.; S. Gosepath and J.-C. Merle (eds.), *Weltrepublik. Globalisierung und Demokratie* (Munich: C. H. Beck, 2002); M. Lutz-Bachmann and J. Bohman (eds.), *Weltstaat oder Staatenwelt? Für und wider die Idee einer Weltrepublik* (Frankfurt a.M.: Suhrkamp, 2002); D. Held and A. McGrew (eds.), *Governing Globalization. Power, Authority and Global Governance* (Cambridge: Polity Press, 2002); D. Held and M. Koenig-Archibugi (eds.), *Taming Globalization. Frontiers of Governance* (Cambridge: Polity Press, 2003).

[15] Cf. Franck, *Fairness*, 173ff.; A. Buchanan, *Justice, Legitimacy, and Self-Determination. Moral Foundations for International Law* (Oxford University Press, 2004), 233ff.

international and global affairs.[16] A number of thinkers, including Rawls,[17] advocate the view that distributive justice does not have any significance in the context of international or global justice. I want to contradict this view and argue for a concept of global justice that integrates distributive justice in a differential way. Accordingly, the international order is subject to distributive justice to the extent in which it has distributive effects in regard to the communal affairs of different nations or humankind as a whole. In the context of this interpretation, it is clear that the impact of distributive justice on international relations depends on contingent facts, namely the actual structure of the world, especially the degree of international and global interdependencies. The more the individual nations and peoples become mutually interconnected and interdependent by the external effects of their domestic political orders, their activities across borders, and their cooperation based on division of labour, the greater is the domain of their communal affairs that create problems of distributive justice. When we consider the present constellation of the world, we encounter at least three issues that concern communal affairs among nations and, therefore, give rise to the demand for distributive justice: the extent of political autonomy of individual nations, the negative effects of societal activities across borders, and international economic cooperation.

The first issue, the *extent of political autonomy of the nations*, is already present in a world where the countries' national economies are relatively separated and independent, but its importance increases with the process of globalisation. I assume that a just international order ought to grant to each nation the right to equal political self-determination to the greatest extent that is compatible with certain internal and external requirements. As to these requirements, I interpret them in a rather weak way as follows: internally, a domestic political order must respect and protect the basic human rights, including social and economic rights; and externally, it must not be detrimental to a peaceful co-existence among nations.[18]

The second issue, the *negative effects of societal activities across borders*, concerns the social and economic affairs of individual societies

[16] See Buchanan, *Justice*, 191ff.

[17] J. Rawls, *The Law of the Peoples* (Cambridge, MA and London: Harvard University Press, 1999), 113ff.

[18] Cf. U. Marti, 'Globale distributive Gerechtigkeit', in Kohler and Marti (eds.), *Konturen*, 345–61.

whose ways of production and consumption have negative effects on other countries and even the whole world. For the time being, a great deal of natural resources that belong to the common heritage of humankind are endangered by industry, traffic and leisure activities; many other natural goods are progressively exploited and decimated; and there is also an increasing proliferation of technical facilities, such as energy plants and military systems, that cause significant dangers and injuries across borders or even threaten humankind as a whole. All these facts raise distributive problems among nations which imply the demand for a just distribution of the benefits and costs of border-crossing social and economic activities. In my view, this demand requires that, insofar as useful activities unavoidably cause negative effects across borders, the distribution of these effects among nations must be in proportion to the benefits which the individual nations get from those activities. If such a distribution cannot be achieved by market regulations, the nations who fare better ought to pay appropriate compensation to those who are worse off.[19]

Third, there is the issue of *international economic cooperation* which results from the fact that individual nations, though not all to an equal extent, increasingly grow together to more comprehensive units of social and economic cooperation based on division of labour in which all of them contribute to a certain degree to the production of earthly wealth, but also become more and more dependent from each other. Even though this cooperation is mainly coordinated through market transactions, it creates a need for distributive justice, because market processes alone can never secure a just distribution of their outcomes. On the one hand, markets already presuppose a just initial distribution of assets among their participants, in order to generate just outcomes; and, on the other, even if they start from a just initial distribution, they may lead to unacceptable outcomes, since their inherent dynamics, such as rationalisation processes, shifts in production lines and locations, and business cycles, can create self-enforcing economic, social and political inequalities that distort the subsequent market transactions. Consequently, the demand of distributive justice also applies to the benefits and burdens of any close international cooperation based on division of labour.

[19] Cf. B. Barry, 'Humanity and Justice in Global Perspective', in B. Barry, *Democracy, Power and Justice. Essays in Political Theory* (Oxford: Clarendon Press, 1989), 434–62, 448ff.; P. Singer, *One World. The Ethics of Globalization* (New Haven and London: Yale University Press, 2002), 14ff.

Perhaps, this demand can be put in a rough way as follows: the global order has to make sure that the international economic cooperation is to the benefit of all peoples, in particular the less developed and poor nations. And this does certainly not admit that some nations take the benefits, while others are left with empty hands.[20]

Corrective justice – international wrongs

Is it plausible to apply corrective justice to international affairs at all, if the wrongs under consideration were committed by nations or states rather than particular human individuals? If organised nations or states are conceived of as collective bodies that act through their political powers or authorised agents on the basis of their rules or collective decisions, there are in fact good reasons to assume that they are responsible for gross wrongdoings that were committed on their behalf. And, in principle, it seems also plausible that a state that has inflicted serious harm on another nation or its members by violating valid norms of international law or fundamental duties of humanity should, as a whole, be liable to appropriate restitution or compensation. In practice, however, this demand raises considerable difficulties that grow with the time-distance to the respective wrongs.[21]

Even in most cases of a recent or current wrong inflicted by a nation on another it is extremely difficult to determine the precise scale of appropriate compensation, because there are no widely accepted and sufficiently concrete normative standards of corrective justice and, very often, there is also considerable disagreement about the relevant empirical facts. The situation becomes much worse in cases of historical wrongs committed by nations a long time ago. The demand for a correction of such wrongs involves not only the problem of how to assess the scale of the wrongs under consideration and their appropriate compensation, but also the danger that it may create a great deal of international conflict, rather than peace. Therefore, one should be cautious in raising the demand of corrective justice in the context of international affairs. At any rate, it should not be taken as a requirement of primary importance.

20 Cf. Singer, *One World*, 51ff.

21 See E. Barkan, *The Guilt of Nations. Restitution and Negotiating Historical Injustices* (Baltimore and London: Johns Hopkins University Press, 2001); O. O'Neill, *Bounds of Justice* (Cambridge University Press, 2000), 129ff.; L. H. Meyer, *Historische Gerechtigkeit* (Berlin and New York: Walter de Gruyter, 2005), 135ff.

However, it may serve as a subsidiary argument that can support and supplement the other demands of justice.

So much about the demands of international and global justice flow from the basic principles of general justice by applying them to international affairs and the global order. In my opinion, these demands combine to create a substantial conception of international and global justice which provides us with a solid ground for a critical assessment of the present international system.

Injustices in the present international system

When I speak of the international system, I conceive of it in a comprehensive way that comprises both international law as its normative order and international politics as its actual practice. Now, I want to look at the present international system against the background of the demands of global justice previously mentioned in order to identify its most severe injustices. For this purpose, however, I need to make use of various empirical assumptions which I shall simply take for granted, since I cannot discuss them here in detail. Again, I am going to deal with the various sorts of justice step by step.

Global markets – international trade and credit system

When we take a closer look at the global economy, it becomes pretty clear that it grossly violates the requirements of transactional justice, in particular as far as the relationships between rich and poor countries are concerned. I just want to mention two striking features of the present global economic system that reveal its blatant injustice: one is the liberalisation of the world market and its management, the other the international credit system and the politics of its leading institutions.

The ongoing *liberalisation of the world market*, which has been pursued for some decades with GATT and other international agreements, has certainly provided significant advantages to many countries and fostered their economic development, but it has also led to an increased worsening of the situation of a great many less developed and poor countries whose economies have been ruined because of their insufficient competitiveness in international markets. Furthermore, it turns out that the World Trade Organisation (WTO), that has been established for the enforcement of the rules of free trade, operates in a way that systematically favours the interests of the mighty and rich countries to the disadvantage of the poor, because it provides the rich countries with free access to the markets of the poor, whereas it does not prevent them from protecting their own economies against international competition by export subsidies and import restrictions, particularly in sectors where the poor countries would have competitive advantages, like in agriculture, textiles and low-skill industrial products.[22]

The existing *international credit system* often contributes to a further deterioration of the socio-economic situation of poor countries, rather than improving it. This system includes two parts. One part consists in the official financial institutions associated with the United Nations, particularly the World Bank (IBRD) and the International Monetary Fund (IMF), which are almost completely dominated by the rich countries. Despite their function to support countries in cases of economic emergency with favourable credits, their actual lending policy works to the opposite effect, because they usually make their loans dependent on the condition that the borrowing countries pursue a rigid cost-cutting policy which mostly shortens their expenditures for education, healthcare, social security and public services at the cost of the lower classes of their population, particularly the poor.[23] The other part of the international credit system is represented by private banks that want to make profit and, therefore, are in the habit of tying the interest rates for their credits to the economic performance of the borrowing countries, so that poor countries have to pay the highest rates. Although this policy is pretty reasonable from the economic viewpoint of the banks involved, it is not only a major cause of bad government in poor countries, but also leads to the bizarre constellation that the expenditures which poor countries annually spend only on the interest of their loans highly exceeds the entire amount of money which they gain from foreign trade. So there is a permanent flow of wealth from the poor to the rich countries.[24]

[22] See N. Woods, 'Order, Globalization, and Inequality in World Politics', in A. Hurrell and N. Woods (eds.), *Inequality, Globalization, and World Politics* (Oxford University Press, 1999), 8–35; World Bank, *Globalization, Growth, and Poverty. Building an Inclusive World Economy* (New York: Oxford University Press, 2002), 3ff.; Oxfam, *Rigged Rules*, 64ff.; Singer, *One World*, 51ff.; Stiglitz and Charlton, *Fair Trade*, 1ff.

[23] See J. Stiglitz, *Globalization and its Discontents* (New York: Norton, 2002); Oxfam, *Rigged Rules*, 122 ff.; Oxfam International, *Kicking the Habit: How the Word Bank and the IMF are Still Addicted to Attaching Economic Policy Conditions to Aid* (Oxford: Oxfam, 2006, Briefing Paper 96).

[24] Cf. W. Hinsch, 'Die Verschuldung ärmster Entwicklungsländer aus ethischer Sicht', in M. Dabrowski, A. Fisch, K. Gabriel and C. Lienkamp (eds.), *Die Diskussion um ein*

Transnational politics – distorted structure of international power

That the present international system is far from satisfying the demands of political justice is common knowledge. When we just look at the global level, we encounter a peculiar situation: on the one hand, there is a global legal institution, namely the United Nations, which, in principle, would be responsible for coping with the global evils previously mentioned; yet, it is obvious that this institution is not only greatly ineffective, but also suffering from highly arbitrary and distorted decision-making procedures. On the other hand, there is a very small group of real super powers, particularly the United States and China, who successfully dictate the course of global affairs according to their own alleged national self-interest rather than the common good of the global community.

As a result, the present international system is characterised by a power structure that fails to meet the demands of political justice in a twofold way by containing both too little and too much power: it comprises too little authorised power which an effective and impartial transnational politics would require, and it includes too much informal and arbitrary power which makes such a politics impossible.[25]

Global community – national sovereignty and unequal benefits

In my view, distributive justice applies to the international system to the extent in which this system involves common affairs among various nations with distributive effects. I have argued that there are a number of such affairs, including three issues: the nations' political autonomy, the negative effects of societal activities across borders, and international economic cooperation. Here, I restrict myself to the first and the second.

As to *political autonomy*, the prevailing international system, that is based on the principle of national sovereignty, assigns to the government of any state two rights, which, following Thomas Pogge, may be addressed as the 'resource' and 'borrowing' privileges: first, the right of exercising control of its country's natural resources at will, including

Insolvenzrecht für Staaten (Berlin: Duncker & Humblot, 2003), 17–43; N. Hertz, *I.O.U. The Debt Threat and Why We Must Defuse It* (London: Fourth Estate, 2004); Oxfam International, *Beyond HIPC. Debt Cancellation and the Millennium Development Goals* (Oxford: Oxfam, 2005, Briefing Paper 78).

[25] Cf. Franck, *Fairness*, 218; E.-O. Czempiel, *Weltpolitik im Umbruch. Die Pax Americana, der Terrorismus und die Zukunft der internationalen Beziehungen* (Munich: C. H. Beck, 2002), 108ff.

selling them (resource privilege); and second, the right of raising credits on behalf of its country that bind future governments (borrowing privilege). These two rights certainly do not satisfy the demand that the nations' political autonomy ought to be compatible with the protection of basic human rights and international peace. In fact, they represent fundamental structural defects of the existing international law, since they not only entice corrupt regimes to enrich themselves at the cost of the people by disposing of their land's resources and raising credits, but they also encourage warlords to usurp political power with the means of military force in order to plunder the land's riches as they like.[26]

The second issue, the *border-crossing negative effects of societal activities*, ought to be dealt with in a way that a nation's costs and disadvantages from such effects are in proportion to the benefits which it derives from those activities. There is plenty empirical evidence which clearly shows that the current practice greatly violates this requirement. I mention just a few examples: the enormous demand for energy in developed countries not only increases the costs of energy, but also contributes to a change of climate conditions to the disadvantage of developing regions; huge fishing companies in industrialised countries exploit the seas all over the world at the cost of poorer nations who cannot afford the technical facilities in order to compete; the mighty nations take measures to improve their military systems by establishing new technologies whose risks are increasingly externalised to weaker regions; and there are many other cases to the same effect.[27]

Correcting wrongs – historical wrongs and continuing harm

As, in my opinion, corrective justice is not of primary importance in international relations, I restrict myself to a few remarks concerning the wrongness relationships between the rich countries in the North and the least developed countries in the South. There are two plausible reasons to maintain that the peoples in the South who are suffering from extreme poverty have a legitimate claim to some compensation from the rich northern nations: first of all, the *historical wrongs* that European and North American nations have inflicted on peoples in Africa, Latin America and South Asia through wars of conquest, colonialism, slavery,

[26] T. Pogge, *World Poverty and Human Rights. Cosmopolitan Responsibilities and Reforms* (Cambridge: Polity Press, 2002), 112ff., 146ff.

[27] Cf. Singer, *One World*, 14ff.; Wuppertal Institut für Klima, Umwelt, Energie (ed.), *Fair Future. Begrenzte Ressourcen und globale Gerechtigkeit* (Munich: C. H. Beck, 2005).

genocide and imperialism; and second, the *continuing harm* which the poor in the South incur because of various injustices of the present international system to the benefit of the rich nations in the North.[28] Even though, in the light of these reasons, the present international system appears also unjust from the viewpoint of corrective justice, it remains highly unclear how to deal with this fact in a reasonable way. However, since corrective justice, when applied to global affairs, widely overlaps with the demands of transactional, political and distributive justice, it may be used in order to support and strengthen these other demands.

If my previous considerations on the normative requirements of global justice and my empirical assumptions about the present international system are by and large sound, then it appears pretty obvious that this system is suffering from gross injustices, because it actually violates each of those requirements to a considerable extent. And this assessment becomes even more evident when one considers that these injustices mutually reinforce and strengthen each other due to the fact that virtually all of them work to the benefit of the rich and mighty nations at the cost of the poor. Consequently, I think it still true that our task is not only to interpret the world, but also to change it.

Conclusion

The proposed analysis of the injustices of the existing global system provides a rough guideline on a policy of its reform. I would like to conclude my chapter with some preliminary remarks on a policy of reform by which this system could be changed in a gradual way that would decrease its injustices. The requisite measures of such a reform policy may be split into three steps according to their political feasibility: relatively simple remedies for the biased practices of the international trade and credit system; more far-reaching measures aiming at a repair of the international economy; and a comprehensive renovation of the basic structure of the global political order.

First of all, there are some *relatively simple remedies* that could be taken in order to rid the present international trade and credit system of its most blatant moral deficiencies. Here, I contemplate mainly the following points: the abolition of protectionist practices on the part of industrialised countries, such as import restrictions and export subsidies for agricultural and low-skill industrial products; an appropriate

[28] See Pogge, *Word Poverty*, 201ff.

representation of poor countries in the relevant international institutions, especially the WTO, the IMF and the World Bank; and, furthermore, an effective regulation and control of transnational companies in developing countries, particularly their strategies of direct investment, their working and social standards and their conduct towards domestic subcontractors.

Second, a policy of making the present world system more just also requires a number of *more far-reaching measures* of reform. I assume that these measures should include the following elements: a limitation of the resource and borrowing privileges of national governments by making these privileges dependent on a government's proper conduct, namely its respect and protection of basic human rights; a global regulation of the use of international natural resources that guarantees all peoples a fair share of these resources and evens out unequal border-crossing negative effects of their use; and redistributive transfers for diminishing the inequalities which result from the biased structure of international economic cooperation, for instance by establishing a global fund dedicated to support poor countries in improving their educational, medical and social systems.

Finally, the developing idea of global justice will demand a further step, namely a *comprehensive renovation of the whole global political order*. In my view, its main target has to be the creation of a system of effective and impartial transnational politics that must gradually replace the traditional international system based on the principle of national sovereignty in order to cope with the challenges of the ongoing process of globalisation. In this context, two tasks are of particular importance: a global authority for the maintenance of peace, the protection of human rights and arms control on the one hand, and a transnational regime for the governance of international economic and ecological affairs on the other. Since there already are a number of international institutions, such as the UN, the ILO and the UNCTAD, that were designed to fulfil these tasks, but have not yet become sufficiently effective, it may appear a promising way to pursue that goal through a progressive extension and strengthening of those institutions.

I should add that the previous classification of the steps to reform the present international system merely focuses on their technical degree of difficulty without paying attention to their actual political probability which depends on the open question of whether a sufficient number of national governments are willing to take the respective measures. I guess, however, that, at the time being, this is not even the case in regard to the relatively simple measures of the first step. If so, the prospects of a rapid change of the prevailing situation are actually quite limited. In view of this fact, one cannot do much more than to contribute to the emergence of a worldwide social movement that may be able to put growing pressure on the relevant national and international powers to build up a better global order according to the demands of justice.

References

Barkan, E. 2001. *The Guilt of Nations. Restitution and Negotiating Historical Injustices.* Baltimore and London: Johns Hopkins University Press.

Barry, B. 1989. 'Humanity and Justice in Global Perspective', in Barry, B., *Democracy, Power and Justice. Essays in Political Theory.* Oxford: Clarendon Press, 434–62.

Bhagwati, J. 2002. *Free Trade Today.* Princeton and Oxford: Princeton University Press.

Buchanan, A. 2004. *Justice, Legitimacy, and Self-Determination. Moral Foundations for International Law.* Oxford University Press.

Chwaszcza, C. and Kersting, W. (eds.) 1998. *Politische Philosophie der internationalen Beziehungen.* Frankfurt a.M.: Suhrkamp.

Coleman, J. 1992. *Risks and Wrongs.* Oxford University Press.

Czempiel, E.-O. 2002. *Weltpolitik im Umbruch. Die Pax Americana, der Terrorismus und die Zukunft der internationalen Beziehungen.* Munich: C. H. Beck.

Dasgupta, P. 1993. *An Inquiry into Well-Being and Destitution.* Oxford: Clarendon Press.

Feinberg, J. 1973. *Social Philosophy.* Englewood Cliffs, NJ: Prentice-Hall.

Franck, T. M. 1995. *Fairness in International Law and Institutions.* Oxford University Press.

Gijsel, P. de 1984. 'Individuum und Gerechtigkeit in ökonomischen Verteilungstheorien', in *Ökonomie und Gesellschaft. Jahrbuch 2: Wohlfahrt und Gerechtigkeit.* Frankfurt: Campus, 14–66.

Gosepath, S. and Merle, J.-C. (eds.) 2002. *Weltrepublik. Globalisierung und Demokratie.* Munich: C. H. Beck.

Hayek, F. A. 1976. *Law, Legislation and Liberty, vol. 2: The Mirage of Social Justice.* London: Routledge.

Held, D. and Koenig-Archibugi, M. (eds.) 2003. *Taming Globalization. Frontiers of Governance.* Cambridge: Polity Press.

Held, D. and McGrew, A. (eds.) 2002. *Governing Globalization. Power, Authority and Global Governance.* Cambridge: Polity Press.

Hertz, N. 2004. *I.O.U. The Debt Threat and Why We Must Defuse It.* London: Fourth Estate.

Hinsch, W. 2003. 'Die Verschuldung ärmster Entwicklungsländer aus ethischer Sicht', in Dabrowski, M., Fisch. A., Gabriel. K. and Lienkamp, C. (eds.), *Die*

Diskussion um ein Insolvenzrecht für Staaten. Berlin: Duncker & Humblot, 17–43.

Höffe, O. 1987. *Politische Gerechtigkeit. Grundlegung einer kritischen Philosophie von Recht und Staat*. Frankfurt a.M.: Suhrkamp.

Höffe, O. 1999. *Demokratie im Zeitalter der Globalisierung*. Munich: C. H. Beck.

Jackson, J. H. 1997. *The World Trading System. Law and Policy of International Economic Relations*. Cambridge, MA and London: MIT Press.

Kapstein, E. B. 2006. *Economic Justice in an Unfair World. Toward a Level Playing Field*. Princeton and Oxford: Princeton University Press.

Kaul, I., Grunberg, I. and Stern, M. A. (eds.) 1999. *Global Public Goods. International Cooperation in the 21st Century*. New York and Oxford: Oxford University Press.

Kohler, G. and Marti, U. (eds.) 2003. *Konturen der neuen Welt(un)ordnung. Beiträge zu einer Theorie der normativen Prinzipien internationaler Politik*. Berlin and New York: Walter de Gruyter.

Koller, P. 2001. 'Zur Semantik der Gerechtigkeit', in Koller, P. (ed.), *Gerechtigkeit im politischen Diskurs der Gegenwart*. Vienna: Passagen, 19–46.

Koller, P. 2003. 'Soziale Gerechtigkeit – Begriff und Begründung', *ErwägenWissenEthik* 14, 237–50, 307–21.

Koller, P. (ed.) 2006. *Die globale Frage. Empirische Befunde und ethische Herausforderungen*. Vienna: Passagen.

Krugman, P. 1996. *Pop Internationalism*. Cambridge, MA and London: MIT Press.

Luper-Foy, S. (ed.) 1988. *Problems of International Justice*. Boulder and London: Westview Press.

Lutz-Bachmann, M. and Bohman, J. (eds.) 2002. *Weltstaat oder Staatenwelt? Für und wider die Idee einer Weltrepublik*. Frankfurt a.M.: Suhrkamp.

Marti, U. 2003. 'Globale distributive Gerechtigkeit', in Kohler, G. and Marti, U. (eds.), *Konturen der neuen Welt(un)ordnung. Beiträge zu einer Theorie der normativen Prinzipien internationaler Politik*. Berlin and New York: Walter de Gruyter, 345–61.

Meyer, L. H. 2005. *Historische Gerechtigkeit*. Berlin and New York: Walter de Gruyter.

Miller, D. 1976. *Social Justice*. Oxford University Press.

Moellendorf, D. 2002. *Cosmopolitan Justice*. Boulder and Oxford: Westview.

Nordhaus, W. D. 2000. 'Global Public Goods', in Krull, W. (ed.), *Debates on Issues of Our Common Future*. Weilerswist: Velbrück, 143–54.

O'Neill, O. 2000. *Bounds of Justice*. Cambridge University Press.

Oxfam International 2002. *Rigged Rules and Double Standards. Trade, Globalisation, and the Fight against Poverty*. Oxford: Oxfam.

Oxfam International 2005. *Beyond HIPC. Debt cancellation and the Millennium Development Goals*. Oxford: Oxfam, Briefing Paper 78.

Oxfam International 2006. *Kicking the Habit: How the Word Bank and the IMF are Still Addicted to Attaching Economic Policy Conditions to Aid*. Oxford: Oxfam, Briefing Paper 96.

Pogge, T. 2002. *World Poverty and Human Rights. Cosmopolitan Responsibilities and Reforms*. Cambridge: Polity Press.
Pogge, T. (ed.) 2001. *Global Justice*. Oxford: Blackwell.
Przeworski, A., Alvarez, M. E., Cheibub, J. A. and Limongi, F. 2000. *Democracy and Development. Political Institutions and Well-Being in the World 1950–1990*. Cambridge University Press.
Rawls, J. 1971. *A Theory of Justice*. Cambridge, MA: Harvard University Press.
Rawls, J. 1999. *The Law of Peoples*. Cambridge, MA and London: Harvard University Press.
Sautter, H. 2004. *Weltwirtschaftsordnung. Die Institutionen der globalen Ökonomie*. Munich: Franz Vahlen.
Sen, A. 1981. *Poverty and Famines. An Essay on Entitlement and Deprivation*. Oxford: Clarendon Press.
Singer, P. 2002. *One World. The Ethics of Globalization*. New Haven and London: Yale University Press.
Sterba, J. P. 1980. *The Demands of Justice*. Notre Dame and London: University of Notre Dame Press.
Stiglitz, J. E. 2002. *Globalization and its Discontents*. New York: Norton.
Stiglitz, J. E. and Charlton, A. 2005. *Fair Trade for All. How Trade Can Promote Development*. Oxford University Press.
Trebilcock, M. J. and Howse, R. 2005. *The Regulation of International Trade*. 3rd edn. London and New York: Routledge.
Walras, L. 1990 [1896]. *Etudes d'économie sociale: théorie de la répartition de la richesse sociale*. Paris: Economica.
Woods, N. 1999. 'Order, Globalization, and Inequality in World Politics', in Hurrell, A. and Woods, N. (eds.), *Inequality, Globalization, and World Politics*. Oxford University Press, 8–35.
World Bank 2002. *Globalization, Growth, and Poverty. Building an Inclusive World Economy*. New York: Oxford University Press.
Wuppertal Institut für Klima, Umwelt, Energie (ed.) 2005. *Fair Future. Begrenzte Ressourcen und globale Gerechtigkeit*. Munich: C. H. Beck.
Zampetti, A. B. 2006. *Fairness in the World Economy*. Cheltenham, UK and Northampton, MA: Edward Elgar.
Zürn, M. 1998. *Regieren jenseits des Nationalstaats. Globalisierung und Denationalisierung als Chance*. Frankfurt a.M.: Suhrkamp.

7

Global justice: Problems of a cosmopolitan account

HERLINDE PAUER-STUDER

Introduction

The current debate between cosmopolitans and the defenders of a so-called political conception of justice[1] focuses mainly on two questions: first, what is the site and scope of justice; and second, whether problems such as drastic worldwide economic inequalities and vast differences in life chances between the members of wealthy and poor countries can be tackled only by transcending the traditional nation-state order.

Cosmopolitans argue that issues like world poverty and the severe unfairness of social opportunities amount to problems of justice, moreover global justice, since their moral relevance transcends ethnic as well as state borders. The claim of cosmopolitans concerns the *site* as well as the *scope* of justice. World poverty and severe social and economic inequalities are global problems since they cannot be explained and understood apart from the current system of international economic relations and agreements (regulating access to markets, market subsidies, trade barriers, flow of capital, currency exchange conditions, creditworthiness). These agreements and regulations, enacted and controlled by powerful global institutions like the International Monetary Fund, the

I would like to thank Thomas Nagel, Richard Pildes, Thomas Pogge, Joan Tronto and David Velleman for critical comments on an earlier version of this paper. I also thank the participants of the conference on 'Justice, Legitimacy, and Public International Law' at the University of Bern in December 2006 for critical discussion.

[1] For a cosmopolitan position see T. Pogge, *World Poverty and Human Rights*, second edition (Cambridge: Polity Press, 2008) (all further references are to the second edition of Pogge's book); C. R. Beitz, 'Cosmopolitanism and Global Justice', *The Journal of Ethics*, 9 (2005), 11–27. A political conception of justice (following Rawls) is taken by, for example, T. Nagel and M. Risse. See T. Nagel, 'The Problem of Global Justice', *Philosophy and Public Affairs*, 33 (2005), 113–47; M. Risse, 'How Does the Global Order Harm the Poor', *Philosophy and Public Affairs*, 33 (2005), 349–76.

World Bank and the WTO, do have, cosmopolitans point out, substantial effects on the life prospects and economic opportunities of individuals. The strong impact of these international organisations on the social and economic conditions of persons allows us therefore to assume the existence of a global basic structure.

In addition to this empirical thesis about the global site of justice, cosmopolitans adopt a normative premise concerning the scope of justice. Since problems like poverty and inequality are mainly due to the currently unjust global economic order, they create strong moral obligations and duties of justice on the side of those better off who eventually profit from the unfair status quo.

Cosmopolitans are also critical of the nation-state system. Since nation-states display strong partiality towards the interests of their members (for example, by enacting restrictions on immigration, residence, citizenship and entrance to labour markets), they present an obstacle to the achievement of global justice. An additional reason why cosmopolitans think that issues of justice should be addressed independently of the nation-state perspective is this: if nation-states were the parties to a global contract or agreement on principles of justice, then intrastate discrimination against particular individuals or specific ethnic or social groups who live under unjust and unfavourable conditions would not become visible.[2] Therefore individuals, not institutions like the nation-state or political unions like peoples, should be the moral units of theories of global justice. What is relevant is the way individuals' basic rights are respected or violated and their autonomy for leading a decent and worthwhile life is enhanced or thwarted.

Defenders of a political conception of justice claim that justice applies to the basic structure of a particular society (nation-state), and, moreover, that duties of justice in a strict sense hold merely between the members of a particular society (nation-state). We do have obligations to severely poor and marginalised people outside our nation-state; these obligations, however, are of a humanitarian kind and not duties of justice in a strict sense. Duties of justice are associative obligations, obligations owed to those with whom we have political relations within a state order. Defenders of a political conception of justice basically follow Rawls's

[2] A. Buchanan objects that Rawls's conception, as Rawls develops it in the *Law of Peoples*, does not allow issues of intrastate conflict and ethnic autonomy aspirations to be dealt with. See A. Buchanan, 'Rawls's Law of Peoples: Rules of a Vanished Westphalian World', *Ethics*, 110 (2000), 697–721, here 716–20.

position as he outlined it in the *Law of Peoples*: peoples do have a duty to assist 'other peoples living under unfavourable conditions that prevent their having a just or decent political social regime'.[3] However, there are no duties of justice created by an application of a cosmopolitan or global principle of distributive justice. Rawls's arguments for rejecting distributive responsibilities on the global level are as follows: first of all, global inequalities are mainly due to the internal political organisation of a society and its social and cultural traditions; and second, there might be no cut off point in transfers of wealth and income from better off to worse off societies which might create unjust burdens on the side of better off societies.[4] Recently, defenders of a political conception of justice have added a further argument why humanitarian duties of assistance, but not strict duties of justice, hold on the global level: the realisation of actual justice demands coercion by the state; since such a global coercive sovereign power does not exist, the idea of global justice in a strict sense cannot be defended.[5]

In the current literature, political conceptions of justice have been sharply criticised. A main objection is that advocates of political conceptions of justice are stuck in a historically outdated framework of a 'vanished Westphalian World' and have missed recent global developments.[6] Moreover, the distinction they draw between duties of justice and duties of assistance amounts to a scandalous ignorance towards the moral weight of grave inequalities in the social global order: poverty can,

[3] J. Rawls, *The Law of Peoples* (Cambridge, MA: Harvard University Press, 1999), 37. Rawls uses the term 'peoples' to indicate his distance to the traditional conception of sovereign states (as determined by rational self-interest and having the right to go to war) and to stress that his central aim in the *Law of Peoples* is to construct a political morality for international relations. Buchanan objects that Rawls would have been clearer if he had used the term 'peoples organised in states'. Buchanan, 'Rawls's Law of Peoples', 699.

[4] One might say that Rawls applies the principle of luck egalitarianism (individuals only deserve compensation for brute bad luck, not option luck) to the case of societies. He offers the following example: two societies, A and B, start with an equal level of wealth but choose different policies. The first society opts for investment, industrialisation and a high rate of saving; the second society chooses none of these policies with the result that some decades later the first society would be much wealthier than the second society. A global distribution principle (along the line of a cosmopolitan difference principle) would require that transfers are made from A to B; Rawls thinks this to be unjustified. See Rawls, *The Law of Peoples*, 117.

[5] For such a position see Nagel, 'The Problem of Global Justice'.

[6] See Buchanan, 'Rawls's Law of Peoples'; A. J. Julius, 'Nagel's Atlas', *Philosophy and Public Affairs*, 34 (2006), 176–92.

and does, entail the loss of life. Equally, the connection between justice and coercion has been rejected.[7]

In this chapter I take a closer look at the controversy between cosmopolitans and the advocates of a political conception of justice. I will defend a political conception of justice, although I suggest some revisions. A cosmopolitan approach is often connected with *monism*, i.e. the claim that the same sort of normative principles should apply to institutions and to individual choices. A political conception of justice presupposes *dualism*, namely a separation between the principles of justice guiding the design of institutions and the moral principles applying to individual choices. In the second section of the chapter I discuss Thomas Pogge's cosmopolitan position and try to show that Pogge shifts from a dualistic account of justice to a monistic account when it comes to the problem of world poverty; therefore Pogge's treatment of world poverty is vulnerable to the objections which he himself raises against monism. Moreover, in the third section, I argue that Pogge's exclusive focus on negative duties is implausible and creates excessively heavy burdens on the side of better-off individuals. In the fourth section I argue that there is no need to consider the nation-state as a hindrance to the realisation of a more global justice. I end with some suggestions as to how a political conception of justice can be modified to meet some of the criticisms cosmopolitans have rightly raised.

Monism, dualism and world poverty

Even if we consider the basic structure as the primary object of justice, it is still controversial whether we should also accept the strict distinction some theorists of justice, for example Rawls, draw between those normative standards which ought to guide the design of institutions and those standards that are meant to regulate individual practices and actions. Some philosophers have argued that a thorough concern with issues of justice requires us to apply the same sort of principles to institutional design and to individual attitudes and choices.[8] A problematic consequence of that strategy is that requirements of justice addressed to institutions are translated into very demanding individual moral obligations.

[7] See A. Abizadeh, 'Cooperation, Pervasive Impact, and Coercion: On the Scope (not Site) of Distributive Justice', *Philosophy and Public Affairs*, 35 (2007), 308–58, esp. 352, 321.

[8] A prominent example is G. A. Cohen. See G. A. Cohen, 'Where the Action Is: On the Site of Distributive Justice', *Philosophy and Public Affairs*, 26 (1997), 3–30.

A paradigm case motivating such a transfer of normative obligations from public or political morality to individual morality is the problem of world poverty.[9] World poverty is considered by many moral philosophers as the most pressing moral issue at present. The dramatic differences in the living standard and levels of wellbeing are striking.[10] The urgency of the problem is certainly intensified by the fact that one small part of the world population is not only well off, but exceptionally better off than a large group of other people. The facts are so grave and depressing that many philosophers consider the policy of delegating the problem to a reform of current institutions or a set-up of new institutions to be morally intolerable. In their view more efficient and immediate relief seems necessary. It often seems to make more sense to care directly for the wellbeing of others than to delegate the problem to the normative construction of institutions, as Liam Murphy points out:

> But it could not be right that an individual, rich First Worlder is required to devote her resources to the Quixotic task of promoting just international institutions. Such a person could clearly do so much more to alleviate suffering or inequality by doing what she can on her own – by giving money to humanitarian aid agencies.[11]

Consequently, many have sympathised with an account that puts remarkable weight on the moral duties of individuals. It is quite common among cosmopolitans to hold that requirements of global justice have to be discharged to a remarkable extent by individuals.

Does the urgency of a problem like world poverty suggest that we should give up the separation between the principles guiding our promotion of just institutions and those guiding our personal choices? A closer look at the distinction between monism and dualism helps to clarify the question.

Monism holds that those normative principles that guide the sphere of public morality equally ought to guide our personal choices and ways of

9 By 'individual morality' I mean those principles and norms that apply to our personal actions and attitudes; the terms 'public morality' and 'political morality' refer to the norms and principles of justice that determine the basic structure of society.

10 Thomas Pogge cites the following numbers: '[I]t is estimated that 830 million human beings are chronically undernourished, 1,100 million lack acces to safe water, 2,600 million lack access to basic sanitation, 1,000 million lack adequate shelter, and 1,600 lack electricity. About 2,000 million lack access to essential drugs, some 774 million adults are illiterate, and there are 218 million child laborers.' See Pogge, *World Poverty and Human Rights*, 2.

11 L. B. Murphy, 'Institutions and the Demands of Justice', *Philosophy and Public Affairs*, 27 (1998), 251–91, here 281.

acting. In the version put forth by G. A. Cohen, monism amounts to a modification of Rawls's theory of justice: the principles of justice that guide our design of institutions should equally apply to the set of informal practices that determine and structure our personal relations to others. Within the basic structure of society, so the argument goes, there is room for informal discriminatory practices that sum up to severe injustices. A theory of justice must also reflect these patterns of informal discrimination that are expressions of personal attitudes. According to Cohen's account, not only institutions but also the attitudes of persons belong to the realm of justice. Cohen argues that monism allows us, for example, to consider the harmful consequences of sexist or racist attitudes as questions of justice.[12] Social justice, as he emphasises, cannot be gained merely by creating just institutions; it also requires a *social ethos* which is created if individuals apply the principles of justice to their personal conduct and attitudes.[13] So the difference principle should also guide the attitudes and choices of individual persons:

> It is generally thought that the difference principle would be used by government to modify the effect of choices which are not themselves influenced by the principle, but, so I claim, in a society of wholehearted commitment to the principle, there cannot be so stark a contrast between public and private choice. Instead, citizens want their own economic behaviour to satisfy the principle and they help to sustain a moral climate in which others want the same.[14]

Dualism maintains a strong distinction between the spheres of individual morality and public morality. The paradigmatic example of a dualist account is Rawls's theory of justice. Rawls's principles of justice, i.e. the principle of equal freedom, the principle of fair equality of opportunity, and the difference principle, apply to the normative structure of institutions but

[12] The case of gender injustice in the family despite appropriate family legislation has been one issue that motivated Cohen's defence of monism.

[13] Cohen is aware of the limits of legal regulations in fighting problems of discrimination. Therefore, he emphasises the impact of justice-based ethical conventions and practices that bind us and form our attitudes (*social ethos*). The regulative effect of these conventions and practices should ideally be as powerful as legal regulations. Cohen does not want persons whose social practices do not conform to the principles of justice to be prosecuted; social sanctions, he argues, should be enough. The problem is that this suggestion, if put into practice, might create a terrible social climate of control and reproaches.

[14] G. A. Cohen, 'Incentives, Inequality, and Community', in S. Darwall (ed.), *Equal Freedom: Selected Tanner Lectures on Human Value* (Ann Arbor: The University of Michigan Press, 1995), 331–97, here 380.

are not relevant for the guidance of individual actions.[15] The principles and standards of personal morality are different from the principles of justice.[16] Rawls's main argument for this separation is that otherwise implausible consequences and normative ambiguities would result. The obvious objection against monism is that the principles of justice apply, as in Rawls's theory, merely to the basic structure of society, i.e. the political constitution, the system of property rules, and the family. The reply of Cohen is that if patterns of discrimination are persistent despite existing legal restrictions and regulations, the basic structure argument seems to lose its plausibility.

A similar frustration with a basic structure account of justice in the case of global inequality and world poverty motivates cosmopolitans to come close to monism, by putting more weight on individual duties and applying the principles of justice to individual choices. Interestingly enough, when it comes to the problem of world poverty, we find such a tendency towards monism in the work of authors who otherwise are critical of monism, such as Thomas Pogge.

In the general debate between dualists and monists Pogge sides with dualism. Pogge rejects the view that the moral assessment of social institutions should depend on a comprehensive moral conception that also governs personal conduct. Principles of personal conduct should be distinguished from the principles of justice guiding the design of institutions.[17] According to Cohen, a social ethos would develop if the difference principle guided the choices of individuals as well. As an example of a specific moral climate created by a commitment to the difference principle, Cohen cites the relatively moderate differences between managers' and workers' salaries in post-war Germany compared with the striking differences in incomes between managers and workers in the post-war US; Cohen attributes the lower income differentials between

[15] See J. Rawls, *Political Liberalism* (New York: Columbia University Press, 1993): '[T]he principles of justice, in particular the difference principle, apply to the main public principles and policies that regulate social and economic inequalities' (282).

[16] In *A Theory of Justice* Rawls states: 'There is no reason to suppose that the principles which should regulate an association of men is simply an extension of the principle of choice for one man ... [T]he correct regulative principle for anything depends on the nature of that thing.' See J. Rawls, *A Theory of Justice* (Cambridge, MA: The Belknap Press, 1999), 25. Rawls uses this passage to argue against utilitarianism; however, his remarks can be taken as a general warning to confound principles for the normative design of institutions with principles guiding personal choices. Compare also Rawls, *A Theory of Justice*, § 19, 98ff. and § 51, 293ff.

[17] T. Pogge, 'On the Site of Distributive Justice: Reflections on Cohen and Murphy', *Philosophy and Public Affairs*, 29 (2000), 137–69, esp. 139.

managers and workers in post-war Germany to the stronger social ethos in the German *Wiederaufbau* area.

Pogge considers Cohen's hope that a social ethos might have inequality-reducing effects as unrealistic. He objects that the lower income differentials in post-war Germany were simply a consequence of different tax laws: US tax laws allow higher salaries for managers.[18] In opposition to Cohen's social ethos conception Pogge affirms the basic-structure argument and the regulative power of laws and institutional decrees.

Pogge, moreover, rejects the idea of applying the difference principle to individual choices altogether. His critical argument is that an application of the difference principle to individual choices would require highly talented and efficient people, who might contribute substantially to the improvement of the situation of the worst off, to adopt jobs that they do not want to accept.[19] Pogge's objection amounts to saying that monism entails a violation of a basic principle of political liberalism, namely the right to choose one's form of life. However, in Pogge's work on world poverty the principle of liberal autonomy seems restricted in a way which is open to his own objections against monism.

An interpretation of Rawls's theory along monistic lines clearly results, I think, in a nightmare of responsibilities and demands, if applied to the problem of global inequalities. The difference principle, in particular, would make demands on persons that are highly implausible: persons in one country who are better off, maybe only slightly better off, than persons in another country would have to devote their moral strength to improving the situation of others. Therefore, persons slightly better off in China would have to do all they can to improve the situation of poor people in India who are worse off. But what if the people in India whom they helped were to experience an economic boom shortly afterwards and become much better off than the Chinese? The problematic consequence is not only an excess of responsibilities, but also an absurd game of giving and demanding on a piecemeal basis which does not reflect our common understanding of justice.

The adoption of the difference principle as a guideline for individual behaviour would severely restrict the autonomy of individuals to develop and pursue their own plan of life. They would have to pursue life plans that contribute to an increase of social goods so that the situation of the worst off members of society can be improved. However, the right to

[18] *Ibid.*, 149–51. [19] *Ibid.*

choose one's form of life is a basic principle of a society which guarantees basic liberties. Autonomy in the sense of having the (economic) means to pursue a plan of life is also considered by many cosmopolitans as the benchmark of a global conception of justice.[20]

To conclude: monism seems an implausible position facing several objections:

a) The way monism blurs the distinction between public and individual morality leads to implausible consequences.
b) The adoption of the difference principle as a principle of personal choice results in unclear, but probably also excessively demanding, requirements and burdens. Exactly what contributes to the advantage of the worst off person? What do we have to do in order to promote the advantage of the worst off?
c) Strengthening the moral requirements on the side of individuals might not have the desired effect – not because moral motivations are too weak or contingent as such, but because they might have no impact on underlying structures.[21]

The strategy of putting more weight on personal duties also proves unhelpful in the case of global inequalities. Nevertheless, there is a strong tendency among cosmopolitans to pursue that line. Given the pressure of a severe problem like world poverty, many are tempted to discharge the moral burden in terms of strong individual moral obligations. Pogge's work on world poverty is an example.

Global justice and individual moral duties

In his book *World Poverty and Human Rights* Pogge combines cosmopolitanism with an institutional account: the primary moral units are individuals; institutional reforms, however, are the prior means of fighting global inequalities and world poverty. Severe poverty is a violation of basic human rights. Human rights, including social and economic rights, are the basic normative parameter for developing a just world order. The main goal is not redistribution on a global level, but 'an economic order

[20] See, for example, Martha Nussbaum's position in M. C. Nussbaum, *Frontiers of Justice. Disability, Nationality, Species Membership* (Cambridge MA: Harvard University Press, 2006), ch. 5.

[21] See D. Jamieson, 'Duties to the Distant: Aid, Assistance, and Interventions in the Developing World', *The Journal of Ethics*, 9 (2005), 151–70, for striking examples of problematic consequences of direct transfers of aid and assistance.

under which each participant would be able to meet her basic social and economic needs'.[22] The normative aim of Pogge's position is to guarantee all humans a life beyond marginalisation, poverty, hunger and death due to malnutrition. The focus is on a threshold of a minimally decent life, not on redistribution as such.[23]

Pogge develops an 'institutionalist interpretation' of human rights according to which human rights are claims against those social orders that have the power of enforcing their regulations. Yet human rights also place demands in regard to personal choices and duties of citizens. If a social order does not meet its obligation to guarantee human rights, then individuals who profit from this system have a duty to engage in activities to reform it. As Pogge writes:

> The normative force of others' human rights for me is that I must not help uphold and impose upon them coercive social institutions under which they do not have secure access to the objects of their human rights. I would be violating this duty if, through my participation, I helped sustain a social order in which such access is not secure, in which blacks are enslaved, women disenfranchised, or servants mistreated, for example. Even if I owned no slaves or employed no servants myself, I would still share responsibility: by contributing my labour to the society's economy, my taxes to its governments, and so forth.[24]

Pogge considers two negative duties as crucial, namely, the duty not to violate and undermine just institutions, and the duty not to participate in the upholding of unjust institutions or to profit from them. Individuals do have a collective responsibility to ensure that the institutions they help sustain are just. If other persons die because of poverty, then this amounts to a violation of a negative duty, namely to respect the basic right to life and bodily integrity. To help poor people therefore cannot be a positive duty in the classical sense of a duty of beneficience or of assistance.

The reason why Pogge postulates the duty towards poor people as a negative one is clearly to emphasise the moral urgency at stake. His

22 Pogge, *World Poverty and Human Rights*, 182.

23 The basic parameters of global justice are human rights, more so: economic rights. On the global level it is important for Pogge 'to choose or design the economic ground rules that regulate property, cooperation, and exchange and thereby condition production and cooperation' (Pogge, *World Poverty and Human Rights*, 182). Pogge holds that this offers 'a standard for the moral assessment of alternative feasible schemes of economic institutions' which is independent of 'the idea of already owned resources to be *re*-distributed' (*ibid.*).

24 Pogge, *World Poverty and Human Rights*, 70.

argument seems to be: if we consider the duties towards poor people as positive duties, then the injustice suffered by the global poor would not receive the moral attention it deserves.

Is Pogge's move to impose on individuals living in developed countries a negative duty towards people in poor countries convincing? Usually the distinction between negative and positive duties is drawn in the following way: negative duties are duties to refrain from doing something; positive duties are duties to do something: they involve positive action. On Pogge's account of negative duties, however, the distinction between active and passive collapses, since his negative duties do involve positive actions. The negative duty of individuals not to violate the human rights of people in poor countries by profiting from an unjust economic world order has to be discharged by certain positive actions, for example, by protesting against the unfair regime of international organisations, possibly also by moving to other places and leaving one's country. As Pogge writes:

> I might honor my negative duty, perhaps, through becoming a hermit or an emigrant, but I could honor it more plausibly by working with others toward shielding the victims of injustice from the harms I help produce or, if this is possible, toward establishing secure access through institutional reform.[25]

Two objections come to mind. First, one might be tempted to object that Pogge's position amounts to a confusion of negative and positive duties since negative duties are duties to refrain from doing something and not duties to take positive action. This criticism depends on the stringency of the active/passive distinction. However, this distinction is a notoriously fragile one. In specific circumstances, the negative duty not to endanger the life of others can be discharged only by a positive action: if someone is drowning, and we are in a position to help, we violate the negative duty towards the drowning person by not taking positive action. So the possible argument that Pogge mixes up negative and positive duties in an illegitimate way is not convincing.

A second objection is more to the point. In his analysis of the moral claims posed by world poverty Pogge tries, as already pointed out, to avoid the consequences of reading positive duties as being weaker than negative duties.[26] The way in which he spells out the claims of poor

[25] Pogge, *World Poverty and Human Rights*, 72.

[26] This quite common interpretation is often (erroneously) justified by referring to Kant's distinction between perfect and imperfect duties.

people apparently appeals only to negative duties. Pogge sees in the lack of help for poor people a much stronger violation of a duty than occurs when a person has not fulfilled her positive duty of assistance or beneficence. In order to escape the classical problem that positive duties allegedly do not have the moral weight of negative duties, he tries to avoid the appeal to positive duties altogether.

Pogge is certainly right to complain that the moral weight of the problem of world poverty is not recognised adequately. Yet the urgency of the issue of world poverty can also be emphasised if the classical distinction between negative and positive duties remains. In Kant's framework, for example, the moral strength of positive duties and negative duties is equal; positive duties are not weaker. Moreover, there is an important reason why Kant separated negative from positive duties, which we should take seriously. By ignoring this Kantian point, Pogge comes close to violating some fundamental liberal premises in regard to the scope of moral obligation.

Kantian duties of justice are different from duties of virtue in the following respect: duties of virtue are directed towards ends, i.e. ends which the individual recognises as right and appropriate according to practical reason. The ends are not set arbitrarily; they are normatively prescribed: one's own perfection and the happiness of others.[27] Duties of virtue are wide duties; duties of justice are strict or narrow duties. Duties of justice are of strict obligation because they demand or forbid a *specific action*. They are negative duties, so-called duties of omission (*Unterlassungspflichten*). A duty of omission can only be discharged by not doing a specific action.

Duties of virtue, however, demand the realisation of ends, whereby it is left to the judgment of the individual person in which way to fulfil these requirements. The reason why duties of virtue are classified as wide duties is that they express a broad moral obligation which need not be discharged by a specific action. The leeway in fulfilling positive duties of virtue is due to moral epistemology: individuals are, given their

[27] See I. Kant, 'Introduction to the Doctrine of Virtue', in Kant, *The Metaphysics of Morals. Part II: Metaphysical First Principles of the Doctrine of Virtue*, edited by M. Gregor (Cambridge University Press, 1996), 150f. (Academy edition: 6:387, 6:388). For a highly insightful discussion of Kant's account of virtues see C. M. Korsgaard, 'An Introduction to the Ethical, Political, and Religious Thought of Kant', in C. M. Korsgaard, *Creating the Kingdom of Ends* (Cambridge University Press, 1996), 18–22; cf. also Korsgaard, 'Kant's Formula of Universal Law', in Korsgaard, *Creating the Kingdom of Ends*, 82–4.

knowledge of the particular situation and circumstances they are in, better judges about how best to fulfil their moral obligation than a universal law procedure that generalises over cases could tell them.[28] The moral law establishes the obligation as such, while determining the details of how to live up to it must be left to individual judgment.

Positive duties differ from negative duties because the idea of universal moral legislation does not tell one in which way the normative obligation can and should be fulfilled in a specific context and situation. So the inevitable particularity of living up to such demands is the reason why duties of beneficence are a positive duty, i.e. an imperfect duty in Kant's terminology. The moral judgment of the person is necessary to determine in which form he or she can fulfil this obligation.

The Kantian specification of negative and positive duties is highly relevant for assessing which duties the problem of global justice implies. To defend an account of global justice that allows for positive duties does not amount to a weakening of normative force. It merely means that the obligation to take measures against global poverty creates on the side of individuals an obligation to do something, though in which way individual persons fulfil this requirement is a matter of their personal moral judgment. This is the case because individuals do have the competence to decide in which form they can best discharge the general moral obligation, given the particular context they are situated in. A universal prescription of justice as it is given in the case of negative duties would restrict the individuals' autonomy in pursuing their moral ends. The political conception of justice, which distinguishes clearly between principles of justice and individual moral duties (including positive duties), grants that autonomy; but a version of cosmopolitanism like the one Pogge defends – which recognises merely negative duties – limits this autonomy in a problematic way.

Negative duties are duties of justice. They drastically limit the freedom of individuals to set their own ends. This is justified if basic rights of others, for example their right to life and bodily integrity, would be violated directly by specific actions of individuals. Pogge claims that persons who profit from an unjust social and economic order do have a negative duty to protect the victims of this unjust order and to work towards a reform of it. The question is: what kind of duty is the negative duty appealed to here? It is certainly not a duty of justice in a juridical sense. We do not imprison people in rich countries if they neglect their

[28] Korsgaard, 'An Introduction to the Ethical, Political, and Religious Thought of Kant', 21f.

duty to work towards a reform of social institutions. Pogge concedes this point when he emphasises that he promotes a version of a moral, not a legal, cosmopolitanism.

In the sphere of morality – and global justice is a question of morality on Pogge's account – there is no recourse to the use of force. It is, however, a characteristic of negative rights and duties that there is strong reason to enforce them by state power. Positive duties cannot be enforced this way, at least not within a fairly liberal framework.

If people's individual choices in developed countries were normatively determined by the Rawlsian principles of justice, at least by the difference principle, then their way of living would have to be organised around the aim and end of reducing serious economic inequality. This might result, as pointed out, in excessively high demands and requirements on the side of individual persons. Why should persons have the duty to give up their form of life and accept a rather arduous way of living? Do they really have a conclusive reason to regard their form of life as wrong, especially if they do not have a luxurious lifestyle and could not afford it anyway? This sceptical question becomes even more urgent because many individual efforts to eliminate global inequalities are undermined by structural factors and disastrous political developments.

So two aspects of Pogge's account seem to me problematic. First, there is a conceptual difficulty in the way he defines and uses the notion of a negative duty. The duties he postulates as negative ones amount structurally to positive duties. Second, Pogge's inadequate use and application of the notion of a negative duty has the consequence that his account entails excessive requirements on the side of individuals.

People in economically well-off countries violate a negative duty, according to Pogge, by profiting from a social order that has unjust and harmful consequences for persons in other areas of the world. So they have a negative duty to protest against such an unjust economic order. However, individuals cannot be under an obligation to forego an action which they have not undertaken – namely to harm other persons directly by one of their actions. Though individuals are not directly responsible for global inequality, Pogge's account subjects them to heavy burdens which, I think, are unjustified.

Pogge's argument, for example, requires each person who profits from the currently unjust global economic order to take action against the unjust practices of global institutions. Pogge emphasises that there are several possibilities to fulfil the negative duty of not doing harm to poor people in poor countries. However, the possibilities he offers – organising political action, protesting, and even emigrating to another country – are in their daily consequences harsh alternatives. Not everyone is in a situation that allows her to fight constantly against the WTO, the World Bank and the IMF. Many people could not live their lives in such a context of permanent protest. Those who have to care for children or for elderly or sick people cannot fulfil this programme. And the demand that one morally ought to emigrate to another country because one's own country is involved in possibly harmful practices seems absurd.

One might argue that Pogge allows leeway for individuals in judging how they best live up to the obligation. This is correct: Pogge mentions that there are several ways to fulfil the negative duty of not doing harm. However, to argue this way just amounts to saying that the duties at stake are positive duties. The characteristic element of positive duties is, as I have pointed out, that they admit of a contextual interpretation whereas negative duties require refraining from a specific action.

Pogge's construction of negative duties on the side of individuals profiting from an unjust economic order is implausible. A theory of global justice cannot require a negative duty on the side of individuals to engage in permanent resistance or civil disobedience against unjust international organisations. The right of having autonomy in choosing one's plan of life is not compatible with a position that demands permanent political struggle against social and political orders, especially when their responsibility seems to be not always clearly given.[29]

The result of my discussion of Pogge's position is that we should be careful in giving up the conceptual separation between principles of justice addressed to institutions and the moral duties of individuals. A monist account is, as I pointed out, not a satisfactory alternative. Therefore, a combination of the normative design of institutions with an account of the moral duties arising on the side of individuals is more promising. Such a normative conception would need to prescribe both the institutional measures to fight poverty and the individual moral duties that would further the effect of such institutional measures.

Pogge, in a way, keeps to the separation between principles of justice guiding institutions and principles guiding individual choices, but in his

[29] In which way can an unemployed factory worker whose previous employer transferred the production of the company to a country with cheap labour, be made responsible for the condition of the inhabitants of a developing country? Moreover, how can she be made collectively responsible for violating a negative duty, namely not to harm or kill other people?

account of negative duties he undermines it. In this respect the political conception of justice is more plausible as it distinguishes clearly between those normative principles which are guidelines for institutions and those principles which guide individual choices.

To conclude: a main feature of Pogge's account is his rejection of the classical understanding of duties to help other people as so-called positive duties.[30] The idea is that an interpretation of our duties to poor people as positive duties amounts to a status quo justification rather than a remedy to the problem of world poverty. However, understanding positive duties as being weaker than negative duties – an assumption Pogge shares – depends, as I tried to show, on a mistaken reading of Kant's account of positive duties. A political conception of justice need not be committed to the thesis that negative duties have more normative strength than positive duties. Once we concede that negative duties and positive duties have equal weight, one of the main objections Pogge raises against a political conception of justice loses force.

But in another respect the political conception (at least some versions of it) is not convincing: its tendency to limit justice and accountability to state borders is indeed highly problematic. In the next section I will argue that this deficiency can be corrected without giving up the basic framework of a political conception of justice.

Global justice and national boundaries

Recent political theory has questioned the legitimacy of the nation-state system. According to cosmopolitans, the nation-state is in many ways a hindrance to a just global normative order. National borders, so the criticism goes, are not compatible with a global moral outlook and the

[30] Pogge criticises, for example, Rawls's classification of the natural duty of justice, i.e. the duty of assistance, as a positive duty. Rawls, he argues, thereby gives our duty to help others in need insufficient normative weight. See T. Pogge, *World Poverty and Human Rights*, 140, 292 (n. 211, 212). This criticism of Rawls (which depends on Rawls's interpretation of positive duties in *A Theory of Justice*) is justified as far as Rawls's reading of individual positive duties is concerned. (Rawls assumes in *A Theory of Justice* that individual positive duties are weaker than negative duties.) But Pogge's objection does not touch on Rawls's position as he outlines it in *The Law of Peoples*. In *The Law of Peoples* Rawls claims that peoples do have a duty of assistance towards burdened societies. However, that duty of assistance is not a natural or 'weak' positive duty; it is simply a normative guideline for the way societies ought to shape their international relations. Pogge confounds what Rawls says in regard to institutions and institutional policies with what Rawls says in regard to individual morality.

inclusion of all the members of the world society.[31] Political and social rights – for example, citizenship, residency and the right to work – are not granted universally; they are granted to certain people, and the nation-state is the institution that has the authority to confer or withhold these privileges. The partiality nation-states show towards the wellbeing of their citizens does not sit well with the demand that all people have an equal moral standing and an equal right to moral consideration. These quite familiar cosmopolitan arguments raise the question as to whether the nation-state is a precarious institution from the point of view of justice.

A political conception of justice, as we find it in Rawls's work, does not question the nation-state order. Its main focus, namely to formulate the principles and conditions of the just basic structure, presupposes implicitly that societies are organised in state units. Rawls's extension of his political conception to the international sphere in *The Law of Peoples* does not challenge the nation-state system as such, either.

Some defenders of a political conception of justice, however, have made a stronger claim, namely, that a state order is a necessary framework for social justice. One philosopher who has recently defended a political conception of justice along this line against a cosmopolitan reading of global justice is Thomas Nagel. He proposes a coercion-based version of political justice: justice has to be backed by state authority and requires 'government as an enabling condition'.[32] Nagel justifies this assumption with the connection between sovereignty and justice:

> What creates the link between justice and sovereignty is something common to a wide range of conceptions of justice: they all depend on the coordinated conduct of large numbers of people, which cannot be achieved without law backed by a monopoly of force.[33]

Nagel links justice to the state structure because he assumes that justice can be realised only by state coercion. Accordingly he limits the scope of justice:

> The full standards of justice, though they can be known by moral reasoning, apply only within the boundaries of a sovereign state, however

[31] Pogge argues that from the standpoint of cosmopolitan morality national sovereignty in its classical form is no longer defensible. Pogge, *World Poverty and Human Rights*, 126–51. Seyla Benhabib equally takes a critical stance towards the nation-state; she diagnoses a 'disaggregation of citizenship' as a consequence of migration and a dissociation of citizenship and cultural identity. See S. Benhabib, 'Democratic Iterations. The Local, the National, and the Global', in Benhabib, *Another Cosmopolitanism* (Oxford University Press, 2006), 45–80.

[32] Nagel, 'The Problem of Global Justice', 114. [33] *Ibid.*, 115.

> arbitrary those boundaries may be. Internationally, there may well be standards, but they do not merit the full name of justice.[34]

Nagel holds that justice refers to the basic institutions of society; justice cannot apply to individuals outside the realm of the nation-state. Justice is, therefore, an 'associative obligation', only owed to those with whom we have strong political relations. We do not have a full obligation to those with whom we have not yet established political relations within a sovereign nation-state which subdues us to its coercive power. We can speak of egalitarian justice regarding the internal structure of the nation-state, but absent a global coercive power (which for Nagel clearly is not in place) there can be no global justice – neither in the sense of individual relations between persons nor between global institutions.

Nagel acknowledges, of course, the existence of institutions and organisations on a supranational level. He denies, however, that these new developments of global interaction do away with the significance and priority of the nation-state. International organisations are, as he points out, simply tools for establishing ways for nation-states to 'cooperate to better advance their separate aims' and he adds that 'they rely on the enforcement of the power of the separate sovereign states, and not on a supranational force that is responsible to all'.[35]

Nagel's argument goes against the line of much of current theorising, especially the global horizon and global governance rhetoric we often encounter in this field.[36] His standpoint looks stunningly conservative. The criticism of Nagel's coercion-based account has been sharp.[37]

34 *Ibid.*, 122. 35 *Ibid.*, 140.

36 For a good criticism of that rhetoric cf. Jean Cohen, 'Whose Sovereignty?: Empire versus International Law', in C. Barry and T. Pogge (eds.), *Global Institutions and Responsibilities: Achieving Global Justice* (Oxford: Blackwell, 2005), 159–89, here 164–70.

37 One critic has argued that Nagel's coercion-based political theory of justice 'rests on a perverse normative principle'. See Abizadeh, 'Cooperation, Pervasive Impact, and Coercion', 351. The perverse normative premise is, according to Abizadeh, Nagel's claim that demands of justice arise only if a person is subjected to state coercion 'regulated by a system of law carried out in her name, i.e. actively engaging her will' (*ibid.*, 351). This assumption entails, Abizadeh criticises, that a state can avoid accountability in terms of justice 'by denying to those whom it coerces any standing as putative authors of the system of coercion'; a consequence which seems 'perverse' in regard to the force states enact against foreigners and possible immigrants (*ibid.*, 351). This criticism seems only justified if Nagel would hold that states can enact immigration regulations arbitrarily, without any need to account for them. Yet Nagel merely claims that states have the duty to enact those laws with an eye to the will and consent of the members of that state. One might criticise that such a conception inevitably leads to rather restrictive immigration laws, but the assumption as such certainly does not seem perverse.

However, I think Nagel's account offers, aside from the limited way Nagel himself understands it, a normative standard for the assessment of international organisations and relations.

A main objection against Nagel's coercion-based political conception of justice has been that Nagel completely ignores the existence of coercion on the global level: force is not exclusively an element of the nation-state structure. International organisations – for example, the IMF, the WTO – are coercive as well; agreement to their terms is not always voluntary.[38] For example, states often have no choice but to comply with the regulations and policies of those organisations, and they often have no exit option. Moreover, international organisations are, as critics point out, rule-generating bodies enacting norms and guidelines, and non-compliance with imposed trade and finance agreements entails often substantial sanctions. Transnational institutions have intergovernmental power since they have an impact on national decision-making and national normative standards. So Nagel's idea that states join these organisations only to pursue their individual self-interests, and that they remain completely sovereign actors controlling the enforcement of regulations by their national enforcement power, underestimates completely the inevitable transformations on the national level. As Joshua Cohen and Charles Sabel note:

> In joining the WTO in order to participate as fully as possible in the global economy, member states are not agreeing to substitute the domestic rules that they have settled on with the universal laws of efficient commerce. Rather, they are agreeing to remake their rules, in domain after domain, in light of the efforts, recorded in international standards regimes, of all the others to reconcile distinctive domestic regulations with general standards that are also attentive to the interests of others elsewhere.[39]

Some critics take this line of objection, pointing out the existence of coercion on the global level, to be sufficient to reject Nagel's coercion-based account.[40] But such a complete dismissal of Nagel's coercion-based account seems too quick. Nagel's argument, though he himself does not

[38] For a discussion of the no-choice situation of poor countries against IMF policies see J. E. Stiglitz, *Globlization and its Discontents* (New York, London: Norton & Company, 2002), chs. 2 and 3.

[39] Joshua Cohen and C. Sabel, 'Extra Republicam. Nulla Justitia?', *Philosophy and Public Affairs*, 34 (2006), 147–75, here 172.

[40] One example is A. Sangiovanni, 'Global Justice, Reciprocity, and the State', *Philosophy and Public Affairs*, 35 (2007), 3–39. Sangiovanni defends a relation-based version of a

pursue that line, can be extended to the international sphere and can be interpreted as providing a quite useful normative guideline for interactions on the global level.

Nagel's thesis about the connection between sovereignty and coercion entails that the state has a specific responsibility towards those persons who are subject to its coercive power: the state owes its subjects a justification for the way they are treated. As Nagel writes:

> A sovereign state is not just a cooperative enterprise for mutual advantage. The societal rules determining its basic structure are coercively imposed: it is not a voluntary association. I submit that it is this complex fact – that we are both putative joint authors of the coercively imposed system, and subject to its norms, i.e. expected to accept their authority even when the collective decision diverges from our personal preferences that creates the special presumption against arbitrary inequalities in our treatment by the system.[41]

Nagel emphasises that most people have no choice in that respect. But their being members of a political society is connected with 'a special involvement of agency or the will': they have the dual role of being subject to authority but also – ideally – giving their consent to the exercise of authority qua 'participants in the general will'.[42]

What Nagel formulates here is not merely an empirical premise about the connection between justice and coercion, but a normative standard of when coercion is legitimate. Coercion is justified if those who are subject to it could give their consent. Understood in this way, Nagel's coercion-based account has the potential for a normative standard in the international sphere. Are the terms on which states enter international organisations and treaties fair enough for them to give their consent? Are the agreements fair? Is their accountability and justification

political conception of justice: states provide basic collective goods; for example, protection from physical attack and maintenance of a system of property rights; therefore we have special obligations of egalitarian justice to fellow citizens and residents who support the system providing these goods. Sangiovanni's relation-based account seems to me not so different from a coercion-based version of the political conception; the distinction he draws up between the two positions seems artificial. The decisive point in Sangiovanni's defence of a relation-based political conception of justice can only be that the state provides *secure access* to certain goods that others living in this community contribute to create. The production of collective goods within a state-community, however, does not work exclusively on the basis of voluntary commitment, but includes enforcement. So a coercion-based account is at the basis of a relation-based version of the political conception.

[41] Nagel, 'The Problem of Global Justice', 128f. [42] *Ibid.*, 128.

given towards those who are subject to sanctions if they do not comply with the agreements and rules?

The problem with Nagel's account is that he restricts coercion and therefore justice to the sovereign state. Cohen and Sabel rightly criticise Nagel for making no room for 'normatively motivated worries about whether global institutions are fair, or accountable and relatively transparent, or democratic, or about how to structure greater participation or representation in their decision making'.[43] That ignorance is not a necessary presupposition of a coercion-based account; it is rather due to Nagel's specifically limited reading of such a position. There seems to be no need to understand the connection between justice and coercion in such a narrow sense. Nagel's version of a political conception of justice associates 'justice' mainly with its realisation in the policies, institutional regulations, and the legislation of a nation-state. Justice is connected with state coercion and is bound to the law backed by a state order. However, a political conception of justice allows us to understand the concept of justice in a wider sense. Standards of justice like reciprocity and fair equality of opportunity are principles of public morality: they are guidelines not only for the design of nation-state institutions but also for the normative and moral assessment of institutions that we create on the global level.[44]

Nagel, we can conclude, is wrong about the site as well as the scope of justice. Issues of justice are not confined to the basic structure of nation-states but arise also in regard to the evolving global basic structure, i.e. those international organisations which do have substantial impact on the social and economic conditions in various countries. International institutions are powerful norm-generating bodies that equally must meet standards of justice, fairness and accountability.[45]

[43] Cohen and Sabel, 'Extra Republicam. Nulla Justitia?', 156.

[44] Nagel's worry seems to be that including problems of global inequality among problems of justice would make it possible to legally coerce individuals who are better off to help those worse off. And that might be objectionable. However, such a consequence might be objectionable also from the point of view of a political conception of justice that recognises problems of global justice and the existence of a global basic structure.

[45] One might argue that the concept of legitimacy which is weaker than the standard of justice might be more apt to assess the policies of international organisations. For such a proposal see F. Peter, 'Global Justice and Legitimacy', paper presented at the 'Absolute Poverty and Global Justice' conference, Erfurt, 18–20 July 2008.

An additional problem of Nagel's account seems to be that he presupposes also a quite restricted conception of legitimacy. See Nagel, 'The Problem of Global Justice', 140, 145. Nagel sees human rights as a part of a minimal humanitarian morality outside the realm of justice. This does not sit well with the standing that human rights as a convention of

Yet extending the limits of Nagel's account in that way does not mean that we have reason to do away with the institution of the nation-state as such. There are several arguments why there is no need to reject the nation-state system in order to reach more justice on the global level. A first argument appeals to the structural advantages of the nation-state. Nation-states are established orders. They are sometimes the result of a long history and difficult struggles. They have a stabilising function and their eruption or dissolution might come at a high cost. Nation-states are not necessarily bad actors and, especially if they incorporate a democratic order and system, they are a basis for culture and identity.[46] To break up such orders might be politically risky and might create less protection in terms of security, guarantees and rights.

A second argument is that there is simply no moral duty for an enlargement of state borders or an elimination of such borders. The requirement for global justice cannot entail the dissolution of the nation-state to be obligatory, since this dissolution does not necessarily lead to more justice. Extensions of state borders often create new injustices.[47] Greater economic equality, as Rawls's important axiom of lexical priority reminds us, might not be a justifying reason to upset existing normative orders, especially if these orders grant basic political rights on the basis of an 'equal freedom' standard.

international law actually possess. Human rights are the standard by which legal orders but also institutional structures and the work of international organisations are assessed. Human rights are connected with the idea of legitimacy in an important way. Human rights are, as Habermas puts it, a necessary component of the concept of legitimacy, because human rights 'ground an inherently legitimate rule of law' (J. Habermas, 'Remarks on Legitimation through Human Rights', in J. Habermas, *The Postnational Constellation. Political Essays* (Cambridge: Polity Press, 2001), 113–29). For an illuminating discussion of the relationship between legitimacy and human rights see also A. Buchanan, *Justice, Legitimacy, and Self-Determination. Moral Foundations for International Law* (Oxford University Press, 2004), chs. 3, 5, 6.

46 There is a justification of the nation-state *on the grounds* of culture and identity. That is not the approach I put forward here. One can provide a neutral justification of the nation-state that does not rely on cultural arguments, which somehow create problems of exclusion. For a justification of the nation-state on the basis of cultural and national identity see D. Miller, *On Nationality* (Oxford: Clarendon Press, 1995) and D. Miller, *Citizenship and National Identity* (Cambridge: Polity Press, 2000).

47 There has been, for example, serious criticism in the Maghreb countries (based on appeals to 'equal consideration') that the EU integration of Eastern European countries will diminish the EU support for structural reforms in North Africa. See R. Chennoufi, 'Kulturelle Differenz. Toleranz und Demokratie', in P. Koller (ed.), *Die Globale Frage. Empirische Befunde und ethische Herausforderungen* (Vienna: Passagen Verlag, 2006), 401–17.

A third argument is that the idea of nation-states as autonomous political entities freely consenting to the policies of international organisations – organisations set up as tools for international cooperation, coordination and a better global order – is a powerful normative criterion to assess the legitimacy of these global institutions. Certain nation-states, as has often been pointed out, are in such a weak political and economic position that they cannot display their sovereignty and autonomy in international negotiations and agreements. Therefore the way to go, it seems, is to confirm and secure their equal status and not take an additional step to undermine their autonomy by demanding their disaggregation and dissolution. The idea of equal sovereignty, as Jean Cohen argues, is a criterion for a rule of law regime on the global level:

> The concept of sovereignty is a reminder not only of the political context of law but also of the ultimate dependence of political power and political regimes on a valid, public, normative legal order for their authority.[48]

Should we really be so impressed by the idea of global governance that we would think its emerging possibility gives us a decisive reason to prefer it to the traditional form of state government? Would it bring more justice? The fancy and flattering way with which global governance is sometimes advocated should not deceive us about the possible lack of control, transparency or legitimacy in the decision-making processes of transnational institutions. Certainly, I do not want to raise objections against the existence of these international organisations per se. I also do not want to claim that nation-states as such are always legitimate. However, what I would like to argue is that a strong condition for the political legitimacy of transnational institutions is the free and voluntary agreement of the nation-states that created these institutions by consent. International organisations are accountable to states and their citizens.[49]

Institutions to promote justice are, as Hume tells us, artificial virtues, they are tools we invent and construct to help secure our wellbeing. And Hume adds that concern with the wellbeing of those affected, 'a sympathy *with public interest*', as he phrases it, '*is the source of the moral* approbation, *which attends that virtue*' of justice.[50] Considered that way, some of the controversies between cosmopolitans and philosophers

[48] Jean Cohen, 'Whose Sovereignty?', 173.

[49] For an explanation of accountability from the perspective of a global governance account see A.-M. Slaughter, *A New World Order* (Princeton University Press, 2004), 231–5.

[50] D. Hume, in L. A. Selby-Bigge and P. H. Nidditch (eds.), *A Treatise of Human Nature*. Second edition, edited by L. A. Selby-Bigge and P. H. Niddich (Oxford: Clarendon Press, 1978), 499f.

defending a political theory of justice – for example, the question whether individuals or institutions should be the relevant moral units of global justice – seem not as dividing as sometimes proposed.

References

Abizadeh, A. 2007. 'Cooperation, Pervasive Impact, and Coercion: On the Scope (not Site) of Distributive Justice', *Philosophy and Public Affairs* 35: 308–58.

Beitz, C. R. 2005. 'Cosmopolitanism and Global Justice', *The Journal of Ethics* 9: 11–27.

Benhabib, S. 2006. 'Democratic Iterations. The Local, the National, and the Global', in Benhabib, *Another Cosmopolitanism*. Oxford University Press, 45–80.

Buchanan, A. 2000. 'Rawls's Law of Peoples: Rules of a Vanished Westphalian World', *Ethics* 110: 697–721.

Buchanan, A. 2004. *Justice, Legitimacy, and Self-Determination. Moral Foundations for International Law*. Oxford University Press.

Chennoufi, R. 2006. 'Kulturelle Differenz. Toleranz und Demokratie', in Koller, P. (ed.), *Die Globale Frage. Empirische Befunde und ethische Herausforderungen*. Vienna: Passagen Verlag, 401–17.

Cohen, G. A. 1995. 'Incentives, Inequality, and Community', in Darwall, S. (ed.), *Equal Freedom: Selected Tanner Lectures on Human Value*. Ann Arbor: The University of Michigan Press, 331–97.

Cohen, G. A. 1997. 'Where the Action Is: On the Site of Distributive Justice', *Philosophy and Public Affairs* 26: 3–30.

Cohen, Jean. 2005. 'Whose Sovereignty?: Empire versus International Law', in Barry, C. and Pogge, T. (eds.), *Global Institutions and Responsibilities: Achieving Global Justice*. Oxford: Blackwell.

Cohen, Joshua and Sabel, C. 2006. 'Extra Republicam. Nulla Justitia?', *Philosophy and Public Affairs* 34: 147–75.

Habermas, J. 2001. 'Remarks on Legitimation through Human Rights', in Habermas, J., *The Postnational Constellation. Political Essays*. Cambridge: Polity Press.

Hume, D. 1978. *A Treatise of Human Nature*. Second edition, edited by L. A. Selby-Bigge and P. H. Nidditch. Oxford: Clarendon Press.

Jamieson, D. 2005. 'Duties to the Distant: Aid, Assistance, and Interventions in the Developing World', *The Journal of Ethics* 9: 151–70.

Julius, A. J. 2006. 'Nagel's Atlas', *Philosophy and Public Affairs* 34: 176–92.

Kant, I. 1996. 'Introduction to the Doctrine of Virtue', in Kant, *The Metaphysics of Morals. Part II: Metaphysical First Principles of the Doctrine of Virtue*, edited by M. Gregor. Cambridge University Press.

Korsgaard, C. M. 1996. *Creating the Kingdom of Ends*. Cambridge University Press.

Miller, D. 1995. *On Nationality*. Oxford: Clarendon Press.

Miller, D. 2000. *Citizenship and National Identity*. Cambridge: Polity Press.

Murphy, L. B. 1998. 'Institutions and the Demands of Justice', *Philosophy and Public Affairs* 27: 251–91.

Nagel, T. 2005. 'The Problem of Global Justice', *Philosophy and Public Affairs* 33: 113–47.

Nussbaum, M. C. 2006. *Frontiers of Justice. Disability, Nationality, Species Membership*. Cambridge, MA: Harvard University Press.

Peter, F. 2008. 'Global Justice and Legitimacy', paper presented at the 'Absolute Poverty and Global Justice' conference, Erfunt, 18–20 July.

Pogge, T. 2000. 'On the Site of Distributive Justice: Reflections on Cohen and Murphy', *Philosophy and Public Affairs* 29: 137–69.

Pogge, T. 2008. *World Poverty and Human Rights*. Cambridge: Polity Press.

Rawls, J. 1993. *Political Liberalism*. New York: Columbia University Press.

Rawls, J. 1999. *A Theory of Justice*. Cambridge, MA: The Belknap Press.

Rawls, J. 1999. *The Law of Peoples*. Cambridge, MA: Harvard University Press.

Risse, M. 2005. 'How Does the Global Order Harm the Poor', *Philosophy and Public Affairs* 33: 349–76.

Sangiovanni, A. 2007. 'Global Justice, Reciprocity, and the State', *Philosophy and Public Affairs* 35: 3–39.

Slaughter, A.-M. 2004. *A New World Order*. Princeton University Press.

Stiglitz, J. E. 2002. *Globlization and its Discontents*. New York, London: Norton & Company.

8

The responsibility to protect human rights

DAVID MILLER

I start from the assumption that the responsibility to protect human rights is an international responsibility. Protecting human rights is not just a matter of each state protecting the rights of its own citizens, even though this is one of its primary functions and (arguably) a condition of its legitimacy. For various reasons that I will come to shortly, making human rights protection purely an internal responsibility of states is not going to be effective in many cases. So the wider responsibility falls on that rather elusive entity 'the world community'. Now let me immediately specify, for purposes of the present discussion, the scope of the responsibility to protect. First, the human rights at stake are to be understood in a fairly narrow sense, as basic rights – rights to life, bodily integrity, basic nutrition and health, and so forth. When we invoke the international responsibility to protect, we are thinking about those all-too-familiar instances in which human beings are being placed in life-threatening situations, in which they are being starved, or terrorised, or evicted from their homes, or are dying from disease – in other words are caught up in what we have learnt to call humanitarian disasters. We are not primarily thinking in this context about rights that fall outside this core, such as rights to free speech or political participation, important though these may be in other respects.[1] Second, we are talking about cases in which human rights

This chapter began life as a short paper for the Workshop on Global Governance held at Princeton University in March 2006. A fuller version was presented to the International Symposium on Justice, Legitimacy and Public International Law, University of Bern, 15–17 December 2006, and later to The Centre for the Study of Social Justice at the University of Oxford. It was also given as a lecture in the Dee Lecture Series on Global Justice, Poverty and War at the University of Utah. On all these occasions I received very helpful critical feedback from the participants. I should particularly like to thank Daniel Butt, Jerry Cohen, Colin Farrelly and Lukas Meyer for their written suggestions.

[1] There is some disagreement about whether this wider set of rights should be seen as human rights proper, or as something else – rights of citizenship, for example. My reasons

are being violated on a large scale, not about individual violations such as will, regrettably, occur on a daily basis in most states. It is only when the scale of rights violations crosses a certain threshold that the idea of an international responsibility to protect human rights comes into play.[2]

That idea, I believe, is fast gathering strength as part of what we might call positive international morality, if not yet international law.[3] One reason why it is not yet included as an international legal norm is that it appears to conflict directly with the idea of state sovereignty – in particular with the idea that intervention in the internal affairs of states is never legitimate unless the state in question itself authorises the intervention. Whether in any given case there is indeed a direct clash between the responsibility to protect and state sovereignty may depend on why it is that human rights are being violated: here it may be worth considering the various different scenarios in which the responsibility to protect human rights might be invoked. Without claiming to have produced an exhaustive catalogue, let me distinguish:

a) Natural disasters – earthquakes, floods, droughts etc. – that leave people without food, shelter and other necessities of life.
b) Deprivation that arises as the unintended consequence of government policies, for example disastrous economic policies that leave many people destitute.
c) Systematic rights violations on the part of governments, for example the incarceration of political opponents, punishment of their supporters, use of torture or other degrading modes of treatment.

for favouring the latter view can be found in D. Miller, *National Responsibility and Global Justice* (Oxford University Press, 2007), ch. 7. But for present purposes it is not essential to resolve this disagreement, so long as we are clear about the substance of the rights that generate the responsibility to protect.

2 I shall not in this chapter investigate the source of this responsibility. I shall take it for granted that where large-scale violations of human rights are occurring, everyone who is able to do something to prevent that happening has a responsibility to do so: it would be morally wrong – a denial of equal human worth – simply to stand by and do nothing. This basic premise does not, however, settle either the extent of this responsibility or how it should be distributed among persons. For that reason I use the language of responsibility rather than obligation – obligations are concrete moral requirements that arise when the two issues just canvassed have been settled.

3 For contrasting views on the question whether a right of humanitarian intervention now forms part of international law, see N. Wheeler, *Saving Strangers: Humanitarian Intervention in International Society* (Oxford University Press, 2000) and S. Chesterman, *Just War or Just Peace? Humanitarian Intervention and International Law* (Oxford University Press, 2001). For discussion, see J. Welsh, 'From Right to Responsibility: Humanitarian Intervention and International Society', *Global Governance*, 8 (2002), 503–21.

d) Rights violations resulting from wars between states, of civilians caught up in the fighting, displaced by it, or unable to satisfy basic needs on account of it.
e) Rights violations arising in circumstances of state breakdown or civil war – massacres, ethnic cleansing and so forth.

As we work through this list, we see immediately that interventions to protect human rights would challenge state sovereignty most directly in cases b) and c). These are cases in which the state itself is responsible for the rights violations, either directly or indirectly, and in which intervention must therefore take the form of challenging and trying to reverse the policies in question – which might also mean a change of government or regime. In case a) intervention may be welcomed by the receiving state, so long as it retains some control over the way that it is carried out. In cases d) and e) the very existence of the state as a body having a monopoly of legitimate authority over a well-defined territory is being put in question by events on the ground; if the state is not, in fact, an effective sovereign, then intervention cannot be ruled out by an appeal to the norm of sovereignty.

But in any case, the idea that state sovereignty is a trump card that defeats all other moral and legal considerations has been challenged in recent years, and not only by political philosophers. Belief in the overriding importance of human rights was encapsulated in a semi-official document, *The Responsibility to Protect*, the title of a report issued by the International Commission on Intervention and State Sovereignty in 2001 in response to the debate over humanitarian intervention sparked by interventions that had happened in the previous decade, such as NATO's intervention in Kosovo, and others that had failed to happen, such as, notoriously, in Rwanda.[4]

The Commission's Report interprets intervention in quite a broad way, covering aspects of humanitarian action that go well beyond the military intervention that might halt a civil war or a genocide. Nevertheless its central focus is on cases of military intervention by outside bodies in the internal affairs of sovereign states, and for this reason the questions that chiefly concern it are questions of international law: first, under what

[4] *The Responsibility to Protect: Report of the International Commission on Intervention and State Sovereignty* (Ottawa: International Development Research Centre, 2001) and *The Responsibility to Protect, Research, Bibliography, Background: Supplementary Volume to the Report of the International Commission on Intervention and State Sovereignty* (Ottawa: International Development Research Centre, 2001).

circumstances may the normal presumption of the integrity of sovereign states be set aside by virtue of the human rights violations that are taking place within their borders, and, second, who is authorised to intervene? Is it a necessary condition that the intervention has been approved by the UN Security Council, for instance? These, one might say, are questions about the legitimacy of intervention. There is, however, another question that seems to me equally if not more important, and that prompts the present discussion, namely who has the *responsibility* to intervene. It is one thing to say that when large-scale violations of human rights are taking place, there is a diffused responsibility on the part of humanity as a whole to protect the victims; it is another to say more precisely where this responsibility falls and how it can be made effective. Such discussion of this question as the Report contains tends to focus on the question of whether states should be disqualified from intervening when they have some material interest in the outcome – on which it takes the realistic view that mixed motives are inevitable in international relations as elsewhere, and that it may be necessary for domestic reasons for intervening states to claim that their own national interests are served by their intervention. Elsewhere it laments the Security Council's past inability to mobilise UN member states to act in circumstances where intervention was clearly both legitimate and essential.

Yet despite this neglect, one might think that this problem of assigning responsibilities is central to establishing an effective international human rights regime. Intervening to protect human rights is typically costly, in material resources in every case, in human resources in many cases (when soldiers, peacekeepers or aid workers are killed or taken hostage), in political capital (when intervention is construed by third parties as motivated by self-interest or imperial ambitions, leading in some cases to reprisals against the intervening state or its citizens). So states have good reasons to avoid becoming involved if at all possible, particularly democratic states where the government will come under heavy domestic fire if the intervention goes wrong. The fact that there are often many agencies – states, coalitions of states, or other bodies – that might in principle discharge the responsibility to protect makes the problem worse. We might draw an analogy here with instances in which individuals are confronted with a situation in which they would have to perform a Good Samaritan act – say going to the rescue of somebody who collapses in the street. Empirical studies of situations like this reveal that the more potential rescuers are present, the less likely anybody is to intervene – so the victim stands a better chance of being picked up if there is only one passer-by at the time he collapses than if there are, say, six people nearby.[5] Several factors may combine to produce this outcome: people interpret other people's inaction as a sign that the problem is less serious than it might appear; there is a parallel normative effect whereby each person takes the others' behaviour as defining what is expected or right under the circumstances; but perhaps most importantly, responsibility is diffused among the potential helpers: if the victim were to die, no one in particular could be held responsible for the death.

This problem of diffused responsibility leading to inaction can potentially be solved in two ways. One is the appearance of an authority with the capacity to single out agents and assign them particular tasks. In the street collapse case we might imagine a policeman arriving on the scene and asking bystanders to do specific things to help the victim. Obviously this can only work in cases where enough of those present recognise the authoritative status of the person who is doing the assigning. The second is the emergence of shared norms that identify one person in particular as having the responsibility to take the lead. These norms do not have to carry all of the justificatory load needed to support the intervention. After all we can probably assume that every bystander looking at the victim would agree that 'somebody should help that man'. What is needed is an additional norm that can tell us who that somebody is. If we return to the case of the international protection of human rights, there is, as we have seen, an emerging (though not yet complete) consensus on the principle that where systematic violations of human rights are taking place, some agency should step in to prevent them. The problem is to identify the particular agency.

In moving from cases which involve the responsibility to rescue a particular individual to collective interventions to protect human rights, we face an additional difficulty. Given the nature and scale of such interventions, they will in practice nearly always have to be undertaken by states, or by coalitions of states (I shall defend this assumption shortly). But these states are coercive bodies, at least in relation to their own citizens. When they intervene, they impose requirements on people – for example they send soldiers or aid workers to the areas where the rights violations are taking place, often at some considerable risk to the people who are sent. Even if there is no risk to persons,

[5] I have considered these studies, and their normative implications, in D. Miller '"Are they *my* Poor?": The Problem of Altruism in a World of Strangers', *Critical Review of International Social Philosophy and Policy*, 5 (2002), 106–27.

resources are required, and these of course are raised by compulsory taxation of the citizens. So the question arises whether interventions that impose requirements of this kind can ever be justified. It is one thing to say that as human beings we all share in a responsibility to protect the human rights of the rest of mankind; it is another to say that we can be forced to discharge this responsibility via the agency of the state.

Should we then leave states out of the picture and instead embrace a purely voluntary model of international rights protection, leaving such protection entirely in the hands of bodies staffed by volunteers and funded by voluntary contributions? We can find instances where something like this model already applies. Much human rights work is done by aid agencies like Oxfam and volunteer groups like Médecins sans Frontières. But without in any way diminishing the importance of such work, it is hard to see this voluntary model as the solution to all human rights disasters. Its limitations are fairly obvious. Where states themselves are the primary source of the human rights violations, as in our cases b) and c) above, no voluntary body is likely to have the capacity to stand up to the delinquent state; we know, for example, that aid agencies already face acute dilemmas when, in order to carry out their humanitarian work, they have to go along with government policies in the target state that they find objectionable. Furthermore, when the risks to human life rise above a certain threshold, voluntary agencies quite reasonably decide to pull their people out, so if anything is going to be done in cases of type e), involving state breakdown or civil war, it must involve intervention by outside agencies that are themselves able to wield coercive power sufficient to separate the warring parties and re-establish social order – in other words by states, or international bodies made up of states. Finally, intervention by voluntary bodies faces familiar problems of accountability: who is to say that a particular form of intervention is legitimate, if undertaken by a body that is not democratically accountable, except perhaps to its self-selected members? This issue becomes troubling whenever intervention is seen to have an impact on the outcome of an internal struggle in the society where the rights violations are occurring. Of course intervening states too can be, and often are, partisan in their actions, but at least they remain accountable for what they do, to their own citizens and to international organisations.

In response to such difficulties, we might propose an alternative version of the voluntary model. Suppose the United Nations, or some other international body of similar scope, were to create a taskforce for humanitarian intervention. Money raised by a global tax would be used to recruit soldiers and others willing to act under UN authorisation. Because of the tax element, this model is not a purely voluntary one, but it could be argued that everyone would merely be contributing their fair share of the costs of discharging a universal obligation to protect human rights. Since the members of the taskforce would be recruited on a voluntary basis, no untoward coercion is involved.

Such a model is prima facie attractive, but we have to ask about the realism of its underlying assumptions. If a force is to be created with sufficient capacity to take on delinquent rights-violating states, as in scenarios b) and c), or to re-establish order in the event of state breakdown, it would require an enormous investment not only in manpower but in armaments, delivery systems and so forth – it would need in other words to replicate the armed forces of a mid-size contemporary state, at the very least. We must ask whether the UN, or its equivalent, is likely in the near future to command the resources and the authority to bring such a force into existence. We must also ask about the decision procedures that would allow it to be deployed. Would it, for example, require the universal consent of all member states bar the delinquents? Observing the present difficulties in obtaining UN authorisation for even relatively small-scale peacekeeping operations inevitably induces scepticism about this version of the voluntary model.

If such scepticism is justified, it follows that the responsibility to protect human rights must in practice be discharged primarily by states, or by international institutions like NATO that represent coalitions of like-minded states. How, then, can it be made legitimate from the point of view of those who are forced to bear the costs of intervention? We might envisage a *contractual* model of international responsibility as an alternative to the voluntary model. The model would look something like this. Citizens, understanding that they have a responsibility towards the human rights of people worldwide, agree to authorise their states to discharge this responsibility on their behalf, an agreement that involves consenting to be taxed for this purpose and/or being sent in some capacity to deal with human rights violations on the ground. Having themselves been authorised in this way, states would then contract with each other to distribute the responsibility – for example forming coalitions in order to create intervention taskforces of different kinds. If this model could be put in place, it would clearly resolve the problem that I identified earlier – the problem, namely, that each state is understandably reluctant to take on the responsibility to protect human rights itself, given the likely costs of discharging that responsibility. According to the terms of the model, each state would be contractually bound to contribute, and if its citizens protested, they could be reminded that they had contracted to authorise the state to act on their behalf.

But does the model really provide a feasible solution to the problem? We need to look more closely at the reasons citizens might have for agreeing to the contract that is being proposed, given that *ex ante* they have no coercively enforceable obligation to protect the human rights of outsiders. Much depends here on which of the five scenarios outlined above we are contemplating. Consider scenario a) – cases in which human rights are put at risk by natural disasters such as floods and famines. Citizens might well sign up to an international contract of mutual aid in response to such situations, because, first, although the likelihood of falling victim to such disasters varies considerably from place to place, still in principle any region of any society might at some time find itself facing a natural disaster, so the contract appeals not only to altruism but also to risk aversion; second, the expected cost of the contract, for any individual or any society, remains moderate. When one society is hit by a natural disaster, other societies would be expected to supply relief funds whose cost can be spread widely across all members of the contributing states, while those who are sent to implement the relief effort are not, normally, in great personal danger themselves. Contrast this with the case of military intervention in response to civil war or genocide. For liberal societies especially, there is virtually no element of mutual aid here; their citizens cannot reasonably anticipate being rescued from civil war or genocide themselves under the terms of the contract. It is sometimes argued that they may benefit in other ways – for example by virtue of facing a lesser threat of terrorism if the conflict situation is resolved. But recent experience surely casts considerable doubt on this proposition. Intervention may benefit large numbers of people whose lives are currently being threatened by civil war or genocide, but at the same time it is likely to arouse hostility among those who lose out in the process, and their sympathisers in other countries – so there is a real risk that violent action may be taken by way of retribution against the intervening state. Moreover the cost of intervention may be high, and very unevenly distributed. Citizens might very reasonably wish to set limits to their future liability, and therefore decline to issue a general authorisation to their states of the kind proposed; they would want to retain the right to decide on each intervention case by case, taking account of the likely costs involved when set against gains to human rights that the intervention would bring. This in turn would prevent states signing up to any arrangement that would oblige them to intervene regardless of the current wishes of their citizens.

The conclusion to this line of thought is that interventions can only be made legitimate by the direct democratic authorisation of the citizen body. Such authorisation might be given in different ways – through a referendum, for example, or through more normal processes of democratic politics whereby governments submit themselves to popular vote if the policies they want to pursue provoke large-scale resistance. This would have the practical drawback that rapid intervention would be difficult unless it was clear that public opinion was strongly in favour, in which case governments could act first and win their mandate later. Whether an intervention would be authorised or not would also be less predictable, which might mean that rogue states, or ethnic groups within those states, were less deterred from embarking on courses of action that would justify the intervention (such as policies aimed at ethnic cleansing). Moreover this approach would not solve the multi-agent problem at international level: assuming that in any particular case, several states, or several different coalitions of states, could carry out an intervention successfully, their citizen bodies would find themselves in the position of bystanders at an accident, each hoping that somebody else will step in to help while being willing to shoulder the responsibility themselves as a last resort. So from the human rights point of view, it can only be regarded as a second best, given that neither the voluntary model nor the contractual model passes the test of feasibility. More fundamentally, we may wonder whether a democratic vote in favour of intervention necessarily solves the internal legitimacy problem. Can a majority vote in favour of some policy justify the imposition of substantial costs upon a minority of citizens who may have voted against the policy?

In general, the answer to this question must surely be 'yes'. The essence of democratic politics is that minorities are obliged to accept the outcome of a majority vote even if this is to their disadvantage. On the other hand, the legitimate authority of the majority is usually understood to be circumscribed in various ways. Minorities have rights too: their human rights cannot be infringed; they are owed various kinds of equal treatment, and so forth. The question, then, is whether decisions involving interventions to protect the human rights of non-citizens are to be seen simply as part of normal politics within those constraints, where majority votes can legitimately bind minorities, or whether they raise deeper questions, such that a more inclusive form of consent is needed to make them legitimate.

Allen Buchanan, in an illuminating discussion of the internal legitimacy of humanitarian intervention, has posed the problem in the following way.[6] Suppose we were to see the authority of the state as stemming from a hypothetical agreement among its members to create an association that serves their interests; then humanitarian intervention becomes problematic, except in the unlikely event that it receives unanimous support from the citizens. Since the purpose of the intervention is to protect the human rights of outsiders, it falls outside the scope of the hypothetical contract, and those opposed to the intervention who would have nevertheless to bear some of the costs are entitled to refuse to do so. Thus soldiers can be required to fight in national defence, or more widely in pursuit of national interests, but not merely to protect the human rights of outsiders – a view famously articulated by Samuel Huntington, who said, in relation to the US intervention in Somalia in 1992, 'it is morally unjustifiable and politically indefensible that members of the Armed Forces should be killed to prevent Somalis from killing one another'.[7] To get beyond this point, a more expansive conception of the state is needed, which Buchanan labels 'the state as an instrument for justice'. On this view, the state is seen as a mechanism which individuals can use to discharge the 'natural duty of justice' that they owe to foreigners as well as to compatriots. The natural duty of justice is the duty to help ensure that all persons have access to institutions for the protection of their basic rights, so long as this can be done without incurring excessive costs.

Because of the limitation contained in the last clause, Buchanan's understanding of the natural duty is consistent with the idea that citizens can justifiably display some degree of partiality for their compatriots – they do not have to weight the protection of non-citizens' rights equally with the protection of citizens' rights.[8] Suppose that most citizens interpret the natural duty in this way: they give priority to protecting the human rights of compatriots even while recognising some responsibility for the human rights of vulnerable foreigners. Even so, acts of humanitarian intervention would seem to be justifiable so long as the costs and

[6] A. Buchanan, 'The Internal Legitimacy of Humanitarian Intervention', *Journal of Political Philosophy*, 7 (1999), 71–87.

[7] Cited in J. L. Holzgrefe, 'The Humanitarian Intervention Debate' in J. L. Holzgrefe and R. O. Keohane (eds.), *Humanitarian Intervention: Ethical, Legal and Political Dilemmas* (Cambridge University Press, 2003), 30.

[8] I have defended such a position in 'Reasonable Partiality for Compatriots', *Ethical Theory and Moral Practice*, 8 (2005), 63–81.

the benefits were proportionate – if, for example, the number of lives saved or amount of suffering averted was considerably greater than the overall cost in death or injury to members of the intervening state. But the problem with this approach is that it treats the citizens as a homogeneous bloc and overlooks the possibly very unequal distribution of costs within that group. It does not, in other words, consider the position of the soldier or civilian worker who is killed or injured in the course of what, overall, may be a relatively low-cost intervention.

It may be said in reply to this that soldiers – and a similar argument might be made in the case of certain categories of civilians – when they join the armed forces undertake an open-ended contract to fight and risk their lives as and when necessary. They may join up primarily to serve their country, in the sense of defending its interests, but once they have enrolled, they have put themselves at the disposal of the state, and they are no longer entitled to judge for themselves when and for what purposes they are going to be deployed. If this is not clear to them already, it should be spelt out in their contracts of employment. Obviously this argument applies only to the case of volunteer or professional armies, not to conscripts, and we might therefore conclude immediately, with Michael Walzer, that only volunteers can be used in humanitarian interventions.[9] But does it apply even to them? For the argument from consent to go through, we would need to be convinced that those who join the military do so out of choice, not necessity, and with a reasonable grasp of the risks they are likely to incur. Perhaps they have been seduced by rosy advertisements of the life of adventure that today's soldier enjoys, or the high-tech equipment he or she will be operating, at a safe distance from the enemy. These advertisements may be justifiable on balance, because there is certainly a problem of finding enough people willing to join the armed forces in a society where military life no longer has the cachet it once had, but we need to ask whether the recruits' consent is firm enough to silence concern about the risks they may be exposed to in the course of humanitarian intervention.

Even if we can show that soldiers have freely consented to be exposed to risk of death or serious injury, moreover, it does not follow that the state that has received their consent is entitled to expose them to any risk, no matter how large. Although no longer civilians, they are still citizens, and are owed what, following Dworkin, we can call 'equal concern and respect'. It can perhaps expose them to a reasonable degree of risk, in

[9] M. Walzer, 'The Argument About Humanitarian Intervention' in D. Miller (ed.), *Thinking Politically* (New Haven: Yale University Press, 2007), 243.

pursuit of a sufficiently good purpose (which would include the protection of human rights). But what counts as a reasonable degree of risk? How many lives may one justifiably anticipate sacrificing in an intervention that if successful would save life on a large scale? There is, as far as I know, no clear answer to these questions to be found in the literature of moral and political philosophy. But if in place of this we look to the practice of democratic states, and to public opinion in those states, the implicit answer is that in the case of humanitarian interventions where no national interest is at stake, the anticipated risk must be quite low. Once a few hundred soldiers have been killed or seriously injured, opinion shifts rapidly against the intervention.[10] Huntington's position remains an extreme one, but popular opinion trails not very far behind it: it is not willing to accept that *many* Americans should be killed to prevent Somalis from killing one another.[11]

It may seem that popular opinion here is simply falling victim to an unthinking form of nationalism, perhaps even racism, that sets the value of (dark-skinned) foreigners at close to nothing. But before rushing to this conclusion, we should step back a bit to reflect. Return for a moment to the duty of rescue considered now as a responsibility of the individual – the duty to pull a drowning person out of the river, for instance. As this is usually expressed, it is a duty to rescue endangered persons when this can be done at little cost to oneself – in other words there is built into the duty a very considerable tilt in favour of the intervener, who has no obligation to incur a risk of the same magnitude as the risk to which the victim is now exposed. (This tilt is reflected in the law of those states with 'Bad Samaritan' laws that impose a legal duty of rescue. The duty applies only where the victim is facing a threat of death or serious injury; the rescuer is required to intervene only when he can do so without incurring significant risk; and often he is given a choice between carrying out the rescue himself and contacting the relevant authorities, for instance the police.[12])

10 For some discussion of this point, with references to supporting empirical evidence, see J. Goldsmith, 'Liberal Democracy and Cosmopolitan Duty', *Stanford Law Review*, 55 (2002–3), 1667–96.

11 In case this should be thought of as mere selfishness, remember that the issue is not what individual people may be willing to do themselves to save the lives of potential victims – we have enough evidence of heroic personal altruism to lay that question to rest – but how far they are prepared to require *others* – their fellow-citizens – to engage in risky humanitarian rescues.

12 See, for example, J. M. Ratcliffe (ed.), *The Good Samaritan and the Law* (Garden City, NY: Anchor Books, 1966); M. A. Menlowe and A. M. Smith (eds.), *The Duty to Rescue: The Jurisprudence of Aid* (Aldershot: Dartmouth, 1993). For discussion of the arguments

Again what counts as a 'reasonable cost' in these circumstances is left undefined, but one helpful suggestion is that one should be willing to incur risks of the kind that one runs anyway in the course of daily life: crossing roads, driving cars and so forth.[13] Suppose we were to use this as our benchmark: it would still be possible for someone to refuse to intervene on grounds of risk, even though the risk involved was only a little higher than the risks he would be taking anyway as he went about his daily business. If this is the correct understanding of moral duty in cases where there is only one rescuer, and so responsibility rests entirely with that person, what should we say about cases in which there are several potential rescuers, and so the additional question of how to allocate responsibility arises – which is normally the position when large-scale violations of human rights are threatened?

There are, in fact, at least two variants on the multi-agent scenario. In the first, the rescue is best carried out by a single agent, and the problem is one of identifying that agent: if several rescuers leap into the water in an attempt to rescue the drowning person, they get in each other's way and make a successful rescue less likely. What is needed here is to pick out, for example, the strongest swimmer among those standing on the river bank. In the second, cooperation between the rescuers increases the chance of success and/or reduces the potential cost to each rescuer: if the water is fast-flowing but not too deep, a human chain could be formed reaching out to the victim. It is easier to escape responsibility in the first case than in the second, because each person may reasonably believe that some other bystander is better qualified than he to leap into the water, whereas once the chain begins to form, it will be hard to find good reasons not to join it. Which variant better represents the case of international intervention to protect human rights? At first sight, it seems that this is a case of scenario two: intervention will be more effective, and less costly to each political community, when undertaken by a multinational force. But in practice this may not always be so. First, an effective intervention is likely to involve only a small number of states, and so there is still the problem of how the list should be drawn up, with

for and against such legislation, see J. Feinberg, *The Moral Limits of the Criminal Law, Vol 1: Harm to Others* (New York: Oxford University Press, 1984), ch. 4; H. H. Malm, 'Bad Samaritan Laws: Harm, Help or Hype?', *Law and Philosophy*, 19 (2000), 707–50; A. Ripstein, 'Three Duties to Rescue: Moral, Civil, and Criminal', *Law and Philosophy*, 19 (2000), 751–79; C. Fabre, *Whose Body is it Anyway? Justice and the Integrity of the Person* (Oxford: Clarendon Press, 2006), ch. 2.

13 For this suggestion, see Fabre, *Whose Body is it Anyway?*, ch. 2.

each state having an incentive to minimise its contribution, or better still not be involved at all.[14] Second, coordination may be difficult if different contributing states impose different cost limits on the intervention – for instance some states are only willing to accept a very low risk of their personnel being killed or injured. Under these circumstances there may be heated disputes about what form the intervention should take, leading to paralysis. For these reasons, the first scenario may better capture the problem of distributing responsibilities at international level.

Let me now attempt to draw the threads of the argument together. I began from the premise that we all share in a general responsibility to protect human rights that crosses national borders. As human beings we cannot simply sit back and watch as others are deprived of their rights to life, subsistence, bodily integrity and so forth. But for this responsibility to become effective, it has to be assigned to particular agents, who are then given the duty to protect the rights of specific groups of people. The primary assignment is to states, whose claim to sovereignty rests in part on their ability to protect the human rights of their own citizens. But where this breaks down, either through state incapacity or because the state adopts policies that violate the rights of its own people, a further assignment of remedial responsibility to outside bodies has to be made. The issue then is how this should be done, particularly in light of the fact that the costs agents are asked to bear in the course of their intervention must be reasonable ones. I then looked at two possible solutions to the problem. The first was the voluntary model, where each person is left to decide for themselves what contribution they will make towards protecting human rights, either directly, by say volunteering to become an aid worker, or indirectly by offering financial support to aid organisations. This, I suggested, was likely only to work in a subset of cases, where the costs of intervention were not high, and intervention did not require a direct confrontation with a state that was itself responsible for violating human rights. The second was the contractual model, where citizens commit themselves in advance to discharge the responsibility to protect, preferably via a binding international agreement that would require states to intervene when asked to do so either on their own or as part

[14] As an illustration, consider the difficulties involved in putting together a 15,000-strong force for peacekeeping duties in South Lebanon in the summer of 2006: even among those countries who declared themselves willing to participate, the numbers offered were remarkably low, France leading the way with an initial promise of 200 troops, later increased after considerable pressure to 2,000.

of a multinational force. I argued that citizens would be unlikely to agree to this, and this would be reasonable in light of the prospective costs – it would be like binding oneself to rescue drowning swimmers regardless of how many of them there were, and how fast the river was flowing. One can accept the duty of rescue, but justifiably retain the right to decide when the costs of a rescue are too high, at least within certain limits.

Since neither of these two models seems likely to deliver what it promises, what we are left with is this: the responsibility to protect human rights is primarily a responsibility of states, which must however retain the right to decide when they will undertake an intervention in defence of these rights. Where states can join forces and work together to offer protection, that is all to the good. But they cannot bind themselves to enter such coalitions in advance, not least because the intervention must be justified internally, to their own citizens, in light of the fact that the costs are going to fall upon those citizens, and often very unequally upon different sub-groups. It is important that those who face the greatest risks should do so willingly, but I argued that one should not take the fact that the army, say, is recruited on a voluntary basis as justification for requiring soldiers to take part in an intervention regardless of the likely cost. The upshot is that in some situations there is likely to be what we might call a protection gap: there are people who can legitimately demand protection, because their rights are being violated by forces that they are unable to resist, whether forces of nature or human agents, but those who might protect them can legitimately refuse, because the costs they are being asked to bear are too great, either absolutely or in relation to those being borne by others. I won't try to judge which real cases – Rwanda, Darfur etc. – might fit this description.[15]

I want to end by drawing out two general corollaries of the position I have been defending. First, as I noted earlier, most discussion of humanitarian intervention, in the specific sense of *military* humanitarian

[15] This idea of a protection gap has been challenged on the grounds that all (genuine) rights must have corresponding duties, so in cases where it turns out that no agent has an obligation to intervene (on grounds of risk, say) it follows that no right has been infringed. Putting the same point another way, all rights, including human rights, have inbuilt limitations that mirror the limited obligations of potential rights-protectors – so my right to life does not extend to the right to be rescued from a fast-flowing river if no suitably powerful rescuer is present. I reject this view. It is true that rights are subject to feasibility constraints, so that, for example, one has no right to a life-preserving resource that it is beyond human power to provide, but more mundane cases of scarcity reveal that the mere absence of an agent with a corresponding duty does not invalidate a right. I have developed this point in Miller, *National Responsibility and Global Justice*, ch. 7, sect. V.

intervention, has been preoccupied with the question of legitimacy: who has the *right* to intervene in any particular case. Reading this literature, one can get the impression that there are too many states eager to intervene who have to be kept in check by some principle of due authorisation. However the gist of my argument has been that, if we are looking at cases that are simply humanitarian and do not have significant geo-political aspects, then the likelihood is that we shall have too few rather than too many willing interveners – that states will be playing games with each other to minimise the risk to themselves in contributing to the relief of what is clearly a humanitarian disaster. From this perspective I share Michael Walzer's view that we should not try to lay down in advance conditions for who may intervene, but rather be guided by the simple maxim 'who can, should'.[16] I speculate here that the reason most authors want to impose legitimacy conditions on humanitarian intervention is that they are thinking about the issue of intervention *in general*, and quite properly want to lay down restrictions on that. In other words, one may think that states should not interfere in one another's internal affairs even for good purposes, such as promoting or safeguarding democracy, and therefore support general principles of non-intervention, but want to make a clear exception for cases of the kind I identified at the beginning of the chapter, where basic human rights are being violated on a significant scale. The solution, therefore, is to worry less about the question 'who has the right to intervene?' and more about the question 'when are human rights being violated on such a scale that anybody who can has the right to intervene? What is the threshold beyond which we are clearly facing a humanitarian disaster?'.

My second corollary concerns the role of international law in protecting human rights. To what extent can the responsibility to protect human rights be turned into a legal obligation? It follows from what I have argued that there could not be a general legal obligation of this kind – there could not be an obligation to engage in humanitarian intervention that would parallel the 'Bad Samaritan' laws that in some states impose a duty of rescue on individuals. This does not mean that international law has no role to play in protecting human rights. Its main role, however, is surely to restrain potential violators of these rights. Since most states have now signed up to the original UN Declaration and the subsequent charters of human rights, one can say that there is at least the basis for a legal obligation to respect these rights. The problem, as we all know, is

[16] Walzer, 'The Argument About Humanitarian Intervention', 241.

how to make international law effective in the absence of a powerful enforcing body, which does not exist now and is unlikely to exist in the foreseeable future. But perhaps international law might first be given normative force, in the form of *rulings* about acceptable and unacceptable human rights practices, even though such rulings could not in the immediate future be enforced. As bodies such as the International Criminal Court become better established, the effect would be to serve notice on the rulers of rights-violating states that they might in the future find themselves liable to prosecution. In this way international law could play some part in preventing human rights disasters that fall under headings c), d) and e) on my original list.

International law could not, however, resolve the problem of how to allocate responsibility for protection in cases where the human rights disaster is already occurring. Unless a scheme of voluntary cooperation between states arises – again unlikely in the short run – the best hope seems to be the emergence of norms that would pick out particular states, or groups of states, as bearing special responsibility for each individual case. The problem, as I have argued elsewhere, is that the norms we might find plausible do not, unfortunately, all point in the same direction.[17] In the international case we might think, for example, of geographical proximity – states, or groups of states, should have a special responsibility for protecting human rights in their own region; cultural similarity – Islamic states, say, should have a special responsibility for rights violations in other Islamic states; historic connection – states should have a special responsibility towards countries they have interacted with over time, for example their ex-colonies; and special capacity – states that have a particular kind of expertise or resources should assume responsibility when that expertise or those resources are needed. We can observe cases where each of these norms has come into play. But clearly their reach is going to be patchy, they will point in different directions in some cases, and following them would distribute the burden of intervention in arbitrary ways – some states being called on to intervene more often and at much greater cost than others.[18]

[17] See my paper 'Distributing Responsibilities', *Journal of Political Philosophy*, 9 (2001), 453–71.

[18] Unequal distribution of costs may not be arbitrary where it can be shown that the intervening state bears some historic responsibility for the human rights violations that are now occurring – for example if it is an ex-colonial power that has previously supported one faction in a state that is now experiencing civil war.

For the time being, therefore, the best we can hope for is something like the following: first, there should be a clearer international understanding of what counts as a human rights disaster, such that the general norm of non-intervention can be set aside. The states directly involved are of course likely to resist being labelled in this way, since they will have their own political agendas to pursue which may well be contributing to the disaster, but that does not matter so long as there is wide international agreement, in the UN and elsewhere, that the scale of human rights violation has crossed the threshold.[19] Then there should be communication between states with the capacity to intervene with the aim of applying norms such as those listed in the last paragraph to pick out one or more states as responsible agents. Perhaps in the longer term it might be possible to work out a system of burden sharing so that the costs of intervention can be more evenly spread – though this will undoubtedly be difficult. (Even in what might appear to be the much simpler case of distributing the burden of admitting refugees – simpler because this can be characterised crudely just as a matter of the numbers to be admitted – coming up with a generally acceptable scheme has proved problematic.[20]) One reason for this is that the present capacity of states to contribute to human rights interventions, particularly interventions that involve the use of force, is heavily influenced by the past policies of these states, in building up their military capability, or choosing not to do so. These policies in turn will reflect different conceptions of national identity, and can be defended by appeal to national self-determination. What, for example, should we say about a country like Switzerland which for historic-cum-cultural reasons has developed a system of national defence that is precisely that and nothing more, and whose contribution

[19] At present such agreement exists in the case of genocide – even those developing countries that are generally reluctant to accept any breaches of the sovereignty norm are willing, in principle, to allow intervention to prevent an impending genocide (they may object to the particular agents who undertake the intervention). Clearly the threshold is here being set very high; there are many large-scale human rights disasters that do not take the form of genocide – for instance ideologically driven policies that lead to mass starvation. I am grateful to Carolyn Haggis for information on the evolving attitude of African states in particular to interventions aimed at stopping genocide.

[20] I have discussed this question briefly in 'Immigration: the Case for Limits' in A. Cohen and K. Wellman (eds.), *Contemporary Debates in Applied Ethics* (Oxford: Blackwell, 2005). I refer there to proposals discussed in J. C. Hathaway and R. A. Neve, 'Making International Refugee Law Relevant Again: A Proposal for Collectivized and Solution-Oriented Protection', *Harvard Human Rights Journal*, 10 (1997), 115–211 and P. Schuck, 'Refugee Burden-Sharing: A Modest Proposal', *Yale Journal of International Law*, 22 (1997), 243–97.

to peacekeeping efforts overseas is therefore unavoidably minimal? Or of countries such as Germany and Japan whose constitutions place narrow limits on military activities? Could they be brought into a burden-sharing scheme by being asked to make larger contributions in other areas, such as reconstruction in the aftermath of an intervention?

In the absence of such a scheme, and given that the UN can only encourage and not require member states to take action even in cases where it has resolved that intervention is justified, there is not much to rely on apart from diplomacy and the moral imperative to protect human rights, made more pressing by media reports of the unfolding disasters. Under these circumstances it seems inevitable that what I have called the protection gap will persist: hundreds of thousands of people will continue to have their rights infringed because the responsibility to protect them remains undistributed.

References

Buchanan, A. 1999. 'The Internal Legitimacy of Humanitarian Intervention', *Journal of Political Philosophy*, 7: 71–87.

Chesterman, S. 2001. *Just War or Just Peace? Humanitarian Intervention and International Law*. Oxford University Press.

Fabre, C. 2006. *Whose Body is it Anyway? Justice and the Integrity of the Person*. Oxford: Clarendon Press.

Feinberg, J. 1984. *The Moral Limits of the Criminal Law, Vol 1: Harm to Others*. New York: Oxford University Press.

Goldsmith, J. 2002–3. 'Liberal Democracy and Cosmopolitan Duty', *Stanford Law Review* 55: 1667–96.

Hathaway, J. C. and Neve, R. A. 1997. 'Making International Refugee Law Relevant Again: A Proposal for Collectivized and Solution-Oriented Protection', *Harvard Human Rights Journal* 10: 115–211.

Holzgrefe, J. L. 2003. 'The Humanitarian Intervention Debate' in Holzgrefe, J. L. and Keohane, R. O. (eds.), *Humanitarian Intervention: Ethical, Legal and Political Dilemmas*. Cambridge University Press.

International Development Research Centre 2001. *The Responsibility to Protect: Report of the International Commission on Intervention and State Sovereignty*. Ottawa.

International Development Research Centre 2001. *The Responsibility to Protect, Research, Bibliography, Background: Supplementary Volume to the Report of the International Commission on Intervention and State Sovereignty*. Ottawa.

Malm, H. H. 2000. 'Bad Samaritan Laws: Harm, Help or Hype?', *Law and Philosophy* 19: 707–50.

Menlowe, M. A. and Smith, A. M. (eds.) 1993. *The Duty to Rescue: The Jurisprudence of Aid*. Aldershot: Dartmouth.

Miller, D. 2001. 'Distributing Responsibilities', *Journal of Political Philosophy* 9: 453–71.

Miller, D. 2002. '"Are they *my* Poor?": The Problem of Altruism in a World of Strangers', *Critical Review of International Social Philosophy and Policy* 5: 106–27.

Miller, D. 2005. 'Reasonable Partiality for Compatriots', *Ethical Theory and Moral Practice* 8: 63–81.

Miller, D. 2005. 'Immigration: the Case for Limits' in Cohen, A. and Wellman, K. (eds.), *Contemporary Debates in Applied Ethics*. Oxford: Blackwell.

Miller, D. 2007. *National Responsibility and Global Justice*. Oxford University Press.

Ratcliffe, J. M. (ed.) 1966. *The Good Samaritan and the Law*. Garden City, NY: Anchor Books.

Ripstein, A. 2000. 'Three Duties to Rescue: Moral, Civil, and Criminal', *Law and Philosophy* 19: 751–79.

Schuck, P. 1997. 'Refugee Burden-Sharing: A Modest Proposal', *Yale Journal of International Law* 22: 243–97.

Walzer, M. 2007. 'The Argument About Humanitarian Intervention' in Miller, D. (ed.), *Thinking Politically*. New Haven: Yale University Press.

Welsh, J. 2002. 'From Right to Responsibility: Humanitarian Intervention and International Society', *Global Governance* 8: 503–21.

Wheeler, N. 2000. *Saving Strangers: Humanitarian Intervention in International Society*. Oxford University Press.

9

The threat of violence and of new military force as a challenge to international public law

MATTHIAS LUTZ-BACHMANN

The foundation of a new international public law

After the dark experiences of two destructive world wars in the twentieth century it has been the constitution of the United Nations Organization by which the foundation stone was laid for a positive change in international relations. But even if we have to admit that the UN couldn't meet all political expectations one can recognise a lasting reform of international public law by the UN Charter. It inserted new directions into the framework of international law. The prohibition of a threat or use of military force in international relations – as constituted by UN Charter, article 2, 4 for all member states of the UN[1] – has a deep impact on the legitimate character of the activities and the role of states as well as on the former concept of state sovereignty. While the traditional order of '*ius gentium*' after the Westphalian Peace Treaty in 1648 did include the legal option for all sovereign states to enter into war against the other members of the international community of states, the UN Charter excludes that right in general, limits the 'inherent right' of self-defence of a member state of the UN to the temporal condition 'until' the Security Council of the UN has decided on appropriate measures,[2] and transfers the legal questions concerning peace and war to the system of 'collective security', represented by the political body of the United Nations itself.

These directions have initially changed the conceptual frame of international public law in a fundamental respect. From a philosophical perspective one could say that the prevailing legal international order meets the normative imperative for legitimacy which was defined by Immanuel Kant at the end of the eighteenth century. In his famous essay

[1] See *Charter of the UNO*, Chapter I, art. 2, 4. [2] *Ibid.*, Chapter VII, art. 51.

'On Perpetual Peace'[3] Kant stated the necessity for a new constitution of international law which should overcome the traditional legal and moral doctrines on a just warfare not only by the implementation of a strict and unconditioned prohibition for all states to go to war against each other but also by the constitution of a 'league of peace', which means a federation of peacekeeping states giving up the original right to carry out their political agenda by the means of warfare.[4] But while Kant presupposed in his arguments that only republics with a basically democratic order were allowed to join the suggested international league of peacekeeping states, the Charter of the UN does not set up such a criterion like a republican or democratic order of a state as an admittance and membership requirement. On the one hand, the decision not to require an inner democratic order was the basic condition for the political success and the factual possibility to constitute the UN among the allies of the Second World War and to form the special admission to the permanent membership in the Security Council. On the other hand, exactly that decision did imply unintended consequences, some of which I would like to address in the following section.

Challenges to international public law

Challenges to international law 'from within'

In early modern times the traditional order of international law was conceived as a '*ius gentium*' or a law among peoples regulating the external relations between sovereign states based on customary law as well as on contract law. Prepared by the previous legal as well as philosophical traditions,[5] the classical doctrine of the '*ius gentium positivum*' became effective with the Westphalian Peace Treaty and applied since then for several centuries, mainly to the external relations of the European states. That legal order reflected juridically the prevailing political structure of power between the modern European states. That function of international public law didn't change in the gradual process of

[3] I. Kant, 'On Perpetual Peace', first edition 1795, in *Kants Werke, Akademie Textausgabe* VIII (Berlin/New York: De Gruyter Verlag, 1968), 354–7.

[4] See the famous book of C. von Clausewitz, *Vom Kriege*, first edition 1832–4 (Stuttgart: Reclam, 1994).

[5] See, for example, M. Lutz-Bachmann, A. Fidora and A. Wagner (eds.), *Lex und Ius. Beiträge zur Begründung des Rechts in der Philosophie des Mittelalters und der Neuzeit* (Stuttgart: Frommann Holzboog Verlag, in press (2009)).

democratic inner reforms or even revolutions within the single states. Beyond the principle of 'indivisible sovereignty' of each single state the legal order of the old '*ius gentium*' contained neither a further legal nor a normative principle or rule in order to protect a state from being attacked by another state. We can therefore conclude that the juridical order of that international public law was never endangered nor challenged *as such* by the conduct of war or the threat of violence in international relations since warfare and the use of force was permitted within its regulations if conducted according to well-specified formal procedures, even if it is true that the emergence and development of 'Humanitarian International Law' in the nineteenth and twentieth centuries achieved success in restricting the legal reasons for nation-states and the legitimate ways to conduct war mutually.[6]

That situation changed fundamentally after the Second World War and the dramatic experiences of a warfare of 'total destruction', including the atomic bomb. The introduction of a new paradigm of international public law succeeding the foundation of the United Nations aimed at the goal of establishing a new international political order based on a few general and fundamental normative ideas which all human beings can and for good reasons should acknowledge as legally binding principles in international politics independent of their political, cultural, religious or non-religious identity: the unconditioned commitment to keep peace, not to dominate other states or political communities and to observe the basic human rights. The intentional threat of violence and the use of military force are therefore, if they happen to occur, not only challenges to the given order of power and of states but additionally challenges to the prevailing order of international public law. Accordingly the 'lawful use of force' in self-defence which is permitted by article 51 of the UN Charter is not only temporally limited but above all restricted to the conditions of a system of 'collective security'.

Like other severe violations of legal orders the evident act of an illegal use of military force in international relations in the case of a military aggression of a member state of the UN could be prosecuted as a criminal act on trial.[7] But the tentative idea of legal jurisdiction suffers not only

[6] See e.g. the Conventions of Geneva (1864), Den Haag (1899) or the Brian-Kellogg-Pact (1928).

[7] See the resolution of the UN General Assembly of 1974: it affirmed that 'aggressions' of states could be called 'crimes' in a proper sense, but that is juridically not the case for all violations of art. 2,4.

from the lack of appropriate international procedures of law enforcement in international legal affairs and from the often disputed unsatisfactory implementation of global political structures, but also from the substantive disagreements among the states over the question how crimes of aggression are exactly to be defined in the international arena. Only new political agreements, improved legal commitments as well as advanced implementations of structures for peaceful and effective political interventions would hopefully prevent the international escalation of aggression and intervene early enough before military acts are carried out by states, either against foreign countries or even against parts of their own population like in the former Yugoslavia, Somalia, the Congo or Sudan today. What might happen in recent times in cases of hot international conflicts, upcoming crises and already ongoing military conflicts, wars and the severe violation of human rights if one (or even more) standing members of the UN Security Council vetoed appropriate measures? Often nothing! As we know, exactly that occurred too often in the past sixty years and it will continuously happen in the future due to the insufficient structure of UN legislation and of jurisdiction within the legal order of international law. I call that the *first challenge* to international law 'from within' the prevailing legal order.

The often documented incapacity of the UN to protect peace in international crises has become even more problematic in recent years. Due to the legal developments within international law like the general assertion of states to the character of '*ius cogens*' for basic principles in international law or to the 'erga omnes'-obligations according to the 'Vienna Treaty on the Law of International Treaties'[8] single actors like states or state-based organisations may much more often feel obligated to intervene in cases of severe violations of human rights than happened before. These legal developments within international public law helped to improve discussions in Western democracies not only on the justification of 'humanitarian interventions' but also on the 'justified use of military force' in international relations. Some political philosophers claimed for themselves and their political systems high moral standards, political legitimacy and argued for a 'moral foundation' for international law.[9] But we have learned that these legal developments increased the

[8] See *The Vienna Convention on the Law of Treaties* (VCLT), 23 May 1969.

[9] See, for example, A. Buchanan, *Justice, Legitimacy, and Self-Determination. Moral Foundations for International Law* (Oxford University Press, 2004).

inherent tensions of international public law, especially with regard to the prohibition of the use of military force beyond the UN system of collective security in the name of a self-authorised obligation of states. There can be no doubt that these developments have led to many even more complicated international crises in recent years. I call these tendencies the *second challenge* to international public law 'from within'.

Finally I would like to address the decisions made by the unanimous vote of the UN Security Council itself, like the decision on the 'War on Terrorism' after the events of 9/11. One can doubt to what extent terrorist organisations like Al-Qaida are subject to international law but it seems to be obvious that the declaration of a 'war' against private actors implies an introduction of new elements in the system of international law, represented by the definitions of the UN Charter and previous UN legislation. The rationale of legitimate war of states against dangerous but private actors in the name of the UN Security Council as the representative of the system of collective security not only adds further conceptual uncertainties into the order of international law, it also helps to develop and to legitimate political concepts like the 'preventive' or even 'pre-emptive use of military force' since it seems to be impossible to fight 'a legal war' against an almost totally invisible enemy without legalising to a certain degree even 'pre-emptive' military strikes. I call that slippery road from a legal war on terrorism to the pre-emptive use of military force in the name of legitimate self-defence which was opened by the decisions of UN itself the *third challenge* to international public law 'from within'.

Challenges to international law 'from outside'

In addition to these three challenges to international law resulting partly from its interior constitution and partly from its legal evolution I refer now to three different challenges arising from recent developments 'outside' the sphere of law. I do so in focusing first on the emergence of a cultural dimension of conflicts among states and populations in the age of globalisation, second on the fact of an ongoing proliferation of nuclear weapons and additional weapons of mass destruction which will very likely increase in the next few years, and third on the problem of how to deal with aggressive political regimes in the world in accordance with the normative ideals and the legal order of the prevailing international public law.

One of the – perhaps unintended – consequences of the political agenda of the UN itself has been the emergence of a 'cultural dimension' within many international conflicts. One might prove whether or not it has something to do with the politics of cultural identity which had been supported by the UN in the time of the anti-colonialist and anti-apartheid decisions. But in contrast to these former political issues the cultural impact on conflicts today goes far beyond a local or regional relevance. Cultural and especially religious (or at least seemingly religious) identities play a growing role in international conflicts and sometimes they produce the willingness of actors not only to use violence in the name of their highest moral good but also to sacrifice their own lives. As we know it is hard to see how the traditional instruments of legal coercion like a rightful punishment by a criminal court could ever be effective against persons who are determined to carry out suicide attacks against others. I call this the *fourth challenge* to the order of international law emerging from 'outside' the legal sphere today.

The proliferation of nuclear weapons and other weapons of mass destruction and their spread to tyrannical regimes as well as to international private organisations, which both might be willing to use these weapons, is probably the most significant and threatening challenge to the order of the international legal system we are confronted with worldwide today. It seems to be obvious that the international 'Treaty on the Nonproliferation of Nuclear Weapons' (NPT)[10] and the 'International Atomic Energy Agency' (IAEA) are not able in the long run to prevent the proliferation of these weapons to unlawful regimes or to private organisations like terrorists, warlords or even ordinary criminals. If that is going to happen one can easily predict that the global public, as well as the international legal order, might be taken as hostages of illegal persons. And even more dramatically we might experience outbreaks of nuclear warfare among states and among private actors which could destroy the basic principles of international public law and its institutional global structures. Insofar as these considerations are rational I would like to call this possible future scenario the *fifth challenge* to prevailing international law since it already preoccupies the political agenda of global diplomacy if we refer to the examples of India and Pakistan, North Korea or Iran.

Finally, regarding the international political interaction of states and powers we are confronted with the problem of whether or not the legal

[10] See *Treaty on the Non-Proliferation of Nuclear Weapons (NPT)*, 1 July 1968; Review Conference 2–27 May 2005, New York.

order is able to really integrate the relevant actors. Due to the fact that there are quite a few states which lack an inner reform towards republican structures and democracy like Kant asked for in his political philosophy one may have severe doubts regarding the reliability of these actors. In accordance with the theory of Kant who required first an inner reform and a democratic constitution for a state in order to become a member in the 'league of nations', one might call these states 'unjust legal orders'[11] or even 'outlaw regimes',[12] like John Rawls did. Even if these states belong formally to the UN as full members we have good reason to suspect that their governments do not respect the normative implications of international public law nor fully recognise its goals, namely a reliable global order of peace, prohibition of warfare and protection of human rights. One may therefore conclude that at least some of those regimes are willing to violate the legal international order if they think that in a given situation they may gain strategic benefits in doing so. If the analysis of the inferences between a lack of inner democracy and a lack of obedience to international law is true one may count even permanent members of the Security Council among these states like China or Russia. I call this problem of reliability the *sixth challenge* to international public law.

Two proposals from political philosophy: Michael Walzer's and Allen Buchanan's arguments for the use of military force in international affairs

The threat of violence and of new military force in international relations has set off various debates within political philosophy on the question of how to react rationally to these challenges. Among the different contributions one can identify new interest in the idea of finding solutions from a *legal* discourse to, at least for many jurists, an unexpected *moral* argument. The recent revival of the just war theory is only one indicator for this development. In this paragraph I refer very briefly to the position of two influential political philosophers, namely to Michael Walzer and Allen Buchanan. They both advocate different versions of this general shift to an ethical legitimation of a

11 See Kant, 'On Perpetual Peace' and cf. additionally I. Kant, 'On the Proverb: That May be True in Theory, but Is of No Practical Use', in Kant, *Akademie Textausgabe* VIII, 307–13.

12 J. Rawls, 'The Law of Peoples', in S. Shute and S. Hurley (eds.), *On Human Rights* (New York: HarperCollins, 1993), 72ff.

'justified warfare', conducted by democratic states and allegedly legitimate in an act of self-empowerment by an *ultima ratio* reflection. Walzer says that this kind of use of military force by single democratic states acts 'beyond humanitarian intervention' in a global society and Buchanan speaks about a 'preventive' use of military force. Of course, both represent quite different traditions in political philosophy but they have in common a moral reading of the core content of human rights which seems to be the normative starting point of their argument in favour of a self-legitimation of single states to use military power in international affairs.

In his Minerva Lecture, held in 2004 at the University of Tel Aviv with the title 'Beyond Humanitarian Intervention: Human Rights in Global Society', Walzer addresses some of the obvious deficiencies of the international order which I cited above as 'challenges to international public law', and in doing so he focuses his arguments especially on three problems: the first problem is marked by the question of which rational status 'human rights' might claim in the international arena – beyond the sphere of the so-called 'decent states'. The second problem is indicated by the question of who might be responsible for the fulfilment of the universal validity claims of these 'human rights' in the sphere of international political relations, and the third problem is raised by the question of what should be done for the enforcement of 'human rights' in the realm of international politics.

In answering these questions Walzer starts with what he calls a 'minimal conception' of human rights. In his view human rights primarily refer to the right to life and liberty, including the basic normative statement 'that mass murder, ethnic cleansing, and the establishment of slave camps are not just barbarous and inhuman acts but violations of human rights'.[13] Walzer favours what he calls 'a short list' of human rights, and he states that there is no public addressee responsible for the enforcement of human rights in the international arena. In his view that marks the decisive difference to the protection of human rights within the legal order of 'decent states' governed under the rule of law. It is evident that Walzer is following here the line of the political philosophy of Montesquieu and Hegel in rejecting the idea that the given international political order might represent a perhaps incomplete but already existing and binding public *legal order*, including basic human rights

[13] Michael Walzer, *Beyond Humanitarian Intervention*, 1; I quote Walzer's text from the version of his manuscript.

today. Walzer argues that a political discourse on rights without a corresponding structure of an implementation of these rights in effective social and political structures is not only incomplete but even fallacious. He therefore gives up the idea of an internationally binding *legal* order and concludes a '*moral postulate*' which functions as a substitute for the supposed lack of effective or reliable basic rights in the international sphere. That postulate claims the *moral* commitment that all those democratic states which are able to intervene in cases of severe human rights violations in the international arena 'should intervene, militarily if all else fails',[14] since 'all people at risk of massacre or enslavement have a right to be rescued'.[15] That postulate addresses the democratic states and contains a moral legitimation for the self-empowerment and self-entitlement of single states to act militarily.

Referring to Hannah Arendt's famous statement that the idea of human rights stands for the claim of human persons 'to have rights' within the given legal order of a single state, Walzer postulates additionally not only something like an original '*moral right*' for all people to live in a 'decent state' but also the more far-reaching '*moral obligation*' for states in the international order to foster state building everywhere in the world in the name of a coercive protection of human rights since a protection of human rights is for Walzer only effective within the legal order of a nation-state. Accordingly, the attempt to protect human rights in the international arena seems to him to be futile.

Allen Buchanan presents another kind of answer to the new threats and challenges which endanger the given international legal order today. He basically shares Walzer's reading of human rights beyond the scope of the *legal* order of single 'decent states' as a source for a *moral* commitment which claims a normative validity 'independently of whether they are enshrined in legal rules or not'.[16] According to Allen Buchanan human rights claim a universal validity since they express and define certain general and necessary conditions without which humans are not able to conduct a good or decent life. The commonly shared '*interests*' of all humans in the protection of those general conditions is for Buchanan the final moral reason for the universal validity of human rights. One may doubt whether or not that argument is able to explain the normative content of the moral and legal claim of validity of human rights sufficiently. But nevertheless, according to Buchanan it is necessary to specify

[14] *Ibid.*, 7. [15] *Ibid.*, 8.
[16] Buchanan, *Justice, Legitimacy, and Self-Determination*, 119.

the reference to these 'general conditions' in order to be able to apply human rights to the very different individual social and political situations humans live in: 'Even if the existence and basic character of human rights can be determined by moral reasoning without reference to the particular features of any legal system, institutionalised efforts to monitor and improve compliance with these rights are needed to specify their content, if they are to provide practical guidance, and these must be context specific.'[17]

The practical impact of human rights as binding rules or norms is primarily a negative one. For Buchanan human rights are *moral norms* 'expressing basic moral values that place constraints on institutional arrangements rather than ... prescriptions for institutional design'.[18] Nevertheless, the primarily negative function of human rights does include at least some positive requirements like the affirmative right of all humans to live under conditions of a 'democratic governance'. In regarding that right as a basic norm which belongs to the 'core' of international law Buchanan obviously goes far beyond the concept of Michael Walzer. According to Buchanan the postulate of 'democratic governance' doesn't just apply to the legal order of the single states[19] but additionally to the sphere of legitimacy of the international legal order as a whole.

The condition of a 'minimal democracy' is, according to Buchanan, a postulate which addresses the single states and their active role within the international arena. His argumentation corresponds to the idea of a normative primacy of the validity of human rights over the sovereignty principle claimed by the single states. For that reason Allen Buchanan postulates a clear commitment for the democratic states to employ, if possible, 'preventive military force' in international affairs in cases of an imminent severe violation of human rights. That moral postulate does not only express the legitimate possibility for the use of preventive military actions in opposition to the prevailing international public law but also an obligation to act accordingly. Buchanan suggests a number of legally ordered procedures including some '*ex ante*'- and '*ex post*'-evaluations which have the task of guaranteeing an 'impartial proof' for the justification of the use of 'preventive military force' by single states. In his article 'The Preventive Use of Force: A Cosmopolitan International

[17] *Ibid.* [18] *Ibid.*, 127.

[19] See *ibid.*, 143: 'All persons have the same fundamental status, as equal participants, in the most important political decisions made in their societies.'

Proposal', published together with Robert O. Keohane,[20] Buchanan additionally proposes an institutional framework which should aim to protect 'vulnerable countries against unjustified interventions without creating unacceptable risks of the costs of inaction'.[21] That proposal is designed as an international contract or even as a global treaty which has the task of implementing prevailing UN law with new legal procedures. They should help the democratic states in cases of imminent or already ongoing severe human rights violations to examine by themselves their specific moral duties if the UN Security Council fails to decide or to act for whatever reason. The proposed list of '*ex ante*'- and '*ex post*'-evaluations contains some more or less precise criteria for democratic governments in order to judge themselves on the question not only *if* but also *how* they should fulfil their alleged 'moral commitment' concerning the human rights of endangered foreign people. These criteria are something like the normative core for a reform of international rules which aims at a new international 'system of accountability'.

Towards a global public law: an argument for a reform of the UN

For our discussion on the meaning and relevance of the challenges to the international public order it seems to be of the highest importance that Michael Walzer and Allen Buchanan argue – like others in political philosophy – within the conceptual framework not of legal duties but of moral obligations, and in doing so they support a moral reading of the validity claims of human rights. As a result of their arguments they suggest the idea of a legitimate self-empowerment of single democratic states in order to use military force for the sake of endangered human rights in international affairs. Before I present my own considerations I would like to address some problems in the argumentation of both Michael Walzer and Allen Buchanan.

Concerning Walzer's contribution it seems obvious that he is ignoring the fact that there has been an evolution of international public law in the last sixty years which has led to a legal sphere of reliable international law even if its mechanisms aren't effective enough. Against that background it seems to be counter-intuitive to reject any juridical content of the

[20] See A. Buchanan and R. O. Keohane, 'The Preventive Use of Force: A Cosmopolitan Institutional Proposal', *Ethics and International Affairs*, 18 (2004), 1–22.

[21] *Ibid.*, 1.

meaning of 'human rights' in the international realm of politics as well as in the global public as he does. His rejection of a reliable legal importance of human rights 'beyond' the order of single democratic states seems to have much more in common with the prejudices of the so-called 'realists' in the theory of international relations than Walzer might agree with. But even if we would accept Walzer's analysis it would remain unclear what a 'moral obligation' of a democratic state to act militarily in the international arena could mean precisely. A self-empowerment of a single democratic state is by no means a contribution in favour of a reliable legal order since it necessarily would not only produce massive tensions among states but also between legal orders, international treaties and organisations. I fear Walzer's proposal would lead to a new and even more dangerous 'anarchy of states'.

It seems to be obvious that Michael Walzer is avoiding appropriate arguments for his understanding of 'human rights' as a source of moral obligations of juridical entities like nation-states. In his arguments he fails to distinguish between 'moral obligations' and 'legal duties', that means between 'obligations' which address moral subjects like individual actors and 'duties' which bind collective actors like states or international organisations constituted by legal and coercive frameworks. Additionally we can see that Walzer ignores other important distinctions like the difference between a conditioned and an unconditioned obligation or between a duty to act and a duty to refrain from acting and so on. But above all: the plea of Walzer for a moral obligation of single democratic states for the use of military force 'beyond humanitarian interventions' doesn't only endanger the prevailing international public law, it also contains a new version of the just war theory which would lead to many counter-intuitive consequences. I therefore cannot see that his suggestion might be helpful in order to develop solutions for the challenges to the international order which emerge from the threat of violence and of new military force today and tomorrow.

It is quite obvious that Allen Buchanan presents a different proposal. But in his case too I cannot see how his reference to human rights might constitute an 'obligation' at all since the normative core of human rights is constituted in his reading by nothing other than an alleged 'interest' of people. Even if it is true that Buchanan wants to argue in favour of human rights as moral norms, I cannot see how one might infer something like a 'moral norm' from a given 'interest' of somebody. What I am missing in Buchanan's arguments is the proof of the normative and universal character of the human rights as moral entitlements as well as legal claims with an unconditioned obligation for all other actors, whether individuals or states. In my view that normative core of the human rights speech remains unrecognised and unwarranted in Buchanan's reconstruction. Additionally Buchanan seems to neglect the difference among moral obligations and legal obligations for collective actors like states. I see similar problems in the argumentation of Buchanan's proposal as in Walzer's. But whereas Walzer's contribution would politically and legally lead to something like a new and, compared to the world of the nineteenth century, even more dangerous 'anarchy of states' which falls far behind the legal and political order of the UN Charter and its international organisations, treaties and mechanisms, Buchanan's arguments for a new 'system of accountability' are designed in order to support and to complete the prevailing order of international public law. That marks a big difference among both authors. But even if this prospect sounds much more plausible for me, the question remains of whether or not the basic idea of Buchanan's is suitable and convincing, namely his idea of a legitimation of a 'preventive use' of military force by single democratic states in order to protect human rights.

I fear that his proposal would, if realised, not reach its goal, namely to support the universal human rights in international affairs in the long run since the suggested self-empowerment of single states would lead necessarily to unintended results and would help to increase extremely dangerous scenarios of warfare, terrorism and anti-terror activities. The mechanism of self-entitlement of states Buchanan suggests would open the door to a new constellation of 'justified warfare' scenarios with inflationary effects and incentives to an increased use of military force in international conflicts since each state might claim its moral legitimacy and refer to supposed justified reasons for its actions. This leads me to the conclusion that the return to the supposed 'morally' legitimate practice of military intervention and the self-entitlement of states to military action is wrong. On the contrary, what we need is an impartial political authority or even better fair legal public procedures by which the international community of states itself can decide whether or not an international humanitarian intervention or even a preventive use of force might be necessary, reasonable and prudent in order to protect international peace. That presupposes not only global public debates among political representatives but also the implementation of new global democratic structures for decision-making in the international arena on questions of peace and war. Consequently I argue in favour of a reform of the prevailing international political order and for a further development of international public law towards a global public law and a just 'republican order' on the *global level* of the world as an upcoming 'cosmopolis'.[22]

I admit that there are many other challenges to prevailing international public law which I have not even mentioned here. But if one may regard the description of these challenges caused by the threat of violence and of new military force as more or less appropriate or tentatively correct we finally have to look for reasonable answers to such challenging developments. That leads me to the following final four proposals. They presuppose to a large extent philosophical basic arguments which belong to the Kantian tradition – arguments for which I cannot give appropriate reasons here in detail:[23]

(1) For good philosophical arguments, that means for the normative reasons which are explained in Kant's political philosophy and in the Kantian tradition, we have to avoid the misleading conclusion to return to the old strategies of a strong 'national security' policy in the name of the so-called 'political realism' in foreign affairs. There is no reasonable way back to a legal international order like the one before 1945. Thus I reject not only the basic intuitions of 'political realism' but also Michael Walzer's arguments[24] since both neglect the necessity to construct the global political order of peace upon the claims of a just global public law. For the same reason we have to avoid moralising the political and procedural legal problems we are confronted with in the international arena today. We have to adhere to the sharp difference between 'the legal' and 'the moral' as explained in the liberal tradition of political philosophy, and in doing so we have to look out for solutions within the legal frame of the prevailing

[22] See my article 'Kosmopolitische Verantwortung. Über Ethik und Recht in einer globalisierten Welt', in O. Decker and T. Grave, *Kritische Theorie der Zeit* (Springe: zu Klampen Verlag, 2008), 70–7.

[23] For further arguments cf. J. Bohman and M. Lutz-Bachmann, *Perpetual Peace. Essays on Kant's Cosmopolitan Ideal* (Cambridge: MIT Press, 1997); H. Brunkhorst, W. Köhler and M. Lutz-Bachmann, *Recht auf Menschenrechte. Menschenrechte, Demokratie und internationale Politik* (Frankfurt: Suhrkamp Verlag, 1999); M. Lutz-Bachmann and J. Bohman, *Weltstaat oder Staatenwelt? Für und wider die Idee einer Weltrepublik* (Frankfurt: Suhrkamp Verlag, 2002); M. Lutz-Bachmann and A. Niederberger, *Krieg und Frieden im Prozess der Globalisierung* (Weilerswist: Velbrück Verlag, 2009).

[24] See above and my article 'Die Idee der Menschenrechte angesichts der Realitäten der Weltpolitik: Eine Reflexion über das Verhältnis von Ethik und Politik', in J. Szaif and M. Lutz-Bachmann (eds.), *What is Good for a Human Being? Human Nature and Values* (Berlin/New York: De Gruyter Verlag, 2004), 276–92.

international public law and by the means of global legal procedures by which the differences of divergent geo-political and economic interests, cultures and religious identities may become reconciled.

(2) On the other hand we have to overcome the specific inner legal inconsistencies and the institutional weaknesses of prevailing international public law. This postulate implies the necessity for a reform of the institutions of the UN which aims at the constitution of a global public law with reliable transnational rules and institutions as well as regional regimes which are able to execute, specify and apply the general norms of global law, if necessary with a certain degree of coercive power. Such a reform of the institutions of the UN should focus especially on the Security Council as the executive power of the UN which has often been unable in the past to act according to its global responsibility under the directions within the system of 'collective security'. A reform of the UN could *first* restrict the right to membership in the Security Council to democratic states only in the strictest sense, *second* substitute the right to veto by differently qualified majority decisions and *third* prepare mechanisms for a justification of the decisions of the Security Council and its responsibility towards the global public. Additionally a reform of the UN might strengthen the competence of other UN institutions over supposed national or other particular interests in all cases of peace and war. These reforms should bring together the international community of states to something like a new International Legal Order which some scholars in international law describe today as the concept of 'constitutionalism' of international law.[25]

(3) A reform of the institutions of prevailing international law should be embedded in additional efforts to build up something like a global democratic public in the civil societies of the world. That development should be supported by special commitments of the democratic states which may help to build up an 'open public space' of global communication and of the exchange of ideas, information and news in the fragmented world today. That might include an open space for free

[25] See J. Habermas, 'Hat die Konstitutionalisierung des Völkerrechts noch eine Chance?', in J. Habermas, *Der gespaltene Westen* (Frankfurt: Suhrkamp Verlag, 2004), 113–93; A. von Bogdandy, 'Constitutionalism in International Law: Comment on a Proposal from Germany', *Harvard International Law Journal* 47 (2006), 223–42; A. von Bogdandy and S. Dellavalle, 'Universalism and Particularism as Paradigms of International Law', *International Law and Justice Working Paper 2008/3* (New York University School of Law, 2008).

speech for everybody, for easy access to education and exchange programmes for students, free access to mass media, print media, the Internet and other sources of human communication. That might support the emergence and development of something like a well-informed, 'enlighted' global civil society beyond the narrow limits of nations, languages, ethnicities, religions and social classes. Education and a free flow of ideas are the best protection against those ideologies which lead to conflicts, to war and terror like the variety of fundamentalisms, religious or non-religious ones, we are confronted with today. Precisely speaking one should not exclude but permit religious doctrines within the political arena of the secular societies, however they should be admitted within the rules of public reasoning alone which have been explained recently, for example by John Rawls or Jürgen Habermas.[26]

(4) That will help to undermine totalitarian regimes and violent cultures in the long run everywhere in the world since the free flow of ideas and the formation of a global public sphere for deliberative political reasoning will undermine the ideologies and particularities from which most of the aforementioned dangerous challenges to the international public order today emerge. In the long run this might lead to developments of democratisation worldwide and step by step to a general recognition of basic human rights as well as of those principles which we can call philosophically 'reasonable' according to the tradition of Kantian philosophy. I here refer especially to Kant's postulate: 'There is to be no war!'[27] in his 'Theory of Law', and we can add today the following obligations: 'There is to be no threat of violence or of military action in the global, in the international, in the regional and in the national political arena!' These versions of a new categorical imperative of political reason are not only addressing the *general* topic of the normative character of the *fundamental legal principles* we should follow in the international and more and more cosmopolitan or global arena, they are additionally offering single practical solutions for the many often delicate and controversial *particular problems* and decisions concerning the question of peace and war in the international arena. In light of these Kantian imperatives we can namely realise that even in cases of imminent state aggressions or of terrorist

[26] See my recent discussion of the arguments of Rawls and Habermas in 'Demokratie, öffentliche Vernunft und Religion', in *Philosophisches Jahrbuch* 114 (2007), 3–21.

[27] See I. Kant, 'The Metaphysics of Morals', in Kant, *Akademie Textausgabe* VI, 354.

attacks we should never decide in favour of those means which imply a violation or abolition of the basic legal norms on which prevailing international law is built as a whole, such as the prohibition to use military force in international relations apart from the case of self-defence under the well-defined conditions of the system of 'collective security' in Chapter VII of the UN Charter.

The challenges to international public law and the international political order we are confronted with today have to and can be overcome not by the self-contradictory legal admission and self-empowerment to the use of military force in the hands of single states but only by the democratic constitution of a strong global public law and the building of more efficient global political institutions under the rule of law and controlled by the international public through appropriate procedures and global mechanisms.

References

Bogdandy, Armin von 2006. 'Constitutionalism in International Law: Comment on a Proposal from Germany', *Harvard International Law Journal* 47: 223–42.

Bogdandy, Armin von and Dellavalle, Sergio 2008. 'Universalism and Particularism as Paradigms of International Law', *International Law and Justice Working Paper 2008/3*. New York University School of Law.

Bohman, James and Lutz-Bachmann, Matthias 1997. *Perpetual Peace. Essays on Kant's Cosmopolitan Ideal*. Cambridge: MIT Press.

Brunkhorst, Hauke, Köhler, Wolfgang and Lutz-Bachmann, Matthias 1999. *Recht auf Menschenrechte. Menschenrechte, Demokratie und internationale Politik*. Frankfurt: Suhrkamp Verlag.

Buchanan, Allan 2004. *Justice, Legitimacy, and Self-Determination. Moral Foundations for International Law*. Oxford University Press.

Buchanan, Allen and Keohane, Robert O. 2004. 'The Preventive Use of Force: A Cosmopolitan Institutional Proposal', *Ethics and International Affairs* 18: 1–22.

Clausewitz, Carl von 1994. *Vom Kriege*. (First edition 1832–4) Stuttgart: Reclam.

Habermas, Jürgen 2004. 'Hat die Konstitutionalisierung des Völkerrechts noch eine Chance?', in Habermas, Jürgen, *Der gespaltene Westen*. Frankfurt: Suhrkamp Verlag, 113–93.

Kant, Immanuel 1968. *Kants Werke, Akademie Textausgabe*. Berlin/New York: De Gruyter Verlag.

Lutz-Bachmann, Matthias 2004.'Die Idee der Menschenrechte angesichts der Realitäten der Weltpolitik: Eine Reflexion über das Verhältnis von Ethik und Politik', in Szaif, Jan and Lutz-Bachmann, Matthias (eds.), *What is*

Good for a Human Being? Human Nature and Values. Berlin/New York: De Gruyter Verlag, 276–92.

Lutz-Bachmann, Matthias 2007. 'Demokratie, öffentliche Vernunft und Religion', *Philosophisches Jahrbuch* 114: 3–21.

Lutz-Bachmann, Matthias 2008. 'Kosmopolitische Verantwortung. Über Ethik und Recht in einer globalisierten Welt', in Decker, Oliver and Grave, Tobias, *Kritische Theorie der Zeit*. Springe: zu Klampen Verlag, 70–7.

Lutz-Bachmann, Matthias and Bohman, James 2002. *Weltstaat oder Staatenwelt? Für und wider die Idee einer Weltrepublik*. Frankfurt: Suhrkamp Verlag.

Lutz-Bachmann, Matthias and Niederberger, Andreas 2009. *Krieg und Frieden im Prozess der Globalisierung*. Weilerswist: Velbrück Verlag.

Lutz-Bachmann, Matthias, Fidora, Alexander and Wagner, Andreas (eds.) in press (2009). *Lex und Ius. Beiträge zur Begründung des Rechts in der Philosophie des Mittelalters und der Neuzeit*. Stuttgart: Frommann Holzboog Verlag.

Rawls, John 1993. 'The Law of Peoples', in Shute, Stephen and Hurley, Susan (eds.), *On Human Rights*. New York: HarperCollins.

10

Forcing a people to be free

ARTHUR ISAK APPLBAUM

Is forcing a people to be free possible, and if so, is it ever morally permissible? The question cries out for clarification: what is it to be a *people*? What is it for a people to be *forced*? And what is it for a people to be *free*? As with so many questions in political philosophy, the hardest task here is to ask the right one, so I will spend most of my time specifying and clarifying what I am asking. When the question is well posed, it will almost answer itself, or so I hope.

I

The question in some form is very much on our minds, provoked by the war in Iraq and one of its stated justifications: freeing the Iraqi people from tyranny. When 'Operation Iraqi Freedom', as the war was called, began, President George W. Bush announced, 'Our mission is clear: to disarm Iraq of weapons of mass destruction, to end Saddam Hussein's support for terrorism, and to free the Iraqi people'.[1]

Reprinted from *Philosophy and Public Affairs*, 35 (2007), 359–400. Versions of this article were presented at Humboldt University in Berlin and the British Academy in London at conferences led by Lukas Meyer, at the University of Vermont in honour of Alan Wertheimer, and initially at Indiana University's Poynter Center for the Study of Ethics and American Institutions in April 2004. I am grateful to the participants at these venues, and to Brian Barry, Michael Blake, Michael Ignatieff, Frances Kamm, Arthur Kuflik, Lukas Meyer, Richard B. Miller, Mathias Risse, Nancy Rosenblum, T. M. Scanlon, Frederick Schauer, Melissa Seymour, Dennis Thompson, Alec Walen, Alan Wertheimer and Kenneth Winston for their helpful comments. I am especially thankful to the Editors of *Philosophy and Public Affairs* for their probing and constructive criticism. Support for this project has been provided by Harvard University's Edmond J. Safra Center for Ethics and Ash Institute for Democratic Governance and Innovation.

[1] 'President Discusses Beginning of Operation Iraqi Freedom: President's Radio Address', Office of the Press Secretary, 22 March 2003, www.whitehouse.gov/news/releases/2003/03/20030322.html.

Now that it has been established beyond doubt that Iraq had no weapons of mass destruction at the time of the invasion, and now that the White House has acknowledged that there is no evidence at all of a connection between the 11 September terrorist attacks and Saddam Hussein's regime, the freedom argument must bear all the weight of justification for both the invasion and the extended occupation that has followed. The Bush administration's case for war initially had three legs. Can it stand on one alone? And if 'to free the Iraqi people' is a good enough reason to permit the forceful occupation of Iraq, in what way does the Iraqi people have to be free before such permission runs out?

To be clear, I am not asking about the motives or intentions of politicians and generals, but about right reasons. There are sound theoretical grounds for holding that the rightness and wrongness of actions (in contrast with the goodness and badness of actors) does not ordinarily turn on motives. But even if this is not so, the project of political ethics in the first instance is forward-looking and first-personal: the primary question is what we as political actors should do, and only secondarily how we should evaluate the actions of others. Insofar as we are asking the first-personal question, we are asking what reasons rightly govern our actions, not what motives cause our behaviour. To put it another way: what should we, who in asking this question already are moved (or want to be moved) to do what is right, do next time the opportunity to force a people to be free arises?

Nor am I asking about the means that might be employed to depose a tyrant and suppress his supporters. From the negligent failure to prevent the looting of Baghdad to the sickening abuses of detainees in Abu Ghraib prison, the United States has much to answer for. The overall conduct of and any particular incident in a war and its aftermath may fail the appropriate criteria for *jus in bello*, justice *in* war. Although crucial to an overall moral assessment of the war in Iraq or any war, I set them aside in this discussion. My sole concern is the claim that forcing a people to be free can, under some conditions, satisfy the criteria for *jus ad bellum*, justice *of* war.

To make a related but different distinction, there are first-order moral considerations that matter to the justification of any war, what might be called the substantive merits of the case: how much death, destruction and misery will be inflicted on their soldiers and ours, their civilians and ours, for what reasons and for whose benefit, for how long and at what cost and with what prospects of success? Then there are second-order moral considerations concerning who is to decide upon the first-order judgments: is the target government morally immune from intervention in this way for these reasons by virtue of the moral legitimacy of its rule?

Does this candidate intervener or some other candidate intervener have the legitimacy to intervene in this way for these reasons? I will focus primarily on the first of these second-order questions, the legitimacy and consequent moral immunity of targets, rather than the legitimacy and the consequent moral powers, privileges and duties of interveners.

So I set aside as well the important question of who, if anyone, can and may force a people to be free. There may be good reason to conclude that an ad hoc coalition of the United States, Britain and thirty-two other countries (from Italy's 3,000 troops to the no doubt brave twenty-four man Moldovan fighting force) does not have legitimate authority to topple a regime and establish democracy, but some other actor – the United Nations, or a regional treaty organisation – does have such authority. My students often adamantly object to military intervention on the grounds that the usual interveners are too arrogant or too hypocritical to be entrusted with such a mission, but they soften when I propose intervention by the CSSSC – the Coalition of Small Scandinavian States and Canada. My question is whether it is possible and permissible for *any* external actor to force a people to be free, not whether the United States is such an actor.

Nor will I consider here whether there are any circumstances under which forcing a people to be free is or ought to be lawful under international law. Moral principles are discoveries or constructions of reason, not enactments or conventions of political bodies, and sometimes there ought to be a gap between the prescriptions of morality and the prescriptions of institutional rules. Every rule, even when properly followed, will sometimes be either over-inclusive or under-inclusive with respect to its underlying purpose.[2] Also, because rules are not always properly followed, the formulation of the best rule takes into account the consequences of mistaken or manipulative misuse of the rule.

Finally, although the use of lethal force ordinarily is unavoidable in military interventions, force understood as violence is not my central concern. Even if Saddam Hussein's regime could have been toppled without a single shot or drop of blood, our question about forced freedom would still stand. Our main concern is about coercion, whether or not violence is employed.[3] Is it possible to *coerce* a people to be free, to free a people against its will?

[2] F. Schauer, *Playing by the Rules* (Oxford: Clarendon Press, 1991), 31–4.

[3] To be more precise, violence is a presumptive wrong in need of justification for two reasons. First, violence physically harms its target. Second, violent force overwhelms the will of its target, either by physically preventing one from exercising one's will or by threatening severe harm if one does not submit to the will of the threatener. I am concerned here with violence insofar as it is employed to overwhelm the will of its target.

This investigation, then, isolates one claim that has been made in defence of the war in Iraq in order to explore general questions about the possibility and permissibility of forcing a people to be free. If freeing the Iraqi people is indeed the only remaining ground for the war, then establishing the possibility and permissibility of such forced freedom by some actor under some conditions is necessary to justify the war. Clearly, however, the success of this claim is not sufficient.

One might be tempted to complain about both the formality and narrowness of this exploration in light of the messier and wider moral and political issues that the US invasion and occupation have raised, and criticise philosophical fiddling while Fallujah burns. Following Montaigne, however, I make no apologies for making distinctions. 'Should we not dare say of a thief that he has a fine leg? And if she is a whore, must she also necessarily have bad breath?'[4] If the current (mis)adventure in Iraq either is or turns out to be a moral disaster, we will not know if this is a necessary or contingent conclusion without such distinctions. The stakes are high: unwarranted generalisations about failures in Somalia played a part in the shameful neglect of Rwanda. When errors of both omission and commission might be catastrophic, we need more fine-grained distinctions, not fewer.

One response to the objection that an intervention aimed at freeing a people is impermissibly coercive is that, under the appropriate counterfactual, the people would have welcomed the intervention, and so were not coerced after all. Before the invasion of Iraq, Deputy Secretary of Defense Paul Wolfowitz was sure that, had there been some mechanism for showing support, the attack would have been supported:

> If the Iraqi people were free to demonstrate they would be on the streets in the millions now saying, 'Why didn't you come sooner? Don't make us wait any longer.' I don't think there's any question where the feelings of the Iraqi people are.[5]

Posing a slightly different hypothetical, he also said, 'I'm absolutely sure that if you could take a free poll among Iraqis, they would say … "Please come; please do the job, and do it quickly"'.[6]

[4] M. de Montaigne, 'Of Husbanding your Will' (1585–8), in D. M. Frame (trans.), *The Complete Essays of Montaigne* (Stanford University Press, 1958), 766–84.

[5] DefenseLink News Transcript: Deputy Secretary Paul Wolfowitz Interview with BBC TV and Radio, US Department of Defense, 19 February 2003, www.defenselink.mil/transcripts/transcript.aspx?transcriptid=1936.

[6] DefenseLink News Transcript: Deputy Secretary Paul Wolfowitz Interview with ITV London, US Department of Defense, 17 February 2003, www.defenselink.mil/transcripts/transcript.aspx?transcriptid=1934.

We do not know what Iraqis would have said to pollsters before the war. Asking the question requires a careful posing of the counterfactual. We can safely guess how Iraqis would have answered an actual poll had they faced the prospect of arrest for answering wrongly, but that of course is not the counterfactual Wolfowitz had in mind. If the aim is to justify the invasion by appeal to implicit but actual consent, however, neither can the right counterfactual be 'How would Iraqis answer a poll had they not had their political views shaped by decades of tyranny?'

Fortunately, we do not have to guess what Iraqis would have said, because we know what they *did* say soon after the invasion and continue to say. The one indisputably enduring contribution of Western democracy to Iraq is the public opinion poll, and, unfortunately for Wolfowitz, there *was* a question about the feelings of the Iraqi people. One fortuitously timed poll was conducted in February 2004, right before the outbreak of hostilities in Fallujah and Najaf that marked the beginning of organised resistance to the occupation, and before the Abu Ghraib revelations.[7] The results showed that support for the invasion and occupation was then mixed. When asked about whether the invasion by US-led forces was right or wrong, 48% answered absolutely or somewhat right, and 39% answered absolutely or somewhat wrong.[8] The most intriguing question asked whether the invasion liberated or humiliated Iraq. Of all Iraqis polled, 42% said liberated and 41% said humiliated.[9] In posing this as a binary choice, the pollsters did not allow for what may be both the best answer and the answer that would have been chosen by most Iraqis: that the invasion *both* liberated *and* humiliated Iraq. One of the purposes of this chapter is to explore how this might be so of a people that is forced to be free.

[7] Oxford Research International, 'National Survey of Iraq, February 2004', for ABC News and BBC.

[8] More recently, in a March 2007 ABC News poll, 52% answered somewhat or absolutely wrong, with wide disparities by faction: 98% of Sunnis, 29% of Shia and only 17% of Kurds. See http://abcnews.com/pollvault.html.

[9] By faction, among Sunnis, 21% said liberated and 66% humiliated; among the Shia, 43% said liberated and 37% humiliated; and among the Kurds, 82% said liberated and 11% humiliated. Oxford Research International, 'National Survey of Iraq, February 2004'.

II

Consider an extended passage from an 1859 magazine article that startles our contemporary sensibilities, John Stuart Mill's 'A Few Words on Non-Intervention'. The main thrust of the piece is to argue against intervention in the civil wars and revolutions of civilised nations, but barbarians are another matter:

> To suppose that the same international customs, and the same rules of international morality, can obtain between one civilised nation and another, and between civilised nations and barbarians, is a grave error …
>
> In the first place, the rules of ordinary international morality imply reciprocity. But barbarians will not reciprocate. They cannot be depended on for observing any rules. Their minds are not capable of so great an effort, nor their will sufficiently under the influence of distant motives.
>
> In the next place, nations which are still barbarous have not got beyond the period which it is likely to be for their benefit that they should be conquered and held in subjection by foreigners. Independence and nationality, so essential to the due growth and development of a people further advanced in improvement, are generally impediments to theirs …
>
> To characterise any conduct whatever towards a barbarous people as a violation of the law of nations, only shows that he who so speaks has never considered the subject. A violation of great principles of morality it may easily be; but barbarians have no rights as a *nation*, except a right to such treatment as may, at the earliest possible period, fit them for becoming one. The only moral laws for the relation between a civilised and a barbarous government, are the universal rules of morality between man and man.[10]

Mill wrote this the very same year that he published *On Liberty*, which remains just about the most uncompromising rejection of paternalism ever written. *On Liberty* argues for toleration of Mormon polygamy in the Utah Territory, although Mill views the practice as a 'direct infraction' of the principle of liberty, 'a mere riveting of the chains of one half of the community',[11] and a 'retrograde step in civilisation'.[12] Still, Mill holds, 'I am not aware that any community has a right to force another to be civilised'.[13]

There is a ready, uncharitable way to explain these texts: in the first, Mill is flacking for the East India Company. His family and his country

[10] J. S. Mill, 'A Few Words on Non-Intervention' (1859), in J. M. Robson (ed.), *Collected Works of John Stuart Mill: Essays on Equality, Law, and Education*, vol. XXI (University of Toronto Press, 1984), 109–24, here 118–19.

[11] J. S. Mill, *On Liberty* (1859), D. Spitz (ed.) (New York: W. W. Norton, 1975), ch. 4, 85.

[12] *Ibid.*, 86. [13] *Ibid.*, 86.

had no financial stake in Salt Lake City. Explanations such as this, however, explain away the need to take a writer's thought seriously. Our concern is with reasons, not motives. There are several ways to reconcile the two passages, although none is entirely satisfactory. Most likely, despite their uncivilised practice of polygamy, Mill simply does not consider the Mormons to be an example of 'those backward states of society in which the race itself may be considered in its nonage'.[14]

Mill's considered view on the matter of intervention in the internal affairs of barbarous nations is not entirely transparent. Our main interest, however, is in the text of 'A Few Words on Non-Intervention' that is so jarring to our ears. What, precisely, is Mill's mistake? Instead of *ad hominem* dismissal, let us engage in perhaps overly charitable reconstruction, and, for every appearance of the quaint (and insulting) term 'barbarous', substitute 'tyrannised', and similarly substitute 'democratic' for 'civilised'. Now the view (which I confess may no longer be Mill's) is much less startling: do not think that the law of nations that applies between democracies also applies between democracies and tyrannies. Tyrannies have no rights as nations, and so no state or government interposes in our moral relations with the persons who live under tyranny. Our duties towards them are direct, governed by 'the universal rules of morality between man and man'.

What resists this easy translation are the references to 'barbarians'. In places, we can substitute 'tyrants', and the meaning is clear enough. But in places Mill is referring to the individuals who populate a barbarous nation, not its leaders, and to substitute 'tyrannised persons' simply will not do. Does a tyrannised person have a mind that is distinctively defective in the way that Mill supposes the barbarian's mind is? Here is Mill's unsalvageable mistake: he thinks that barbarous nations are barbarous because they are composed of barbarians, and barbarians are individuals whose minds are incapable of the great effort of reciprocity and whose wills are insufficiently governed by distant motives. Now, Mill is not claiming genetic inferiority here. Barbarism for Mill is a product of culture, not nature, but the ill effects of barbarous cultures operate through the shaping of the mind of the barbarian. Mill's account, even after our politically correct updating, remains insulting, because it supposes that persons who live under tyrants are likely to have tyrannised minds and wills that lack the capacity to think the thoughts and will the

[14] *Ibid.*, 11.

ends that persons who live in democracies think and will.[15] This is a sweeping factual claim that needs to be backed up by evidence. It may, for some persons in some tyrannies, be true, but it is not a conclusion Mill or we get for free.

Here, then, is the point of our Millian digression: Mill believes that we may paternalise barbarous nations because we may paternalise barbarians. To force a people to be free is to paternalise a people. Does paternalising a people entail paternalising the persons who are members of that people? If so, then justifying the paternalising of a people depends on justifying the paternalising of the persons who are members of that people, and the criteria for the justified paternalism of persons are stringent. If those persons are not proper targets of paternalism, then neither is their people. Yet if it is possible to paternalise a people without paternalising its constituent members, then the argument for paternalising a people does not need to meet the objection of individual persons that they are not proper targets of paternalism. It is humiliating to be paternalised (even, as I will soon argue, when the paternalism is justified). But if we can drive a wedge between paternalising a people and paternalising persons, perhaps feelings of humiliation are, in one respect, unfounded.

III

Consider three ways in which it might be *impossible* to force a people to be free.

Forcing a people to be FREE

The claim is that forcing a people to be free is a conceptual impossibility because if a people is forced, it cannot be free; if free, it cannot be forced. Now, this is true synchronically, unless we entertain a paradoxical

[15] In his early writing, Mill clearly holds that tyranny plays a causal role in the shaping of the minds of its subjects. In 'Cataline's Conspiracy' (1826), he says that an aristocracy 'seldom or never reduces the human mind so completely to the level of the brutes, as a military despotism'. In a despotism, the danger faced by those who cultivate their merits and talents 'contributes most of all to sink the minds of the unhappy subjects of a despotism into the lowest state of brutality and degradation of which human nature is susceptible' (J. S. Mill, *Collected Works of John Stuart Mill: Essays on Equality, Law, and Education*, vol. XXVI. University of Toronto Press, 345f.). In the posthumous 'Three Essays on Religion', he returns to the idea that self-control, unnatural to the undisciplined human being and to children, must be learned. 'Savages are always liars' (Mill, *Collected Works*, vol. X, 395).

understanding of forced freedom that is often attributed to Rousseau. Rousseau infamously writes, 'Whoever refuses to obey the general will shall be constrained to do so by the entire body; which means only that he will be forced to be free'.[16] There is some textual evidence in the *Geneva Manuscript* that suggests Rousseau meant nothing quite as frightening as this sounds, but in any case, I have no use here for accounts of higher freedom.[17] What I mean by freedom is independence, the power of a moral agent to both set and pursue one's own ends without being subject to the domination of another.[18] But there is nothing incoherent about forced freedom understood diachronically. It is not impossible to force a people in time t so that it is a free people in time $t + 1$, unless one holds to a pedigreed conception of freedom under which any force in the history of a people renders it incapable of freedom in the future. On such a view, there are no free people, because, with the possible exception of Plymouth Plantation in the period immediately following the signing of the 'Mayflower Compact', there has never been a political society of any consequence that was freely constituted.

FORCING a people to be free

The second claim of impossibility is empirical, not conceptual: there is no known causal mechanism of regime change that has outside force as one of its inputs and a free people as an output. Attempts to force a people to be free are futile. When Mill writes about civilised as opposed to barbarian peoples, this is the view that he endorses:

> The only test possessing any real value, of a people's having become fit for popular institutions, is that they, or a sufficient portion of them to prevail in the contest, are willing to brave labour and danger for their liberation.
>
> I know all that may be said. I know it may be urged that the virtues of freemen cannot be learnt in the school of slavery, and that if a people are not fit for freedom, to have any chance of becoming so they must first be free. And this would be conclusive, if the intervention recommended would really give them freedom.

16 J. J. Rousseau, 'On the Social Contract' (1762), in R. D. Masters (ed.) and J. R. Bush (trans.), *On the Social Contract: with Geneva Manuscript and Political Economy* (New York: St Martin's Press, 1978), 55.

17 See Rousseau, 'On the Social Contract', 1:7 (138), and 'Geneva Manuscript' 1:3 (164).

18 Here I follow Arthur Ripstein's Kantian account in A. Ripstein, 'Authority and Coercion', *Philosophy and Public Affairs*, 32 (2004), 2–35, and A. Ripstein, 'Beyond the Harm Principle', *Philosophy and Public Affairs*, 34 (2006), 215–45.

> But the evil is, that if they have not sufficient love of liberty to be able to wrest it from merely domestic oppressors, the liberty which is bestowed on them by other hands than their own, will have nothing real, nothing permanent. No people ever was and remained free, but because it was determined to be so; because neither its rulers nor any other party in the nation could compel it to be otherwise …
>
> When a people has had the misfortune to be ruled by a government under which the feelings and the virtues needful for maintaining freedom could not develop themselves, it is during an arduous struggle to become free by their own efforts that these feelings and virtues have the best chance of springing up.[19]

This view is less appealing than might first appear. First, note that Mill conflates establishing a free people through force and maintaining a free people through force. It may be historically accurate that no people ever remained free, 'but because it was determined to be so', but it does not follow that no people ever remained free that had its freedom 'bestowed on them by other hands than their own'.

Second, Mill is not simply saying that if you are not willing to face some risk of dying for freedom then you are not fit for it. If that were the claim, then once a people has shown that its members are 'willing to brave labour and danger for their liberation', why require that they brave it alone? A freedom-loving uprising of courageous but hapless Don Quixotes would then merit outside support, a conclusion Mill rejects. So either Mill's view assumes, falsely, that a brave majority always is strong enough to prevail.[20] Or he holds that the inability to wrest freedom from merely domestic oppressors shows insufficient love of liberty. This, to put it harshly but not inaccurately, implies that if you are not sufficiently willing and skilful to *kill* for your freedom, then you are not fit for it. But it is just a contingent matter of good luck that a popular majority that actually is capable of living free lives in peace and also has

[19] Mill, 'A Few Words on Non-Intervention', 122–3. Elsewhere, Mill goes so far as to turn this into a constitutive rather than an empirical claim. 'The attempt to establish freedom by foreign bayonets is a solecism in terms. A government that requires the support of foreign armies cannot be a free government' (Mill, 'The Spanish Question' (1837), in *Collected Works*, XXI, 374).

[20] The passage in 'The Spanish Question' continues: 'If a government has not a majority of the people, or at least a majority of those among the people who care for politics, on its side; if those who will fight for it, are not a stronger party than those who will fight against it, then it can only have the name of a popular government; not being able to support itself by the majority, it must support itself by keeping down the majority, it must be a despotism in the name of freedom.' Note that Mill simply assumes that the side that has the majority of willing fighters is the stronger.

the strength and expertise and resources to be able to overthrow various kinds of tyranny and oppression. That such instruments of power are intimately connected with a deep desire for freedom and the capacity to carry forward with freedom just seems to be empirically false. One can know how to operate a printing press without knowing how to operate a rocket-propelled grenade launcher.[21]

I see little reason to accept Mill's (and, later, Arendt's and Walzer's) tendency to identify the violent struggle of revolution and civil war with real political voice. Rather, internal violence, though too often enough morally permitted or even required, is the utter failure of politics. The sound of gunfire never is the voice of the people.[22]

The strongest retort to the objection that forced freedom necessarily is doomed to failure, however, is that there have been two spectacular successes: Germany and Japan. Many keys have been stroked arguing that the highly developed political cultures of the pre-war Axis powers render those two cases quite unlike any contemporary attempt at regime change. I do not deny the point. My claim is much more modest: the fact of two successes somewhere under some conditions shows that forced freedom is not impossible somewhere else.[23] Since we know that forcing

[21] How is Gandhi's successful campaign of non-violent resistance in India to be analysed under this reading of Mill? First, let us bracket the fact that the British were outside occupiers, since Mill has a different account of such struggles, and suppose, counter-factually, that the British Raj was a 'domestic oppressor'. I think the Millian stance would have to be something like this. It is admirable that the Indians showed willingness to brave considerable 'labour and danger', and fortunate in two senses for them that this non-violent bravery was sufficient: fortunate in that they have won their freedom, and fortunate in having the good moral luck of not having the extent of their love for freedom put to a more stringent test. Had the British (again, assumed to be a domestic oppressor) crushed the non-violent movement and had the Indians then refused to escalate into violence, that would have shown insufficient fitness for freedom, and no outside power would have been permitted to intervene.

[22] I do mean to make the counter-intuitive claim that the successful violent overthrow of a tyrant, though a moral success, is a failure of politics, if politics is understood in its normative sense as the workings of collective agency. Indeed, as the next section suggests, politics in this normative sense is not possible under conditions of tyranny. If this is correct, then even when both are morally justified, neither internal revolution nor external intervention is an expression of the general will of the people.

[23] It must be said as well that differences in prior political culture are not the only moving explanatory parts. I will refrain from saying much about comparing the effort, skill and commitment brought to bear in Germany and Japan with the current situation in Iraq, except to point out the difference in preparation. The war in Europe was over in April 1945. April also was the month that General George Marshall appointed General John Hilldring to begin training the thousands of military administrators who would govern occupied Germany – but the year was 1943.

a people to be free is possible at least under some conditions, we must address the permissibility question. But first, one last try at rendering forced freedom impossible.

Forcing a PEOPLE to be free

On this view, one cannot force *a people* to be free because an unfree people is a contradiction: if a people, it already is free; if forced, it cannot have been a people.

Now, this view seems to employ an extravagantly demanding conception of a people. It implies that an occupied population ceases to be a people, so that there was no French people in occupied France in the Second World War. For that matter, it implies that there was no French people under Louis XIV, because the French people under an absolute monarchy hardly was free.

Although extravagant, there is something to the claim, which I will soon explore. For a moment, however, simply suppose the claim is correct. If we are then to make sense of our original question, it must be recast as a question about *forcing individual persons to become a free people.* Now, even if it turns out that a people can be unfree without contradiction, this formulation of the question is independently interesting, and has the advantage of being answerable. Surely it is conceptually possible to force individuals to become a free people, so we can ask under what conditions it is morally permissible to do so. What we thought was one question is actually several:

> When can and may we force an individual to be a free person?
> When can and may we force individuals to become a free people?
> When can and may we force a people to be free?

The answers will depend, in part, on the correct account of the practice Mill was so opposed to, at least among the civilised: paternalism.

IV

On the standard textbook account of the concept, A paternalises B when A restricts B's liberty for B's own good. Since an action may be undertaken for a variety of reasons, morally sufficient or insufficient, it is most illuminating to see paternalism as an attribute of reasons for action, rather than an attribute of actions themselves.[24] On this view, to justify

[24] Here I follow D. F. Thompson, *Political Ethics and Public Office* (Cambridge, MA: Harvard University Press, 1987), 153.

paternalism is to show that the paternalistic reason for restricting B's liberty – for B's own good – under the circumstances is sufficient.[25] The question of paternalism need not arise if there are sufficient non-paternalistic reasons for action. So, if preventing harm to C is a sufficient reason for A to restrict B's liberty, the action is justified for non-paternalistic reasons. It may also be the case that the same restriction of B's liberty also is for the good of B. Indeed, if one holds that B has a moral interest in not doing wrong, then to be prevented from wronging C always is for B's own good.[26] Yet it would be superfluous to persist in asking if an action also is justified on paternalistic grounds (and odd for B to demand such a justification) once the action has been justified on the grounds of harm to others.[27]

Paternalism is a presumptive moral wrong in need of justification because the paternalist interferes with an agent's freedom to set and pursue her own ends for a reason that denies or discounts the importance of the agent's self-governance. If A does not claim that B has an impaired will, but merely that B is mistaken about her ends, then A discounts the importance of B's moral agency simply, and so disrespects B. If A claims that B's will is impaired, but is mistaken about this, B has been insulted, and is entitled to be indignant, our characteristic response to being paternalised. It is worth examining exactly why indignation is fitting. By claiming that B is insufficiently capable of choosing or pursuing ends for herself, A is treating B as something less than a full moral agent, a creature with a less dignified status. Unjustified paternalism warrants indignation because it takes a swipe at one's dignity.

Now suppose that A is not mistaken, and B knows that A is not mistaken. A precocious and relatively reflective twelve-year-old girl wants to pierce her tongue just like all her friends, but her parents say no. In a moment of clarity, she acknowledges to herself that she is not a fully mature and competent agent yet, and acknowledges that she still needs her parents to make some decisions for her. This recognition is, in a way, humiliating, because the girl now correctly sees that she is a creature of lower moral status than she had thought. This of course is

25 I focus here on reasons, not motives. Paternalistic motives ordinarily do not enter into judgments of the rightness or wrongness of an action, although they do enter into evaluative judgments of the goodness or badness of the actor.

26 A point I owe to Mathias Risse.

27 On the view sketched here, if A is motivated by insufficient paternalistic reasons and not motivated by the sufficient non-paternalistic reasons that apply, B could complain about A's attitudes, but is not wronged by A's actions.

not to say that she counts for less. Considered as a moral patient, she is no less valuable and her claims on others are no weaker. Considered as a moral agent, however, she is not fully an end-in-herself, because others do not always have a reason to respect her ends merely because they are hers. Indignation is not called for, since her parents are not failing to recognise her moral status, and have not done anything to lower her status. The recognition of the truth of her lesser agency nonetheless carries with it a bit of self-inflicted shame. She is, after all, a little less dignified than she thought.

If A paternalises B when A restricts B's freedom for the reason that it is for B's own good, and if the presumptive wrong in paternalism is that A fails to respect B's capacity for choosing ends, then A's paternalistic action is most likely to be justified when the following three criteria are met: B's freedom already is impaired, the good of B at stake is B's future freedom, and B's retrospective endorsement is likely. The strongest case for paternalism is when the liberty of someone who has an impaired or immature will is restricted in order to develop in her the capacity to have a competent and mature will, and from that competent and mature perspective she will endorse the prior restrictions. I have just described the condition of childhood and the practice of parenting.[28] If we may not paternalise children, whom may we paternalise? Still, as we have seen, even justified paternalism humiliates. So perhaps the Iraqi people were both liberated and humiliated.

V

Is it then possible to paternalise a people without paternalising the individual persons who are members of that people? Recall Mill's mistake about the barbarians. Mill held that uncivilised political societies are uncivilised because they are made up of uncivilised persons, persons who have barbarous minds incapable of enlightened thought. These societies can be paternalised because individual persons within them can be paternalised. Perhaps these societies cannot be forced to be free, since they are incapable of freedom; but they may be ruled by force, taken under the protection of a civilised society, until the individuals reach political maturity. Can we avoid Mill's mistake and recognise that individual adults who are said to make up a people are perfectly mature, competent moral agents, but still make the case that the people itself lacks the capacity to exercise competent moral agency?

[28] See T. Schapiro, 'What Is a Child?', *Ethics*, 109 (1999), 715–38.

Let us return to the extravagant claim that there cannot be unfree peoples. Surely this is false if by 'people' we mean the social fact of common sentiments, shared language, culture and religion that lead individuals to form bonds of solidarity and identify as members of a people. As a matter of social science, it is plausible to think that when it comes to peoplehood, collective thinking makes it so. On what I shall call the *anthropological sense* of peoplehood, of course the French under German occupation and under the reign of Louis XIV are a people. And it is no small irony that, in this anthropological sense, Iraq may fail to be one people, since it is deeply divided along religious and linguistic lines in ways that make a common Iraqi cultural identity largely illusory.[29]

Peoplehood, however, can also be understood as a normative concept. On the normative view, the anthropological markers of common sentiment and shared cultural material are neither necessary nor sufficient. Rather, what makes for normative peoplehood is the capacity for shared agency. A people in the *normative sense* must be capable of willing as a people. What do I mean by this, and why do I think it is so?

I want nothing to do with spooky accounts of the general will here. A group agent is not a metaphysical entity, and collective willing is not a mental state in some group mind. Yet neither is a group agent a simple aggregation of the preferences of individuals. To be fully capable of competent shared agency, individuals have to be properly constituted, incorporated, represented or personated. A natural individual is capable of agency, of willing ends, when there is a unity of the self, the capacity for reflecting on desires and for endorsing some and not others. Without such a capacity, one is what Harry Frankfurt calls a wanton, a creature that simply follows the vector of his desires, rather than a person.[30] When a collection of individuals

[29] Indeed, over the course of writing and revising this article, the moral disaster of civil war has increasingly threatened. But an outright civil war in Iraq would not show that anthropological peoplehood is a necessary condition for normative peoplehood. Deep cultural division is not conceptually incompatible with the thinner shared commitments to legitimate and just law that collective political agency requires, and we have examples of divided societies that flourish as unified polities. I also believe, as an empirical matter, that what distinguishes divided societies that violently fragment from those that hold together is not the depth of the cultural divisions, but rather contingent shocks to mechanisms of social order, trust and cooperation. (Yes, the destruction of a tyrant's mechanism of order without immediate adequate replacement would be such a shock.) But this, I confess, is a rather whiggish view of the possibilities for reasonable pluralism.

[30] H. G. Frankfurt, 'Freedom of the Will and the Concept of a Person' (1971), in H. G. Frankfurt, *The Importance of What We Care About* (Cambridge University Press, 1988), 11–25.

has this unity of will and capacity for second-order reflection, it is capable of group action and what comes along with action: the group itself is a proper subject for moral evaluation. (The conditions under which such evaluation properly distributes to the individual constituent actors is a further question.) Without a shared will, there are only the individual wills of individual persons, which may show statistical regularities, may be coordinated in various ways, and which always result in some vector that is the consequence of individual actions, but none of this makes for shared agency. To use Christine Korsgaard's image, a bag filled with mice will move, but it will not act. This is the difference between the results of a public opinion poll and the results of an election: a public opinion poll is a mere aggregation of individual preferences. An election (when the conditions for its legitimacy are met) is performative, the action of a shared agent.

What, more precisely, do I mean by normative peoplehood? A normative people is a set of individuals that (1) has sufficient size, density of interaction among the members of the set, and differentiation from members of other sets (despite gradation, ambiguity, and overlap) to fit our common-sense, non-normative notions of a society, and that (2) is itself the proximate locus of respect and responsibility, and so is an entity that can make genuine moral claims on others and of which others can make genuine moral claims. Note that the first condition is not demanding in the way of common sentiments, solidarity or shared identity, and so may be satisfied when the conditions for an anthropological people are not satisfied. Most of the interesting work is done by the second condition. When peoplehood is invoked in political discourse, some combination of the second condition's normative attributes typically is claimed.

Can there be normative peoples, understood as societies that are bearers of respect and responsibility, and if so, what properties must they have? First, if the idea of a normative people is to be taken seriously, then all of the moral claims a people can make and all of the moral claims that can be made against it cannot merely be direct pass-throughs for the separate and several moral claims by and on the natural individual persons who make up the normative people. If that were so, talk of a normative people would simply be a convenient shorthand, a manner of speaking.

Yet the idea of a normative people should not be taken seriously in the wrong way, and be given moral standing unconnected to the moral standing of the natural persons that constitute it.[31] In ways that are

[31] So, although a normative people is not merely instrumentally valuable, the source of its value is extrinsic. On the distinction, see C. M. Korsgaard, 'Two Distinctions in

often complex, claims against a normative people distribute into claims of some sort against at least some of its members; claims against one set of individual members sometimes generate claims against the normative people as a whole, and these in turn may distribute onto a different set of individual members; at least some claims by individual members generate claims by the normative people; and at least some of the claims of individuals can be discharged by satisfying claims made by normative people (even though the substance of the claim of the natural person may fail to have been met).

In short, if normative peoples are possible, any normative status they have must be in virtue of the normative status of natural persons. If peoples in some measure are owed respect and can be held responsible in some ways, this is because they are made up of natural persons who are owed respect and can be held responsible. But there is no simple reduction or one-to-one correspondence from the claims attached to persons and the claims attached to peoples.

I take it to be a conceptual truth that anything that properly can be held responsible is (or at some time was or will be) capable of action. So a normative people, if it is to have the properties specified above, must be an agent of some sort, and it must be an agent in virtue of the connection it has with the individual agents of which it is constituted. Something that is an agent, in turn, must have three capacities or their functional equivalent:

(1) considering: the capacity to respond to considerations for action, endorsing some and rejecting others;
(2) willing: the capacity to intend or to decide to act (or not act); and
(3) doing: the capacity to behave in ways guided by these considerations, intentions, or decisions.

So a complete account of normative peoplehood would show how individual capacities for and instances of considering, willing and doing can combine to constitute an entity with sufficient unity of the right sort to count as an agent that itself considers, wills and acts.

If a people succeeded in forming such an agent, then one of the important moral claims it would make against others is a claim of immunity from outside interference in its internal affairs. A competent collective agent would claim the respect owed to any competent agent,

Goodness', in C. M. Korsgaard, *Creating the Kingdom of Ends* (Cambridge University Press, 1996), 249–74.

who ordinarily has the right to exercise self-governance in ways that are harmful only to oneself. Just as it is disrespectful to overrule a competent natural agent's self-governed choice among ends, even when that choice is mistaken, the claim is that it is disrespectful to overrule a competent collective agent's self-governed choice among the claims of its constituent members, even when that choice is mistaken. As is the natural agent's, the collective agent's entitlement to immunity from interference is limited in both scope and force. Clearly, the actions of a group agent that will wrong or harm those outside the group have no protection under this sort of immunity claim any more than a natural agent who is prevented from harming another can cry paternalism. Moreover, even when only constituent members are affected, the group agent's complaint of disrespectful interference need not trump all other moral considerations. In particular, as I argue later, a group that violates the basic human rights and political liberties of some of its members is an impaired or even a failed collective agent. From a properly constituted collective agent, however, the claim that interference disrespects is weighty.

I do not have a complete account of agency, individual or collective, but I can offer one necessary condition: *agents must be sufficiently free.* A natural agent must have an adequate set of freedoms necessary to have the three capacities of considering, willing and doing, and a collective agent must be made up of sufficiently free natural agents whose individual capacities for considering, willing and doing mesh in a way that renders the collectivity sufficiently free to have the capacities of considering, willing and doing.

A natural individual can fail to be a moral agent in degree, hence the notion of an impaired or incompetent person. Children and those who are demented, mentally ill or mentally retarded are still persons. Similarly, shared agency can fail in degree. So the account of normative peoplehood would also specify the minimal capacities for considering, willing and doing that make a collectivity an agent at all, and, as with individual natural agents, specify the thresholds that distinguish competent from incompetent collective agency. I do not need to deny that the French under German occupation were a normative people. Understood as a group agent, however, occupied France was impaired, incapable of effective willing. This can be so, of course, even if every single French individual had a mature and competent will. Here, I side with Hobbes and Kant against Locke: there can be no legitimate political society prior to legitimate political institutions.[32] So, here is the truth in the extravagant claim: an aggregation of individuals that does not meet even minimal threshold conditions does not count as a shared agent at all, and so does not count as a normative people at all. Since the conditions for normative peoplehood and anthropological peoplehood may be different, a people in the anthropological sense may fail completely to count as a normative people. The extravagant claim remains extravagant, however, because it does not admit that an aggregation of individuals can meet the minimal threshold conditions for shared agency and so for normative peoplehood, but fail to meet the more demanding conditions for competent and effective shared agency. A collective agent can fail the test of sufficient freedom, either because the natural persons that make it up are not sufficiently free, or because their individual capacities for considering, willing and doing have not combined in the ways needed to form a collective agent that is sufficiently free. So not all normative peoples are already free peoples.

The question that began this section can now be answered. It is possible to paternalise a people without paternalising the individual

[32] In what way are the French under occupation a normative people at all? Both in the occupied north and the unoccupied south, both after Germany's military occupation of the entire country in 1942 as well as before, the Vichy state had quite a bit of continuity with what came before, and Vichy exercised substantial autonomy. Much of the legal system and the civil administration of France continued unchanged. The government, though no longer democratic, was responsive to its (non-Jewish) citizens, and was not a mere puppet of Berlin. France was not Poland. Here, I follow the now standard accounts by S. Hoffmann, 'Collaborationism in France during World War II', *Journal of Modern History*, 40 (1968), 375–95, and R. O. Paxton, *Vichy France: Old Guard and New Order, 1940–1944* (New York: Knopf, 1972). One should not press the analogy to impaired persons too far, in part because it is hard to draw a sharp distinction between natural individuals who are seriously impaired persons and those who are not persons at all. But I am supposing that a natural individual whose capacity for self-governance is seriously impaired, but who nonetheless has remaining domains of meaningful, purposeful action responsive to reasons and desires and has enough psychological continuity among these domains, can still be considered an agent, although an impaired one. If the analogy holds, a normative people whose institutions and practices that make it a group agent are seriously undermined but survive in part and show appreciable continuity with what came before can still be considered a group agent, although an impaired one. Not much turns on establishing the possibility of an impaired or unfree normative people, however, since mere normative personhood is not a sufficient condition for political legitimacy, which is a more demanding standard. With its reversion to authoritarianism and its willing persecution and deportation of French Jews, Vichy could hardly be considered legitimate. I take no stand on its *legality*, for the legal validity of the legislative vote that accepted the armistice, terminated the Third Republic, and installed Pétain does not settle the matter of legitimacy one way or the other.

persons who are members of that people, and the conditions that would justify such paternalism can be offered. A set of individuals who make up a society, by having some measure of group agency, can succeed in being a normative people that is itself an entity entitled to some measure of respect, but still fail to be a competent group agent. As an agent with independent (but not intrinsic) moral standing, a normative people is the sort of entity that can possibly be paternalised, because it has a will that can be forced for the reason that such force is for its own good. That this will already is impaired and that the good in question is the people's future freedom would both count towards the justification of such paternalism. This justification would not extend to restrictions on the liberty of individual members of the normative people who are themselves capable of competent willing. But though such restrictions of liberty need justification, a justification of *paternalism* is not needed, since the reason for the restriction on the liberty of the individual agent is not for the individual's own good, but for the good of the collective agent. This might seem to be an excessively formalistic answer, for though the collective agent is an entity with independent moral standing, such standing ultimately comes from the standing of the natural agents that constitute it. Recall, however, that one of the defining attributes of a genuine collective agent is that the distribution of moral claims from and to its constituent members is no mere pass-through. Although a collective agent has interests and a will only because its constituent members have interests and wills, it is not the case that anything done for the sake of the collective agent is done for the sake of each constituent member. The short answer why an individual forced to constitute a free people need not be paternalised is that such force need not be for the individual's own sake, but for the sake of others. The non-paternalistic justification for such force is offered in Section IX below.

VI

So far, I have said little about what the conditions for shared agency are. We need a conception of shared agency to plug in here, but we may disagree about the correct conception, and so disagree about the correct criteria. Here, I will simply sketch the beginnings of such a conception. If you do not like it, plug in your own. Only two claims are essential to my overall view. First, we cannot do without *some* conception of normative peoplehood. Second, a society ruled by a tyrannical regime either is not a people at all in the normative sense, and so is incapable of shared agency, or else is profoundly impaired as a shared agent, and so is as compromised as a normative people can be and still have the name.

How does an aggregation of individual 'I's somehow go *POOF!* and become 'We', a unified moral agent capable of shared action and that is the proper proximate subject of moral appraisal? Two sorts of answers are needed. One answer should be sufficiently general so that, when we look at aggregations as diverse as marriages, string ensembles, baseball teams, street demonstrations, universities, hospitals, business enterprises, professions, organised crime families, governments, ethnic groups and political societies, we are able to say which have the capacity for shared agency and which do not. Then we need an answer that is sufficiently specific to the kind of aggregation in question, so that we can specify the necessary and sufficient conditions for success as a shared agent of that kind. Conditions for succeeding at 'playing the Mendelssohn octet' may be different than conditions for succeeding at 'amending the Constitution'.

Unified, shared agency can come about in at least three general ways. Every plausible account of which I know follows these three routes, either singly or in combination.

Meshed aims and plans

The structurally simplest route to shared agency is through the intermeshing of aims and plans.[33] Very roughly, a 'we' is formed that plays Mendelssohn when each of us aims to play the piece together, knowing that each of us has that aim, and with each of us planning to (and knowing that each plans to) adjust our actions (tempo, pitch, dynamics, phrasing) to mesh with the actions of others as necessary to support each other to achieve our shared aim. Because no organisational or procedural structure needs to be relied upon for the intermeshing of aims and plans, the paradigm cases are face-to-face, small-scale and synchronic (although more complicated collective agency is not precluded). Note how this simple collective agent succeeds at being the proximate locus of responsibility. The octet itself is a proper subject of evaluation, to be praised or

[33] Michael E. Bratman has what I think is the most plausible account in M. Bratman, *Faces of Intention* (Cambridge University Press, 1999), chs. 5–8. I loosely follow his view. Margaret Gilbert has written the seminal works on this topic, but I am not persuaded by her holism or by her views about how involuntary commitments are formed. See M. Gilbert, *Living Together* (Lanham, MD: Rowman & Littlefield, 1996), and M. Gilbert, *Sociality and Responsibility* (Lanham, MD: Rowman & Littlefield, 2000).

criticised, and this praise and criticism to some extent distributes onto the individual players in a way that is not simply an evaluation of the individual contribution of each. This is captured by locutions such as 'We did it!' after a good performance: 'we', all together, the weakest player and the strongest, did one thing, 'it'. But note too that, if the intermeshing of aims and plans is the only route to shared agency relied upon here, if the eight string players are a subset of a larger chamber orchestra, the woodwinds and horns who stayed home did not 'play the Mendelssohn octet'. For the stay-at-home players to be authors of this action in any way, so that some sort of responsibility for the performance could distribute on to them, recourse to one of the other two routes to shared agency is needed.

Representation

The second route to shared agency relies upon representation and impersonation. Hobbes of course is the great propounder of the view that unity of agency is achieved only through the unity of the natural agent.[34] A shared agent is formed and can act as one only if each of many individuals severally authorises a natural individual to represent each, or, in Hobbes's phrase, to impersonate each. The core idea here is that, under certain conditions, A can act for B in a way that makes B the author of the action, and so the proper locus of responsibility for the action. Via this route, collective agency comes about when a natural agent is authorised to act in the same way on behalf of each of many. There need not be coordination or intermeshing of the plans of the many, or even common knowledge of the multiple representation (although one might make authorisation contingent on the authorisation of others, in which case common knowledge would be necessary). Notice how the route of intermeshing plans and the route of representation can combine. A multitude of unmeshed individuals can be represented by a team with intermeshed plans; or we can together, through an intermeshed plan, appoint a single representative to act for us.

[34] 'A Multitude of men, are made *One* Person, when they are by one man, or one Person, Represented; so that it be done with the consent of every one of that Multitude in particular. For it is the *Unity* of the Representer, not the *Unity* of the Represented, that maketh the Person *One*. And it is the Representer that beareth the Person, and but one Person: And *Unity*, cannot otherwise be understood, in Multitude.' T. Hobbes, *Leviathan* (1651), R. Tuck (ed.) (Cambridge University Press, 1996), ch. 16: 'Of Persons, Authors, and Things Personated'.

Procedure

The third route to shared agency relies on procedures, practices or organisational structures. The various capacities of considering, willing and doing are functionally accomplished by the combined efforts of many, though perhaps no one natural person has considered, willed or acted in a way that matches the shared action.[35] A mechanism that produced an authoritative decision or action out of (and sensitive to) practical inputs of individual agents would be such a procedure. A shared action produced by a procedure could be relatively simple, such as friends choosing a movie by majority vote, or as complex as the rendering of law in a legal system in which the admission of evidence, factual determinations given the evidence, legal rulings given the factual findings, and appellate review given this and other precedential legal rulings are produced by many actors, not one of whom may will the outcome for a consistent set of factual and legal reasons. Complex instances of shared agency typically will rely on all three routes. A corporation or association might form through the intermeshing of the aims and plans of its founders, appoint representatives to make decisions through procedures, and then delegate the implementation of plans to intermeshed teams of workers. To make sense of 'amending the Constitution' as an act of a shared agent, the web of intermeshed aims, representations and procedures would have to be even more elaborate.

For each of these routes to shared agency, we must ask what gives it its authority in Hobbes's sense: what makes any particular natural agent an author of the group agent's actions, and so a candidate for distributed responsibility? The mere existence of a procedure is not sufficient to create a shared agent out of those natural agents whose practical capacities and functionings are taken to be inputs. Your neighbours may, to

[35] Indeed, one tempting test of whether a procedure constitutes a shared agent is that the outcomes of the procedure meet some appealing standards of rationality even when the collective choice is at odds with the individual choices appealingly aggregated. Philip Pettit has fruitfully pursued this line of argument. See especially P. Pettit, 'Responsibility Incorporated', *Ethics*, 117 (2007), 171–201; P. Pettit, 'Groups with Minds of Their Own', in F. Schmitt (ed.), *Socializing Metaphysics* (New York: Rowman & Littlefield, 2004), 167–93; and C. List and P. Pettit, 'Aggregating Sets of Judgments: An Impossibility Result', *Economics and Philosophy*, 18 (2002), 89–110. For a precursor, see H. Raiffa, *Decision Analysis* (Reading, MA: Addison-Wesley, 1968), who relies on a result later published in A. Hylland and R. Zeckhauser, 'The Impossibility of Bayesian Group Decisionmaking with Separate Aggregation of Beliefs and Values', *Econometrica*, 47 (1979), 1321–36.

your surprise, announce a procedure whereby each house on the block is to be painted the colour preferred by the majority, and under that procedure, after duly taking your fondness for blue into account, the colour of your house is to be changed from blue to yellow. Yet surely something more than the counting of your preference as an input must tie you to this procedure before you assume any authorship in or responsibility for the alleged shared agent that has arrived on your doorstep with cans of yellow paint. If instead of employing a procedure, your neighbours appointed as representative a natural agent to make the neighbourhood painting decisions, what is she to you? Or if a neighbour appears with a couple of yellow paintbrushes in one hand and a shotgun in the other, you may find it prudent to join him in painting your house yellow and – one eye on the gun – take pains to do it right, meshing your plans with his. Although you would be taking the action of painting your house yellow, you would not, in any normatively important sense, have formed a shared agent to paint your house yellow.[36]

Authorship of a shared agent's actions is attributable only in two ways: one is if the natural agents who constitute the group agent, under uncoerced and informed circumstances, commit to constituting a group agent in this way for this purpose, either by consent, promise, or

[36] What are we to say about string players in a concentration camp ordered to play Mendelssohn for the guards? Autonomous individual action can be nested inside a generally coercive background. An individual cellist ordered to play the Bach solo suites for the guards may be forced to do something she would not voluntarily choose to do, but, against that forced background, she may out of defiant pride or simple pleasure amid misery decide to exercise the discretion that remains hers to play her best, and then, again within limits, she is a responsible competent agent. So too, eight prison musicians may form a locally autonomous group agent whose purpose is instrumental survival, or defiant pride, or a bit of happiness amid the misery. They do not form a collective agent, however, with the guards. Is a collective agent formed with a guard who also is a good violinist and orders that the prisoners play with him? Under some circumstances and for some circumscribed purposes, yes. If, nested inside the larger coercive background, the prisoners have and exercise local autonomy in performance with the guard, then for purposes of aesthetic praise and criticism, they are acting collectively with him. If the guard also is a musical bully who demands obedience note by note under threat of punishment, then no. Either way, the prisoners do not form an all-purpose group agent with the guard that is responsible, as a group agent, for all of the consequences of the forced performance. Suppose the performance also served as the signal to commence atrocities elsewhere in the camp. Performing under those circumstances may or may not be excusable, but this is a direct assessment of responsibility to be made of each musician taken as an individual natural agent, rather than an assessment of distributed responsibility for the action of a group agent. Group agency is a normative ascription that supervenes on some descriptive facts, but is not itself a descriptive fact of the matter.

some other sort of voluntary action. (Voluntary action short of agreement could constitute participation in a collective agent if the natural agent voluntarily accepts the benefits of a cooperative venture or if the agent voluntarily and intentionally assures others in their expectations concerning his actions.[37]) The second is if commitment to constitute a shared agent in something like this way for this purpose is a practical necessity, in that it is either constitutive of or a precondition for acting upon the natural agent's prior uncoerced and informed commitments, and the natural agent, knowing that this is so, either cannot or will not give up these prior commitments. These are demanding conditions for authorship, but such demandingness is needed to bring about an entity with the moral standing and powers of a group agent. Recall that a group agent is a proximate locus of respect and responsibility that both bears, in some ways, the moral claims made by and against its constituent members, and distributes over its constituent members, in some ways, the moral claims made by and against it.

The kind of shared agency that is of greatest interest to us, of course, is political agency. Political action has profound effects on the freedom and interests of those subject to it because it nearly always involves coercion, and seeks to change the normative status of its subjects by imposing duties or liabilities. Because of these high moral stakes, the conditions for successfully constituting a political 'We' from a multitude of 'I's are going to have more moral content than what it takes to constitute a string ensemble. For how can a people be *my* people unless, in some way, whoever speaks and acts for the people speaks and acts for me, representing in a morally adequate way both my will and my basic interests across the broad range of freedoms and interests that governments claim the right to regulate?

When the collective agent in question claims the normative power to coerce its constituent natural agents, the criterion that these natural agents be sufficiently free is threatened. Governments, by imposing and enforcing laws, appear to restrict the freedoms of the governed. So governments must either show that these restrictions on freedom nonetheless leave the governed sufficiently free, or show that the enactment and enforcement of law does not, despite appearances, actually restrict

[37] For voluntary acceptance of benefit, see John Rawls's account of the principle of fairness in J. Rawls, *A Theory of Justice* (Cambridge, MA: Harvard University Press, 1971), 108–14, 342–50; for voluntary assurance of expectations, see T. Scanlon, 'Promises and Practices', *Philosophy and Public Affairs*, 19 (1990), 199–226.

freedom. One strategy for showing that restrictions on freedom leave natural agents sufficiently free is to show that restrictions are for the sake of realising and protecting these same freedoms, for there is no condition of anarchy or other scheme of government under which these freedoms would be more inviolable or less violated, and so no other condition under which natural agents in general would have greater capacities for agency. One strategy for showing that apparently coercive law does not restrict freedom is to show how the subject of law can also be, from some normatively appropriate point of view, its willing author who therefore is not coerced. These are not two separable strategies, however, but two turns of the same justificatory argument.

One of the central questions of modern political philosophy is how, if at all, collective self-governance is compatible with individual freedom. The correct answer, I believe, has both a substantive and a procedural component, because it needs to address agents both from their perspectives as subjects of law and their perspectives as authors of law. The agent viewed as the subject of coercive law must be given adequate justification, and the most promising strategy of justification is to show that a fully adequate set of freedoms for all requires such limits on the freedom of each. The agent viewed as the author of coercive law must be free enough in the relevant ways to count as an author. Only if individuals are free enough to count as authors can the collective body constitute a shared agent. How free is free enough? No more constrained than is necessary to guarantee other constituent members of the collective body the freedoms they need to have the capacity to be authors. To establish that subjects also are authors, we do not look for free founding moments; even if such foundings were not myths, they would not by themselves do the job needed. Rather, we look for virtuous circles in which subjects are free enough to have the capacity to be authors of collective acts, procedures and institutions that realise and protect the freedoms that make them free enough to have the capacity to be authors.

VII

This chapter has explored the conditions for achieving free collective agency, but has not yet said why this achievement is so important. What, one might wonder, is the great moral significance of becoming a normative people? This is a very large question indeed, and here I shall attempt only to present a typology of answers, some more prosaic and some more lofty, that have some initial plausibility. These answers are not mutually exclusive, so insofar as acting together is morally important, its importance may be over-determined.

First, the achievement of free collective agency could realise a good necessary for survival or basic functioning. So, perhaps prudence universally demands that we end the state of nature's war of all against all. Or free collective agency could realise a contingent good whose importance depends on the ends that persons pursue. The aspiration to flourish as a distinct linguistic community may be an end no more necessary than the aspiration to climb Everest, but the right sort of social cooperation is necessary for success in both. Or the achievement of free collective agency could fulfil a moral duty. So, argues Kant, we have a duty to engage in collective self-rule once we have disputes about what our rights are.

Second, these duties or goods could be connected to collective agency instrumentally, in that collective action is the means to fulfilling a pre-existing duty or realising a pre-existing good. Life, liberty and happiness, independently valued ends, might be best achievable if we act together. Or the duties and goods could be connected to collective agency constitutively, in that they are conceptually possible only under collective agency. This is tautologically true if acting together is a great good in itself. More subtly, we may have a duty to enter into a political relation that gives us duties to each other that we would not and could not otherwise have.

Third, the requirement that group agency be *free*, in that the conditions for genuine collective agency outlined above are met, could be a requirement in three senses. Freedom could be an instrumental requirement, in that only free collective agency is the sort of social coordination that works to fulfil pre-existing duties or realise pre-existing ends. For example, perhaps it is the case that warships staffed with volunteer sailors who choose their own officers outsail and outfight ships of impressed seamen whose coordination is extracted by threat of flogging. So, if a seaman is to go to sea, then his interest in survival is best instrumentally realised by joining a free crew of free sailors. Or freedom could be a constitutive requirement, in that the goods realised or the duties fulfilled are made conceptually possible only by free collective agency, and not by mere social coordination. Or freedom could be an independent normative requirement, in that the only morally permissible forms of social coordination are free ones, whether or not forced coordination instrumentally or constitutively realises goods or satisfies other duties.

To summarise, free group agency may have importance because it realises a necessary good, a contingent good, or fulfils a duty. Group agency may be instrumental to these goods or duties or constitute them. And group agency must be free either because freedom is instrumental to the realisation of the goods or fulfilment of the duty, or because freedom constitutes the goods or duties, or because freedom is an independent normative constraint. These distinctions yield twelve possible combinations. Not all are of interest, but the standard arguments for the importance of social cooperation are usefully differentiated by locating them on the resulting grid. Note too that there are many ways to find moral importance in free group agency that do not depend at all on communitarian, collectivist or participatory democratic premises that see deciding and doing things together as somehow intrinsically more valuable than deciding and doing things individually.

VIII

I have been offering necessary conditions for collective political agency, but notice that these conditions do double duty as criteria for a normative conception of political legitimacy. This should come as no surprise. If the concept of political legitimacy is, very roughly, the right to rule, then one plausible account of the criteria for the legitimacy of a government is that only governments constituted as shared agents authored by their subjects have the right to rule those subjects, because only then is the puzzle of how we can remain self-governing when governed by others solved. Yet note that, if the account of shared agency above is correct, then the correct account of political legitimacy has substantive as well as procedural requirements. Only free enough natural agents can constitute a shared agent, and no procedure can make a natural agent free enough who is not free enough already. This is why, to be legitimate, procedures of governance must be constrained by substantive preconditions (for example, constitutional rights that limit majority rule).

On the conception of political legitimacy that I believe is correct, the test of legitimate government is two-pronged, just as the test of shared political agency is two-pronged. There needs to be an adequate connection between the governors and the governed (the procedural prong), and there needs to be adequate protection of at least basic human rights (the substantive prong). At a minimum, legitimacy requires those political freedoms and basic protections that are constitutive of or instrumentally necessary for the individual moral agency of the members. *A necessary condition for a free (enough) people is that it be made up of free (enough) persons.* We do not have to be too precise about the thresholds here. Perhaps something less than democracy will satisfy the political freedom prong, and perhaps something less than the full complement of liberal rights will satisfy the human rights prong. But on no plausible normative account of group agency and therefore of legitimacy does a tyrannical regime that recognises no constraints on the arbitrary will of the tyrant and that systematically violates basic human rights personify the people it rules.

Might a tyrannical regime personify a subset of the population it rules, or might subsets constitute their own shared agent? First, consider the case of a separatist or revolutionary movement. Surely, once members of such a movement are the targets of massive human rights violations, they do not constitute a shared agent with their persecutors, even if the initial rebellion was unjustified. It would be utterly perverse to think that a regime that engages in mass atrocities against groups of subjects personifies those subjects. The victims of atrocity are not the authors of their own victimisation. It does not follow, however, that such secessionists or revolutionaries have succeeded in constituting a new shared political agent. Political legitimacy does not follow some law of conservation under which it can neither be created nor destroyed, but only changed from form to form. The social solidarity that both makes large-scale political dissent possible and makes group-based suppression instrumentally rational may underwrite anthropological peoplehood, but there is no normative peoplehood without the institutions and procedures necessary for the formation of large-scale shared agency.

Second, consider the case of a favoured group that is not subject to massive atrocity. One might think that such subjects constitute a smaller shared political agent personified by the regime. Under sufficiently repressive regimes, however, where all political dissent is stifled and where one's basic wellbeing is unprotected and insecure, this is not so even of those who are faring well. No one who lives in fear and must curry favour to avoid the arbitrary whims of an unconstrained, absolute ruler is free enough to constitute a shared agent. A regime that considers everything about you violable and has the absolute power to violate you does not represent or personify you, even if in fact you are not violated. Well-treated cattle do not share agency with their rancher.

Finally, could a ruling class, party or bureaucracy constitute a group agent? Perhaps. Officials in a tyrannical regime may have met the necessary and sufficient conditions for constituting a shared agent of its kind, an organised crime syndicate, and so would be capable of unified agency that makes its individual members responsible authors of the regime's actions. But such a regime does not personify the people it rules.

In a tyranny, the tyrant does not personify the people, and there is no other candidate. Although I will subscribe to a part of Kant's political philosophy in the next section, I do not subscribe to his view that the legislative head of state must never be resisted because only the legislature can speak for the general will.[38] It may be the case that, although no body other than a current head of state can possibly speak for the general will, neither can the current head of state. The general will in some circumstances may simply not exist; it may never have existed or it may have gone out of existence. It does not follow from there being a duty to leave the state of nature that it is impossible to be returned to the state of nature, or that one must act as if it is impossible.[39]

If the tyrant does not speak for the people, the people is mute, and incapable of competent, unified moral agency – incapable of competent willing. Sufficiently determined pollsters or social scientists conceivably could measure public opinion in a tyrannised society, but a poll merely aggregates; it cannot unify. Poll results no more speak for the will of a people than a listing of a person's desires speaks for the will of a person.

So Mill almost has it right about barbarous peoples. He is just wrong about the barbarians. A people that is not capable of shared agency simply is an aggregation of individuals who exist in a state of nature with each other and with other peoples. So, he is right that 'the only moral laws for those relations are the universal rules of morality between man and man'. Yet without further argument, such men are presumed to be competent moral agents.[40]

[38] See I. Kant, 'Doctrine of Right' (1797), in M. J. Gregor (ed.), *The Metaphysics of Morals* (Cambridge University Press, 1991), 131; Prussian Academy edition AK 6:320.

[39] Indeed, in a passage that generally denies the legitimacy of revolution in order to reform a despotism, Kant implies that the general will can dissolve through natural causes: 'Thus political wisdom, in the condition in which things are at present, will make reforms in keeping with the ideal of public right its duty; but it will use revolutions, where nature of itself has brought them about, not to gloss over an even greater oppression, but as a call of nature to bring about by fundamental reforms a lawful constitution based on principles of freedom, the only kind that endures.' I. Kant, 'Toward Perpetual Peace' (1795), in M. J. Gregor (ed.), *Practical Philosophy* (Cambridge University Press, 1996), 311–52; here 341, AK 8:374.

[40] Presumptively competent individual agents may fail to form a competent group agent due to a number of causes – physical danger, language barriers, lack of necessary infrastructure – that do not call into question their individual competence as agents. But might some causes of their failure to form a group agent count against their individual competence as well? If so, then a barbarous people could be evidence of barbarians, and I have been uncharitable to Mill. How might this be so? On a thick view

We now can give a partial answer to the question of whether setting a people free is a reason for coercion that meets the criteria of justified paternalism. (This laboured formulation reminds us that paternalism, as used here, is an attribute of reasons for action, not of actions themselves.) A society whose members are deprived of the most basic rights and freedoms might not count as a normative people at all. If what I have called the extravagant view is supported by the morally relevant political facts, there is no normative people to paternalise – there is no shared agent that is the locus of respect and responsibility – so the complaint of unjustifiably paternalising a people does not arise. The invaders are subject only to the 'universal rules of morality', standing in relation to each person as one stands to individuals in a state of nature. Alternatively, if such a society is to be counted as a normative people, it is a seriously impaired people, incapable of competent and effective shared agency and self-governance. Insofar as such a people has a will that is subject to being coerced by external military intervention, it is a will whose freedom is not very valuable, and a will that, by hypothesis, is overborne by the intervener for the sake of its own future freedom. Although such a people is capable of being forced for paternalistic reasons, such reasons under the circumstances overcome the ordinary presumption against paternalism. Of course, much more is needed to justify a military invasion than showing that objections to paternalism can be met.

IX

Individuals could concede that the people of which they are members has no ground to complain about being paternalised, but this hardly robs individuals of all moral complaint. Each can complain that as a mature, competent individual agent it is up to each to decide whether to accept the grave risks of violence, destruction and upheaval that an invasion and occupation would bring. Even if the risks to personal safety and restrictions on personal freedom that military intervention imposes are less onerous than life under tyranny, ordinarily it is no defence against the

of competent moral agency, failure to recognise one's interest in overcoming coordination problems to form a group agent (when indeed one has such an interest) may count as a form of irrationality, and failure to be properly motivated by such an interest may count as weakness of will. On an even thicker, moralised view of competent individual agency, failure to recognise the moral law or to be properly motivated by the moral law may count as irrationality and so be a failure of competent agency. I have in mind a thinner view of irrationality here, under which prudential and moral mistakes are not per se impairments of agency.

charge of wrongdoing that one has replaced a worse wrongdoer. The conditions for justified paternalism by and large are not met in the individual case. So we still have not established that it is morally permissible to force individuals to become a free people.

The best response is to deny that the reason individuals are forced is for one's own sake, and so deny that the invasion paternalises individuals. True, each is being forced to constitute a free people, but this is being done for the sake of one's neighbours, or one's children, or one's neighbours' children. To see why this is a plausible non-paternalistic account of the reasons for intervention, we turn to Kant.

Unlike his social contract predecessors, who saw leaving the state of nature as the rational or prudent thing to do, Kant held that it was also a duty to do so. Once we interact in a way that might lead to disputes about our rights, we each have a duty to each other to enter into a civil condition, so that we are not judges in our own case. 'When you cannot avoid living side by side with all others, you ought to leave the state of nature and proceed with them into a rightful condition.'[41] Only in that way do we treat each other with the respect that we are owed. Furthermore, 'each may impel the other by force to leave this state and enter into a rightful condition'.[42] To realise my rights and yours, I may, and perhaps must, coerce you into meeting the conditions for shared agency.

For Kant, once a right has been established, there is no further question of whether the coercive enforcement of that right is justified. Rather, to have a right just is to have the authority to force compliance, and, correlatively, to have a strict duty of justice simply is to be subject to coercive enforcement.[43] Ordinarily, when one is justified in using force – say, in self-defence – one also is justified in enlisting the forceful aid of others. I do not have to stand by and watch you defend yourself against wrongful attackers. (Whether I have a duty to defend you or not depends in part on the risks and burdens I face.) On a vastly different scale, if you are justified in forcing your neighbours in a state of nature to do their duty and enter into a rightful condition with you, I do not have to stand by and let you force them alone. Perhaps in the self-defence case you may refuse my help and I must respect your refusal. If that is so, then if there is unanimous agreement among those in a wrongful state of nature that they want to stay that way, or that they do not want outside help in forcing each other into a rightful condition, then perhaps they too may

[41] Kant, 'Doctrine of Right', 121, AK 6:307. [42] *Ibid.*, 124, AK 6:312.
[43] *Ibid.*, 57, AK 6:232.

refuse external help and outsiders must respect that refusal.[44] As a formal matter, however, just one person wrongfully kept in a state of nature would have the authority to invite the world's help in forcing her neighbours into a rightful condition, and, also as a formal matter, the intervener would then have a non-paternalistic reason to force individuals to be free. First-order moral considerations surely would tell against this being an all-things-considered sufficient reason for military intervention in such an unpromising case, but the example demonstrates the point: individuals may sometimes be forced to do their duty, and when that is so, they are not forced for their own sake, but for the sake of those to whom the duty is owed.

Kant admittedly is silent on whether we are permitted to force distant others who do not have a duty to enter into a civil relation with us to enter into one with each other, but it is precisely this extension of the view that would have to be made in order to justify forcing natural persons to constitute a free people. If this extension can be made, then the reply to the individual who complains about being paternalistically forced to constitute a free people is that, though indeed forced, he is not paternalised. Rather, he is being forced to comply with his natural duty to his fellow countrymen.

Now, Kant clearly repudiates forced colonisation, which might suggest that he would reject this extension:

> Lastly, it can still be asked whether, when neither nature nor chance but just our own will brings us into the neighbourhood of a people that holds out no prospect of a civil union with it, we should not be authorised to found colonies, by force if need be, in order to establish a civil union with them and bring these men (savages) into a rightful condition (as with the American Indians, the Hottentots, and the inhabitants of New Holland) … But it is easy to see through this veil of injustice (Jesuitism), which would sanction any means to good ends. Such a way of acquiring land is therefore to be repudiated.[45]

But Kant here does not address colonisation in order to force savages to enter into a rightful condition with *each other;* rather, he rejects colonisation to force savages to enter into a civil union with *us*. In any case, the thrust of the passage is to put limits on the acquisition of land, rather than limits on the use of force.[46]

[44] I say perhaps, because the analogy to refusing help in the self-defence case is not perfect. The duty to leave the state of nature may not be reciprocally waivable.

[45] Kant, 'Doctrine of Right', 86f., AK 6:266.

[46] I am grateful to an Editor of *Philosophy and Public Affairs* for directing me to this passage.

Because Kant's treatment of private right in a state of nature largely concerns the acquisition and transfer of external objects, one might be tempted to think that the sole purpose of public right is to adjudicate conflicts in the acquisition and transfer of property. If that were so, then a Kantian defence of a military intervention would depend, strangely enough, on whether the target regime has adequate civil courts to adjudicate property disputes. This is an excessively narrow reading of why Kant holds that we must leave the state of nature, however, and therefore an insufficiently demanding account of what it takes to enter (and I would say remain in) a rightful condition. To be secure in one's possessions is important in Kant because control over things secures our freedom. But the civil condition secures us more generally against the 'maxim of violence' that follows from the right of each in a state of nature to do what seems right and good.[47] Threats to our freedom can arise from many sources, including 'the inclination of men generally to lord it over others as their master'.[48] The provisional rights that a civil condition makes actual are not only rights to things, but rights to persons in the household, the limits of which mark off the correlative rights of wives, children and servants *against* mistreatment by their master. Such dependent persons, or passive citizens, never lose their natural liberty and equality. 'On the contrary, it is only in conformity with the conditions of freedom and equality that this people can become a state and enter into a civil constitution.'[49]

The necessary conditions for the formation of a general united will among the active citizens are considerably more stringent:

> In terms of rights, the attributes of a citizen, inseparable from his essence (as a citizen), are: lawful *freedom*, the attribute of obeying no other law than that to which he has given his consent; civil *equality*, that of not recognising among the *people* any superior with the moral capacity to bind him as a matter of Right in a way that he could not in turn bind the other; and third, the attribute of civil *independence*, of owing his existence and preservation to his own rights and powers as a member of the commonwealth, not to the choice of another among the people. From his independence follows his civil personality, his attribute of not needing to be represented by another where rights are concerned.[50]

So a society in which large numbers of persons are denied their natural liberty and equality and in which perhaps no one possesses the three

[47] Kant, 'Doctrine of Right', 123, AK 6:312. [48] *Ibid.*, 122, AK 6:307.
[49] *Ibid.*, 126, AK 6:315. [50] *Ibid.*, 125, AK 6:314.

attributes of a citizen arguably remains a Kantian state of nature, even if there are mechanisms for the orderly transfer of property.[51]

Lest I be accused of conscripting Kant into a cause he would not recognise, let me be clear about my claim and its limits. My own view is that there is a non-paternalistic reason to force individuals who live side by side to become a free people: they each have a duty to leave the state of nature and enter into a civil relation with each other. If such a reason is sufficient to justify the force involved, then it does not matter that entering into a civil relation also is for the good of each. If there are sufficient non-paternalistic reasons for using force, it is otiose to inquire about the sufficiency of the paternalistic reasons. Kant does not address whether there is such a permission, let alone a duty, for any outsider to force others into a rightful condition. One might think that, since Kant insists that the legitimacy of existing authority not be questioned and that forced colonialism is repugnant, he cannot be enlisted in support of such a view: Kant would either deny that people living under tyrannical rule can be judged to not be in a rightful condition or deny that outsiders have any right to force them into a rightful condition. I have argued, however, that Kant puts fairly demanding conditions on what it takes to enter into a rightful condition, and that the case of the colonial land grab that he repudiates can be differentiated from our case: his savages have no duty to enter into a rightful condition with colonists before the colonists' arrival, but the savages do have a prior duty to enter into a rightful condition with each other. So my claim that there could be sufficient non-paternalistic reasons to force individuals to become a free people is not, as far as I can tell, inconsistent with Kant's political philosophy.[52]

[51] I am grateful to an Editor of *Philosophy and Public Affairs* for pressing me on this point.

[52] Permission to intervene is one thing, a duty to intervene another. Since there are limits on the sacrifices morality requires us to make for each other, and since military intervention almost always is costly in blood and treasure, intervention often may be a sacrifice too great for morality to require. Surely Lord Byron had no duty to give his life for Greek independence. When the would-be intervener is a group agent, we must be careful in the aggregation and distribution of burdens across its members to assess sacrifice correctly. Monetary cost can be distributed widely, but death and injury are concentrated. The technical calculations of generals and the political calculations of elected officials about 'acceptable' casualty rates often involve morally unacceptable aggregation across lives that fails to treat individuals with respect. Each battlefield death must be justifiable to the soldier who is to die, and that is no easy matter. The justification goes something like this: from some morally appropriate *ex ante* point of view, the risk of death that you face is reasonably proportionate to the moral importance of the ends at stake, fairly distributed, and decided under institutions or practices or

X

I have said a lot about the criteria for entrance, but nothing about the criteria for exit. How free does a people have to be before the intervener must withdraw?[53] An obvious worry about a claim that interveners may or must stay until a well-functioning democracy has been established is that there are precious few well-functioning democracies around the globe. Does the argument for democratic institution-building underwrite a frighteningly broad permission to engage in never-ending democratic jihad wherever there are defects in collective will formation?

The worry is misplaced, and would be misplaced even if it turned out that *no* country in the world meets the test of legitimacy. This is because even if there are no governments that are morally immune from intervention by virtue of respect accorded to them in light of the respect due to the subjects they represent, first-order moral considerations will ordinarily forbid intervention, because intervention will do more harm than good, destroy more than build, and inflict misery and danger on innocents that cannot be justified to them.

procedures that are connected to you in ways that respect your equal freedom. The argument for the correct point of view is crucial: if too *ex ante* and general, the separateness of persons is threatened and too much individual sacrifice is permitted; if too *ex post* and particular, nearly all have vetoes and not enough individual sacrifice is permitted. Justifying sacrifice for the end of repelling an existential threat to one's own normative people is easier than justifying sacrifice for the end of establishing the normative peoplehood of others. Why? Recall that to be both a free enough author and a free enough subject of the collective agent for this purpose in this way, one either has to have consented, or have voluntarily benefited from the cooperation of others, or have intentionally created reasonable expectations, or face a practical necessity. Dangerous military service is a practical necessity primarily in defence of one's own people, and the other conditions are less likely to be met in the case of intervention as well. So group agents may be prohibited from requiring its members to fight in otherwise permissible interventions. A volunteer force fares better in this regard than a conscript army, but there are substantive limits to the risks that can be imposed even on recruits, just as there are limits to the risks that can be imposed on voluntary employees. Let us then isolate the question of whether there is any sort of presumptive duty upon outside powers to force others into a civil condition with each other from the question of how much sacrifice is beyond the call of duty. Suppose the fantasy of the gunboat diplomat came true, and some intervener had the absolute power to force others into a civil condition by making a nearly costless but credible threat that puts none of the intervener's soldiers at the slightest risk. If there is any sort of duty of rescue among unconnected strangers of the pull-the-drowning-baby-out-of-the-puddle variety, then there is a duty of intervention in this case too. But such pure cases are implausible.

[53] I thank Melissa Seymour for pressing me on this point.

There are second-order considerations that tell against democratic jihad as well. An advantage of the view presented here is that there is an important asymmetry between conditions for entrance and conditions for exit. Suppose that there were some form of theocracy in which the conditions of normative peoplehood and of political legitimacy, though far from ideal, surpass the threshold that immunises that regime from outside intervention. Or suppose that there were some form of rule by an autocrat that met the threshold conditions.[54] Further suppose that constituting a normative people along the lines of a theocracy or an autocracy is the preferred option among an occupied population, and would also be both quicker and less costly in blood and treasure to bring about.[55] It still does not follow that the intervener must, or even may, aim at theocracy or autocracy. By assumption, both of these forms of rule, if established, would be owed respect and so be immune from intervention. But until a normative people is constituted, there is no competent will of the people that is owed such respect. The fact that most want a theocracy or an autocracy is simply that: a social scientific fact that by itself has no legitimate authority at all. Strange as it may sound to ears that conflate cultural sensitivity with political respect, until individuals are constituted in the normative sense as a free people, nothing is owed to the people in the anthropological sense qua people.

Much, of course, is owed to individuals. There are limits to how much each can be asked to sacrifice for the freedom of his neighbour. Just as first-order moral considerations and the probabilities of success may tell against intervention in the first place, first-order moral considerations

[54] There are two separate thresholds at play: minimal normative peoplehood and minimal political legitimacy. A collectivity can count as an impaired normative people but fail to have political legitimacy. Here I am assuming that the theocracy and the autocracy meet both tests. Both forms of government would have to minimally satisfy both the human rights prong and the representativeness prong of the test for political legitimacy. In the case of the theocracy, this would require, among other matters, that women be granted more personal freedom than is commonly the case in societies ruled by Islamic law today, and that non-conforming religious beliefs and practices, though politically disfavoured, be tolerated. In the case of the autocracy, the ruler would need to be not only responsive to the interests of his subjects but also, in some measure, responsive to their wills, as Louis XVI appeared to be when he called for the Cahiers de Doléances in 1789. I have in mind forms of rule that meet Rawls's notion of a decent consultation hierarchy, rather than what he calls benevolent despotism. See J. Rawls, *The Law of Peoples* (Cambridge, MA: Harvard University Press, 1999).

[55] In Iraq, we do not need to suppose. In the March 2007 ABC News poll, only a 42 per cent plurality of Iraqis thought a democracy was best for Iraq, with 34 per cent opting for a strong leader for life and 22 per cent for religious rule.

and the probabilities of success may tell against a more ambitious plan for regime change. Although the anthropological facts have no intrinsic normative force, they of course matter instrumentally. Though Mill is wrong about impossibility, surely he is right to worry that free institutions externally imposed are less likely to take root. So the changer of regimes must take into account blood, treasure and odds. And surely there is a diverse set of political institutions to choose from that are free enough and just enough. Over that range, respect for individual self-governance would trump the intervener's views about ideal collective self-governance – though how disagreement among individuals is to be resolved necessarily is underspecified in the absence of legitimate decision rules for resolving disagreements. But these all are what I have called first-order moral considerations. Until properly constituted as a shared agent, occupied persons simply are individuals owed respect as individuals. Therefore – here is the crucial point – this range of free enough and just enough political arrangements is likely to be narrower and more demanding than the range of constitutions and institutions that, once in place, are morally immune from intervention. Hence the asymmetry of criteria for going in and getting out.

The implication is striking: an occupying force may, and perhaps must, prevent the formation of some forms of government that it would not have been permitted to overthrow, had they existed.[56] So we have reached the surprising result that, in Iraq, US forces may and perhaps must prevent the formation of a minimally legitimate government in order to hold out for more extensive political freedoms and human rights protections, even if that is not what most Iraqis presently want. Although only the hardhearted can fail to be moved by the purple-fingered voters who braved political violence to participate in peaceful

[56] I am not proposing that powers that have not yet intervened must forcefully stop the formation of legitimate but less-than-just institutions around the world. That indeed would be a counsel for global democratic jihad. Rather, once a power has chosen to intervene with force, and thereby has assumed responsibility for the fate of an occupied population, it acquires a presumptive obligation to forge not merely legitimate but also just institutions. This presumption can be rebutted on various grounds: the higher standard may be impossible to reach under the circumstances, or require too much sacrifice by the intervener, or impose too many burdens on the population. It is a mistake, however, to think that because fairly low levels of sacrifice by a would-be intervener are enough to make intervention merely optional, the same low level of sacrifice is enough to permit withdrawal. Even though it may be optional for an intervener to take a population under its protection, it is not equally optional to withdraw that protection.

elections in Iraq, the adoption of a constitution by referendum and the election of a parliament do not yet constitute a minimally legitimate government. They do not because a government is legitimate only when it can and does act to secure and protect a minimally adequate list of rights and freedoms on behalf of its free (enough) constituent individuals, and surely a government unable or unwilling to prevent widespread sectarian warfare has not met these conditions. Although protection of the basic rights and freedoms of Iraqis is of the utmost moral urgency, if my argument about the asymmetry of entry and exit is correct, the provision of this protection *by a minimally legitimate Iraqi government* may be considerably less urgent. The onset of legitimate government is not an unalloyed good, for one should not be indifferent between the establishment of a minimally legitimate government and a just and democratic government.[57] These, I hasten to add, are theoretical considerations. I make no claims about the actual capacity of this occupation force to bring about any positive political change whatsoever under the present circumstances.

XI

All foundings are forced. If we, collectively, are free, it is because we too have been forced to be free. In a state of nature, there are no legitimate procedures that can bootstrap us into legitimate government, although rhetoric that makes believe that there is such a procedure is a useful lubricant for achieving legitimate government. When some of us force others of us to be free, the victors look back with pride, the defeated beget political orphans, and so the next generation can tell a just-so story about freedom's origins that is often useful, largely harmless, and nearly always

[57] Admittedly, a principle that, for the sake of bringing about self-governance, prescribes an *indefinite* protectorate would be self-undermining in cases where legitimate but unjust self-governance is possible. Rawls says that the end of a just war is a just peace (Rawls, *The Law of Peoples*, 94). Similarly, intervention must have an end, with the temporal end driven by its purpose. In purely humanitarian interventions the end is protecting basic human rights, and this may require, without contradiction, indefinite occupation if self-rule that protects human rights is impossible. But an intervention that aims at forcing a people to be free has misfired if it finds itself permanently preventing possible legitimate self-governance. As with so many questions in non-ideal theory, reasonable people may make different judgments about how long an intervener may hold out for not merely legitimate but just self-rule before the intervention becomes self-undermining. I thank an Editor of *Philosophy and Public Affairs* for pressing me on this point.

false. But when they, the foreigners, force us to be free, shame replaces pride, and the just-so story is harder to tell. This is why the just-so stories about home-grown freedom are not entirely harmless – they set up founding expectations elsewhere that are normatively too demanding. The truth is different: sometimes a people must be humiliated before it can be free.

References

Bratman, M. 1999. *Faces of Intention*. Cambridge University Press.

Frankfurt, H. G. 1988. 'Freedom of the Will and the Concept of a Person' (1971), in Frankfurt, H. G., *The Importance of What We Care About*. Cambridge University Press, 11–25.

Gilbert, M. 1996. *Living Together*. Lanham, MD: Rowman & Littlefield.

Gilbert, M. 2000. *Sociality and Responsibility*. Lanham, MD: Rowman & Littlefield.

Hobbes, T. 1996 (1651). *Leviathan*. Tuck, R. (ed.). Cambridge University Press.

Hoffmann, S. 1968. 'Collaborationism in France during World War II', *Journal of Modern History* 40: 375–95.

Hylland, A. and Zeckhauser, R. 1979. 'The Impossibility of Bayesian Group Decisionmaking with Separate Aggregation of Beliefs and Values', *Econometrica* 47: 1321–36.

Kant, I. 1991. 'Doctrine of Right' (1797), in Gregor, M. J. (ed.), *The Metaphysics of Morals*. Cambridge University Press.

Kant, I. 1996. 'Toward Perpetual Peace' (1795), in Gregor, M. J. (ed.), *Practical Philosophy*. Cambridge University Press, 311–52.

Korsgaard, C. M. 1996. 'Two Distinctions in Goodness', in Korsgaard, C. M., *Creating the Kingdom of Ends*. Cambridge University Press, 249–74.

List, C. and Pettit, P. 2002. 'Aggregating Sets of Judgments: An Impossibility Result', *Economics and Philosophy* 18: 89–110.

Montaigne, M. de 1958. 'Of Husbanding your Will' (1585–8), in Frame, D. M. (trans.), *The Complete Essays of Montaigne*. Stanford University Press, 766–84.

Mill, J. S. 1963–1991. *Collected Works of John Stuart Mill*. Robson, J. M. (ed.). 33 vols. University of Toronto Press.

Mill, J. S. 1984. 'A Few Words on Non-Intervention' (1859), in Robson, J. M. (ed.), *Collected Works of John Stuart Mill: Essays on Equality, Law, and Education*. Vol. XXI. University of Toronto Press, 109–24.

Mill, J. S. 1975. *On Liberty* (1859). Spitz, D. (ed.). New York: W. W. Norton.

Paxton, R. O. 1972. *Vichy France: Old Guard and New Order, 1940–1944*. New York: Knopf.

Pettit, P. 2004. 'Groups with Minds of Their Own', in Schmitt, F. (ed.), *Socializing Metaphysics*. New York: Rowman & Littlefield, 167–93.

Pettit, P. 2007. 'Responsibility Incorporated', *Ethics* 117: 171–201.
Raiffa, H. 1968. *Decision Analysis*. Reading, MA: Addison-Wesley.
Rawls, J. 1971. *A Theory of Justice*. Cambridge, MA: Harvard University Press.
Rawls, J. 1999. *The Law of Peoples*. Cambridge, MA: Harvard University Press.
Ripstein, A. 2004. 'Authority and Coercion', *Philosophy and Public Affairs* 32: 2–35.
Ripstein, A. 2006. 'Beyond the Harm Principle', *Philosophy and Public Affairs* 34: 215–45.
Rousseau, J. J. 1978. 'On the Social Contract' (1762), in Masters, R. D. (ed.) and Bush, J. R. (trans.), *On the Social Contract: with Geneva Manuscript and Political Economy*. New York: St Martin's Press.
Scanlon, T. 1990. 'Promises and Practices', *Philosophy and Public Affairs* 19: 199–226.
Schapiro, T. 1999. 'What Is a Child?', *Ethics* 109: 715–38.
Schauer, F. 1991. *Playing by the Rules*. Oxford: Clarendon Press.
Thompson, D. F. 1987. *Political Ethics and Public Office*. Cambridge, MA: Harvard University Press.

INDEX